Christ is All!

A Joyful Manifesto on
the Supremacy of God's Son

A Joyful Manifesto on
the Supremacy of God's Son

CHRIST
Is All!

David Bryant

Join a Campaign to Recover
ALL the Hope We Are Meant to Have!

**NEW
PROVIDENCE
PUBLISHERS**

Published by
New Providence Publishers Inc.
P O Box 770
New Providence, NJ 07974-0770

Design and Layout
Sahlman Art Studio Inc.
50 Christy Drive
Warren, NJ 07059

Scripture taken from the following:
THE MESSAGE. Copyright 1993, 1994, 1995, 1996, 2000, 2001, 2002.
Used by permission of NavPress Publishing Group.

The Holy Bible New International Version. Copyright 1973, 1978, 1984 by International Bible Society. Used by permission of the International Bible Society.

The New Testament in Modern English, Translated by J. B. Phillips. Copyright 1964.
Used by permission of The Macmillan Co. (New York).
Library of Congress Catalog Number: 2004107040
International Standard Book Number (ISBN) 0-9755038-1-2
Printed in the United States of America

"...Christ is all..."

Colossians 3:11

"These three words are few, short and
soon spoken; but they contain great things.

These three words are the essence
and substance of Christianity.

These three words give to Christ
His rightful place."

– Bishop J.C. Ryle, c. 1870

DEDICATION

TO THE GLORY OF GOD
this *Manifesto* is dedicated to:

THE LORD JESUS CHRIST
whose very Person dominates its every page.

ROBYNE L. BRYANT
who has spent a lifetime pursuing its truths with me.

ADAM SAMUEL BRYANT
BETHANY MEERA BRYANT
BENJAMIN DHEERAJ BRYANT
to whose generation belongs the awakening that must come.

A "FACULTY" OF CHRISTIAN LEADERS
whose minds and hearts helped give shape
to the hope in Christ it proclaims.

PRAYING CHRISTIANS EVERYWHERE
whose heart-cry to God for a fresh awakening in the Church
to Christ and the full extent of His supremacy
compelled me to write it in the first place.

**"I have just seen the Lord Christ.
Now I know all I have written is straw."**
– SPOKEN BY THOMAS ACQUINAS,
SHORTLY BEFORE HIS DEATH, WHILE ATTEMPTING TO COMPLETE HIS OWN BOOK
ON THE SUPREMACY OF CHRIST.

CONTENTS

VOLUME ONE
CHRIST AND SUPREMACY
What Is the Hope We Must Recover?

(continued)

VOLUME TWO.
THE CRISIS OF SUPREMACY
Where Is the Hope We Must Recover?

VOLUME THREE
A CAMPAIGN OF HOPE
Recovering All the Hope
We Are Meant to Have

Saint Paul

On Hope and
the Supremacy of God's Son

We look at this Son and see the God who cannot be seen.
We look at this Son and see God's original purpose for everything created.

For everything, absolutely everything,
above and below, visible and invisible,
rank after rank after rank of angels —
***everything* got started in him**
and finds its purpose in him.
He was supreme in the beginning, and
— leading the resurrection parade —
He is supreme in the end.
From beginning to end he's there,
towering far above everything, everyone.

So spacious is he, so roomy,
that everything of God finds its proper place in him without crowding.
Not only that, but all the broken and dislocated pieces of the universe —
people and things, animals and atoms —
get properly fixed and fitted together in vibrant harmonies,
all because of his death, his blood that poured down from the Cross ...

The mystery in a nutshell is this:
Christ is in you,
Therefore you can look forward to sharing in God's glory.

It's that simple. That is the substance of our message.
We preach *Christ* ...

— from chapter 1 of Colossians (The MESSAGE)

Defining the Hope Shaped by
the Supremacy of God's Son

*"... that in everything He might have **THE SUPREMACY**."*
— *Colossians 1:18*

It is a hope shaped by
who Christ is as the Son of God ...
this is the *FOCUS* of His Supremacy.

It is a hope shaped by
where Christ leads in the Purposes of God ...
this is the *FULFILLMENT* of His Supremacy.

It is a hope shaped by
how Christ imparts the Resources of God ...
this is the *FULLNESS* of His Supremacy.

It is a hope shaped by
what Christ receives from the People of God ...
this is the *FERVENCY* of His Supremacy.

The **CENTRALITY** of Christ expresses His right to be kept at the center of who we are, where we are headed, what we are doing and how we are blessed.

But the **SUPREMACY** of Christ expresses so much more. It is about His right to keep us at the center of who HE is (focus), where HE is headed *(fulfillment)*, what HE is doing *(fullness)*, and how HE is blessed *(fervency)*.

Only in the supremacy of God's Son can we recover ALL the hope we are meant to have.

LOOK BEYOND

An Introduction

THE THRESHOLD!

Have you looked beyond the threshold ... *recently?*

For over 30 years I've watched the Holy Spirit move His Church toward a "kairos" moment that waits for us, just beyond the threshold. First as a pastor, then ministering to university students, followed by a decade of mobilizing Christians for world evangelization coupled with 15 years of raising up prayer among the nations, I've witnessed an unparalleled groundswell toward worldwide revival throughout the Body of Christ. Today I sense it is truly at hand. The Spirit beckons us on.

Therefore, I was not surprised when, in the opening months of the 21st century, a group of 70 national leaders — from business, political, educational and church arenas — extended *"An Open Letter to the Church"*, putting their own signatures to it. Listen to part of their appeal for a Church-wide movement of renewal:

> "Today, the Spirit is increasingly speaking to the Church worldwide
> about our need for a revitalized hope
> defined by the supremacy of Christ in all things.
> God is preparing many Christians to be 'reconverted' to His Son
> at much deeper levels in their lives and ministries.
> Jesus Christ must be lifted up before the Church as never before.
> The fullness of His reign must be proclaimed
> with renewed passion to believers everywhere."

In the same spirit, dear reader, I come to encourage you: It's time to get ready. *It's time to look beyond the threshold!*
We do dwell at a threshold, you know. We are on the edge of what many leaders, like those mentioned above, are hoping for. We stand at a doorway. Beyond it beckons a wide-scale awakening to God's Son throughout the Body of Christ. It is an awakening for which many have longed and labored for years. We are poised at the sunrise of extraordinary answers to the cries of the modern day global prayer movement, a movement unprecedented in Church history. Many are catching the crest of a wave, leading them to the cure for a major crisis in this hour among God's people — what I call a "crisis of supremacy". This wave can lift us into fresh hope, passion, worship and mission for the glory of the Lord Jesus.

Saying it another way: We are gathered at the launch-point of a grand *campaign*. It is a campaign to proclaim the name of God's Son to *Christians* everywhere — doing so in such a way that every facet of discipleship, church life and outreach will be radically (and wonderfully) transformed in the process. We have come to the crossroads of a crucial cause. As we're about to see, it requires the flooding of the Church with *Messengers of Hope* who will raise up *Prisoners of Hope* and bring together *Vanguards of Hope* to form the frontlines of renewal and outreach for a whole generation.

As you step into the pages of this *Joyful Manifesto,* therefore, *I invite you to look beyond the threshold.*
Something new — something *joy*-filled — is about to unfold. This document invites you to prepare for the thrilling adventure God intended for you all of your life. Here you'll find an opportunity to minister a marvelously compelling message to multitudes of spiritually hungry people. Here you'll learn to be the kind of *Christ-proclaimer* your fellow believers so desperately need you to be for them. In so doing, you will discover how to help the Church recover all the hope we are *meant* to have.

As you do this, one reality will possess you above all others. It flows from nearly every page of this book. And, it can be summarized in just three little words taken from Colossians 3:11:

"*Christ is all!*"

This verse defines what I see beyond the threshold. But the vision is not new for me. Let me tell you why.

Even now I chuckle as I think about how this phrase first got hold of my heart. As a young pastor just starting out, I was determined to shape my ministry in unique ways. One goal I set, for example, was to compose a moniker that would make a unique theological statement every time I signed personal correspondence. I wanted a special phrase, something beyond an everyday "sincerely yours".

Then, one morning it came to me. In my private devotions I stumbled on three little words in Colossians 3:11: "... Christ is all ..." It resonated instantly. I sensed it should become the fundamental focus of a lifetime of service for the Lord Jesus. So later that week I concluded the very next pastoral letter to my congregation with this tag: *"Christ is All! Pastor David."*

Conservatively speaking, over the past 30 years in a ministry that has circled the globe I've probably sealed nearly 85,000 personal letters with "Christ is All!" stretched banner-like above my signature. However, as I did this, I must admit that a *campaign* was the farthest thing from my mind.

But no longer! A *campaign* is now what I'm on! I'm restless. I'm in motion. I want to help fellow believers see what it actually means to call the Redeemer our EVERYTHING. I want to do whatever I can to encourage each of us to re-engage with Christ more fully for who He really is. Bottom line, I'm committed to proclaim to *Christians,* in every way possible, the *full* extent of the supremacy of God's Son. I'm happy to give the rest of my life to this mission. As I do, I know this phrase will remain the refrain for my campaign: *"Christ is All!"* I believe the same could happen to you. I've seen it happen to many others.

In fact, over the years close friends, imitating my approach to letter writing, have redesigned their own correspondence sign-offs with similarly short statements, composed to exalt Jesus for their readers. For example:

- Christ Over All!
- Christ For All!
- Christ Before All!
- Christ In All!
- Christ Above All!

Each phrase is compelling. Still, I'm sticking with "Christ is All!" In truth, it sums up all the others. CHRIST IS ALL! states succinctly the truth that God's Son, in His grand majesty, must be the centerpiece of who I am, where I'm headed, what I do and how I'm blessed. It speaks of His "centrality."

However, the refrain speaks of more. It also captures the *ultimate destiny* the Holy Spirit is pursuing with every Christian — that we live every day at the center of Who *Christ* is, where *He's* headed, what *He's* doing and how *He's* blessed. That's what His "supremacy" demands.

That's Why I Call this a "JOYFUL MANIFESTO"

As already hinted, from every quarter of the contemporary church Christian leaders are starting to confess it's time to restore to Christians worldwide a larger vision of our Redeemer's triumphant glory. The conviction is growing that God can and must awaken His people to Christ for ALL that He is. As we're about to discover a vast company-of-the-committed are already praying and proclaiming this hopeful message across the Body of Christ.

Believers of every stripe must revisit their vision of the Victor. For the sake of Christ's global cause our number one priority must become exalting our Savior more consistently to one another *as Christians*. We must spread throughout our churches and ministries a message of God's Son that will explode the boundaries of our current hope in Him while, at the same time, re-ignite renewed passion for the pursuit of His Kingdom in all things, among all peoples.

**To take us beyond the threshold, I present to you this
"Joyful Manifesto".**
"Joyful" is not too strong a word for such a document. It alerts the reader to the thrilling threshold-moment in which we stand. It urges the reader to gaze at the Kingdom-sized Christ who has come to bring us tidings of great

joy about *Himself*. Therefore, it gives the reader scores of reasons to celebrate:

- Reasons to celebrate all that Jesus is as the Lord of the nations.

- Reasons to celebrate the multiple dimensions of His dominion.

- Reasons to celebrate the full hope He brings to the Church and the world.

- Reasons to celebrate the promise of greater insights from the Holy Spirit of Jesus' glory to impact our generation.

- Reasons to celebrate the way all of this can revitalize for us a spirit-filled walk with Him.

But, as its name suggests, this is also a *manifesto*. It was written to be shared. It announces great possibilities for those seeking to re-engage with Christ personally in more exciting and productive ways. It sets forth new directions for those praying for the restoration of delight and devotion toward our Lord, both in their lives and in their churches. Additionally, this manifesto provides a blueprint for a *"Campaign of Hope"* aimed at fulfilling the cries of many hearts. It calls for a movement that could ultimately change the face of our nation — and beyond.

As a manifesto, therefore, this book contains:

- A grand *exposition* of the consummation of all things in Christ.

- A robust *resolution* to re-form our vision of Christ and His supremacy.

- A personal *invitation* to join Empire-wide celebrations of the King of Kings.

- A broadcast *appeal* for renewed passion for the sole Lord of the universe.

- A public *proclamation* of magnificent promises by which the Holy Spirit can stir up in us fresh hope in Christ.

- A decisive *declaration* to Christians to revive their expectations for the Kingdom.

- A verbal *challenge* to believers to bring Kingdom changes to the status quo now.

- A compelling *call* for agents of renewal to be mobilized throughout the Church.

I think of Paul's own manifesto to the Colossian Christians. It, too, was filled with joy, as he wrote:

" ... make known among the Gentiles
the glorious riches of this mystery,
which is
Christ in you, the hope of glory.
WE PROCLAIM HIM,
admonishing and teaching everyone,
so that we might present everyone
perfect in Christ."

His was a joyful vision of Christ! His was a joyful manifesto about Christ. His was a joyful mission for Christ! As a result, his was a joyful hope held out to God's people everywhere! The same vision, manifesto, mission and hope fill this book with joy, too.

So, Where Is This
"Joyful Manifesto" Headed?

For a fuller answer to that question, turn to **Appendix I: *How to Make This Manifesto Work for You*** along with **Appendix II: *How to Facilitate Small Group Discussions***. Together they provide an excellent map for the next twelve chapters. But let me summarize what is ahead:

Volume One (chapters 1-5) takes the first steps to lay out a larger vision of Christ — of who He is to us and to the Church, as well as for all the ages to come. It investigates what Christian leaders have for centuries termed *"Christology"* — that is, the study of who Christ is as God's Son, where He leads in God's purposes, how He imparts God's resources and what He receives from God's people. No wonder Paul calls Him "Christ Jesus our hope" (1 Timothy 1:1). Volume One is about ALL the hope we are meant to have — about waking up to Christ for ALL that He is.

Though brief, each chapter provides an overview on God's Son you'll find both Biblical and (I believe) breath-taking. Frankly, you need to be ready to encounter Him in four major ways that are fairly unique for many believers (supported, however, by hundreds of Scriptures — see *Appendix V*): Christ as the summation, consummation, approximation and consuming passion of Christian hope.

Volume Two (chapters 6-8) explores what I define as the greatest crisis in the Church today — the "crisis of supremacy". It surveys the attendant impact this crisis has on hope and passion in the Christian movement. We uncover who and what this crisis is about, how it touches profoundly every aspect of fruitful life and ministry for Christ, and what it will take to cure the crisis and re-awaken the Church to Him for *all* that He is. You'll learn why concerned Christians today are eager to — indeed, must — deal with this crisis straight on, and without delay. Volume Two concludes by calling for a *Campaign of Hope* to deliver a potent cure for the crisis.

Volume Three (chapters 9-12) introduces the larger message this movement must declare to the Body of Christ today. Then, it unpacks the three-fold strategy for every Campaign of Hope — what I call "three compelling cures" for the crisis: *Messengers* of Hope, *Prisoners* of Hope and *Vanguards* of Hope. These concluding chapters will help you get a grip on practical ways to grow a more dynamic discipleship for yourself and fellow believers, one that restores all the hope we are meant to have — the hope shaped by the supremacy of God's Son.

Reflection/study questions are embedded throughout each chapter. They double as side-headings to introduce each unit of a chapter. Each question is my way of saying to the reader: (1) Here's the next topic. (2) Take some time to reflect on what *you* think about the topic. (3) If you're in a small group, discuss the topic using the question as a guide. (See more on this in *Appendix I and II*.)

Author's Permission:
Feel free to skip around!

Although I recommend you begin with chapter 1, no one necessarily needs to read the additional eleven chapters in sequence. *Joyful Manifesto* is specifically designed to let readers explore issues in whatever order seems most appropriate for them. Each chapter is written to stand alone.

For example, you might read chapters 2-3 (Christ as Summation and Consummation), then look at chapter 6 (a deeper analysis of the crisis of supremacy), then jump over to chapter 9 (how to tackle the crisis as a Messenger of Hope). Then, you might decide to scan chapters 4-5 to read more on Christ's supremacy, or return to chapters 7-8 to dig deeper into the crisis, or continue on with 10-12 so as to get an overview of the entire strategy for healing the crisis. *Or,* you might simply choose to read all of Volume Two as soon as you finish chapter 1. It all depends on your personal interests and needs.

Whatever approach you take, the main thing is this: You will be preparing yourself for what lies beyond the threshold as you link up with a campaign that offers tremendous potential for renewal. More importantly, you will be stepping into an exciting new way for disciples to respond to their Savior as the Lord of all.

That's really what matters most in the end, isn't it?

Author's Invitation:
Feel free to visit!

It would be a delight to hear from you! Tell me how God is using this book in your life. Let me know of developments with any "Campaign of Hope" unfolding where you live. Share with me the ways hope in the supremacy of Christ is starting to increase in the life of your congregation. Report results from a small group that has worked through *Joyful Manifesto's* embedded discussion questions. You can reach me at *ChristIsAllBook@aol.com.*

And, if you would like to explore how the ministry of PROCLAIM HOPE! might serve you, your church or your community, please visit us on the web at *www.DavidBryantDirect.com.*

To order additional copies of this book, please visit
www.ChristIsAllBook.com.
To purchase discounted quantities for small group studies of the book
please call **18MOREBOOKS** (1-866-732-6657).

"What's the very next thing I should do?"

Good question. I have a suggestion: Take a moment to re-examine your *own* vision of God's Son Before crossing the threshold, reflect on the degree of hope *you* hold toward Him personally.

To help you do this, turn to the next section titled Prelude. It's a masterful declaration about God's Son! It was composed by one of the great African-American preachers of our country (recently deceased), Bishop S.M. Lockridge. Read this "sermon-poem" aloud, either privately or with a small group. Then, using your own words (or borrowing some from Bishop Lockridge) pray its vision back to the Father. In a brief time of worship and praise meditate on Lockridge's powerful insights. This will prepare you to appreciate the more comprehensive portrait of Jesus the upcoming 3-books-in-1 paint for you.

For, you see, whenever you look beyond the threshold, you will always be moved, first of all, to (as the *Prelude* proclaims): ***"Put Your Hope In Christ!"***

You must make your choice. Either this man was, and is, the Son of God; or else a mad man or something worse. You can shut Him up for a fool; you can spit at Him and kill Him as a demon; or you can fall at His feet and call Him Lord and God.

(C.S. Lewis)

---

*Prelude**

PUT YOUR HOPE IN CHRIST!†

Adapted from a poem-sermon delivered by the distinguished
20th century African-American pastor

Bishop S.M. Lockridge⁺

Christ is enduringly strong,
He is entirely sincere.
He's eternally steadfast,
He's immortally graceful.
He's imperially powerful,
He's impartially merciful.
No barrier can hinder Him
from pouring out His blessing.

He's God's Son.
He's a sinner's Savior.
He's the centerpiece of civilization.
He's the greatest phenomenon
Ever to cross the horizon of this world.
I'm trying to tell you, Church —
PUT YOUR HOPE IN CHRIST!

He does not have to call for help,
and you can't confuse Him.
He doesn't need you and he doesn't need me.
He stands alone in the solitude of Himself.
He's august and He's unique.
He's unparalleled, and He's unprecedented.
He's supreme and He's pre-eminent.

He is the loftiest idea in literature.
He's the highest personality in philosophy.
He's the supreme problem of higher criticism.
He's the fundamental doctrine of true theology.
He's the cardinal necessity of spiritual religion.
He's the miracle of the ages.
He's the superlative of everything good you can call Him.
I'm trying to tell you, Church —
PUT YOUR HOPE IN CHRIST!

He can satisfy all of our needs,
and He can do it simultaneously.
He supplies strength for the weak.
He's available for the tempted and tried,
He sympathizes and He sees.
He guards and He guides.

He heals the sick,
He cleanses the lepers.
He forgives sinners,
He discharges debtors.
He delivers the captives,
He defends the feeble.
He blesses the young,
He regards the aged.
He rewards the diligent,
He beautifies the meek.
I'm trying to tell you, Church —
PUT YOUR HOPE IN CHRIST!

* You are encouraged to read it audibly either by yourself; in unison as a whole group; or responsively, with the leader reading the light print and the group responding with *"Put Your Hope in Christ!"*

† It was originally titled, "You Can Put Your Trust in Him!"

(continued)

Prelude
PUT YOUR HOPE IN CHRIST!

(continued)

He's the key to knowledge.
He's the wellspring of wisdom.
He's the doorway of deliverance.
He's the pathway to peace.
He's the roadway to righteousness.
He's the highway to holiness.
He's the gateway to glory.
PUT YOUR HOPE IN CHRIST!

He's the Master of the mighty.
He's the Captain of the conquerors.
He's the Head of the heroes.
He's the Leader of the legislators.
He's the Overseer of the overcomers.
He's the Governor of the governors.
He's the Prince of princes.
He's the King of kings.
He's the Lord of lords.
PUT YOUR HOPE IN CHRIST!

His office is manifold.
His promise is sure.
His life is matchless.
His goodness is limitless.
His mercy is everlasting.
His love never changes.
His Word is enough.
His grace is sufficient.
His reign is righteous.
His yoke is easy.
His burden is light.
PUT YOUR HOPE IN CHRIST!

I wish I could describe Him to you!
He is indescribable
because He's incomprehensible.
He's irresistible, and He's invincible.
You can't get Him off your hands.
You can't get Him out of your mind.
You can't outlive Him,
and you can't live without Him.

Herod couldn't kill Him,
Death couldn't handle Him,
And thank God the grave couldn't hold Him.

There was nobody before Him,
There will be nobody after Him.
He had no predecessor,
and He'll have no successor.
You can't impeach Him,
and He's not going to resign.
Listen to me, Church —
PUT YOUR HOPE IN CHRIST!

VOLUME ONE

CHRIST AND SUPREMACY

What Is the Hope We Must Recover?

Joy to the world! the Lord is come; let earth receive her King;
Let every heart prepare Him room, and heav'n and nature sing.

Joy to the earth! the Savior reigns; let men their songs employ;
While fields and floods, rocks, hills,
and plains repeat the sounding joy.

No more let sins and sorrows grow, nor thorns infest the ground;
He comes to make His blessings flow far as the curse is found.

He rules the world with truth and grace,
and makes the nations prove
The glories of His righteousness, and wonders of His love.

— *Isaac Watts*

1

THE GLORY OF THE SUPREMACY OF GOD'S SON

ALL the Hope We Are Meant to Have

Does God *really* have a son? If so, what do you think about the son God has?

Broadcasting worldwide over CNN, Larry King has been voted "the most remarkable talk-show host on TV ever". Throughout his five decade career King has interviewed over 40,000 people. Raised in a Brooklyn Jewish home, he remarked once that the one interview he would most like to land is with God Himself. If this happened, he said, he would ask God just one simple question: "Do you really have a son?"

I'm no Larry King! But if I could interview 40,000 *Christians,* I would want to ask them a similar simple question: "What do you *really* think about God's Son?" If offered a follow-up question, I would add: "What is one word you would use most often to describe the glory of God's Son?" And, if allowed a final probe, I would continue: "What is the greatest impact the glory of God's Son brings to your daily walk with Him?"

If you would corner me with those same three questions, here's how I would answer:

(1) Christ is all.

(2) Therefore, "supreme" is the theme of His glory.

(3) That's why hope defines the scope of His impact on my life.

It's important for you to know this about me. Because essentially this entire *Joyful Manifesto* orbits around these three questions and the implications of my answers to them.

To get us started, this opening chapter will consider:

- **The most significant crisis emerging today among Christians and churches everywhere.**

- **The profound cure this crisis requires: spreading a more comprehensive vision of Christ's supremacy throughout the Church.**

- **Broad "brushstroke" definitions for the glory of His supremacy (to be explored in-depth in subsequent chapters).**

- **How the re-awakening of hope and restoration of passion toward Christ is dynamically tied to our vision for ALL that He is.**

- **Why our most strategic step for renewing the Church's engagement with Jesus as Lord is to launch a *"Campaign of Hope".***

Stumbling Over His Supremacy
(Luke 23:13-53)

Issuing this *Joyful Manifesto* comes none too soon. It tackles what many Christian leaders consider to be the major crisis of our times.

There is an emergency. As we're about to discover here (and more so in Chapters 6-8), a host of believers are already caught in its grip. Some call it a "crisis of Christology". I prefer calling it a *crisis of supremacy*. Either way, it signals a serious shortfall in how we see, seek and speak about Christ. For many believers it feels like an aching absence of the dynamic relationship with the Lord Jesus God promised us — like a forfeiture of the holy, happy hope in Him we thought we were meant to have.

I imagine this crisis could produce a pretty disappointing interview on the topic of God's Son with not a few members of your own congregation ... even if Larry King conducted it!

THINK WITH ME ...
What are different ways Christian leaders identify the current crisis?

Already, the "crisis of supremacy" lurks in the shadows. One of the foremost evangelical statesmen of our times, Dr. John R.W. Stott, has heard it. Recently he identified the crisis as he surveyed the Church's battle with religious pluralism. Addressing readers of *Christianity Today*, the Anglican theologian urged them to confront actively all "fuzzy, fallow thinking about our Savior" by insisting at every turn on "the uniqueness of Jesus (he has no competitors) and his finality (he has no successors) because nobody else has his qualifications".

Dr. Timothy George, dean of Beeson School of Theology, has heard the knock: "The erosion of Christ-centered faith threatens to undermine the identity of evangelical Christianity. Real revival and genuine reformation will not be built on flimsy foundations." University of Southern California professor, Dr. Dallas Willard, has amplified this concern: "Why is today's church so weak? Why are Christians indistinguishable from the world? The poor result is not in spite of what we teach and how we teach, but precisely because of it. The power of Jesus and his gospel has been cut off from ordinary human existence." Could this be one reason an interdenominational national clergy network recently called upon Christians to take all crosses off their churches as a gesture of reconciliation with other religions, because other faiths regard it as a "symbol of oppression and perceived superiority"?

QUOTABLE QUOTE

In the United States, Jesus is widely hailed as the "King of Kings". But it is a strange sort of sovereign who is so slavishly responsive to his subjects ... The American Jesus is more a pawn than a king, pushed around in a complex game of cultural (and countercultural) chess, sacrificed here for this cause and there for another.

(DR. STEPHEN PROTHERO)

Former Dallas Seminary president, Dr. Charles Swindoll, identified the wolf-at-the-door another way in his book *The Grace Awakening*. He warned that the greatest heresy shadowing the evangelical movement may be our over-emphasis on what we should be doing for God, rather than on what God has done and is getting ready to do for us in Jesus Christ. Premiere reformed theologian Dr. J.I. Packer has likened the modern Church's vision of Christ to "Humpty-Dumpty" — broken into a hundred fragments! Everyone has a piece of the picture. But few are trying to put all the pieces back together so as to give God's people a comprehensive message about His Son sufficient to transform congregations and their mission to the world.

THINK WITH ME ...
How much do we actually talk about God's Son to one another?

Writing out of his own extensive travels in evangelical circles, Jonathan Graf, editor-in-chief of NavPress's popular *PRAY!* magazine, editorialized not long ago that he finds, with rising alarm, the name of Jesus Christ *seldom even mentioned* inside many churches these days. After over 30 years itinerating into various parts of the Body of Christ across the globe, I must admit that often my own experiences have mirrored Graf's.

More than once, I've participated in half hour worship sessions where (unintended, I'm sure) specific references to our Savior were virtually absent in the choruses we sang. More than once, I've listened to widely respected preachers deliver Biblically-grounded messages that barely referenced our Lord Jesus, let alone bring the congregation to bow at the feet of their King. More than once I've monitored the between-session conversations of delegates at major Christian conventions, hoping for even a hint that God's Son was somehow vital to their discussions, only to be disappointed time and time again.

In all honesty, Sunday after Sunday how much of the general conversation in our churches actually honors Jesus in a manner comparable to how Paul talked? How often do we say to each other words like: "For me to live is *Christ*" (Phil. 2)? Or, "We proclaim *Him,* admonishing and teaching everyone with all wisdom, so that we might present everyone perfect in Christ" (Col. 1)? Or again, "For I resolved to know nothing while I was with you except *Jesus Christ* and him crucified" (1 Cor. 2)? In our times of fellowship do we seek to "take captive every thought to make it obedient to *Christ*" (2 Cor. 10)?

Recall for a moment a recent exchange you had with a fellow believer.

QUOTABLE QUOTE

Anyone who believes that Jesus is Lord can not avoid the implications of such a confession in every sphere of life. This is clearly one reason why the early Christians suffered and died. They dared to challenge the political authority of Rome by saying "Jesus is Lord!" They did not defy Rome's every law, but they did refuse to say anyone but Jesus was Lord.

(DR. JOHN ARMSTRONG)

Taking your cue from 1 John 1, did the time together give both of you a greater vision of the glory of Jesus as "the eternal life which was with the Father and has appeared to us"? Did you try to encourage each other with "what we have seen and heard" of Christ? Was there a shared effort to help each other enter into deeper "fellowship with the Father and with his Son" and, thus, have your joy "made complete" (1 John 1)? If your experience was like most of mine, probably not.

Too many of us, I'm afraid, have become comfortable simply conversing about benign concepts of God. We allow ourselves to sidestep deeper encounters with Jesus as *Lord*. Yet, there's no getting around the fundamental principle of Romans 10:17: "Faith comes from hearing the message, and the message is heard through the word of *Christ*." This process is as equally true of believers — in some ways even more so — as it is of unbelievers. What *Christians* hear about their Savior from one another, as a steady diet, determines a good deal of the depth of hope and passion they express toward Him.

THINK WITH ME ...
In what sense is Jesus *missing*
in the evangelical movement today?

Incidentally, this quietly persistent diminishment of Christ's preeminence in our churches has not gone unnoticed by secular society around us. For example, in its wrap-up issue for 2003, *U.S. News and World Report* ran a front cover story titled: *"The New Evangelicals: Their Bold Take On Christianity Is Changing America"*. What their research uncovered, and how they interpreted it, should give all Christians pause.

The editors employed quite a constellation of descriptive words and phrases to identify the evangelical movement which, they said, includes four out of ten Americans. Here is a sampling:

- Serious about religion
- Diverse and complex
- Spiritually accessible to all
- Experientially and emotionally engaging
- Therapeutic in its impact
- Vigorous in its propagation

- Faith-based in its social initiatives
- Pro-Life and Pro-Family
- Pro-America and its manifest destiny
- Entrepreneurial and improvisational
- Market-savvy in its expansionism
- Theologically fuzzy and ambivalent

U.S. News reported that much of what it saw was positive. The movement has caused America to become the most religious of all modern industrial nations. But what should have thundered at any thoughtful reader — conspicuous by its absence — was this: There wasn't *any* suggestion, anywhere in the five-page report, that giving Christ primacy was the (or even "a") predominant distinctive of evangelical faith. In fact, apart from one phrase referencing "Christ's redemptive role" as a long-held doctrine, the entire article never even mentioned His name!

Shouldn't this raise red flags for us? How could such a report contain this profound oversight? Where has the Church failed to make our Lord the preeminent definition of our identity before others? Must not evangelicals accept major responsibility for what is missing in our testimony — for *Who* is missing?

Not long ago a brochure landed on my desk that troubled me a good deal. It was produced by a major national evangelical ministry. The large, colorful eight panel promotional piece invited Christians to an event that anticipated tens of thousands of participants. It billed itself as a "motivational conference", full of "humorous and dramatically engaging presentations" by powerful "motivational speakers". The event's theme, splashed across the front panel, consisted of a phrase taken from a popular verse of Scripture. But, unfortunately the phrase was quoted out of context, neglecting the portion of the sentence that referred to Christ's matchless role for the Church at the Throne of God. Even more astounding was this: *Nowhere* on any of the eight panels was the Lord Jesus even mentioned. Not one time! A few uses of "God" were the extent of references to deity.

Please don't misunderstand. I know for a fact this national conference was convened by leaders who dearly love our Savior with all their hearts. Which is what leaves me even more dumbfounded: Why was the name of Jesus abandoned in their promotional effort? At the very least, why was He not given a visibility comparable to that provided for each of the ten major speakers whose faces and "bio's" were featured? Why was only a generic "God" used in a brochure about a decidedly Christian event?

And why over the years, visiting in many nations, have I seen a similar pattern repeated in not a few public relations pieces produced for various evangelical causes? Why is that?

In a *People* magazine cover story on "religion in Hollywood", TV and movie actress Patricia Heaton (herself an evangelical Presbyterian) suggested one answer: "Most people have some kind of faith. However, I think Jesus is a scary subject. 'God' you can make into anything you want. But confronted with Jesus you have to say I believe that or I don't. That's very powerful." Sadly, this avoidance can be seen too often *inside* our churches. We talk *around* Jesus more than we talk *about* Him.

I'm not surprised Graf concluded his editorial with this plea, one we all need to heed: "As people of prayer we must pray fervently that the head, the Lord Jesus Christ, would be lifted up again in our churches; that the Lord Jesus Christ, the Beginning, would once again be proclaimed from our pulpits; that publishers, pastors and prophets would not be afraid to point directly to the supremacy of the Lord Jesus Christ, no matter what it does to their popularity."

I agree. The time has come to pray for the Holy Spirit to restore to the Church a "*Person*-driven" walk with the everlasting Son of the Father. What would this look like if God answered? And how might it make things different for us?

THINK WITH ME ...
How does one demonstrate a "Person-driven" approach to discipleship?

Lately, mega-church pastor Rick Warren has introduced into Christian vernacular the helpful phrase "the purpose-driven church" and "the purpose-driven life" (selling over 20 million books on the topic). These are great concepts! But, let me ask: How many of us have discovered, first of all, what it means to be *Person*-driven in our churches and lives? How many of us are drawn into the prior issue, a passion for the *person* of the supreme, sovereign and all-sufficient Son of God — for whom the *purpose* for our churches and our lives exists to begin with?

Let me ask this in some other ways: How many of us possess a deepening sense of the imminent consummation of all things in Christ, in which we have a strategic part? Do we long to be a part of a movement toward the glorious climax of history in Him? Do we sense that we're on a mission that even now tastes of the powers of the Age to Come because Jesus Christ is in our midst? Who among us ties our true destiny directly to the Hour when heaven and earth will be "summed up" in God's all-consuming Son (Eph. 1 and Col. 1)? And, how often do we Christians ever share such a vision among ourselves?

> ## QUOTABLE QUOTE
>
> **He is indeed proved to be the Son of His Father. But He is found to be both Lord and God of all else. All things are put under Him and delivered to Him. For He is God, and all things are subjected to Him. Nevertheless, the Son refers all that He has received to the Father. The Father is the source of His Son Himself, whom He begot as Lord.**
>
> (NOVATIAN [C. 235], A ROMAN ELDER AND THEOLOGIAN.)

Let's be candid: When all is said and done, evangelicals may not be the *Person*-driven people we thought we were. For example: How many of us follow Jesus daily with the exciting conviction that what He will be Lord of *ultimately* He is Lord of *even now;* that every believer is being led by Him in triumphal procession today toward the Grand Finale over which He will fully triumph at The End? How often do we *say so* to each other, and with boldness?

We talk *around* Jesus more than we talk *about* Him.

Tragically, for multitudes of Christians there appears to be little of a compelling, *Person*-driven core to their sense of God's purpose. Motivation based on Christ for ALL that He is, remains marginal. Relatively few of us are propelled with a hope and passion worthy of God's Firstborn and ignited by Scripture's teachings on His Lordship in everything. Instead, far too often we find ourselves stumbling over His supremacy.

We talk *around* Jesus more than we talk *about* Him.

Without a doubt, Christ fulfills our everlasting future. He embodies our blessed hope. He provides the guarantee for all we could ever become or do for God. And, He offers to be this for us in Himself alone (1 Tim. 1 and Titus 2). But I ask you: Is this normally, consistently, how we talk about Him with each other? Are we *driven* by this Person and the promises He encompasses? Do we find it impossible to be silent about Him, most of all with believers?

What if the Savior whom Christians bank on appears, instead, to be almost the opposite? *What If* — what if He usually seems to be indifferent to securing meaningful solutions for the struggles of our lives? What if He comes across to us as offering little immediate hope for broken relation-ships, or financially besieged families, or bungled battles with addictions, or our beaten-up sense of self-worth, or the breathless bustling of our churchly activities, or the moral bankruptcy of our communities? What if the Jesus we call Lord is *perceived* frequently as incapably involved with us when we are drowning in dark moments of despair? Why would we want to make Him a major topic of conversation when we gather together? Why would we rather not talk around Him instead of about Him?

Is our most pressing spiritual ambition simply to "flee the wrath to come" (Lk. 3)? Or is it much more? Is it also to seek the glory of the One who is to come (1 Thess. 1)? If mostly the former, then why should we be surprised that Sunday schools, for example, are far more intent on discussing Biblical solutions to day-to-day survival issues than exposing students to the successes of a Sovereign who, right now, is saturating the nations with the triumphs of His grace?

THINK WITH ME ...
In what other ways does our stumbling
over supremacy show itself among us?

Such confusion about Jesus forms a major part of the crisis of supremacy. It helps explain the worrisome spiritual malaise that plagues many of our congregations. It provides one solid insight into the various deep-seated disappointments with Christ that eat away at passion for His Kingdom in so many of our people. It is a prime source of growing despair over endless battles with sin and evil. It reinforces our persistent suspicion that even if Christ is on the move, most of us will still be left behind when He acts.

Without an adequate view of the incomparable majesty of our Redeemer King, Christians quickly revert to the role of spiritual "couch potatoes". We survey God's purposes in Christ *remotely*. We're involved with Him at arm's length, at best. Jaded by the immensities and complexities of modern society, we forfeit expectations of being "surprised by joy" again (as C.S. Lewis described the effect of encountering Christ). For many of us "amazing grace" has ceased to be genuinely amazing because, for many of us, our vision of God's Son is no longer genuinely amazing.

George Barna, respected demographer of American Christianity, concluded extensive research a short time back with this troubling summary: "Overall, Christian ministry is stuck in a deep rut. Too many

Christians and churches in America have traded in spiritual passion for empty rituals, clever methods and mindless practices. The challenge to today's Church is not methodological. *It is a challenge to resuscitate the spiritual passion and fervor of the nation's Christians.*"

Why would there ever be a need for spiritual "resuscitation" if Christians were truly following Jesus as nothing-less-than the King of Glory, the Lord of the Universe, the Hope of the Nations? Could it be that our affections languish because Christ is not preached *inside* our churches for ALL that He is? Are we "stuck in a rut" (to use Barna's phrase) because we've stumbled over the issue of His supremacy? Some, I'm sure, would challenge that last statement. They would insist that in most evangelical churches today "Christ *is* preached".

But is He? A closer look may reveal that our messages, more often than not, are about how Christ fits into who we are, where we are headed, what we are doing and how we are blessed. That's important, of course. But is that adequate? As the rest of *Joyful Manifesto* will argue, to "preach Christ" — in the full view of His supremacy — is something else altogether. It involves helping Christians discover how they fit into who *Christ* is, where *Christ* is headed, what *Christ* is doing and how *Christ* is blessed.

THINK WITH ME ...
In what sense do we view Jesus
as a *mascot* more than a *monarch?*

I attended a high school that is football-crazy. It boasted a stadium seating 20,000. This Ohio institution has produced nearly twenty-five state championship teams. Voted national champions more than once, our team was recently given a full page story in the *New York Times* along with a two-hour special on ESPN. The team is called the Massillon Tigers. Our mascot requires a taller student to dress up like a tiger — I mean, wearing a *real* tiger skin! He inherits a name of affection: Obie the Tiger.

Here's how a mascot works. At times, in the midst of a game, if we're falling behind, the coach signals time-out. Because the crowd needs to be stirred to cheer more enthusiastically for the team's victory, the uniformed tiger runs his stripes onto the field. Seeing Obie doubles the crowd's determination to celebrate the champions we hope to be. After all, we are the Massillon Tigers! In turn, this reinforces the team's confidence in itself. They charge back to the scrimmage line ready to put bold plays into action,

to redouble the struggle, to win the game on their terms. At every succeeding time-out, the mascot reappears, paws lifted triumphantly toward the
skies. The roar of the crowd goes up once more. The team regains courage
and resolve.

But at each appearance, interestingly, Obie's performance is very brief.
Then he disappears, sent to the sidelines, put on hold until the next setback.
He has served his useful purpose well. We're so proud of him. Everyone
feels better now. The game can proceed with new momentum.

Still in the final analysis, the tiger never really gets involved beyond re-
igniting cries of confidence, beyond giving us an identity to boast about. To
be sure, Obie stirs up a certain kind of passion. But it is not really about him.
It's really about the team, and even more about the fans. The team designs
the plays, runs the patterns, throws the blocks, reaches the goal, claims the
credit. The fans jump with joy, declare their superior skills over the losers,
and boast that *they* are "the Massillon Tigers". Then we all go home
satisfied.

Now, here's the kicker: What happens the moment our team hits a
losing season? What good is the mascot then? The zeal it inspires suddenly
feels hollow, even foolish. We are left with little else but embarrassing
thoughts of our team's helplessness and hopelessness. Then, how quickly
passion heads south — for Obie, for our team, for our future, for the game
itself.

*In so many of our churches, I fear, Jesus is regularly deployed as our
mascot.* Once a week on Sunday, for example, we "trot Him out" to cheer us
up, to give us new vigor and vision, to reassure us that we are "somebodies".
We invite Him to reinforce for us the great things we want to do for God. We
look to Him to reinvigorate our celebration of victories we think we're
destined to win. He lifts our spirits. He resuscitates our souls. He rebuilds
our confidence. He gives us reasons to cheer. He confirms for us over and
over that all must be well. We're so proud of Him! We're so happy to be
identified with His name. Enthusiasm for Him energizes us — for awhile.

But then, for the rest of the week He is pretty much relegated to the
sidelines. For all practical purposes we are the ones who call the shots. We
implement the plays, scramble for first downs, and improvise in a pinch.
Even if we do it in His name, we do it with little reliance on His person.
There's scant evidence that we think of ourselves as somehow utterly
incapable of doing anything of eternal consequence apart from Him.

Promises of fuller displays of His dominion leave our daily discipleship un-phased. We evidence little desperation for increased manifestations of His majesty among us.

As contradictory as it may seem, many of us have redefined Jesus into someone we can both admire *and* ignore at the same time! To be our *mascot*, we've re-designed Him to be reasonably convenient — someone praisewor-thy, to be sure, but overall kept in reserve, useful, "on call" as required.

Without promoting an overriding passion for Christ as our Monarch — as our *everything* — why would we ever openly celebrate Him as anything other than our mascot? The truth is, Jesus' claims to the Monarchy make Him the opposite of an Obie character. Instead, He encompasses in *Himself* the coach, quarterback, playbook, team, uniforms, cheerleader, goal post and final championship — the "whole nine yards" (as we say) — wrapped up in one person alone. Does our vision of His lordship take on such exalted dimensions *inside* the Church? Does it express such grand themes? Does it promote an exclusive love for Him — an enthusiasm not unlike what rises from thousands at a Super Bowl — a zeal for His glory evident in our daily routines in the marketplace as much as in our churchly schedules on weekends? Is the Spirit truly having *His* way with us?

I suspect we have found far more fascination with the evangelical game itself — with how *we* are playing it and whether *we* are winning — than we have with the One in whose name, and for whose sake, the "game" exists at all. Which may explain the reports: The membership in 80% of U.S. churches is either stagnant or dying. Tens of thousands of congregations are wrestling with a leveling off of financial giving, with a growing shortfall of laborers, and with an atmosphere of apathy toward evangelism, compassion ministries and the global mission of Christ's Kingdom that seems endemic.

THINK WITH ME ...
How might we begin to recover a vision
for the supremacy of God's Son?

But the good news is this: If we turn back to exalt once again in our Savior as the Monarch He is — if we spread this grander message about God's Son to God's people, inviting them to re-discover in His reign all the hope we are meant to have — we can create a life-saving paradigm shift inside the Church. We can trigger a re-ignition of our passion for Him as Lord of all. This effort can help bring an end to our scandalous stumblings over Christ's supremacy. It can return us to the dynamics of a *Person*-driven discipleship.

Recently, a Florida pastor attempted to stir up a national movement that he called "America Say Jesus". His goal? To get every Christian in the U.S. to say the name of Jesus three to five times daily. Said he, "Just think what a revival would break loose if Christians all across America started saying the name of Jesus to their friends, family and neighbors. The name of Jesus is so often shunned, even ridiculed. I believe God would honor the Lord Jesus in our nation and send us a spiritual awakening if we took up this effort, even beginning among ourselves as believers."

As a strategy for revival, repeating the name of Jesus throughout the day may seem a little far-fetched to some. But, I suggest to you, the crisis we've just begun to explore *does* require a campaign of similar vein. We *do* need fresh initiatives to expand how most Christians view and value God's Son. We need to summon fellow believers to embrace the full scope of the hope of His supremacy. We need to make His glory the dominating theme in everything we do together as the Body of Christ, not only in how we seek Him but also in how we speak of Him.

Volume Two explores the crisis of supremacy in much more depth, exposing it fully for what it is: the greatest crisis of our times. But I chose to at least touch on it at the outset in order to set the stage. The preceding pages have hung a backdrop for the decisive drama about Jesus' dominion waiting to unfold throughout the remainder of **Volume One**.

So now, let the drama begin! Let it unfold, beginning with the rest of this chapter. Here the Holy Spirit can help you re-discover a greater vision of Jesus' everlasting praise so you might speak of Him to each other in more powerful ways. Here you'll thumb through stirring "snapshots" of the Lord Jesus Christ that you could start sharing with other believers right now. Then in chapters 2-5 we'll go back through the "photo album" more carefully, taking time to enjoy all the beauty that we find in the Son of God.

QUOTABLE QUOTE

It pleased God, in His eternal purpose, to choose and ordain the Lord Jesus, His only begotten Son, to be Mediator between God and man, the Prophet, Priest and King, the Head and Savior of His Church, the Heir of all things, the Judge of the world; unto whom He did from all eternity give a people, to be His seed, and to be by Him in time redeemed, called, justified, sanctified, and glorified.

(FROM THE WESTMINSTER CONFESSION OF FAITH)

Snapshots of His Supremacy
(1 John 4:1-3; 5:6-11)

A leading U.S. cereal company recently championed their primary product, available in grocery stores everywhere for over one hundred years, with a catchy new slogan. It sent sales through the roof:

"CORNFLAKES: Taste them again, for the first time."

Not to be trite, but many in our churches today need to be similarly called back to the foundation of our faith. We might say it this way:

"JESUS CHRIST: Meet Him again, for the first time."

To be blunt: Many Christians need to meet God's Son again. As we do, it may feel as if it were happening for the first time, because of how far from His glory we have wandered. However, as a result the crux of our crisis — the magnitude of what's missing in the message of Christ heard *inside* the Church — will become unavoidably apparent.

THINK WITH ME ...
How would *you* define a Biblical vision
of the supremacy of Christ?

Within the Trinity, the Father Himself is so thoroughly consumed with the primacy of His Son that He insists, throughout the New Testament, on being known as "the Father of our Lord Jesus Christ". Can we choose to be any less passionate about this same Person? Should we not be inspired by how the Father both exalts His Son and exults in His Son?

QUOTABLE QUOTE

For nothing counts with God, except His beloved Son, Jesus Christ, who is completely pure and holy before Him. Where He is, there God looks and has His pleasure.

(MARTIN LUTHER)

Colossians 1:18 reports that for God the bottom line of every constellation He's created — the stunning climax of every facet of salvation He offers — comes down to this: " ... *that in everything Christ might have the supremacy*". If securing Christ's reputation is such a big deal to Heaven, should it not be equally a big deal for all of Heaven's citizens? Should we not eagerly join with the Spirit in His role to promote Christ's preeminence in all things? Jesus explained it this way: "The Spirit will bring glory to me by taking from what is mine and making it known to you. All that belongs to the Father is mine. That's why I said the Spirit will take what is mine and make it known to you" (Jn. 16).

Surely it is in order, therefore, to revisit the one word Paul uses to gather up the whole panorama of Christ's glory: *"supremacy"*. I wonder: How would *you* define "supremacy" to encompass all it includes? Maybe you'd like to try this easy-to-remember sentence on for size. This definition has proved quite helpful to me over time:

> *The SUPREMACY of Christ includes*
> *Who He IS as the Son of God,*
> *Where He LEADS in the Purposes of God,*
> *How He IMPARTS the Resources of God,*
> *What He RECEIVES from the People of God.*

When you get right down to it, the supremacy of Christ is really not as complicated as one might suspect. Though profound in its implications, the concept can be shared initially in just these few words. This one sentence alerts us to four major themes that summarize virtually all that the Bible teaches us about our Lord Jesus Christ. (And we're talking about thousands of verses here.) To review: Who Christ **is**, where He **leads**, how He **imparts**, what He **receives**.

The personal implications of this definition are unavoidable, as well. In His supremacy, God's Son wants us to know Him directly — even intimately — through four life-changing encounters with Him: with the glory of His person **(Son)**; with the thrill of His mission **(Purpose)**; with the wonders of His grace **(Resources)**; and with the significance of His service **(People)**.

THINK WITH ME ...
What are the four dimensions
of a "wide-angled vision" of Christ?

But there's more to add to this definition. I've learned to take my thinking on supremacy one additional step. I turn to what I call the *Four F's*. They make the meaning of His majesty even more manageable. They give us a second handle on it:

- **Focus**

- **Fulfillment**

- **Fullness**

- **Fervency**

Here's how the Four F's work: The **focus** of Christ's supremacy for His Church consists, above all, of our preoccupation with who He IS, for time and eternity, as God's Son. The **fulfillment** of everything His supremacy guarantees to His church flows from where He LEADS us in God's purposes. The **fullness** of His supremacy results from how He IMPARTS to His Church all of God's resources. The **fervency** of His supremacy springs from the ways His people respond to him with loving, even passionate, surrender and service.

Now, let's put together all these "snapshots". When we do, our definition of supremacy expands to say this:

Who Christ **IS** as the Son of God

defines the FOCUS of His supremacy.

Where Christ **LEADS** in the Purposes of God

defines the FULFILLMENT of His supremacy.

How Christ **IMPARTS** the Resources of God

defines the FULLNESS of His supremacy.

What Christ **RECEIVES** from the People of God

defines the FERVENCY of His supremacy.

Based on these four themes it is clear that supremacy is fundamentally about Jesus' **rights**:

As the Son of God (that is, being the One who is in eternal union with the Father and the Spirit) He has the *right* to occupy our full attention and keep it fixed on Him, exclusively as Lord. He's the *focus* for our lives.

In the Purposes of God (that is, in the Father's plan to sum up everything in Heaven and among the nations under the Son's everlasting dominion) He has the *right* to keep us involved with the advance of His mission, exclusively as Lord. He's the *fulfillment* of our calling.

Owning the Resources of God (that is, being the Supreme Ruler over the outpouring of God's triumphant grace) He has the *right* to keep our full dependence on Him, exclusively as Lord. He's the *fullness* in our fellowship.

As the One who dominates the People of God (that is, being the Regent of God to whom the affection and allegiance of every subject belongs) He has the *right* to gather up the devotion of His servants for His everlasting glory, exclusively as Lord. He's the *fervency* of our labors.

Don't you find that just a little bit thrilling when you stop to think about it? *Our Redeemer is all those things, wrapped into one Person!* Therefore, in the hands of the Holy Spirit each phrase can enrich, at very practical levels, the meaning Christ brings to your daily walk with God? (You'll see how well this works in **Volume Three**).

It is a little like what former Senator John Ashcroft (subsequently Attorney General) once called "the basketball approach to life". Great NBA stars, he noted, develop a "wide-angled vision". They are able to see the whole court at once so they can exploit, at a moment's notice, every option available to them. Ashcroft remarked that as soon as great players like a Michael Jordan spring into mid-air toward the basket, success no longer depends on his coach or his shoes or his other teammates. It depends on his ability to see the larger picture and make instant moves that put the ball in the hoop.

Similarly for all of us, catching a wider vision of Christ's supremacy increases our options for achieving a victorious Christian life. It helps us start "playing the game" in view of *everything* Christ brings to the "court" as Son, and Leader, and Resource, and Heir. The implications of this outlook are extraordinarily life-giving. "Wide angle vision" enlarges the content of worship. It empowers moral perseverance within a decadent culture. It inspires renewed efforts at racial reconciliation, at reaching and serving the poor, at rearing godly children, at setting Biblical priorities in our spending, at performing with excellence on the job, or at spreading the Gospel among the nations. It fills us with abounding hope in God even in the darkest moments of the daily battle we all face.

THINK WITH ME ...
How can snapshots of supremacy
ever capture the "mystery of God"?

Truly, if the term "Christology" means "the study of Christ", then what a rich study He provides! What a rigorous pursuit He rightfully deserves! What a marvelous cure for our crisis awaits us as we meet Him like this ... again ... for the first time!

Please don't misunderstand, however. Even with all of these beautiful words and phrases, so logically organized, we've just begun to unveil the full extent of who He is. These snapshots are really little more than *signposts*. They help us get better bearings on what Scripture teaches about God's Son. In no way am I suggesting this resumé comes close to exhausting all we can know of Him. In fact, if we were to research the nearly 17,000 books on Jesus housed in the Library of Congress — more than any other historical person — we would still be only at the threshold of defining the glory of His supremacy.

Let's not forget how pointedly Paul tells the Colossians that Christ is the "*mystery* of God". In Colossians 1 he writes about "the glorious riches of this mystery, which is Christ in you". In Colossians 2 he speaks of "the mystery of God, namely Christ in whom are hid all the treasures of wisdom and knowledge". Without question the Lord of Eternity, though plainly revealed in time-and-space-and-history, remains at the same time profoundly inexhaustible, incomprehensible, uncontainable as well as thoroughly unsearchable (as Paul specifically tells us in Ephesians 3). In other words, being supreme in Heaven and earth means there will always be "an air of mystery" about Him. There will always be so much more of Him to know than anyone can completely fathom. No set of categories will ever fully encompass the one "in whom all the fullness of the Godhead dwells in bodily form" (Col. 2). In that sense, He will always be a "magnificent mystery".

Yet on the other hand, I do believe simple tools (such as the four phrases discussed above) can equip us to explore more effectively the brilliance with which Scripture presents Him from cover to cover. Applied to the promises and prophecies of God's Word, such tools can reveal much of what our souls are desperate to re-discover of Him (longings we may not yet have the courage to admit). By them the Holy Spirit can help us capture Grand Canyon-style vistas on King Jesus. This will become increasingly evident as we break down our four-part definition over the next four chapters.

THINK WITH ME ...
Where does the *suffering* of Jesus fit into the supremacy of Jesus?

At this point, some readers may question (and properly so): Where does the *Cross* come into this enthusiastic emphasis on glory, and hope, and supremacy? Is not the Lion exalted foremost as a *Lamb* (Rev. 5)? After all, didn't Paul protest to the Corinthians that he wanted to know nothing among believers except "Jesus Christ and Him *crucified*" (1 Cor. 2)? If those six hours of incomparable suffering form the pinnacle of our Lord's ministry for us all (and they do), shouldn't His holy humiliation predominate in any emphasis on His regency?

Good questions. We will return to them more than once in coming chapters. But for now please note: The Cross, in fact, was the *definitive display* of Christ's eternal dominion. It was the *supreme* revelation of His sovereignty. Because of it, slaves of the Fall are liberated. Because of it, Satan's minions are bound. Because of it, death is destroyed, sin is demolished, judgment is absorbed and fear is banished. Because of it, all who believe are conquered by grace and transferred into the Empire of the Son. If the fruits of the Tree do not magnify the full extent of Christ's Kingship, then surely nothing else does. Nothing else *can*.

As to Paul's statement to the Corinthians, remember: He committed himself to proclaim both the *Christ* ("anointed one" referring to His divine appointment as Master of the Universe) as well as His *Cross* (the fundamental foundation undergirding His victorious throne). In point of fact, both parts of Paul's message were really about the supremacy of God's Son! As he amplifies in 1 Corinthians 2:8, it was no less than "the Lord of glory" who was crucified. Centuries later, his outlook was accurately reflected in the preaching of the Puritans who, as J.I. Packer puts it, "measured Christ's mercy by His majesty. They magnified the love of the cross by dwelling on the greatness of the glory He left for it." And, I would

> ## QUOTABLE QUOTE
>
> *Tetlesthai* — it is finished! The most significant single word in the Greek New Testament translates to the most triumphant declaration! It contains both a prophecy and a verdict. On the cross Jesus, the Son, anticipated the Father's verdict and His ultimate intervention. The dawn of the world's redemption had broken, and with it the chains of human slavery to sin, shame and condemnation were shattered.
>
> (Dr. Jack Hayford)

add, by dwelling on the greatness of the glory He *inherited* because of it.

It is hard to deny a double meaning in Jesus' promise in John 12: "And I, if I am lifted up, will draw all people to myself." When He promises to "draw all to Me", He's talking supremacy — how the redeemed of all the ages will marshal to Him as willing subjects. When He refers to being "lifted up" He not only pictured hanging on the Cross (as John notes). He also spoke of His resurrection and ascension and coronation, when the Father invited Him up to assume the position He now holds in the universe (Acts 1). Forever, He is the One lifted up to the right hand of God — precisely because of the victory of the Cross — to reign in life over all who surrender to His cleansing blood and saving power. Forever, He is exalted as salvation's all-sufficient sacrificial offering, the precious Lamb of Glory, whose glorified body still bears the marks of His sufferings.

Even a cursory reading of the passion passages, such as Luke 23, reveals that supremacy comprised a central theme. Re-read sometime Luke's account of Jesus' farewell words about the Kingdom in the Upper Room, or the Sanhedrin's charges based on His claims of authority, or His own brief defense predicting His return in clouds of glory, as well as the thief's desire for the Kingdom that Jesus answered with dying breath. Or read the very words placed above His head as He hung between Heaven and earth proclaiming Him to be "King of the Jews". Throughout the whole chapter, Luke was careful to ensure that his readers never viewed the Cross apart from the Ascension.

THINK WITH ME ...
How does the supremacy of Christ
take us beyond the *centrality* of Christ?

It should be obvious by now that expanding our definition of supremacy like this — including how we look at the Cross — may require a significant shift in how Jesus is viewed by many followers. The Scripture points toward much more than what we commonly refer to as the *centrality* of God's Son. Does that insight surprise you?

Of course, "centrality" remains an important Biblical concept. It characterizes a whole set of Jesus' lordship claims. It affirms Him as the center of everything, meant to be in the middle of everything, surrounded by everything. And, *that* He is! As Dietrich Bonhoeffer named Him, He is by nature "Christ, the Center". We must never cease to sound this note loud and clear.

But "supremacy" takes our vision of Him to a whole new level. Similar to "centrality", His claims to "supremacy" rise from His very nature as God's Son. This dimension gives our Redeemer even higher homage. To worship Him as supreme in the universe moves beyond centrality. As supreme, our Lord is not only surrounded by everything, but He also *surrounds* everything with Himself. As Lord, He *encompasses* all of us within His rule.

Of course, Christians properly profess (as you and I have often said) that "Jesus is the center of my life". And that's true! But *which* Jesus is at the center of my life? — that's the issue. Is it the one whose glory *enfolds* my life, and *consumes* my life, and *defines* my life because He alone thoroughly *sums up* my life — both its meaning and its destiny — and sums it up in Himself?

Here's how Eugene Peterson pictures "supremacy" in his rendering of Colossians 1:17 in *The Message*:

> He is supreme in the beginning, and
> — leading the resurrection parade —
> He is supreme in the end.
> From beginning to end he's there,
> towering far above everything, everyone.
> So spacious is he, so roomy,
> that everything of God finds its proper place in him
> without crowding.

wow!

> **QUOTABLE QUOTE**
>
> In 1737 I had a view, that for me was extraordinary, of the glory of the Son of God as Mediator between God and man and His wonderful, great, full, pure and sweet grace and love, and meek and gentle condescension. This grace appeared ineffably excellent with an excellency great enough to swallow up all thought and conception ... I felt an ardency of soul to be, what I know not otherwise how to express, emptied and annihilated; to lie in the dust and to be full of Christ alone.
>
> (JONATHAN EDWARDS)

The Messiah that Christians follow is one who is both central *and* supreme, both intimate *and* infinite — a Sovereign who is wholly *above* us while at the same time wholly *among* us. This is how the Church today must see and seek Him once again. This is how we must speak of Him once again. If we're ever to recover fully all that His *centrality* holds for us, it will be necessary to increase our emphasis on the place of His *supremacy*. Given the current crisis in our Christology, we must do so without delay. The effort must receive our highest priority.

THINK WITH ME …
In what sense does Jesus' supremacy
make Him the *circumference* of our lives?

Let me put this distinctive in the form of a metaphor. Christians, we might say, are like an uncapped bottle cast into the ocean. Once the bottle (the believer) is in the ocean (Christ), the ocean can begin to fill the bottle (representing the idea of *centrality*). But that's just the beginning of the adventure. There's still the whole Atlantic to explore, into which to plunge, through which to navigate. This represents our pursuit of fuller dimensions of Christ's *supremacy* for our lives (just as the ocean ultimately surrounds the bottle).

Full of water, the bottle can still be swept by currents out to sea. This pictures a Christian who puts his or her eyes on Christ, seeking His glory and pursuing the manifestation of His kingship in all things, among all peoples Colossians 1:27 combines both aspects: Christ not only dwells in us (just as the ocean gets into the bottle — *centrality*) but Christ is also "the hope of glory" for us (just as the bottle flows out to sea — *supremacy*). Not only does the Holy Spirit want to *fill* our souls with the Living Water, but He also wants to *compel* our souls to venture forth into the Great Deep of God's eternal purposes in Jesus.

To put it another way: There's a world of difference between saying "God loves you and has a wonderful plan for your life", and saying "God has a wonderful plan for the nations, to sum up everything in Heaven and earth under Jesus as Lord, and He loves you enough to give you a strategic place in it." The first promise is about centrality, the second is about supremacy. The second, unfortunately, is woefully neglected among far too many Christians.

In *The Emerging Church* California church planter Dan Kimball agreed. For many Christians, he observed, the gospel they've heard has essentially told them that Jesus died for their sins so that they could go to Heaven when they die. This is, of course, true. It reflects some of the "centrality" perspective. Consider, however, the way Kimball would re-phrase the full scope of God's call: "Jesus died for your sins so that you can be His redeemed coworker *now* in what He is doing in this world, and then spend eternity in Heaven with the one you are giving your life to now." This is one way to give the "supremacy" dimension of the Gospel the priority it warrants.

Missionary statesman E. Stanley Jones understood this larger perspective on Jesus well. Reflecting on how He proclaimed the Savior throughout India for 40 years in the 1900's — doing so among multitudes of devotees to thousands of Hindu deities — Jones found it necessary to remind Indian Christians that Christ was simultaneously their center and their *circumference* (or, to use our terms here, both central and supreme). That was something no village idol could claim. Start with Christ as our center, Jones argued, but then keep moving toward the circumference. However, do so knowing that because He is God and Lord no one should ever expect to reach the "end point" of His reign. "Christ is all infinite and boundless," he declared. That's the language of "supremacy". It is similar to the language of God's Messianic-era promise to Jerusalem in Zechariah 2:5: "I myself will be a wall of fire around it [circumference] and I will be its glory within [center]".

On one hand, centrality calls us to let our lives be *wrapped around* who Jesus is. On the other hand, supremacy requires that our lives also be *wrapped up into* who Jesus is. Without question, there is a delightful difference between these two complementary positions! As one of the opening pages of our *Joyful Manifesto* suggests:

> **Centrality** is about Christ's right to be kept at the
> center of who *we are, where we are* headed,
> all *we* are doing and how *we are* blessed.
>
> **Supremacy** speaks of so much more.
> It proclaims Christ's right to keep us at the center of
> who *He* is (focus), where *He* is headed (fulfillment),
> what *He* is imparting (fullness) and how *He* is blessed (fervency).

Watch how this distinction emerges in five familiar New Testament texts (and there are many more like them): "Christ is all [supremacy], and in all [centrality]" (Col. 3). "For us there is one Lord, Jesus Christ, through whom are all things [supremacy] and through whom we exist [centrality]" (1 Cor. 8). "Therefore, I press on to take hold of that [centrality] for which

Christ has taken hold of me [supremacy]" (Phil. 3). "If a man remains in me [supremacy] and I in him [centrality], he will bear much fruit" (Jn. 15). "His divine power has given us everything we need for life and godliness [centrality] through our knowledge of Jesus our Lord who called us by his own glory and goodness [supremacy]" (2 Pet. 1).

Centrality and supremacy — center and circumference. Any recovery of hope in our churches will begin as we're re-introduced to our Savior as *both*. However, if vast numbers of Christians are to be re-awakened to Christ for ALL that He is, our word to one another must retain its strongest emphasis on His *supremacy*. To paraphrase II Corinthians 3:17: "Where the Spirit of the Lord is, there is supremacy" (which always leads us into genuine "liberty"!).

QUOTABLE QUOTE

THINK WITH ME ...

How does Colossians picture the pinnacle of Jesus' preeminence?

Quite a few times already I've referred to Paul's teachings in the book of Colossians. As I bring this section to a close, it might be helpful to turn briefly to the "snapshots of supremacy" presented there.

First, some background: The little church in Colossae was caught in its own outbreak of the crisis of supremacy! False teachers were attacking their vision of Christ, each insisting that the Savior was not sufficient for their spiritual needs. By implication, however, this meant He was not supreme.

Some of these troublers we call *Gnostics*. They boasted deeper spiritual realities that might start with Christ but extend far beyond Christ. Others we call *Judaizers* who taught that it was good to come to Christ, but that there were many prior steps to be taken before Christ would do them any good. Both teachings called into question various aspects of Jesus' lordship over all things. In both cases, Paul knew they must hold to the grand theme of vs. 27 *("Christ is in you, the hope of glory"),* without compromise, in order to confront these conflicting teachings.

However, the truth of vs. 27 didn't stand in isolation. Behind it resided the reinforcement of Paul's entire first chapter. Throughout he presented a major briefing on the Person of Promise. The snapshots in Colossians 1 were posted to give these new Christians (and us) increased assurance that everything the Father had prepared for His people could be found, in totality, in His dear Son. Christ was sufficient. He was enough. He was all (Col. 3:11).

As Colossians confirms, when God's full glory is finally revealed — in the consummation of everything — we will discover, to our great joy, that all Divine magnificence dwelt in Jesus all along. In fact, Paul reminds us in verse 4 of Col. 3: "When Christ, who is your life, appears then you also will appear with Him in glory". The glory for which we hope is inherent in the Son *now*. That's what makes Him our "all in all" *right now!*

The implications of the Colossian vision are absolutely thrilling. Christ Himself, at this very moment, encompasses the *future* of God's triumphs. Furthermore, He does so as He comes among us, ministering to us foretastes of ultimate victories. What He will be Lord of *ultimately*, He is Lord of *already*. Ten thousand years from today, who He is as the Son of God — as well as where He leads, how He imparts and what He receives — will remain exactly the same as it is today. His glory will be no different at *that* point than what is true of our Savior at *this* point.

Accordingly, as Colossians 1:18 claims, supremacy belongs to Him alone. Nor does this supremacy develop in degrees or go through stages. Our Lord's supremacy displays a sovereignty and sufficiency without exceptions. He is our all, now, because He is all supreme now. That makes Him our one great hope — *now* — just as fully as He will be at the End. To our happy surprise, the everlasting destination of our lives throughout all the ages to come is linked inseparably to the very Person who actively reigns in our lives *today*. (I like Phillips' paraphrase for Paul's message in Col. 1:27: "Christ is in you, the assurance of all the glorious things to come.")

Thus, the Apostle exclaims in Colossians 1: "*Him* we proclaim" (vs. 28). Heralding Christ to *Christians, as God's all-encompassing hope for them*, was Paul's priority ministry with believers everywhere (in vs. 24-26 he calls it his "commission"). Of one thing he was convinced: The strongest evidence Christians could provide, to show they had thoroughly engaged with Christ as Lord of all, was the prevalence in their hearts of *an abounding hope* toward Him (see also Romans 15:13). From the outset, Paul preached hope in Christ not only to pagans but to every *Christian* he met (as his other epistles verify).

But, Paul was not content to just *preach* Christ. He wanted more for his hearers. He wanted believers to become *complete* in Christ (vs. 28). He wrote to the Colossians: "Him we proclaim, teaching every person and warning every person, that we might present every person complete in Christ" (vs. 28). What did that mean? Paul realized that for Christians to impact their cities and their world for the Kingdom, they must be fully engaged with the Lord of their lives in the light of His unfailing reign — in other words, be wrapped up *in* Him as well as wrapped *around* Him! No mission to the nations could be *completed,* he knew, unless those sent to the nations were themselves, first of all, *completed* in Christ.

But, what did the phrase actually imply? Again, Colossians 1 gives the answer. Primarily, Christians become complete (or mature) to the degree they are possessed of (and obedient to) a comprehensive vision of Christ and His supremacy (vs. 18), with eyes fixed on the glorious destiny He is offers them (vs. 27). Whenever convictions concerning Christ's preeminence produce in Christians eager expectations for Kingdom advance, along with the passion to pursue that agenda, those disciples have become "complete in Christ". They aren't perfect, or sinless, or infallible, but they are *complete.*

Paul concludes Colossians 1 by rejoicing in how the Spirit energized him daily for this one specific objective: to bring believers to a decisive devotion to their King (vs. 29). The same joy can be yours, as well. Experiencing that is what I call a "Campaign of Hope". I can't imagine anything the Holy Spirit would rather lead us into in this moment of need and possibilities for a pervasive Christ awakening throughout the Church.

Creating a "Campaign of Hope"
(Romans 9:1-5; 9:30-10:17)

"Everyone's nerves are on edge," remarked a leading cancer surgeon. "No matter where we turn, we're reading about something killing us prematurely." As *The Wall Street Journal* reported, thanks to research labs, tort laws and media hype, danger does seem to "lurk around every corner of life" from children's toys to anthrax to secondhand smoke to AIDS. "Faced with a barrage of warnings — including the color-coded caveats from the new Homeland Security department," concluded the *Journal*, "it's not surprising that in contemporary America, the safest society in recorded history, many people feel as though they have never been more at risk."

Thankfully, despair does not hold the final word for believers in America (or anywhere else), or for America (or any other peoples). The final word — about history, humanity, destiny, eternity, mystery — belongs to God's Son. As we saw in Colossians 1, that final word is forever a word of *hope*. It is an assurance that even *more* of God's glory is waiting to be revealed "in the face of Jesus Christ" (2 Cor. 4). Our message of hope must begin and end by proclaiming *Him* — by pointing to Him as the One to see, seek and speak about for ALL that He is.

Without question, America is fertile ground for a movement toward the *recovery* of hope — we are poised for a *reformation* of hope, if you will. The Church is primed for a major *campaign* to help spread Biblical hope everywhere, first of all by confronting and curing the crisis of supremacy *inside* the Church.

THINK WITH ME ...
Why does a vision of Christ's supremacy always cause hope to grow?

So, maybe we should ask: Why is *hope* so often a chief hallmark of a life or congregation where Christ is worshipped as "all in all"? Why does *hope* rise among those saturated with the truth of Christ's supremacy in everything? It is because Biblical hope is more than a verb (as in "I hope so"). Biblical hope is ultimately a *person* (as in "my hope is in the Lord").

British poet Alexander Pope coined the familiar proverb: "Hope springs eternal in the human breast." Well, hope *does* spring eternal from the breast of God. Romans 15 names Him "the God of hope." Biblical hope gets very personal, when you think about it. Every promise of Scripture is, by nature, eternally *Trinitarian:* Designed by the Father, quickened by the Spirit, and focused on the Son. True hope has the Father as its source, the Son as its theme and the Spirit as its witness. Scripture reminds us that He is not only the God who is and was, but the God who is to come (Rev. 1:8).

Within the Triune God, however, the Son defines the *substance* of all eternal prospects. Only in Him can God's Kingdom purposes be fully understood, measured and entered into. More specifically it is by His supremacy that the future obtains any meaning or holds out any possibilities. His glorious greatness gives us hope because in Him what should be, will be. In Him, healing, reconciliation, justice, holiness, happiness and all goodness will prevail — ultimately supplanting dominions of death and Hades. Put simply: Christ's *person* guarantees His *position* to marshal His *promises*. That's why every promise of God remains forever "Yes!" to us in Christ Jesus (2 Cor. 1).

It is estimated that there are over 7000 separate promises recorded in Old and New Testaments. Assuming that's so, let me ask you three fascinating questions:

- Can you think of any promise God has made in Scripture, based on the person and ministry of His Son, which does not fit naturally into our overall definition of Christ's supremacy?

- Further, can you point to a single promise which does not also require a demonstration of His supremacy to fulfill it?

- Similarly, can you recall any promise which would not make the supremacy of Christ manifestly more obvious and wonderful, to us or to the nations, as God brings it to pass?

There should be little surprise, therefore, that *Joyful Manifesto* makes a "Campaign of Hope" the primary antidote for the crisis of supremacy. One of the greatest benefits derived from reclaiming for Christians an exalted outlook on the Son of God is that the Church regains a strong taste for the promises of God. Let it be stated unequivocally: *Kingdom-shaped hope is always the first evidence of, as well as the premiere blessing from, a reawakening among God's people to the supremacy of God's Son.*

THINK WITH ME ...

**How could a *campaign* to recover hope
become the antidote to the crisis of supremacy?**

Why have I chosen to capitalize on the concept of a *campaign?* Let me tell you a story. A few years back, a U.S. presidential campaign took as its motto: "Hope Is Back!" For months its promoters presented platforms and promises designed to convince countless citizens to swing away from previous political leanings. They urged them to cast their lot with a very charismatic leader. He claimed to offer the finest prospects for securing a prosperous future for America. In the end, *hope* — a political hope based on the credibility, expertise and star-power of one politician — summoned millions to turn and follow. In November, the "Hope Is Back!" campaign triumphed convincingly at the hands of enthusiastic voters.

In a way faintly reminiscent of a run for the White House, this *Joyful Manifesto* summons Christians everywhere to help confront the crisis of supremacy through a *Campaign of Hope.* To be sure, this is quite *unlike* any general election you've ever seen. Our Lord is not a "candidate"! He doesn't need to be "elected" as our Monarch. He already *is* the "Wonderful Counselor, Prince of Peace, Mighty God". Already, the government of the universe is "upon His shoulders", the increase of which "there shall be no end" (Isa. 9).

On the other hand, this campaign is not totally dissimilar to a political endeavor. It too may trumpet gladly that "hope is back" for Christians everywhere. This campaign has the potential of re-igniting ardent zeal for the names and claims and gains of the King of Kings. This campaign can recruit citizens in the Empire of the Son to re-engage with Him — with *His* cause, *His* platform, *His* policies, *His* promises, *His* credibility, *His* administration, *His* eternally supreme star-power — fanning into flame (both in lips and lives) fresh fervor for His Royal Majesty

Those involved in a *Campaign of Hope* will set out to convince fellow believers there is so much *more* — more that Christ deserves, more that He desires, more that He has designed and more that He has decreed — and then get others praying and acting like it, filled with renewed anticipation! Surely, this makes abundant sense. *Hope* is — and always has been — one of the most marvelous manifestations of Christ's reign within any context, for a Christian or a congregation, or for a whole nation.

THINK WITH ME ...
Is the Holy Spirit calling *you* to move forward with such a campaign?

You need to know: I'm convinced a Campaign of Hope is already rising in today's Church! And I pray that you, my reader, will eventually choose to become part of it (if you haven't already). How should you respond to that invitation? Let me answer with another story.

For many years I resided in Madison, the capital of the state of Wisconsin. Center-city Madison is dominated by the state Capital building, with its magnificent rotunda and massive white dome. On the dome's very top stands a golden figure, a woman gilded in robes of antiquity, with her right arm outstretched and finger boldly pointing. She's affectionately referred to as "Miss Forward" because the motto of Wisconsin is one word: *Forward!* Day in and day out, in the midst of commercial activities she seems to stand forth charging us to keep looking ahead, to be full of hope, to advance into the future with courage and expectation — to go *forward*.

When I think of this Campaign of Hope, I'm reminded of her. What a graphic symbol of how the Lord Jesus is rising up in the midst of His church at this very hour, to reveal Himself afresh as our one and only Champion! He's calling us to go *forward*. He wants us to recover the marvelous prospects secured by His reign over Heaven and earth. His message of hope summons us into a future forever sealed in His blood.

At the same time, I foresee an army of proclaimers joining their voices with His, to amplify *"Forward!"* I see them inviting fellow Christians to wake up to Him, to re-discover an abounding hope in Him, and then to move out as captives to His victorious purposes.

Forward! Have you heard Christ's summons?

In the past 20 years, unprecedented numbers of Christians around the world have. They've been faithfully praying for a Christ-exalting explosion in the Church. I've met with thousands of them in my travels, interceding for a spiritual awakening to Jesus within their congregations. Already for *them* the Campaign of Hope has begun. They are already moving forward every time they enter the Throne Room in prayer. The hour is at hand for this army of *seekers* to become an army of *speakers!* They need to infect fellow Christians with the hope in Christ that stirred them to pray in the first place.

What I'm proposing is that a Campaign of Hope could become the culmination to years of intercession for the renewal of our churches.

Doesn't it make sense for all who care enough to *pray* the vision to now step forth to *say* the vision at every opportunity? Who wouldn't want to bear witness to Christ's supremacy among the very Christians for whom they've been faithfully praying, petitioning the Father to re-awaken His children to His Son for ALL that He is? Once those prayers are coupled with a movement of messengers, I suggest to you that millions of petitions will be answered in short order. Would you like to become a Christ-proclaimer to God's people, too? Are you willing to cultivate a Campaign of Hope as a follow up to many prayers? Would you like to move forward with God's Spirit in a ministry that changes strategically the Christian movement for a whole generation? If so, *Joyful Manifesto* exists especially for you!

Fresnel's Fascination
(1 John 1:1-7)

In 1822 the French scientist Augustin Fresnel revolutionized the impact of lighthouses all over the world. For 2500 years, attempts to improve safety for ships at sea focused on increasing fire-power to intensify lighthouse beams. But Fresnel took a totally different tactic. *He studied the characteristics of light itself.* It wasn't long before he discovered light waves. Subsequently, he manufactured glass domes that incorporated several prisms compatible with these waves, refracting them with incomparable brilliance. Known as the Fresnel lens, for the next two centuries his invention was used in lighthouses on every ocean.

What better strategy for the Church in this hour? Call it *"Fresnel's Fascination"*. It's about Christians giving priority to the study of the Light-of-the-World *as* our Light. It's about ceasing exhausting efforts to fuel spiritual fire in our churches with home-made plans and programs and personalities — ceasing long enough to take stock of the glory of the One we're called to share with the nations. Instead of focusing so much of our attention on Christian revival and missions, the "Fresnel's Fascination" encourages us to work, first of all, at enlarging our vision of the Revive-er and Sender Himself.

To revitalize "the whole Church to take the whole Gospel to the whole world" (words from the Lausanne Covenant) we must restore the *whole vision* of God's Son among God's people. We must strive to proclaim a message that "re-converts" Christians back to Christ for ALL that He is — transforming many, once again, into *Person*-driven disciples. In turn, such a campaign can help believers become the *purpose*-driven people we long to be, for the completion of the Great Commission and the consummation of the ages. That's why the next four chapters remain, unapologetically, fascinated with the Light Himself. (I think Fresnel would be pleased.)

The rest of **Volume One** serves you as a *"laboratory"* for studying the Light. It can help you get "traction" on a stronger sense of Jesus' supremacy. These chapters are far more than academic, however. They also offer the opportunity of a *life-changing* experience with Jesus, as well. Notice how the chapter titles follow quite closely the preliminary definition for supremacy laid out in chapter 1:

- *Christ Supreme: The SUMMATION of Christian Hope* (chapter 2) — What can we expect to find if we're living according to the FOCUS of His supremacy? We'll detail many exciting answers rarely mentioned among Christians today.

- *Christ Supreme: The CONSUMMATION of Christian Hope* (chapter 3) — Why should the FULFILLMENT of His supremacy be the greatest single motivation in a Christian's walk with the Savior? We'll find out and put it in terms you can talk about with others.

- *Christ Supreme: The APPROXIMATION of Christian Hope* (chapter 4) — How does experiencing the FULLNESS of His supremacy involve preliminary expressions of the consummation of His reign released into every day life? We'll look at major areas capable of radically changing your approach to ordinary Christian living.

- *Christ Supreme: The CONSUMING PASSION of Christian Hope* (chapter 5) — What does the FERVOR of His supremacy look like in those who pursue Him for ALL that He is? We'll define some of the deepest affections possible in a dynamic Christian experience.

Let me restate my initial invitation: At the end of the Introduction (*Look Beyond the Threshold*), I invited you to skip around. I suggested you do not need to take the remaining chapters in sequence. For example, the first thing you may want to do now is dig a little deeper into the crisis itself. In that case, go straight to chapter 6. On the other hand, you may be anxious to let your vision of the Lord Jesus expand its borders. In that case, chapter 2 is your best choice. It all depends on your personal needs and interests.

Whatever chapter you decide to read next, however, remember that throughout this manifesto we must never cease to " *... fix our eyes on Jesus, the author and perfecter of our faith"* (Heb. 12).

That's precisely the goal of the Triune God for each of us as expressed in Revelation 5, where the seven lamps (the Seven-fold Spirit) cast their inexhaustible and inescapable glow on the Lamb who stands at the center of the Father's throne – before whom all Heaven and earth falls prostrate with hymns of salvation.

QUOTABLE QUOTE

Thus all the way from creation at the beginning, through the incarnation at the centre, to final redemption at the end, God speaks and acts through Jesus Christ. The *love of God* is not any ideal of love, it is that love that in the specific grace of Jesus Christ comes to seek and to save what was lost, to establish at great cost fellowship with those who never had and could not ever have any kind of claim upon it. The *power of God* is not any kind of sovereign omnipotence, it is that specific power by which the Son became man, and which he used with compassion to heal the sick and endure the cross; it is the power by which he rose from the dead. The *truth of God* is not the content of any philosophical world-vision, or mystic communication or charismatic insight; the truth of God is the person and action of his Son who is both Messiah of Israel and Lord of the Church, to whose coming prophets bore witness before, and apostles after, and that witness is interpreted out of scripture by the Spirit in the Church. The *commandment of God* is not an ethical action or religious discipline, it is the commandment of the Father that is defined in this gospel by this Son. The Father has committed all things to the Son and nobody knows the Father except the Son and those to whom he chooses to reveal him.

– Dr. Thomas Smail

2

CHRIST SUPREME:
The *Summation*
of Christian Hope

Recover a Vision Shaped by the
FOCUS of His Supremacy

On her way home from Sunday School, Wendy announced from the back seat of the car: "I guess God must have made the world with His *left* hand." Her mother inquired, "Why would you think that?" "Because today we learned that Jesus is sitting on His *right* hand!" A humorous misunderstanding, to be sure, but one that highlights a beautiful Biblical picture for the high honor God has given His Son.

Jesus' activity at the Father's side was certainly not lost on religious commentators when the Soviet flag was lowered over the Kremlin, indicating the internal collapse of atheistic Communism. Transpiring on Christmas Eve of 1991, it provided further evidence of the great eternal truth: "Jesus reigns!" His Kingdom is decisive in all the affairs of humankind.

As *Time* magazine observed in one of its first front cover stories for the 21ˢᵗ century: "It would require much calculation to deny that the single most powerful figure — not merely in these two millennia, but in all human history — is Jesus of Nazareth." In the same manner, the Christ proclaimed in Scripture, whose dynamic displays of dominion have dominated the past 2000 years, is the only explanation for the endurance and advance of the Church, despite its sailing so frequently "through bloody seas" (as Isaac Watts put it).

But an equal indicator of authority is how Christ intends to dominate the *future*. Just as the course of ages gone by cannot be understood apart from Christ's supremacy, neither can the ages to come. All of God's intentions for the road ahead of us, including the Consummation itself, impinge on the exaltation of Jesus — who He is as the Son of God, where He leads in the Purposes of God, how He imparts the Resources of God, and what He receives from the People of God. "The cosmic Christ" — that's what John R. W. Stott names Him in his commentary on Ephesians 1, and for good reason.

Christ in His reign is the "summation" of every promise God has proclaimed to the world. Understanding this can significantly transform our view of His lordship in general, and of His personal involvement with each of us as individuals. In this chapter we'll find out why as we explore:

- **How Christ's reign is both the center and circumference of God's Kingdom.**
- **How His supremacy sums up Old Testament hope.**
- **How His Incarnation embodies God's promises.**
- **How His Crucifixion secures God's promises.**
- **How His Resurrection unleashes God's promises.**
- **How His Ascension advances God's promises.**
- **How His Return will complete God's promises.**

The FOCUS of His Supremacy
(Daniel 7:9-14)

At her mother's knee, Condoleezza Rice (Secretary of State under President George W. Bush) was taught to see Christ's supremacy in a special way. The daughter (who became an accomplished pianist) was reminded: "Condoleezza, when leading a time of spontaneous worship at church, remember if you play in the key of 'C', which is the foundational key in music, the congregation will always be able to follow you." Recalling that insight, Rice adds: "In the same way, Christ is God's 'C' chord, and that is why we always seem to find our way back to Him, sometimes in spite of ourselves."

THINK WITH ME ...
In what sense is it Christ's very nature to be the summation of all hope?

If we ask, "Who is the *focus* of the future of the universe?" or, more accurately, "Who occupies the *throne* that is the focus of the future of the universe?" Scripture knows only one answer: Our Lord Jesus Christ. Christ supreme! We read: "Then I saw a lamb, looking as if it had been slain, standing in the center of the throne ... and the twenty-four elders fell down before the Lamb ... and they sang a new song: 'You are worthy to take the scroll and to open its seals.... Worthy is the Lamb, who was slain, to receive power and wealth and wisdom and strength and honor and glory and praise' " (Revelation 5:6-9).

His highest title — the Greek word employed by New Testament writers — was *"Lord"* (Kurios). It was also a term used by Greek-speaking Jews to translate the Hebrew word for Jehovah (Yahweh). As Fuller Seminary professor, Ralph Martin, documented: Throughout Scripture "Lord" not only denoted "rulership based upon competent and authoritative power, the ability to dispose of what one possesses.... " but when applied to our Savior, it declared that "Jesus Christ is installed in the place which rightfully belongs to God himself as the Lord of all creation ... the place of cosmic authority."

No wonder Dietrich Bonhoeffer's classic work on the person of God's Son (possibly his greatest legacy before the Nazis executed him by hanging in 1945) was titled unequivocally: *Christ the Center*. He wrote: "It is the *nature* of Christ to be the center." He didn't say that making Christ the center is the goal of God's plan, or that this idea defines the ultimate result of God's activities. Rather, every indication of Scripture, Bonhoeffer concluded, is that centrality is inherent to Christ's very being. He's the One that everything is wrapped around, that everything must come back to. This is *who* He is.

Bonhoeffer died believing this, died less it only true.

But there's even more to our Lord than that. As we saw in chapter 1, it is also His very nature to be supreme. He is the *circumference* — the One in whom everything is wrapped up and summed up; the One in whom all the saints must forever live and move, to find their identity and destiny. Being *supreme,* in other words — being in Himself the *summation* of God's purposes and promises — is equally inseparable from who Christ is, eternally, as the Son of the Father.

For many founders of the first 120 colleges in America, this idea was a prevailing conviction. For example, in the *College Laws* written in 1642 the Puritan benefactors of Harvard University wrote: "Let every student consider well that the end of his life and studies is to know God and Jesus Christ which is eternal life (John 17:3), and therefore to lay Christ at the bottom, as the only foundation of all sound knowledge and learning. Seeing that the Lord giveth wisdom, everyone shall seriously by prayer, in secret, seek wisdom of Him." From its outset this world-renowned academic institution confessed that the most brilliant scholarship would never be able to supercede one overarching truth: *Christ alone sums up in Himself all reality as its supreme focus.*

THINK WITH ME ...
Who do *you* say that He is
and what words would you use to say it?

"We're having a national conversation about Jesus" suggested *Christianity Today* toward the midpoint of the first decade of the 21st century. *New York Times* bestsellers, blockbuster movies, journals and magazines, TV documentaries, Grammy winners — from every direction there seemed to be increased desire to talk about the Savior. But the editorial went on to suggest that we may not be talking about the "real Jesus", stating that "talking about the real Jesus is a dangerous thing". *Christianity Today* concluded: In the New Testament the real Jesus "is a consuming fire, the raging storm, who seems bent on destroying everything in his path, who either shocks people into stupefaction or frightens them so that they run for their lives.... He swirls, a tornado touching down, lifting homes and businesses off their foundations, leaving only bits and pieces of the former life strewn on his path.... We need to talk with biblical honesty about the One who would not only love and forgive us but also demolish all our cultural images of him."

Remember the debate the Twelve had about Jesus as they walked the roads of Caesarea Phillipi? They were responding to Jesus' penetrating question to Peter (Matt. 16):*"Who do you say that I am?"* Finally, Peter answered with the familiar words, "You are the Christ, the Son of the living God." But did he or the others really grasp the full implications of that brief sentence? Based on what many Scriptures teach about the meaning of those two titles — *"the Christ"* and *"Son of the living God"* — Peter's response was equivalent to saying (and this is the vision of Jesus that must be injected into the national conversation mentioned above):

LORD JESUS ... .

- *You are the Superlative One.* Indescribable
  You defy all human categories. No language is adequate to describe You. No analysis can fully record all the roles You must play to advance God's ever-expanding Kingdom. (1 Pet. 1)

- *You are the Incomparable One.* infinitely
  You remain in a class by Yourself — no duplicates, no clones. Your importance will continue to eclipse all others, outranking every other being in Heaven, Earth or Hell. You will reign 'world without end' (2 Thess. 1).

- *You are the Exalted One.*
  For eternity, You will hold the primary focus of our praises, a position of unrivaled distinction, prestige and majesty in the universe. You will be the joy of all peoples, worthy to receive every treasure, every dominion and every ounce of praise (Rev. 5).

- *You are the Preeminent One.* (for all-time)
  In time, in space, in history and throughout eternity, You forever lay claim to the universe. As You held the primacy at the beginning ('firstborn of creation', Col. 1), so You will hold it at the End ("firstborn from among the dead", Col. 1). All things to come are Your possession, to do with as Your Father pleases.

- *You are the Sufficient One.* (in all power & resources)
  Nothing can ever exhaust Your power and resources. You require no 'outsourcing'. You will forever prove totally adequate for all our longings, or fears, or needs, or heart cries. You are the final inheritance of each of God's children (Phil. 3).

■ *You are the Triumphant One.*
None of Your enemies will prevail. You will defeat all foes unconditionally — both human and demonic — to emerge forever
unthreatened, unhindered and victorious over all opposition,
permanently and forever. You are the everlasting Overcomer
(Rev. 17).

■ *You are the Unifying One.*
Bringing all things under Your feet as Lord, You will permanently
redeem and reconcile to the Godhead innumerable sinners from all
the ages and all the nations. In the Consummation, all creation, as
well as the Church itself, will be held together in perfect harmony by
Your irrevocable decrees and Your indestructible
might (Heb. 1).

These things being true (and this is just the
beginning of a list of Biblical attributes implied
by Peter's brief confession), it certainly seems
appropriate to address Him, as well, by saying:
*"You are the Christ, the Summation of Christian
Hope!"*

On that red-letter day Peter was beginning to
wake up to how His Lord was, in Himself, the
focus of everything the Father deserves, desires,
designs and declares. There in Matthew 16,
whether he fully grasped it or not, in essence
Peter confessed: "As *Son of God,* wherever You
dwell all of God's promises are gathered to You,
guaranteed by You and summed up in You. As
Christ you are ordained and anointed as
supreme — absolute and universal in every way.
You are supreme in the appeal You make to
sinners. Supreme in the scope of Your activities
on our behalf. Supreme in the depth of Your
transforming power for all the Redeemed.
Supreme in the irreplaceable ministry of Your
high priestly work for saints in heaven and earth.
Supreme in the eternal relevancy of Your reign
extended throughout the entire universe.

QUOTABLE QUOTE

**We look at this Son and
see the God who cannot
be seen. We look at this
Son and see God's
original purpose in
everything created –
everything got started in
him and finds its purpose
in him. He was supreme
in the beginning – leading
the resurrection parade —
He is supreme in the end.
From beginning to end, he
is there, towering far
above everything,
everyone. All the broken
and dislocated pieces of
the universe — people
and things, animals and
atoms — get properly
fixed and fitted together
in vibrant harmonies, all
because of his death, his
blood that poured down
from the Cross.**

(COLOSSIANS 1 — THE MESSAGE)

Supreme in the magnificently indescribable future into which You are taking all who are Yours."

In another place, the Lord Jesus answered His own question to Peter when He said to John: "I am the Alpha and the Omega, the First and the Last, the Beginning and the End" (Rev. 22). Not only was He at the beginning, but He Himself is the Beginning. Not only will He be waiting for us at the end, He *is* the End. All history streams from Him and is directed toward Him, to be completed by Him. The eternal past has no other eternal future but Christ alone. There is only *one* in the entire universe of whom God has ever said without qualification: "With you I am well pleased" (Luke 3). Thus Christ and Christ alone can insist on being the center and the circumference — the One to whom all supremacy belongs, whose supremacy encompasses all.

That's why Christian hope draws its ultimate meaning from this one unique individual. As we saw in the last chapter, for Christians hope is ultimately a *person*. That person embodies our grandest expectations. He's ready to take us beyond our wildest dreams. Everything needed to secure the promises of God to us has come to pass in Him — by the virtue of who He is, by what He has done and is doing, and by where He is taking us with Himself.

Any human prospects (Christianly or otherwise) that leave Him out of the equation for *all* He really is in Himself, must inevitably dissolve into irrelevance, confusion, emptiness and unmitigated despair. Our future is not preeminently about things, or events, or prophetic dramas, but about Christ. "For me to live is Christ and to die is gain", was Paul's motto (Phil. 1). Or, as J.B. Phillips translates the verse: "For living to me means simply 'Christ', and if I die I should merely gain more of him."

THINK WITH ME ...
In what ways is Christ the *only* focus
for every bit of hope we have?

Martin Luther likened the supremacy of Christ to an antique *magnifying glass* revealing intricate designs on a medieval map. Details at the center of the lens stay crisp and clear. But around the edges, the graphics of the document tend to grow increasingly distorted. Therefore, one must keep the important landmarks at the center of the lens.

Similarly, in order to properly magnify the hope Christ brings us, we need to keep Him as our foremost *focal point*. That's how we study the exquisite map of God's grand purposes among the nations. Jesus is our focal point for history, in church growth, for our mission to the unreached as well as in daily living. He will *remain* the focal point in the Consummation as well. For eternity all reality will be magnified to the thousandth power through the superb perspective He alone gives to those seated with Him "at God's right hand in the heavenly realms, far above all rule and authority, power and dominion, and every title that can be given, not only in the present age but also in the one to come" (Eph. 1).

Here's another metaphor to help make sense of this truth: Consider a *slide projector*. Though we have many pictures to review, just one bulb is needed to project each of them onto the screen. In the same way there are thousands of hope-filled passages in the Bible, but just one Person is needed to make those truths burst into life. Only one Person comes shining through every verse, revealing more of His supremacy every time He does. "The whole of Scripture is one book, and that one book is Christ," concluded medieval Christian leader, Hugh of St. Victor. "The Bible is the cradle in which Christ is laid," observed Luther. "The Scriptures spring out of God and flow into Christ," proclaimed William Tyndale.

In fact, the Scriptures nurture a cornucopia of descriptive names that suggest how Jesus is seen when projected through a myriad of God's promises, such as:

- The Way
- The Truth
- The Rock
- Dayspring from on High
- Son of Righteousness
- Light of the World
- Bread of Life

- The Light
- The Bright Morning Star
- Prince of Peace
- Good Shepherd
- Lion of Judah
- Alpha and Omega
- Name Above All Names

And we could list, literally, a hundred other formal titles that God's Word bestows on our Lord. In other words, our God-given prospects are tied up so comprehensively in this one Person that the Bible requires an entire registry to define for us how and why He is (to use another title) "the Hope of Glory" (Col. 1:27). The titles not only express what Jesus means to us but also what we can expect from Him. Each is a statement of *hope*.

Looking at the breadth of these descriptions, I often like to paraphrase a familiar statement from the brilliant 4th century African bishop, Augustine:

"The one who has Christ has everything.
The one who has everything except for Christ really has nothing.
And the one who has Christ plus everything else
does not have any more than the one who has Christ alone."

Colossians 3:11 agrees. It states this focus succinctly, in just three words — which is why it became the main title of *Joyful Manifesto:* "Christ is all!" Isn't it obvious why I made this choice?

THINK WITH ME ...
Why does it make sense to say our hope in God is "summed up" in Christ?

When you balance your checkbook, there comes a point to "sum up" your account. You add a number of entries together to get the grand total. Even so, in Christ the promises and purposes of all the ages have been "summed up" — brought to their grand total, unequivocally and irrevocably. There's nothing left out. There's nothing more to add to the tally.

Jesus sums up all meaning in current reality. He also sums up all outcomes in *future* reality. He's the source of a New Covenant, a New Creation, and a New Destination — by grace alone, through faith alone, in Him alone. He embodies right now what God's promises will look like when they are fulfilled. Christ is not only the End toward which we move. He is also the *means* to reach that End. Whenever we say "Jesus is Lord", we are confessing both — that He *sums up* the End as well as provides *the means* to it.

Therefore, our primary Message of Hope — which is our greatest tool for confronting and curing the crisis of supremacy in today's Church — must begin with this truth: Christ's supremacy is the *summation* of Christian hope. *God has no hope for us beyond who His Son is.* He is the ultimate focus of every promise. Glorifying the Son is the final outcome — the singular conclusion — of every Kingdom advance God has ordained.

This requires our Savior to be both an *excluder* and an *includer.* On the one hand, as the Bible testifies, He *excludes* every other source of hope. He's all there really is. There's room for no other. He must exclude all those who choose to put their confidence in any other kind of hope. But, on the other hand, He is also an includer. He *includes* in Himself every prospect God has for us, for the rest of eternity. And He *includes* with Himself all who trust in Him to receive those everlasting blessings.

Consider the impact of the Salk vaccine which eradicated polio in the 1950's. Once discovered, it rendered all other medicines and therapies for the disease irrelevant (i.e., it was exclusive). But it also became the harbinger of health for anyone around the world who took it in time (i.e., it was inclusive). The unrivaled preeminence of Christ as the hope of the universe is something like that: Exclusive and inclusive, simultaneously. That's why we say every promise of God must be summed up in Him.

THINK WITH ME ...
Where does the Trinity fit into the hope in Christ we confess?

Finally, before we proceed to unpack how "summation" is short-hand for "supremacy" — how all of God's purposes are gathered up in the Son alone — let me reassure you of my bedrock commitment to the truth of the Triune God. In confessing Christ as center and circumference I'm not suggesting that Jesus is all there is to God; that all deity has been collapsed into Christ alone; that our destiny is *only* about Him. I agree with Dr. Timothy George: "What makes God, God? It is the relationship of total and mutual self-giving by which the Father gives everything to the Son, the Son offers back all that He has to glorify the Father, with the love of each being established and sealed by the Holy Spirit, who proceeds from both. The doctrine of the Trinity tells us that relationship — *personality* — is at the heart of the universe."

Maintaining the supremacy of the Lord Jesus Christ for all eternity — and, in the process, transforming us into people with Christ-focused purposes — will never cease to be a *Trinitarian* project. Every dimension of hope is initiated by the Father, developed by the Spirit, while always exalting the Son. The radiance Christ brings us, as the Son of the Father, is inseparable from the fundamental nature of the Godhead — just as the rays of the physical sun could never exist apart from the sun itself. Ultimately, it is the uniqueness of His relationship to the Father and the Spirit, rather than His saving mission for the Redeemed, that bestows on Him preeminence in everything (Col. 1). Nothing about Christ as the focus of God's promises should ever rob the Father or the Spirit of equal praise.

The early Church understood this. Confessing Jesus to be Lord, the Church confirmed His divinity by its witness to the full panorama of God's attributes, functions, authority, power and rights in Him. The adoration of the Son by early Christians (many of whom were previously monotheistic Jews who abhorred idolatry) was unqualified and wholehearted. Nowhere, observes Donald MacLeod, do we find any debate in the 1ˢᵗ century over His inherent superiority as God. As far as they were concerned, when Jesus taught, God taught. When Jesus healed, God healed. When He wept, God wept. When He suffered, God suffered. When He conquered, it was the triumphant work of the Godhead. Wherever Jesus' reign broke through, the whole Trinity was on display. Culminated under Jesus as Lord, eternity held for them just one additional climactic drama: Everlasting worship of Father, Son and Holy Spirit as the three-in-one.

When men and women surrendered to Jesus to become His disciples, they were initiated into a relationship with the Tri-Personal Being (Matthew 28 commands us to baptize: "in the name of the Father and of the Son and of the Holy Spirit"). And whenever a promise was fulfilled in Jesus' name, the glory belonged equally to the Godhead who made it all possible, working together as One to bring it about. As 1 Pet. 1:2 reminds us, we are: " ... chosen according to the foreknowledge of God the Father, through the sanctifying work of the Spirit for obedience to Jesus Christ and sprinkling by his blood.... "

Even in the Consummation, it will be the mission of the Son to secure before the whole universe the glory *of* the Godhead, *for* the Godhead, in the *midst* of the Godhead. One day, this will come about fully as He will submit Himself (and everything He has conquered), by the Spirit, to the Father's pleasure. Yet even that only can happen once the Father, by the Spirit, has secured for His Son the full recognition of His lordship over everything in Heaven and earth and under the earth (compare Phil. 2:5-11 with 1 Cor. 15:20-28 and Rev. 5). Without qualification (as John records), the Son will prevail steadfastly at the center of the Father's throne, world without end, while the Spirit's fires illuminate Him there, for elders and angels (and all of us) to behold and adore with abandon (Rev. 4, 5 and 21). Permission to live for Him with passion at this very moment springs from the passion that will be required of us when His glory is fully revealed.

As I was waiting to catch a plane not long ago, my attention was arrested by the front page headline on a newsstand rack. *"He's no 'Son of God!' "* leaped from a Minneapolis newspaper. The reporter told of 35 Muslim preachers from the local Islamic Center who fanned out that month to nearly 300 Christian churches and ministries in the Twin Cities to present lectures on their view of Christ. Their challenge to Christians? Here's how one speaker put it: "The Trinity is merely a human lapse toward polytheism.

Christians have become hung up on the Messenger, Jesus, and in the process they have forsaken his message. They should have just stuck with the teachings of Jesus. They should have revered him as the prophet he is, and avoided all the other embellishments."

And I thought to myself: Embellishments? Quite to the contrary. From the Bible's point of view, *who* the Messenger is, in the unbroken fellowship of the Trinity, determines unconditionally the legitimacy and potency of the supremacy He claims and the hope over which He reigns. Therefore, any message He proclaims is woven automatically into who He is as the Son of God. He is the only Prophet ever to appear among the nations who has focused all prophecies and promises on Himself alone. This is how He brings us to God. No Jesus, no hope. The Father won't let us have one without the other.

Six Biblical Themes

Exploring How Christ Is the Summation of Christian Hope

Now, let's get down to specifics. Briefly, I'd like to survey six major themes in Scripture that wrap hope and Christ's lordship together, rendering them permanently inseparable:

1) Old Testament:
   the *foreshadowing* of our hope in Christ

2) Incarnation:
   the *manifestation* of our hope in Christ

3) Crucifixion:
   the *guarantee* of our hope in Christ

4) Resurrection:
   the *anchor* of our hope in Christ

5) Ascension:
   the *advancement* of our hope in Christ

6) Return:
   the *consummation* of our hope in Christ

1) Old Testament:
The *Foreshadowing* of Our Hope in Christ
(Jeremiah 33)

We might paraphrase St. Victor to read: "Even the *Old Testament* is really one book. That book is Christ." If we were to blend together the massive number of Old Testament promises — including sweeping, breathtaking horizons of the Coming Kingdom laid out by a score of prophets — what would we have? *In the final analysis we construct a dazzling portrait of the person of God's Son —* an extensive and vivid description of what His supremacy entails. That's because every vision offered there, without exception — whether of grace or judgment — *requires* Him for its truest meaning and its grandest completion.

THINK WITH ME ...

How do Old Testament texts on creation prepare us for Jesus' majesty?

This is certainly the case when it comes to the abundance of Old Testament reflections on God's glory in creation. Accounts include the vivid dramas that open Genesis; the awesome portrayals that shook Job; Isaiah's visions of natural forces implementing God's judgments; Habakkuk's reassurance that the whole earth will respond with oceans of praises to God; or the many Psalms that tell us (in the words of the 19th): "The heavens declare the glory of God ... like a bridegroom coming forth from his pavilion." The purpose of these texts was to encourage Israel to ponder nature's witness to the greatness and grandeur of God.

Finally, these time-tested reflections on creation served their maximum mission as they added texture to the meaning of Jesus' supremacy — by whom everything was made and from whom everything gained life (Jn. 1). In the flesh, the Savior summed up all the glory to which the heavens testified from the beginning. Drawing on Old Testament understandings of

---

QUOTABLE QUOTE

(God) has now, at the end of the present age, given us the truth in the Son. Through the son God made the whole universe, and to the Son he has ordained that all creation shall ultimately belong. This Son, radiance of the glory of God, flawless expression of the nature of God, himself the upholding principle of all that is, effected in person the reconciliation between God and man and then took his seat at the right hand of the Majesty on high — thus proving himself, by the more glorious Name that he has won, far greater than all the angels of God.

(HEBREWS 1 – PHILLIPS TRANSLATION)

creation's wonders, texts about Jesus like Colossians 1, Romans 1 and John 1 explode with deeper meanings.

For years, thousands of congregations have sung Jack Hayford's uplifting chorus called "Majesty". It starts out, you may recall: "Majesty, worship His majesty, unto Jesus be all glory, honor and praise. Majesty, Kingdom authority, flows from His throne, unto His own, His anthem raise." But what does Jesus' majesty mean? How can we ever properly define it?

Well, listen to Hayford's own answer: "To say our Lord is 'clothed in majesty' is to say that *all creation is window dressing for His excellence. It all points to Him. And just as a king's palace with all its royal décor reflects something of that king's personality, so creation reflects the magnificence of our Lord's nature and character." In other words, exploring creation so extensively, the Biblical writers prepared us for the day God would become flesh and dwell among us in the full display of Jesus' majesty (Jn. 1). Creation is "window dressing" for His supremacy.

But the Old Testament took believers further in their understanding of the expected Messiah, sharing with them heart-stopping foreshadowings of His coming glory.

THINK WITH ME ...
How does Jesus sum up the Old Testament's
"shadows of supremacy"?

My good friend Evelyn Christenson likens the abundance of Old Testament predictions of Christ's supreme place in the purposes of God to an obstetrician's *"ultrasound"*. This computer-generated picture provides a pregnant woman the ability to see the child forming in her womb. Viewing shadowy movements on the monitor brings her unexpected excitement. The mother-to-be can even take the images home as black and white prints. But, Evelyn adds, after the baby is born no one ever hangs a series of framed ultrasound photos on her living room walls, or keeps them in her wallet to show friends. No, after the birth the ultrasound pictures are quickly replaced by an album full of dramatic photos, in living color, of the actual child. As meaningful as prenatal images may be — as faithful as they are in predicting something of what the baby will look like — their value is quickly surpassed the moment the infant is enfolded in the mother's arms. This illustrates the link between God's ancient promises and the Person who was born in a stable to sum them up in Himself.

Let me modify the metaphor slightly. Consider a *shadow*. Referencing Old Testament customs and traditions Paul reminded Christians that "these are a shadow of the things that were to come. The reality, however, is found in Christ" (Col. 2). A shadow can be useful — providing us shade or alerting us to someone approaching. But basically, a shadow calls attention to something beyond itself — to the object that casts it. In the end, Old Testament hopes suggested the shape of Someone far more vivid and tangible and powerful and eternal than any shadow could be.

To borrow a phrase from C. S. Lewis, ancient Scriptures contained the "shadowlands" of Christian hope. Like paper silhouettes, Old Testament dramas, personalities, expectations, predictions, types and themes provided faint but fascinating — even *tantalizing* (1 Pet. 1) — outlines of Christ and His redemptive mission. In virtually every event and story recorded, using texts found in virtually every book, Christ was pre-visioned. He was anticipated. But none of these shadows could be adequately understood until the One who cast them was revealed in Jesus of Nazareth.

The hope held out in such passages was *foreshadowed,* we say. Great expectations awaited their revelation in New Testament teachings about God's Son. Covenant promises were always anchored exclusively in the sovereignty of God's own character and actions. But then, in the "fullness of times" (Gal. 4), they burst forth bodily, revealing unprecedented realities, in plain view of the nations. They sprang into the foreground of world history by the incarnation of a Savior. Early Christians were convinced that Jesus embodied in Himself everything the Bible (Old Testament) claimed about God's greatness, and about the guarantees of His Kingdom. For example, compare the closing verses of Isaiah 45 (" ... before me every knee will bow and by me every tongue will swear ... ") with the opening verses of Philippians 2 (... that at the name of Jesus every knee should bow ... and every tongue confess that Jesus Christ is Lord ... "). This is one of a thousand illustrations of how 1st century believers linked the "shadows of supremacy" with the glory of Jesus' authority over everything.

THINK WITH ME ...
How did Christians look at the Old Testament through "Jesus' glasses"?

Finally, it happened. Full of Holy Spirit joy, Jesus invited His disciples to step out of the shade into the mid-day brilliance of His saving mission among them: "Blessed are the eyes that see what you see. For I tell you that many prophets and kings [Old Testament] wanted to see what you see but did not see it, and to hear what you hear but did not hear it" (Luke 10).

From that moment, it was impossible for believers ever again to study the Old Testament without seeing Christ and His Kingdom permeating its pages. His coming created "Act II" in redemption's drama. The early Christians uncovered significance in Old Testament passages not apparent to ancient Israel, because now they knew Who the story was about, and how the story would conclude. In Christ, the Old Testament is *fulfilled,* we Christians say. What that really means is that now all of its promises are *filled full* — full of the Son to whom everything pointed. Consequently, hundreds of Old Testament verses are woven into the New Testament story by its writers.

Here are few examples of what 1st century believers saw through "Jesus' glasses":

- He is the new *Adam* of a promised re-creation, the overseer of a new race of worshippers to inhabit a new Eden with God's praises (Rom. 5).

- He is the promised seed of *Abraham,* raised up to complete the patriarch's calling to bless all the families of the earth (Gal. 3).

- He is the greater *Moses,* leading us out of sin's captivity into redemption's eternal inheritance (1 Cor. 10).

- He is the superior son of *David,* bringing with Him an everlasting throne and kingdom that conquers all others (Acts 2).

- He is the prophet's *Prophet,* challenging and replacing the status quo, not just in one nation but throughout the whole creation (Heb. 1).

- He is the suffering *Servant,* who sacrificially bears the sins of His people and then extends through them His redemptive, healing mission to all peoples (1 Pet. 2).

QUOTABLE QUOTE

The prophets who told us this was coming asked a lot of questions about this gift of life God was preparing. The Messiah's Spirit let them in on some of it — that the Messiah would experience suffering, followed by glory. They clamored to know who and when. All they were told was that they were serving you, you who by order from heaven have now heard for yourselves — through the Holy Spirit — the Message of those prophecies fulfilled. Do you realize how fortunate you are? Angels would have given anything to be in on this!

(1 PETER 1 — THE MESSAGE)

What, after all, did Jesus mean by His oft-repeated claim that everything He did was "according to the Scriptures"? Quite simply: The Old Testament narrative culminated in His person and His triumphs. Its whole plot pivoted on Him. He was the goal of every redemptive initiative launched there.

In the Consummation, Israel had expected to see her vindication before her enemies; deliverance from all suffering; victory over every evil power; restoration to God's full favor; a whole new beginning stretching into eternal ages. But to everyone's utter amazement The End invaded this present Age through a Nazarene rabbi. In Himself and by Himself, Israel's destiny was achieved in the truest sense God ever intended. Now, those promises await the Great Day when Christ completes them fully and finally — *consummately*, we might say — for His people.

Isn't it curious how on the first Easter, as Luke 24 reports it, Jesus kept coming back to the ancient foreshadowings?

> "And beginning with Moses and all the prophets
> He explained to them what was said in all the
> Scriptures concerning Himself.
> (Then they said), 'Were not our hearts burning within us
> while He talked with us on the road and opened the Scriptures to us?'
> (Then He said), 'Everything must be fulfilled that is written about me
> in the Law of Moses, The Prophets and The Psalms.'
> Then He opened their minds so they could understand the Scriptures.
> He told them, 'This is what is written:
> The Christ must suffer and rise from the dead on the third day, and
> repentance and forgiveness of sins will be preached in
> His name to all nations.' "

It appears that Old Testament hope was the agenda most on Jesus mind when He rose from the dead. In this Risen One, prophetic history had reached its pinnacle, not only for Israel but for all earth's peoples. The sunrise of promised immortality had broken in upon the world stage with a furious blaze (2 Tim. 1). Now, every other promise could unfold. Before the presence of His Royal Highness the shadows could flee once and for all.

No wonder those Emmaus disciples, so filled with despair at the beginning of their journey, found their hearts burning within them, "strangely warmed" (as Wesley described it) by the way Christ unfolded for them how the Old Testament was alive in Himself. This same deliverance from hopelessness — this same encounter with the Lord of Glory — awaits any of us who allow Him to instruct us "along the way".

Thus, as you study Old Testament promises (like those found in **Appendix V**) let this be one of your major goals: See with new eyes how ancient visions of God's awesomeness — whether from Moses or David or Job or Malachi — as well as dramatic stories of God's activities — recorded in Exodus or 2 Chronicles or Daniel or Joel — provide happy hints of more to come. In what sense are such promise-laden texts merely shadows when compared to how they finally found expression and culmination in the person and reign of God's Son? *In other words, how does our Lord Jesus "sum up" and "flesh out" what the Old Testament set forth about the themes of supremacy and hope?*

2) Incarnation:
The *Manifestation* of Our Hope in Christ
(Isaiah 9:1-7)

When Jesus walked among us, He not only brought a more comprehensive *revelation* of hope but also a new *activity* by Heaven to secure that hope. What He did and said in His earthly ministry revealed the determined strategy of the Father to bless the redeemed eternally. In the days of His flesh Christ was the hope of the universe, not "on hold" but "on the move".

Certainly, He was a prophet of glorious things to come — the preeminent Prophet of the ages. But He was a prophet who was also a Son (Heb. 1). Ministering in Galilean hamlets, He was hope-in-*action*, not just hope-in-*words*. In Him, the Kingdom was "at hand" (Mk. 1). In Him the Kingdom was "coming". He vindicated His words by extraordinary deeds of power, representing early stages of the Consummation itself. ("But if I drive out demons by the finger of God, then the Kingdom of God has come to you" Luke 11). Therefore, every force of hopelessness — gripping His hearers' bodies, minds, hearts and spirits — was countered, exorcised and replaced with *Himself*.

THINK WITH ME ...
How does calling Jesus the "Son of Man" magnify hope in His supremacy?

Of all the Old Testament titles Jesus took for Himself, none was used more frequently than *Son of Man*. And for good reason. Taken from the writings of two Old Testament prophets, it permanently married themes of incarnation, supremacy and hope.

Throughout Ezekiel God used the title to describe the seer's humble position in serving captive Jewish exiles. Borrowing the phrase "Son of Man", Jesus likened His experience to that of Ezekiel's humiliation and sufferings. It recalled for His followers the costliness of bringing hope to captives of sin. Being a son of *man* pointed to how He emptied Himself of all divine prerogatives in order to bring spiritual refugees into the prerogatives of divine promises (see Phil. 2).

But the phrase also appears in the book of Daniel. There, *Son of Man* describes something quite different. There we find a human but radiant figure coming on clouds of glory to receive authority over the whole earth on behalf of all peoples (Dan. 7). In a similar way, Christ represented His incarnation as the fulfillment of Daniel's vision. Because He became one of us, a son of *man,* He also became God's climactic word on the reclamation of our race, including the reconstitution of God's creation. As representative Man, He was given all authority over human destiny just as Daniel promised.

> ## QUOTABLE QUOTE
>
> **At the beginning God expressed Himself. That personal expression, that word, was with God and was God, and he existed with God from the beginning. All creation took place through him, and none took place without him. In him appeared life, and this life was the light of mankind. The light still shines in the darkness, and the darkness has never put it out ... so the Word of God became a human being and lived among us.**
>
> (JOHN 1 — PHILLIPS TRANSLATION)

Son of Man, therefore, points to Christ's *servant* role as well as to His *sovereignty* role in God's eternal plan for the nations. It gives the Incarnation and the Kingdom promises common ground. In fact, it weds them as one and the same.

In "the face of Jesus" (2 Cor. 4) everlasting God-ward hope took on temporal, concrete contours. As the express image of God, as the imprint of God's nature (Heb. 1), Christ embodied all God's promises in a human life — for the first time, and the only time, in history.

That's because nothing of deity whatsoever was missing in Him. The Bible tells us He appeared as the permanent depository of divine fullness, laying claim to the full complement of divine attributes (Col. 2). No other being in the entire universe brings human nature and the Godhead together like this, in one single human being.

This is nicely verified in Hebrews 1 when it speaks of Jesus as the "express image" of God. That word picture comes from Roman gold coins engraved or stamped with the image of the Emperor. That image is what gave them their ultimate legitimacy and value. Similarly, we could say that the Servant of God became God's "currency" for distributing His promises to His people. Christ sums up magnificently all Heaven's blessings and deposits them unconditionally to our account. But there's more. This Son, to whom all promises point, in whom the whole universe holds together and to whom has been given every eternal resource one could long for, has *thoroughly* expressed God's nature as *supreme*. He did this by becoming a man who conquered every foe, human and spiritual, and then sat down "at the right hand of the Majesty in heaven" (vs. 3) to reign over God's people and impart His grace forever.

Our hope has been fused to a person who is no less than "Immanuel", God-with-us. Since God dwells in Him fully, and is made fully accessible to us in Him forever, all of God's promises are equally accessible without any diminishment. To paraphrase Luther, Christ incarnate turned out to be God's supremacy fulfilling God's promises "incognito". When God became flesh and entered the world, then (to paraphrase John 1:14) "Eternal *hope* became flesh and dwelt among us, full of (and thus, sovereign in) grace and truth."

THINK WITH ME ...
How does the Incarnation touch
our personal experiences of hopelessness?

Jesus experienced life as one of us (Heb. 2). Unprotected and vulnerable in His humanity, Jesus entered directly into our own painful frustrations, engaged our precarious conditions, tasted our futilities, and embraced our despairs. Think of it: Christ made possible for the Trinity something that they did *not* possess before He became a man — a direct, personal experience of human suffering as well as human triumph over suffering (the victory toward which all God's promises had pointed to start with). Early church fathers thought of it this way: In the God-Man, humility was embraced by majesty, weakness by strength, mortality by eternity.

But He entered into our hopeless condition at an even more profound level. He laid hold of that which perpetrated our worst nightmares. By assuming our sin as if it were His own, He endured the penalty of our rebellion against the promises of God and against the God of all promises. In our place, He entered the black hole of humanity's most horrifying form of hopelessness. "My God, my God, why have you forsaken me?" He cried. Under the judgment of the Cross He shared our desperate straits, drinking our bitter cup to the end. Amazing grace! He paid the ultimate price to allow us to re-enter the Heavenly hope we had forfeited, the hope that Scripture calls eternal life

In human flesh He experienced the humiliation of exile from the throne of the universe. He put His own destiny squarely on the line as He submitted to the Father's will. He emptied Himself — He *donated* Himself! — so that in spite of the godless sinners we are, God might bring to pass, *even in us,* His consummate plan for the ages through the life-giving reign of His Son. What supremacy is His!

Consider further: By taking on human flesh, by abandoning Himself to be the Servant of servants, Christ actually renounced any claim to final control over His own destiny. He placed Himself totally at the Father's disposal. He left in the Father's hands completely the fulfilling of covenant promises. The Son made Himself "nothing" (Phil. 2), because He chose to wait for the Father to vindicate Him, for the Spirit to raise Him, and for lasting lordship to be bestowed upon Him. To be sure, the glory He received as He ascended on high was the same glory He had with the Father and the Spirit from all eternity (Jn. 17). Still, by lifting Him up out of disgrace and despair and destruction, and by giving Him a name above every other name along with a throne above every other dominion, God sealed irrevocably every promise Christ proclaimed (Eph. 1).

The faithfulness of the Father to the Son incarnate, who surrendered so unconditionally to His will, was ultimately displayed when He presented to Him the nations as His inheritance (Ps. 2). The Son has become the *heir* of all for which we could ever hope (Heb. 1). Even so, the Father will manifest the same faithful commitment to everyone who sets his or her hope on the Son and "kisses" Him (as Psalm 2 puts it — an act expressing full allegiance to the crown He wears).

The incarnation provides irrefutable proof that our God is personally committed to the future of humankind. Why? Because, through endless ages a *Man*, delivered from death, will occupy the Praises of Heaven — a Man who is, at the same time, God — One with the Father and the Spirit. As a Scottish theologian once noted: We have hope because "the dust of the earth sits on the throne of the Majesty on High". For the Father to renege on even one of His promises to us is for Him to renege on His promise to glorify His Son. Quite rightly, the old hymn boasts: "Blessed *assurance*, Jesus is mine! Oh, what a foretaste of glory divine!"

3) Crucifixion:
The *Guarantee* for Our Hope in Christ
(Ephesians 1:7-12; 2:12-13)

Let's go back now to look specifically at Christ's *sufferings* in more depth. In doing so, we scale the summit of His supremacy.

Church father Lactantius, serving in the 4th century court of Emperor Constantine, suggested: "No nation is so uncivilized, no region so remote, that either His passion or the heights of His majesty is unknown. So, in His suffering, He stretched forth His hands and measured out the world — so that even then He might show that a great multitude (collected out of all languages and tribes, from the rising of the sun even to its setting) was about to come under His wings!"

In other words, the passions of Christ made the reign of Christ universal. *Hope* holds meaning for a Christian (and for the nations) only to the degree the *Cross* holds meaning. We cannot understand the full breadth of our destiny in Jesus apart from understanding the breadth of His sufferings that guarantees that destiny for us.

All the wealth of God's promises, held out to us by the Gospel, depends entirely upon Calvary to become reality for any sinner. Therefore, Jesus focused His entire earthly life toward the Cross. It was there He was able to secure God's purposes for Heaven and earth, including each of us. How overwhelmingly precious is the certainty of our prospect: "If God is for us, who can be against us? He who did not spare His own Son, but gave Him up for us all — how will He not also, along with Him, graciously give us all things?" (Rom. 8). Every promise God has ever issued to the human race is captured by that phrase: "all things". The Cross, it appears, is the fountainhead of everlasting bounties to be poured out relentlessly upon grateful saints everywhere, for all time and eternity. So great was the sacrifice of God's Son — so marvelous its ramifications, so extraordinary its accomplishments, so all-encompassing its consequences — that every other grace the Father has granted is unconditionally guaranteed in the Son.

THINK WITH ME ...
Why is the Cross the great crossroads for our future?

When you're on a trip, arrival at any crossroads requires decision. At that point, a traveler can't remain neutral. Avoiding a choice will simply prevent you from going any farther.

In our spiritual journey, Christ's death marks the most critical crossroads for a hopeless humanity traveling toward Eternal Judgment. It's the most authentic "*cross*-road" there is. On the harrowing hill of execution, just one single day created the historic moment toward which every promise of Scripture to the nations had pointed, and from which every promise will reach ultimate fulfillment. At the foot of the Cross two themes converged. The glories of God was one, including: all the streams of His blessings, all the triumphs of His grace, all the manifestations of His majesty, all the grandeurs of His holiness, all thunders of His judgments and the all-subduing power of His love. The other theme consisted of deadly dramas dictated by the sins, sicknesses and sorrows of our rebel race.

Then, the Cross provided the pivot-point to turn sinners away from the dead-end of the latter road and toward a dynamic new destination in Jesus. There He took upon Himself creation's futility and decay. He took upon Himself the cancer of our terminal hostility toward God. Through what happened our Lord provided a way of escape out of darkness to bask evermore in the thick brilliance of divine beauty. At that crossroads outside Jerusalem 2000 years ago, our Savior became by Himself the Super Highway back to the Father, where we will never cease to delight in the Lamb's wounds. We will celebrate without ceasing the consummate glory of His agonies. We will forever delight in all the possibilities that His sufferings have turned into realities. If that's not a vision of His *supremacy*, then what is?

No one ever suffered like the Master suffered. In Himself and by Himself, He penetrated the bowels of mankind's miseries. He drank the bitter dregs of our spiritual perdition. What He endured had unfathomable impact on the powers of darkness. For all the redeemed He absorbed and exhausted and displaced, irrevocably, the fatal specter of divine judgment and eternal death.

That's why we call it *Good* Friday. In place of our alienation, estrangement and enmity, that bleakest of days opened for all time *inexhaustible goodness* — so good, in fact, that even former enemies might share in it, eternally, through union with the conquering Redeemer. He satisfied every condition for fully restoring to us our God-ordained calling. By His sufferings, Jesus not only *purchased* our hope for us. He actually *inherited* it for us. The promises are exclusively His, first of all by *right*. But they are also His by *righteousness* — that is, by fulfilling all of God's righteous requirements on our behalf, including the endurance of the Father's just retribution upon our sin (Lk. 3).

His plan from the outset was to act in our stead and on our behalf. He took responsibility to accomplish what we could never do for ourselves. He answered creation's groanings for release from decay (Rom. 8). He freed us from the futile ways of our fathers (1 Pet. 1). Every inheritance we have in God's Kingdom has been bought and paid for by God's Son. We have become heirs of God and co-heirs with Christ, rescued by blood to share in His glory for ages to come (Rom. 8).

At the Cross God offered each of us a *wonderful exchange* that included:

- My depravity ... exchanged for Christ's pure righteousness.

- My mortal death ... exchanged for Christ's immortal life.

- My despair ... exchanged for a joyous destiny summed up in Him.

- My curse ... exchanged for eternal blessings that flow from His wounds.

- My judgment ... exchanged for a safe place inside His Kingdom.

- My defeat and destruction ... exchanged for His inexhaustible victory.

So again I ask you: If Christ's death accomplished all of this, could there ever be any greater display of His all-consuming dominion?

THINK WITH ME ...

How has the Cross eliminated every false hope for us?

What happened at the Cross permanently exposed counterfeit paths to joy. It unmasked the lies inherently found in the world's *false* hopes. Calvary was God's masterful stroke of defiance toward rebel dreams. By it He confirmed that our hopeless estate is far worse than we first dared to believe. Sacred blood bears witness before all peoples that our own efforts are undeniably in vain. Left to ourselves all of us are incapable of satisfying either our longings or God's justice. We are confined instead to a cataclysm called eternal death.

If there was any other way to secure our future, then surely Christ's suffering was an insanely tragic endeavor (to paraphrase Gal. 2:20-21). The reality is just the opposite, however. The Cross challenges all peoples to repent of the foolish illusions of our own pomp and power. At the same time the Cross sets before nations unprecedented prospects as bright (and beautiful) as the promises of God — circumscribed by a slain Sacrificial Animal who, at this very moment, is ruling the universe as a Lordly Lion, carrying everything to its pre-ordained Consummation.

THINK WITH ME ...

Why do Christ's sufferings crown Him supreme over every hope we have?

Ultimately Christ's supremacy does not consist in His ability to *impose* His will uncontested — to break, or take, or shake things up (all of which He will do one day). Rather, His supremacy is preeminently about His ability to *redeem* — to reclaim, to reconcile, to restore, to remake and to re-deploy salvaged sinners to serve Kingdom agendas. Therefore, *the Cross is really His crown.* Final vindication of the Son's right to the Eternal Throne consists of His willingness to lay aside His rights, to obey His Father even to the point of submitting unto death. Hope triumphs not only *through* His travails but also *in* His travails.

QUOTABLE QUOTE

One of the Elders said, 'Don't weep. Look – the Lion from Tribe Judah, the Root of David's Tree, has conquered. There, surrounded by Throne, Animals, and Elders, was a Lamb, slaughtered but standing tall ... and they sang a new song: Worthy! Take the scroll, open its seals. Slain! Paying in blood, you bought men and women, bought them back from all over the earth, bought them back for God. Then You made them a Kingdom, Priests for our God, Priest-Kings to rule over the earth ... the slain Lamb is worthy! Take the power, the wealth, the wisdom, the strength! Take the honor, the glory, the blessing!'

(REVELATION 5 – THE MESSAGE)

In that Great Day when God's promises in Christ reach their climax, the Cross will still dominate. Throughout endless ages Christ's wounds will appear to us, as the old hymn says, as "rich wounds, yet visible above, in beauty glorified". In the New Jerusalem, the victorious Monarch will always be viewed, at the same time, as a bloodied Martyr.

Therefore, the Cross will forever remain the high watermark of all manifestations of Christ's supremacy — unsurpassed, throughout endless ages. At no point will Jesus ever appear to Christians to be more exalted than when He became the sacrifice for our sin. Nowhere will He ever blaze forth in victory more vividly than when He was vanquished on Golgotha's tree. To worship Him as He deserves, focused on Him as supreme upon His *throne,* we must learn first to marvel at Him supreme upon His *Cross.*

What was written on Pontius Pilate's sign nailed above His head? "This is the *King* of the Jews" (emphasis mine). Even then His supremacy bannered His sufferings.

4) Resurrection:
The *Anchor* for Our Hope in Christ
(1 Corinthians 15:17-28)

In the Resurrection Christ's preeminence comes shining through in a whole other way. In the Resurrection He stands unique among all religious leaders of any world religion, whether gurus or prophets. He is the only Master ever to come back permanently alive from the grave, and that by His own power (Jn. 10). In the Resurrection He remains forever unchallenged, utterly superior and totally beyond the pale of all other contenders.

A word of promise *He* speaks, therefore, must retain unparalleled legitimacy. Because He lives, God's purposes and promises are vindicated and validated for all who believe. When God raised Jesus from the dead, the unprecedented prospects He had preached became wonderfully wedded to His very person. The "Message of Hope" and the "Messenger of Hope" merged into one.

In 2004 Mel Gibson's epic film *The Passion of the Christ* stormed the theaters of the world. It was viewed with deeply felt emotions by tens of millions. Many Hollywood critics savaged the movie, however, because to them it seemed to consist of two hours of nothing but mindless brutality. Yet to multitudes of Christians, *The Passion* had the very opposite effect. Why? Because as believers we knew that, first, the sufferings represented on the screen were eternally redemptive, and therefore profoundly precious, for those who call Jesus their Lord. Secondly, we also knew that the story continued right through an empty tomb (as the last few moments of Gibson's film sensitively portrayed), making all the bloody agony of the previous 24 hours foundational for a renovated universe in which our Risen Sacrifice would reign in glory.

THINK WITH ME ...
How many victories did His resurrection achieve?

"Christ is victor!" This is a familiar weekly cry among the world's Orthodox Christians — Greek, Serbian, Russian and others. That's because for this wing of Christendom, everything is thoroughly infected by their vision of the Resurrection. You read it in their theologies. You see it in their dazzling icons. You hear it in ancient liturgies that embrace two worlds at once — they describe the worship of God as a descending of "Heaven to earth". That's how alive Jesus is for them. You note it as well when they speak of the "communion of saints". For them this experience includes a tangible intersecting of believers in glory with believers below. For Orthodox believers, both groups are equally alive in Christ, which is why many have embedded the photographs of loved ones on their tombstones to emphasize how alive the deceased *still* are.

Surely, Christians of every stripe must echo something of the Orthodox perspective on Easter. We must declare with them that *all* our spiritual triumphs draw their vitality from one supreme victory: When Christ rose to destroy the final opponent to every God-given hope, He swallowed up death itself. Our Lord not only brings us forgiveness by His bloody wounds but He also frees us by His risen body. He not only cleanses the sin that eternally separated us from God. He also rose to confound, every day in every way, the sin that would enslave and defeat us even now.

Christ is Victor! Let this truth erupt with undying praise to the Triune God. Christ is Victor! Let this truth place our Savior in His position as the heir of all things past, present and future. Christ is Victor! Let this truth reinforce His role as exclusive source of hope for all humanity, the One we can trust unhesitatingly with our farthest-reaching expectations.

Christ is Victor! Only this explains why the early Church worshipped Him so fervently, bestowing on Him a vast array of royal titles. Only this vision explains why, despite its ghastly horrors, they celebrated His sacrifice, seeing it as the pinnacle of God's promises. This is where they found courage even in the face of mockery and martyrdom. This is why they acted as Kingdom ambassadors to their enemies. Their hearts were held steady by the sure and certain hope of their *own* resurrection in Christ. They walked in life-changing experiences of His death-destroying power. Filled with the very same Spirit that took Jesus out of the tomb, they could not be silent. They could not be contained.

Christ is Victor! — All of God's promises are permanently preserved for us in the risen Prince of Life (Acts 3). This witness alone should cause every Christian today to join the shouts of Heaven and say — "the kingdom of the world has become the kingdom of our Lord and of His Christ, and He will reign for ever and ever" (Rev. 11).

THINK WITH ME ...
In what sense is Christ also now the firstfruits of all our hope?

Crushing the jaws of the tomb, Christ became *firstfruits* — the beginning, the initial wave — of a future resurrection that lies before us all. We may not yet have the whole harvest, but in Him we hold God's pledge of that harvest. In fact, in Him the harvesting has already begun, with additional (and far more extensive) reaping just ahead (1 Cor. 15).

Lazarus was resuscitated by Jesus, only to die again (Jn. 11). But Christ Himself was resurrected with an eternally indestructible body (Jn. 20-21). He, not Lazarus, now reigns as our prototype. He's the *template,* we might say, not only for our individual resurrection bodies but also for the glory that will saturate the entire creation when everything is enveloped by a universal recapitulation back to Jesus, the Consummation.

Out of a borrowed tomb, *a new order of existence emerged within time and space.* Much more than some memorable miracle passed down as a story from ancient times, the Resurrection is the out-breaking of something utterly *new* that remains with us permanently. Nothing could be more contemporary than this. It is the beginning of the ultimate triumphs of God's grace. It is the inception of a victory that's currently spreading across the earth, destined to envelop everything, everywhere, not long from now.

In our risen Lord, the splendor of the New Heaven and Earth was unveiled for His disciples to behold — immediately. The Resurrection was not some freakish intrusion into the natural order of things. It was the anticipation — better yet, the implementation — of an indestructible life (Heb. 7), eternally destined by God for our blessing and His praise.

Just as the incarnation draws its meaning from the *first* creation; just as the crucifixion is necessitated by the helpless condition of the *fallen* creation; even so the Resurrection permanently positions all believers in a *new* creation, even at this very moment (2 Cor. 5).

THINK WITH ME ...
In what way does the Resurrection anchor every other hope for us?

We might say that the risen Christ *anchors* us to all the promises of that new creation. That's what Hebrews 6 concludes. Because of Christ's unparalleled reversal of death, our confidence about the outcome remains steadfast: "We have this hope as an anchor for the soul, firm and secure ... where Jesus, who went before us, has entered on our behalf."

Just as an anchor, though invisible below the waves, firmly tethers a ship in a storm, even so Christ supreme over the grave grips us and holds us, unshakeable, to every single dimension of God-given hope. He "ties" us directly to a future in which "no longer will there be any curse. The throne of God and of the Lamb will be in the city, and His servants will serve Him. They will see His face ... and they will reign for ever and ever" (Rev. 22). He sovereignly binds us to *Himself*, "the hope of glory", with chains of love that cannot be broken (Rom. 8).

His Resurrection encourages us, then, to resist drifting back into hassles of human hopelessness. It gives us a rock to cling to in life's disillusioning floods. It empowers us to endure life's most disheartening storms. It summons us into constant celebrations of the risen life of Christ within us. It reassures us that when our destiny is consummated in Christ we'll discover that not one of our labors for Heaven was ever in vain.

Without question, that day of our deliverance is coming. Soon, we too will be physically raised

---

QUOTABLE QUOTE

Whatever God has promised gets stamped with the Yes of Jesus. In him, this is what we preach and pray, the great Amen, God's Yes and our Yes together, gloriously evident. God affirms us, making us a sure thing in Christ, putting his Yes within us.

(2 CORINTHIANS 1 – THE MESSAGE)

with Christ to reign with Him (1 Thess. 4). As surely as light dawns tomorrow, there's a date scheduled when we will stand *bodily* on the earth, raised incorruptible and immortal (1 Cor. 15).

The ramifications of this for today's Christians are breath-taking. It should provide us incomparable, God-concocted cures for every other crisis we face. It should reverse every shortfall of confidence about His Kingdom as well as any wavering of passion for His glory. It should compel us to lose our lives for His sake and the Gospel — to serve the advance of His global cause among earth's peoples — knowing that in the end because He lives we shall live also (Mk. 8 with Jn. 14).

In the early days of the Bolshevik revolution, the newly empowered communists forced a debate in Moscow at a local university between a party leader and the head of the Russian Orthodox Church. When the priest arose to speak, instead of attempting to refute his atheist opponent, he gazed on his audience briefly, then said this simple phrase: "Christ is risen!" The building shook with a thunderous, spontaneous, unanimous three-fold response: "He is risen indeed! He is risen indeed! *He is risen indeed!*" Then the priest sat down. He knew the auditorium was filled with good Orthodox Christians who recited this liturgical response every Sunday morning. This was their unshakeable conviction. This prevailing hope was the only prospect they needed at such a dark hour for their nation. The communist members on hand that day were silenced. Nothing remained to be said. Christ was all. The Principalities and Powers must have taken notice as well (Eph. 3).

I suspect that "He is risen indeed!" will continue to be a message of hope, proclaimed and praised and practiced by all of us, throughout all of eternity. It's a permanent piece of the Church's vision for the supremacy of God's Son.

QUOTABLE QUOTE

Father, the hour has come. Glorify Your Son now so that he may bring glory to you, for you have given him authority over all men to give eternal life to all that you have given him. And this is eternal life, to know you, the only true God, and him whom you have sent — Jesus Christ. Father, I want those whom you have given me to be with me where I am; I want them to see the glory which you have made mine — for you loved me before the world began.

(JOHN 17 – PHILLIPS TRANSLATION)

5) Ascension:
The *Advancement* of Our Hope in Christ
(Psalm 2 and Psalm 110)

Whenever you ponder the majestic Christological portraits of Scripture — texts such as John 1, Ephesians 1, Colossians 1, Hebrews 1 or Revelation 1 — remember this: They were written just a few short decades after the Crucifixion and Resurrection. They bear witness to the magnitude of devotion and praise Jesus was already receiving as Lord by that point in time. Why was the early Church's vision of the Savior so expansive and so highly exalting?

The simple answer: Beyond His incarnation, crucifixion and Resurrection, 1st century Christians lived daily in the full awareness of Christ's *Ascension* (Acts 2). Their hearts were set on His coronation and current position at God's right hand (Col. 3). They breathed the very air of His active role from the throne of Heaven, holding sway as the King of Kings and Lord of Lords that He already was.

To be sure, Christ inherently possessed the *power* to govern the universe by virtue of His creating it. In addition, He could claim the inherited *right* to preside over it because of His death and Resurrection. But now, seated at God's right hand, He had a *direct role* in the success of His reign due to activities unfolding at His throne every moment. And the early Church knew it because they experienced it.

When Paul wrote about preaching only "Christ and Him crucified" (1 Cor. 2) we mustn't forget: Paul envisioned his message as *Christ* crucified. In other words, the apostle's word about the power of the Cross made no sense apart from the Ascension. We know this, because the technical title given God's Son — that He was the "Christ" or the "Anointed One" — had been reserved for centuries by serious Jews like Paul to be given only to one person: The promised final Sovereign — the ultimate heir of David who would be set apart by God (anointed) as universal King, crowned as Lord of the cosmos, Ruler of the nations and Head of the Church. The Ascension *confirmed* for 1st century disciples like Paul that Jesus was precisely the Supreme Redeemer they had anticipated. Exalted as the mighty Messiah of God, He was ready to reclaim subjects for His Kingdom by the blood of His Cross (Col. 1).

Even pagans took note of this unwavering passion for the current kingship of Jesus, labeling believers as "*Christ*-ians" (Acts 11) which, in the

Greek, implied "people who have become fanatics about the current reign of their Anointed Lord".

THINK WITH ME ...
What practical difference should it make
that Christ is on the throne?

It is true to say the Transfiguration (Mt. 16) *foreshadowed* the glory of Christ's coming Ascension and enthronement. Even more amazingly, we could say the Resurrection, as the spectacular explosion into time and space of a whole new creation provided the *prelude* ("phase one" if you will) for the full "symphony" of Christ's eternal dominion. But the Ascension offered even more. It transformed the Transfiguration and the Resurrection from *momentary acts,* on a mountain top and in a garden, into a *permanent state* to impact everything from here to eternity, both now and later.

Because Jesus ascended, the active advance of God's Kingdom streams out everywhere. It flows forth from one royal Court, through one royal Person, with incomparable precision of purpose. All of life, whether for individuals, churches or nations, plays itself out under the immediate, unstoppable, unavoidable (even if unrecognized) sovereignty of the Son of God. He's the most contemporary ruler there is. He is "the Ruler of the kings of the earth" (Rev. 1).

Our Lord has no serious rivals in the universe. Instead the Father is aggressively uniting all things under His Son's feet this very moment. Christ is not waiting to be crowned as king. He is only waiting to be *recognized* as king. Reigning as its only Sovereign, He is responsible to judge the world and then cleanse it for His own uses, one way or another (Acts 17). Even as you read these words, He is actively restoring all creation, according to God's eternal plan, by the increasing subjugation of all things to Himself (Eph. 1). One day earth's peoples from all the Ages will be convincingly conquered at the great Climax. They will be summed up in our Lord forever, either by *redemption* or by *judgment*. His supremacy comprises the only horizon toward which all of us are moving, whether believers or unbelievers.

The message of the Ascension comes down to this: *What Jesus will be Lord of ultimately, He is fully Lord of now. Whatever hope Jesus' reign will offer the universe ultimately, it offers believers now.* All things are as much under His authoritative oversight at this moment as they will be in the day of His Return. Even now He freely exercises all of His divine prerogatives, executing divine purposes. This is as true today as it will be at the crowning hour of the Consummation.

The great midpoint of history now lies behind us. The future has broken in upon us. Now it unfolds before us day by day. Since Christ's coronation in Heaven, according to Acts 1, the Church not only looks *up* (for His return), and looks *out* (on His missionary advance), but also looks *forward* (to whatever more of His Kingdom is about to be revealed among the nations). God's Word assures us that in every step of our journey His Son continues extending His scepter, enforcing His dominion, validating His victories. That's why we have full assurance that our labors for Him will never be wasted. Our mission to earth's peoples is not a fool's errand. In fact, He's actually going before us as we go.

All of this has very *practical* implications for our personal walk with God's Son. Even before the End our union with Him should bring us powerful *foretastes* each day of who He will be for us then, when He wonderfully wraps up all history and all creation in Himself. "Christ is in you, the hope of glory" (Col. 1) — just this one verse links us experientially, through the dynamics of His indwelling dominion, with the New Heaven and Earth. Consequently, as amazing as it sounds, believers are actually invited to experience life-changing "beginnings of the End", ahead of time. In other words, we can expect "*approximations* of the Consummation" (as we'll term them in chapter 4) because He is already ruling.

At the throne right now, the future has been described and decided — in a Person! Whenever and wherever His reign breaks through into our ordinary routines there's more than meets the eye. His grace toward believers incorporates key themes of His Grand Finale. That's because He Himself defines those themes — whether then or now — by virtue of who He is, where He leads, how He imparts and what He receives. In other words, by virtue of His supremacy.

THINK WITH ME …
Why is Psalm 110 quoted so frequently in the New Testament?

Consider for a moment Psalm 110. It is the most frequently quoted or referenced Old Testament passage by New Testament writers. Why is that? Why, out of all the ancient promises, did the first disciples turn to this ancient hymn time and time again? The answer is obvious. This one text spoke more clearly than most about who they understood their ascended Jesus to be as He worked in His Church. Supremacy, you'll notice, is its central theme:

> "The Lord says to my Lord:
> 'Sit at my right hand
> until I make your enemies
> a footstool for your feet.'
> The Lord will extend your mighty scepter from Zion;
> you will rule in the midst of your enemies.
> Your troops will be willing
> on your day of battle …
> The Lord has sworn and will not change his mind:
> 'You are a priest forever,
> in the order of Melchizedek'…
> He will crush kings on the day of his wrath.
> He will judge the nations.…"

Psalm 110 pinpoints the single greatest reality unfolding around us today. Its drama interprets both the front page of our newspapers as well as the frontlines of our mission. It reinforces that peoples and events everywhere are being woven into Christ's reign, whether they know it or not. No matter how far from the center of divine activity we may seem to be, Christ engages every human domain. He engages kingdoms of finance and commerce, entertainment and education, industry and labor, the arts and sciences, rulers and governments. There is not a square inch of any sphere of existence for which it cannot be said: "Christ rules over *you!*" All ambitions will soon be cut or culminated in Him.

History is not moving in a vacuum. At His footstool, Psalm 110 tells us, we can watch history pursuing one increasing purpose: To bring about the fullest possible expression of Christ's supremacy, to the farthest bounds of earth, to the greatest extent envisioned by the Father. Nothing will ever turn this battle back at the gates.

Our hope in God stands strong because Jesus' reign already stands strong. Installed as Messiah, His promised work of universal restoration is underway. His lordship is becoming increasingly visible among all peoples, as God works through His own. The whole earth boasts wondrous potential for experiencing and expressing God's glory. The Son's victory procession is on the move across the planet, recruiting people from many tribes and tongues.

Therefore, wherever they live and whatever they face Christians can expect to walk daily in ever-increasing demonstrations of His supremacy, by the power of His Spirit in us. No wonder Psalm 110 predicts: "Your troops will be *willing* on your day of battle." In view of what He is up to, enthusiasm for serving Him will be unbounded.

THINK WITH ME ...
How are we a part of Christ's missionary invasion among the nations?

Similar to Psalm 110, Isaiah 9 confirms that "of the increase of His government there shall be no end". No matter what the future holds out to us, we can be sure of this: The impact of Christ's rule will continue to swell and grow — not shrink and shrivel — from age to age, until the Climax of All Things arrives. *This hope has consistently propelled Christ's global cause of world evangelization.*

In the 2nd century, for example, Clement of Alexandria wrote: "The whole world, along with Athens and Greece, has already become the domain of the Word." North African Christian scholar Tertullian, writing around the same time, boldly asserted that "We have filled every place — cities, islands, fortresses, towns, market places, palace, senate, forum" leaving nothing to the pagans "but the temples of your gods". Why? In the same treatise he exclaimed that even peoples inaccessible to Roman armies had become "subjugated to Christ" through the Gospel, adding: "In all these places the name of Christ reigns. Christ's name is extending everywhere, believed everywhere, worshipped by all the nations, and is reigning everywhere." Early Church fathers were convinced that Christ's Kingdom was *advancing*, generation after generation.

Like waves ascending up a beach in the momentum of an incoming tide, despite periods of ebbs and flow, the missionary purpose cannot be stopped.

Its Champion remains undaunted, concerned for all peoples, Lord of all peoples, for all time to come. God has no "Plan B". At this very moment, our lofty Leader is about the business of bringing about unconditional surrender among all the nations through the spread of the Gospel. In our generation this planet-wide mission is one of the most vivid expressions of the all-embracing scope of Christ's Ascension.

From the throne Christ has never ceased directing a 2000-year-old global missionary invasion of the nations with the Gospel. True to His universal presence, there is no place His ambassadors go where He has not gone ahead of them. With full authority He sets the stage for our arrival before we get there. He works through us when we arrive. He sustains the impact of His reign long after we move on.

The Father has given His Son keys to countless doors, in cities and communities, doors just waiting to be opened. There are peoples poised by sovereign grace, even now, to be reached with His salvation. There is no place on the planet Christ cannot and will not lead His missionary Church in its victory parade (Mt. 28). He intends to *fill* the nations with the hope of the Gospel (Acts 1 with Col. 1). Sovereignly rearranging the affairs of mankind as needed to bring everything to pass, the Father has set His heart on countless sinners yet to be drawn to His promises in Christ Jesus (See 2 Cor. 2, 3, 4).

With full determination this mission-sending God has narrowed His sights on *our* generation. He sees more than two billion people still completely unevangelized. He knows there are multitudes who have no knowledge of who His Son is — who have no one like them, near them, even to begin to tell them. But He refuses to leave earth's peoples in this hopeless condition. What is God's *goal?* — to achieve the greatest possible glory for His Son, among the greatest host of humans, to the fullest extent possible, in a way that magnifies forever the triumphs of His mercy and the supremacy of His Messiah.

THINK WITH ME ...
What does opposition to His mission
tell us about His supremacy?

To avoid any spirit of trivial "triumphalism", however, let's be clear on one thing: Christ's missionary cause not only initiates *harvest fields;* it also instigates *battlefields.* Any war is costly, usually bloody. Skirmishes are lost and won. Not every moment in the service of Jesus' Kingdom offers visible, unalloyed advances in His mission. There are Forces of Darkness opposed to God's promises, ready to fight them, and us, to the death.

Still, we can boast in our undiminished hope. Though not physically present, Christ is right now actively subduing His enemies, dethroning Principalities and Powers in many places. Increasingly He is putting limits on their opposition to His dominion among the nations. Though the time of their full destruction awaits the Consummation, God's Son is rapidly rendering them ineffective and unproductive. He is breaking their *stranglehold* on earth's peoples. He is tearing down their *strongholds* against the Gospel. He is upholding His cause to bring saving hope to sinners everywhere (compare Rev. 12:1-12 with Heb. 12:25-29). The increased martyrdom of Christians over the past century alone, in unprecedented numbers, only serves to reinforce how decisively and effectively Christ's redemptive mission is penetrating enemy territory.

In 1948 Dwight Eisenhower published his memoirs on World War II entitled *Crusade in Europe*. As commander-in-chief of the Allied Forces, he faced many pressures to give up his primary goal, to use the beaches of Normandy for an all-out invasion of the Nazi empire at the earliest practical moment. Two sentences on page 48 in his book sum up his story well: "History has proved that nothing is more difficult in war than to adhere to a single strategic plan. Unforeseen and glittering promise on the one hand, and unexpected difficulties or risks upon the other, present constant temptations to desert the chosen line of action in favor of another."

In the same way, *our* Supreme Commander will never waver, despite all the opposition. He will not desert His invasion of the nations. He will not turn back from fulfilling the promises of the Father, or fail to recapture uncontested what is rightfully His. His "one strategic plan" is for every knee to bow, by either redemption or judgment, in the confession of His Kingship over all, to the glory of the Almighty Father (Isa. 45 and Phil. 2).

THINK WITH ME ...

Why is our Ascended Ruler also our chief prayer partner?

Let's return to the teaching of Psalm 110 for a moment. There we read that His reign will reach out through His role as *High Priest*. Heaven-bound in the Holy of Holies, He has taken charge permanently *as a man of prayer*. This may be the most strategic confirmation of His reputation as the summation of Christian hope.

The theme of Psalm 110 is picked up and expanded throughout the book of Hebrews. Jesus' prayers, we learn there, are the *primary* means of expressing His supremacy right now. Fundamentally, they are how He works out the far-reaching ramifications of His Cross and Resurrection, both for churches and for nations.

For example, we read: "He has become a priest not on the basis of a regulation as to His ancestry, but on the basis of the power of an indestructible life.... And a better hope is introduced, by which we draw near to God.... Jesus has become the guarantee of a better covenant.... Because Jesus lives forever, He has a permanent priesthood. Therefore He is able to save completely those who come to God through Him because He always lives to intercede for them" (selected from Heb. 7).

Poised every moment at God's right hand, our Lord Jesus bears on His heart two things: Heaven's promises and the saints' pleas — simultaneously — mingled together. He presents both to the God of all hope. As our Chief Intercessor, He stands up for His people's longings. He claims for us the Father's absolute favor. It is due Him as the Son and as the King of all kings. His perpetual priesthood procures for us God's promises for every godly desire, every act of obedient faith, every redemptive mission, every battle with the Devil — and especially, for every crisis of supremacy we may experience.

But there's more. Because He is supreme, Jesus is also the ultimate *answer* to all of our prayers. That's why the last prayer of the Bible (Rev. 22) simply says: "Come, Lord Jesus." Who He is, in kingly array, will finally bring total satisfaction to every cry of our hearts. His prayers ensure for all of us that the crowning conclusion of our prayers will unfold — as it unfolds for His universal Kingdom — just as the Father ordained from eternity (Rom. 8).

The triumphs of the Empire of the Son, present and future, are inseparable from how the Father delights to respond to the prayers of the Son. This certainty should hold every Christian captive to a Kingdom-sized vision that refuses to let us go. Because He is Lord, as the Bible teaches repeatedly, those who hope in Him (and pray accordingly) "will not be disappointed" (Isa. 64).

6) Return:
The *Consummation* of Our Hope in Christ
(Revelation 19:6-16; 22:12-13)

Kingdom activities that unfold *this* day around the Savior will, on *another* Day, reach cosmic proportions. Just as Christ's lordship has public dimensions now, those same dimensions will be permanently and incomparably magnified in the Hour He returns to culminate the promises of God.

QUOTABLE QUOTE

Just as surely as it is appointed for all men to die once, and after that they pass to their judgment, so it is certain that Christ was offered once to bear the sins of many and after that, to those who look to him, he will appear a second time, not this time to deal with sin but to bring full salvation to those who eagerly await him.

(HEBREWS 9 – PHILLIPS TRANSLATION)

Two discourses in John's Gospel make this point in dramatic fashion. Responding to critics of His Sabbath healings, Jesus exclaimed: "To your amazement [the Father] will show [the Son] even greater things than these. For just as the Father raises the dead and gives them life, even so the Son gives life ... the Father judges no one, but has entrusted all judgment to the Son, so that all may honor the Son just as they honor the Father ... A time is coming when all who are in their graves will hear [the Son of Man's] voice and come out ..." (Jn. 5). With the crowd that sought Him only for the miracle of multiplying loaves and fishes, Jesus did not mince words: "My Father's will is that everyone who looks to the Son and believes in him shall have eternal life, and I will raise him up at the last day ... I am the living bread ... Whoever eats my flesh and drinks my blood has eternal life, and I will raise him up at the last day...." (Jn. 6). In both cases, Jesus tied immediate claims of His supremacy to how His authority would be revealed at the End.

To grasp fuller depths of Christ's glory today, therefore — to understand how He truly sums up all Christian hope in Himself — we must actively mine-out the incomparable truths of what the *fulfillment* of His reign will look like in the Age To Come. The term normally used for the everlasting displays of our Lord's dominion is the *"Consummation"*.

THINK WITH ME ...

How does hope *inaugurated* become hope *consummated*?

In one respect, as we've just seen, His coronation inaugurated the beginnings of the Final Day. But it did so only in *preliminary* forms within the unfolding drama of history (properly re-spelled, *His*-story). Current experiences of Christ's supremacy parallel, but only initially, what we'll behold *more fully* when Jesus comes back to bring forth a New Jerusalem under His triumphant gaze (Rev. 21-22). All foretastes of the promises wait to be "consummated" at that Hour.

Of one thing we can be sure: At this very moment He's preparing for something much grander and more conclusive than we can imagine. There's coming a revolutionary revelation of His reign, when the unbelieving peoples of earth will groan in fear, seeking to flee His face (Rev. 6). Christ will bring down the curtain on the dead-end tragedies of this fallen world, to raise it again on that fabulous Forever Festival that the Bible terms eternal life. Faith will flow into sight. Promises will culminate in ways beyond comprehension, visitation of God we call our Lord's visible return in Glory.

Would you like to understand more thoroughly how Christ's lordship can reinvigorate discipleship *right now*? Then, join me to explore a vision of the final dimensions of His eternal Kingdom. To enter into a truly victorious life with Him day after day, we need to uncover something of the *ultimate scope* of the hope of His Final Victory. To benefit thoroughly from His Headship over the Church in *this* generation, we need to grasp greater measures of the grace by which He will rule His people *later*.

What I'm saying is this: If we want to help the Church discover the full extent of Christ's majesty and power; if we want to re-convert fellow believers back to Him for ALL that He is, it makes sense to devote significant time to learning how He intends to bring our destiny to its Climax.

As we're about to discover in the next chapter, Christ is more than just the *summation* of our hope. He is also the *consummation* of that hope. It is impossible to understand His supremacy — to define adequately what the "all" in the phrase "Christ is all" truly means — apart from understanding what the soon-arriving, decisive Day of His Power will tell us about *Him*. How will we interpret His lordship the hour we see Him coming in clouds of glory (Rev. 1)? I'd like to take the next few pages to talk about it.

PARTING WORDS FROM NAPOLEON

Napoleon Bonaparte's final days were spent in despair and defeat due primarily to his own shameful ambition and lust for power. Yet toward the end of his life the brilliant French emperor remarked, in what may be his most memorable words:

"Everything in Christ astonishes me!
Neither history, nor humanity, nor the ages, nor nature, offer me anything
with which I am able to compare Him
and by which I am able to explain Him.
Here is everything extraordinary."
[emphasis mine]

If only this military general had nourished a heart that acted in concert with such convictions. If only he had submitted to Eternity's Emperor. I'd like to paraphrase Napoleon's insights, suggesting how he might have spoken of Christ had he known Him for ALL that we have just discovered in this chapter:

Everything in Christ astonishes me!
There is no other who can compare with Him.
Nothing in all creation can secure my destiny apart from Him.
Every inexplicable grace the Father offers flows from Him.
Christ Supreme is the extraordinary summation of all my hope.

Is this the One to whom *your* heart belongs? Is this how *you* are prepared to praise Him forever?

3

CHRIST SUPREME:

The *Consummation* of Christian Hope

Recover a Vision Shaped by the FULFILLMENT of His Supremacy

In *The Silver Chair* (one volume in C.S. Lewis' *Chronicles of Narnia*), a dreadfully thirsty little girl named Jill finds herself desperate to drink from a stream of water. Unfortunately, it is guarded by a fearsome-looking lion named Aslan (the Christ figure in the Narnia series). Lewis describes how, overcome by thirst, "she almost felt she would not mind being eaten by the lion if only she could be sure of getting a mouthful of water first." Jill asks and receives permission from him to come and drink. The lion's voice frightens her so much, however, that she wavers over risking another step toward the stream.

"Will you promise not to do anything to me, if I do come?"

"I make no promise," said the Lion ...

"Do you eat girls?" she said.

"I have swallowed up girls and boys, women and men, kings and
emperors, cities and realms," said the Lion ...

"I daren't come and drink," said Jill.

"Then you will die of thirst," said the Lion. "There is no other stream."

It was the worst thing she had ever had to do, but she went forward.

With this incident Lewis illustrates the tension all Christians should feel about their relationship with God's Son.

On the one hand, around Christ flows a river of blessing filled with the riches of His Kingdom. It is sufficient to quench our deepest thirsts as well as satisfy the pervasive longings of a whole creation. Christians are invited to drink with abandon, to consume without hesitation all He promises us. Yet, we do so knowing this: Christ will also consume *us* with Himself in the process. This is the ultimate transaction held out to everyone in the Gospel. This is what Lewis understood so well: God calls us both to consume Christ (never to cease feeding upon the wealth of power and riches in His Kingdom) and to be consumed with Him (like the fiery bush Moses witnessed as it was consumed with the flames of God's glory, yet able to keep on burning).

"Consummation" is the technical word theologians use to define the decisive nature of a Christian's destiny in Christ. In light of Aslan's proposition, we might spell it *"consume*-ation"!

In an exhaustive treatise on New Testament teaching, Professor George Eldon Ladd concluded: "You can't understand God's redemptive work in history apart from the Consummation. *The Consummation is the true focus of all revelation."* In other words, the Gospel is not simply about "how to get to heaven when we die". Rather it summons us to live every day increasingly awake and alive to the lordship of Christ. Why? Because bearing down on top of us is the *fulfillment* of who He is, where He's headed, what He's doing and how He's blessed (the four facets of supremacy). For every believer, the warning is clear: "The End of all things is at hand" (1 Pet. 4).

The Consummation provides one of the most powerful perspectives on the supremacy of Christ. It summons us to take a hard look at how He will show Himself supreme at the Climax. Here's how Paul painted it for a congregation:

> *"For God allowed us to know the secret of His plan, and it is this:*
> *He purposes in His sovereign will*
> *that all human history will be consummated in Christ,*
> *that everything that exists in Heaven or earth*
> *shall find its perfection and fulfillment in Him."*
> — Ephesians 1:10 *(Phillips translation, emphasis mine)*

In this chapter, therefore, we want to:

• **Explore the meaning of the Consummation and how it manifests Christ's primacy in the universe.**

• **Pinpoint how important it is for us to see the fulfillment of all things in Him.**

• **Uncover some of the important dimensions of the Consummation that magnify His supremacy today.**

• **Identify how Christ embodies in Himself, both "then" and "now", the core characteristics of the Consummation.**

• **Apply our new understandings to restoring hope and passion toward Christ within our lives and our churches.**

The FULFILLMENT of His Supremacy
(Revelation 21:1-22:7)

Let's start with some old fashioned candidness. *Is the Consummation the dimension of hope in Christ's supremacy by which you and I are really prepared to live today?*

In other words, based on who the Consummation will one day reveal our Savior to be — the sole subject of our Eternal Bliss — is He the same Person we thought we welcomed when we first gave our lives to Him? How comfortable are we with building an ongoing, intimate relationship with the One who will soon climax human history under His sovereign's scepter? Knowing that the very same Person who inhabits our lives right now, demanding our hearts, is the same King who will consummate everything in Heaven and on earth in His glorious Person, do we actually expect to *enjoy* Him anytime soon?

To ask this another way: Is this Fulfiller-of-All-Things the one with whom we're willing to risk a deepening love (Jn. 15)? In all honesty, is He the kind of "Lion" to whom we truly want to draw near, drinking in His glory as we savor His "river of delights"? Are we prepared to pursue a *personal* relationship with the One enthroned on High (Rev. 5), before whom all nations will come out for disposal, and in whom all of God's purposes will be fulfilled to the uttermost, forever?

Bottom line, I'm asking: Does the concept of "consummation" genuinely express the way we want to know Him, both now and later? Are we willing to consume *this* Lord Jesus and, even more, be consumed *with* Him for ever and ever? And are we equally eager to help other believers experience with us this similar encounter on this side of Eternity?

It is my intention in this chapter to encourage all of us to dare to respond to each of these questions, maybe for the first time, with an unhesitating *"Yes"* ... and see what happens!

THINK WITH ME ...
How should the hope of "consummation" affect our daily lives with Christ?

Privately, from time to time, most people (Christian and non-Christian) reflect on the End of the World, whether on the final state of their own lives or on the wrap up of human history in general. Recent polls, for example, indicate that more than one-third of Americans say they are plugged into international news to see how it relates to what the Bible teaches about the destruction of the world. Seventeen percent believe Christ's return will materialize in their lifetime.

In a front cover story on *The Bible and the Apocalypse, TIME* magazine observed that when mothers tell their children that a situation "is not the end of the world" that becomes the little one's introduction to humankind's basic reference point. "We seem to be born with an instinct that the end is out there somewhere. Just as all cultures have their creation stories, so too they have their visions of the end." Calling the book of Revelation a "Technicolor spectacle" on the climax of history, *TIME* pinpoints a primary paradox for those who believe its predictions: "How should we react — with hope or with dread?"

Properly understood, the End was intended to fill *Christians* with nothing less than reactions of rousing expectations toward our Savior. God wants us to look forward with joy to the future He has planned for us. As psychologist John Eldredge reminds us, a story is only as good as its *ending*. Without a proper outcome the drama of life can easily become a nightmare for any person. Anticipating our Happy Ending in Christ, however, takes away fear and frees Christians to enjoy, this very minute, the spectacular story we're a part of — and more importantly, enjoy the Person who makes that story worth living.

Dread has no place in a Christian's outlook once we understand two fundamental facts: First, "the Consummation" — the glorious climax to history, that is HIS-story — provides the most comprehensive definition for Christ's supremacy and the hope it brings. Second, this has immediate and exciting implications for our walk with Him today, too.

THINK WITH ME ...
How much do you feel a part of history's grand and glorious goal?

Theologians often speak of history as *teleological*. God has a clear goal (*teleos*) in mind for the nations. All human events, moving under God's sovereign hand, flow toward the Appointed Hour when Christ's Kingdom will be all that remains. Nothing in this world is static. Under Christ's current reign everything is in transition toward the fulfillment of that vision. From the moment each human being was conceived, divine destiny has beckoned us, as it has the entire creation, toward Judgment Day. In the same way, from the opening moment of our *new* birth, the consummation of all things in Christ was written into the DNA of the new creation Christians have become in Him (2 Cor. 5).

Scripture, however, does not encourage naiveté about this goal. We shouldn't project parades of progress or methodical marches moving upward toward the blossoming of some utopian dream. From the Fall forward it has remained clear: History knows no evidence of permanent spiritual progress, no means to reclaim our original innocence by our own efforts, no foolproof road map we can improvise to traverse back to Eternal Dwellings. The rise and collapse of previous civilizations substantiate that something outside of the human race must intervene. More specifically, *Someone* bigger than we are must step forth to extract us from both persistent pits of personal despair and terrorizing threats of global disintegration.

Enter God's eternal plan! Enter the promises of Heaven's unprecedented, choreographed rending of the skies! Enter the *fulfillment* of Christ's supremacy — climaxing with an in-breaking that will one day, at the End of all things, permanently establish His reign, in realms both visible and invisible! "God's two creations (writes John Stott) — his whole universe and his whole Church — must be unified under the cosmic Christ who is supreme head of both."

Like a master surgeon's precise incision, Christ will soon "slice open" Heaven and earth to reveal death-defying displays of God's sovereign glory and grace. As already noted, His Coming will be literal and dramatic. Inescapable. Unavoidable. Utterly transforming. And it will be realized with greater specificity than the prophets ever had words to portray.

In fact, the nature of evil is such that the End can come no other way. It is absolutely *required* for Christ to intervene decisively at the close of the conflict of the ages in order to deliver a people helpless to rescue themselves, and hopeless if left to themselves.

The Bible actually stakes God's reputation on His ability to conquer and destroy all evil thoroughly. It makes the revelation of His glory inseparable from His power to reclaim fully His creation back from Dark Powers; to unleash in totality the redeeming work of His Son in all directions; to establish visibly Christ's Kingdom before all beings in Heaven and earth and under the earth; to have the King sit upon His Throne uncontested and unhindered forever. There *needs* to be a Consummation. There needs to be an Hour when everything is compelled to confess and confirm the supremacy of God's Son!

The owner of what many regard as the greatest race horse of the 20th century put it well in the acclaimed movie *Seabiscuit*: "The end of the race is not the finish line. The *future* is the finish line." That's equally true for every disciple who runs the race of life. Our eyes must be fixed on Jesus and the Consummation of everything in Him. It is for this we strive and pray and hope.

THINK WITH ME ...
What Biblical themes define the *Consummation* of Christ's supremacy?

As an historic doctrine of the Church, the idea of the Consummation has been around a long time. The teaching consistently has incorporated the promise that our Redeemer is *supreme enough* ...

- to complete God's plan in every detail.

- to give God's Kingdom its ultimate manifestation.

- to bring about the climax or grand finale of God's promises.

- to dominate fully the New Creation as Heir of the universe.

- to consummate the destiny of God's people with God's glory in God's presence.

In each phrase above, the ultimate outcome is clear. Drawing parallels once again with Aslan in *The Silver Chair:* The Father's intention is that when the Consummation finally breaks upon us, the universe of necessity will become engaged permanently with Christ and no other. We will consume Him and be consumed with Him. Multiple Scriptures predict we will be possessed by His every word, devoured with delight in His majesty, passionately enthralled with His magnificence. We will be caught up in giving Him unending praise in full view of His Throne. (Take a moment to think about that. You will be there to see it!)

The Consummation was certainly familiar to *Old Testament* saints. Scholars note that hundreds of Jewish prophetic expectations about the Climax targeted a handful of major themes, including these:

- No matter how dark the circumstances, God's righteousness will triumph among nations.

- The Kingdom will come forth at God's decree despite all opposition.

- The judgments of God upon the nations will bring permanent justice and peace to earth.

- Believers can expect the return of God's manifest glory to inhabit Zion.

- His presence will rally exiled saints to serve Him there once again.

- Then they'll witness the enthronement of God's King over Zion and all the earth.

- God will make His home among them, defending and saving them from every enemy.

- God will rebuild and fill His temple so He might be worshipped by His people forever.

- God's people will *prepare* for the End because history is moving toward this Grand Finale.

According to *New Testament* writers, in His Son the Father finally intends to bring every one of these ancient themes to glorious completion. He will maximize them in exquisite detail. Christ will oversee unprecedented fulfillments of each prophetic design, even those set in motion thousands of years ago. In that Final Hour all things spiritual and physical will converge around one, overarching revelation of the Second Person of the Trinity in the full power of His Kingdom. That is why it is appropriate to call Christ Himself the *"consummation* of Biblical hope". Our whole future is lodged in Him. It is defined by Him. It is ultimately consummated in Him.

THINK WITH ME ...
How does Christ's second coming add
weight to his supremacy now?

The Church has always lived in the expectation of the renewal and recapitulation of all things in Jesus. Ours is not only a God who "is and was" but also a God who "is to come" (Rev. 1). Christ is both Alpha and Omega. There is a time just ahead of us when He will come to His creation and His people in a more confrontational way than He ever has before. On that Day every hope toward which the committed Christian is invited to press will be brought to culmination.

That's why Martin Luther said that there are really only two days on a Christian's calendar: "today" and "that Day". Without a doubt *that* Day is straight ahead because Christ *is* coming back! When He returns, *all* of us will be involved in His powerful in-breaking, one way or another. When this happens, Christ's reappearance will have as much tangible reality for you as the chair you're sitting on has for you at this moment, as you read this sentence.So, how much of a difference should that make in my walk with Jesus today? A lot! Let me show you why.

Three important Greek words are used in the New Testament to describe this impending, unparalleled revelation of the supremacy of God's Son:

- *Parousia*
  referring to His tangible, even visible, presence when He arrives.

- *Apocalypsis*
  referring to His dramatic unveiling or disclosure at that time.

- *Epiphaneia*
  describing how His appearing will be indisputable, unavoidable and impossible to deny.

But guess what: These words aren't just about Christ's triumphal return. They can also be used to portray what happens any time God steps in to reactivate, in Jesus, deeper experiences of His promises at work among His people.

In other words, whenever God grants a heart's desire for more of Christ's *power* to fill a life, one can expect to experience more of Christ's *presence*, more of His *unveiling*, more of His decisive *interventions* on our behalf. Whenever Christ involves Himself by His Spirit to carry out God's purposes for us, in a sense we could say He "comes" to us. He actually promised us: "I will not leave you ... I will come to you. Because I live you also will live ... obey my teaching. My Father will love [you], and we will come to [you] and make our home with [you]" (Jn. 14).

At the End when Christ's climactic breakthrough takes place, it will be simply the ultimate "*come*-summation". In other words, it will be the grandest of all His comings. It will be the one "coming" that finally and completely sums up every other time He has ever drawn near to His people as Lord! Every other coming of God's Son into our lives by His Spirit, day-by-day, takes its cue from that final "Second Coming".

QUOTABLE QUOTE

This judgment will issue eventually in the final denouement of the personal coming of the Lord Jesus from Heaven with the angels of his power. It will bring full justice in dazzling flame upon those who have refused to know God or to obey the Gospel of our Lord Jesus. Their punishment will be eternal exclusion from the radiance of the face of the Lord, and the glorious majesty of his power. But to those whom he has made holy, his coming will mean splendor unimaginable. It will be a breathtaking wonder to all who believe — including you, for you have believed the message that we have given you

(2 THESSALONIANS 1
— PHILLIPS TRANSLATION)

To put it differently: The Consummation shouldn't be limited in our thinking to some cataclysmic, apocalyptic episode. There's more to it than scenarios spelled out in popular prophetic graphs and charts or by dime-store novels developed around plots about end-times conspiracies. Rather, every time Christ meets a believer's spiritual hunger, or heals broken relationships, or empowers expanded missionary outreach, He supplies us with rich *foretastes* of the day when the Consummation will unfold thoroughly.

Biblically speaking, in this age the Spirit wants His Church to experience preludes of each theme of the Consummation (including justice, healing, community, worship, and divine presence). In this age every Christian is automatically in the thick of a huge cosmic drama, from Creation to Consummation, moving toward victory with every passing day. Even current world events reported on CNN are somehow a strategic part of this all-encompassing epic. In it all, Christ is both the central plot and the chief character ... *now*, the way He will be at the End.

Come to think of it, this fact is by far the most compelling and fastest-breaking international news story CNN could ever aspire to broadcast!

He's Leading Us into Quite a Future!
(Micah 4:1-13)

Library shelves bulge with centuries of books documenting different views on the *drama* of the Consummation. Currently, for example, a popular twelve-volume fiction novel portrays what might happen worldwide (by some interpretations) after Christ "raptures" the whole Church away to heaven (as some teach He will). Imagination-grabbing, these books have sold by the millions, more to non-Christians actually than to Christians.

Throughout Church history debates about the End have sometimes turned quite fierce. Shrill arguments have been waged over the identity of characteristics, activities, characters, plots and props expected to surface in the Final Act of redemption's story. But let's be thankful that on many of the basics Christians remain in agreement (even if we're still not all agreed on what will happen within the timeframe immediately preceding it). This has been especially true when the heart of the discussion has remained centered on learning from prophetic visions more about the glorious greatness of the One whose arrival all of us anticipate. What are some of those points of agreement?

THINK WITH ME ...
What will the consummation of Christ's supremacy *not* include?

To start with, most agree that more is said in Scripture about what the Consummation will not include, than what it will. For example we are told there will be no death, no mourning, no crying. We are told that pain and heartache will pass away. Sin will be banished. Satan will no longer prowl. Why this emphasis on the negative?

On the one hand it is much easier for the Bible to tabulate all the ugly dimensions of a fallen world with which we are so familiar, and then simply declare: "Under Christ's reign, there will be no more of that!" On the other hand, the Grand Finale involves such an all-encompassing, unparalleled unleashing of Christ's supremacy that the vision begs for graphically adequate categories to picture it.

The fact is, the End-of-the-Age incorporates a measure of blessings beyond what we mortals are able to comprehend, let alone verbalize. This should humble us. There will always be a magnitude — a mystery — to Christ's lordship, wherever and whenever it is manifested, that we will never fully grasp, nor ever be able to fully explore. This will be even truer at His return. As Paul writes in Romans 11: "The deliverer will come from Zion; he will turn godlessness away from Jacob.... Oh, the depth of the riches of the wisdom and knowledge of God! How unsearchable his judgments, and his paths beyond tracing out! Who has known the mind of the Lord? Or who has been his counselor? ... For from him and through him and to him are all things. To him be the glory forever!"

THINK WITH ME...
What will the consummation of Christ's supremacy include *for sure*?

All the great prophetic world religions, influencing over half the world's peoples — Judaism, Islam and Christianity — promote breathtaking narratives of the Final State. All three refer to it as "Heaven".

The afterlife's allure has been painted (sometimes literally on canvas) with a spectrum of enticing visions. Some anticipate dark-eyed virgins at the beck and call of faithful martyrs. Some envision gardens and palaces and mansions of gold. All three refer to unending feasts accompanied by angelic choirs with indescribable bliss spawned by a bonanza of God's resplendent beauty. All three talk about reunions with loved ones in a joy that knows no bounds. The Koran, for example, refers to a place with upholstered couches, pomegranate trees, deep green pastures and unlimited opportunities for sensual pleasures. At least three quarters of the American population believe in basic Judeo-Christian pictures of heaven as an actual place, though we seem divided over whether it is a luxurious arboretum or a well laid-out gated community.

This much we know with confidence from the *Bible*: The Consummation will not deposit us on some celestial shore where eons crawl by tediously. More accurately, time will be transformed by eternity. *Simultaneous realizations* of all that God originally designed, desired, deserved and decreed since the beginning of Creation will take place in us and around us, through the reign of His Son. No longer will Christ's kingship be experienced in bits and pieces. Rather, the Consummation will fully exhaust what His dominion is all about. It will display it in one grand, unending panorama that penetrates the most profound longings of our souls.

Canadian theologian John Stackhouse sums up many Biblical pictures of eternity this way: "Heaven, in fact, has not been portrayed as a boring place, but the location of the highest aspirations of the human heart." C.S. Lewis reflected once: "If I find in myself desires which nothing in this world can satisfy, the only logical explanation is that I was made for another world."

In other words, our deepest hungers for happiness should signal to us a great deal about the Coming Ages. They tell us we were made to inhabit another dominion, to relish the blessings of another Kingdom. The Spirit of God tantalizes us with what's ahead for us in Jesus. He activates a wealth of expectations in us that foreshadow the breadth of joys in the coming

Consummation. In doing so, He precludes our ever settling for anything short of the final revelation of the Son of the Father. Reflective of E.T.'s heartcry for his mother planet (the main theme in the Spielberg movie *The Extra-Terrestrial*), the Spirit stirs an inner restlessness that keeps us from allowing anything or any place — or any one — to substitute for the final "Home" for which we were made (Isa. 61-62).

So, we need to take heart. Our yearnings will be fulfilled with God's tangible supplies. According to Scripture, the Consummation is destined ultimately to manifest itself with *historical literalness*. The Father loves to carry out His promises (as well as our longings) in concrete, practical ways. How can we be sure? Just look at how He did this when fulfilling the prophecies related to the *first* coming of His Son. Most Biblical scholars agree that the Bible portrays an eternity which retains an ongoing physical creation, not unlike what God originally intended in Genesis 1.

We won't float way on illuminated cotton clouds. Instead, the current creation will be both emancipated and renovated by Jesus for our full use. To our joy themes derived from the initial Garden of Eden will be reactivated, though greatly expanded. Creation, liberated from the bondage of decay (Rom. 8), will be incorporated into a new world, concentrated within the jeweled walls of a new city fashioned by the Architect of Heaven (as the colorful imagery of the last two chapters of Revelation details for us).

Taking its cue from that vision, the early Church eventually constructed what was termed a *"theology of recapitulation"*. By this they meant God would rebuild His physical creation, restoring it to all He originally designed, yet doing so in a way that outshines the literal grandeur of any previous expressions of the heavens and the earth. With the risen Redeemer at the helm we can anticipate a whole new quality of spiritual life to emerge within the literal creation, further magnifying the essence of His supremacy.

Let's examine this last thought a little more carefully.

THINK WITH ME ...
In what ways will Christ's reign require both *continuity* and *discontinuity*?

As just noted, there will be a strong measure of *continuity* between the original creation and the consummate new creation. The earth, renewed and purified, will still be the same kind of sphere, destined to be covered with praises to God like waters cover the sea (Hab. 2:14). In part Scripture promises that its inhabitants, captivated by the knowledge God's glory "in the face of Jesus Christ" (2 Cor. 4), will radically improve the earth *just by their being there*, filling it with holy passion to bring eternal delight to the Godhead.

Which means, it seems to me, that what will render the Consummation especially *new* is how it will be animated by the Holy Spirit's ongoing ministry of Christ's life to His people. The Spirit will inspire the saints' devotion. He will carry us toward rightful worship of God as well as righteous activities for God. Our glorified bodies, directed by the Holy Spirit ("spiritual bodies" Paul calls them) will be able to participate fully in every other dimension of Christ's final Kingdom — both seen and unseen (1 Cor. 15).

On the other hand, Scripture also teaches an obvious *discontinuity* between the old creation and the new. Turning to Dr. Stackhouse again: "Heaven's most welcoming features seem to correspond nicely to *inhospitable counterparts* on earth." [Emphasis mine.] The Consummation will establish permanent peace versus international chaos. The Bible promises beautiful dwellings to replace earthly squalor; abundance to replace the oppressive poverty of the masses; mutual love to replace the age-old exploitation of one human being by another.

Discontinuity transpires as everything passes through the fire — engulfed in God's holy purgings (2 Pet. 3). We call it Judgment Day. It involves a cataclysmic display of divine revulsion and opposition to all evil. It will fill up and seal all other judgments throughout history. It will publish and finalize every one of God's previous decrees against our fallenness and our rebellion. The inescapable consequences of opposing God's purposes in Christ will be published abroad, ratified as just and true by Heaven's citizens (Rom. 2 and Acts 17). "The kingdom of the world has become the kingdom of our Lord and of his Christ.... The nations were angry and your wrath has come. Time has come for judging the dead ... for destroying those who destroy the earth" (Rev. 11).

In that awesome hour, everything that is not of Christ — everything that remains unyielded to His supremacy — will be consumed by His wrath. ("Hide us from the face of Him on the throne and from the wrath of the Lamb!" Rev. 6) We must never forget that despite God's overflowing favor, there hovers a matching and equally more sobering theme of His fearsome fury. He will banish all things that are incompatible with His Son (Rev. 20).

And the last enemy to be destroyed is Death itself (1 Cor. 15).

In addition the Consummation will instigate another similarly radical break with the present. God will utterly crush Satan and his lethal forces, abruptly bringing to conclusion their ages-old resistance to Christ's dominance. "The great dragon was hurled down — that ancient serpent called the devil, or Satan, who leads the whole world astray.... Then I heard a loud voice in heaven say: 'Now have come the salvation and the power and the kingdom of our God and the authority of his Christ....' " (Rev. 12).

Of course, by death, resurrection and ascension, Christ's victory over the Devil has *already been won*. But sinners and demons alike still must *concede* that victory. Though Christ claims full kingship, reigning at God's right hand He must, and will, *prevail* one day as King everywhere. Not only has He inherited the Kingdom, but He must also return in timely fashion to *establish* it, pervasively, until His dominion obliterates the jaws of Hades itself. In that day, the final revelation of Christ's victory over Hell's hoards will be as comprehensive as the rebellion they have waged against Him all along.

This too is part of the fulfillment of His supremacy. Resting in Jesus' lordship, a Christian will always nurture vision for the maximum destruction of the demonic.

THINK WITH ME ...
How will the fulfillment of Christ's supremacy
be expressed in community?

Coalesced around the Son in the presence of the Everlasting Father and in the bonds of the Holy Spirit, God's children will enter into a quality of life we might best term "community unity" or even "Trinity unity". It is the consummate answer to Jesus' prayer for the Church in John 17 as He prayed for oneness precisely *because* it was the divine destiny for God's redeemed from the beginning.

The fulfillment of Christian hope will always be visibly *social*. "Behold, I will create new heavens and a new earth.... I will create Jerusalem to be a delight, and its people a joy. I will ... delight in my people.... They will build houses and dwell in them" (Isa. 65). Following Judgment Day, the Consummation will inaugurate an unprecedented fellowship. Earth will be filled with exultant saints from all the ages, ready to become dearest neighbors forever. The Bible teaches that history's final chapter will

QUOTABLE QUOTE

In the re-creation of the world, when the Son of Man will rule gloriously, you who have followed Me will also rule, starting with the 12 tribes of Israel. And not only you, but anyone who sacrifices home, family, fields — whatever — because of Me will get it all back a hundred times over, not to mention the considerable bonus of eternal life. This is the Great Reversal: many of the first ending up last, and the last first.

(MATTHEW 19 — THE MESSAGE)

introduce one single, world-sized society, comprised of people from every tongue and nation. Together forever, the redeemed will not cease to thrive in the presence of a creative, innovative, inexhaustible, unlimited and uncontainable God of love. The Father will be forever revealing to us more and more of His incomprehensible glory to those welcomed in the Beloved One (Eph. 1).

Such wonder-filled Providence will show no partiality. Whatever He reveals of Himself, and whatever agendas He may call us to advance in His eternal purposes in Christ, will come to us *in community*. It will require us to pour out ourselves in love for each other, without reservation, as we seek to honor God's Son with one heart and voice (compare Rom. 15 with 2 Peter 3 and Rev. 22). Just as hope and faith will remain, so love will remain — with the greatest of the three, the most visible expression of them, being love not only for the Triune God but for all the saints who love Him too. (1 Cor. 13). The authors of both Isaiah (65-66) and Revelation (21-22) coined a fascinating term for this phenomenon: *New Jerusalem*. The image draws together a wealth of prophetic streams from Old and New Testaments regarding the final shape of the "people-hood" of the saints.

Consisting of multiple cultures of the world, purged of all depravity and rebellion, one congregation will emerge to inhabit the Heavenly Habitat. The Church Triumphant, as theologians call it, will unveil the manifold grace of God in Christ through varieties of creative worship and service. Washed in His blood, a marvelously mystical mosaic will lay invaluable treasures before the Son in everlasting, unceasing, all-consuming concern for His glory (Rev. 5 and 21). Made up of "living stones" (1 Pet. 2 and Eph. 2), this timeless tabernacle will consist not of mortar but of immortals — people like you and me — rallied before God's face in undistracted devotion to the Lamb on His Throne.

Because of the preeminence of Christ and His cross, everything in heaven and earth will remain forever reconciled in perfect harmony (combine Col. 1

with Eph. 1). Peace on earth, coupled with peace with God, will unite the saints in peace with one another as the incomparable Peacemaker dwells in their midst in royal splendor. What more desirable destination could we hope for?

THINK WITH ME ...
Why must Christ's reign climax in a
ravishing vision of the Godhead?

Without question, the heart and soul — the apex — of the Consummation will be the *renewed vision* of the Triune God reflected in the radiance of the triumphant Son. We read: "The Throne of God and of the Lamb will be in the city, and His servants will serve Him. They will see His face and His name will be on their foreheads" (Rev. 22).

Beyond every other ecstatic enjoyment of the Age to Come, none will surpass its zenith: Christ's presence, displayed for us to marvel at, welcoming us into encounters with the Living God as a result. We will be enraptured with Christ's glory straight on, but unafraid.

You may ask, what about the passage that describes how, at the End, the Son delivers up the Kingdom to the Father (1 Cor. 15)? The answer is not complicated. To be sure, when the End comes He will subordinate Himself and His Kingdom to the Father just like a devoted Son would be expected to do. Nonetheless He will remain exalted as our Mediator-Monarch, still actively leading us in salvation's saga throughout all ages to come. Christ will continue His role as the New Adam of our race. He will remain the Husband to the Bride (Eph. 5). Wherever God's inexhaustible grace continues to pour out on the New Heaven and New Earth, the One who is the "glory of the Father, full of grace and truth" (Jn. 1) will remain at the forefront of the action. He will never cease to be lifted up before the saints so we can worship His matchless majesty. This in turn will bring unending honor to the Father who gave Him up for us all (Phil. 2). As a result, the Triune God will appear to be even more "all in all" to His redeemed people (1 Cor. 15).

Imagine, you and I will actually witness every bit of this! Not long from now! One day soon, we will be thoroughly alive to Him, seeing Him and interacting with Him on the most intimate terms. And this experience will never end.

In ancient times the Greek word *apocalypsis* (which, as we've seen, is used in the Bible to refer to the Consummation) was originally coined to describe a special occasion at the climax of a week of wedding festivities. It was the moment when the veil of the virgin bride was lifted so that the groom and all the guests could finally look upon her beauty. Interestingly, this always took place immediately before the next big event when the couple would slip away to the honeymoon suite. There they would consummate their marriage in sexual union.

Even so, when the Book of Revelation calls the Consummation the "Marriage Supper of the Lamb", it is borrowing from this ancient tradition. It is pointing us toward that moment when, at Christ's return, we will be ravished together by what lies "behind the veil". Out of this unprecedented revelation of God's glory to us — as well as out of the unveiling of Christ's finished work in us — we will enter into greater intimacy with the risen Redeemer than we have ever dreamed existed. That will be a *consummating* experience to say the least!

THINK WITH ME …
So, who will be consumed with Christ
and who will just be consumed?

No wonder "consume" lies at the heart of the English term "Consummation". Biblically speaking it appears there are one of two profound destinies for all of God's creatures: Everyone will either be consuming Christ and consumed with Him — or they will be just plain *consumed*. One or the other.

In the "Consume-ation" everyone not consumed with Christ as their Redeemer Lord will be irrevocably banished from His presence. Inevitably the fate of those who permanently reject God's offer to be consumed *with Him* will be consumed *by Him* — by His judgments, that is. Our Lord is likened to "consuming fire", Hebrews 12 tells us. When He comes back, we're told, He will be "revealed with fire from Heaven against all ungodliness" (2 Thess. 1). The Lion will banish into outer darkness those who refuse to participate in the gift of eternal life, abandoned to everlasting weeping and gnashing of teeth (Matt. 25). This will overtake countless sinners from all the nations and all the ages.

This tragedy should make every believer weep as well. For it will be, literally, the *death of hope* for the unsaved, forever. The Lost will be consigned to the appalling atmosphere of stifling, irreversible hope-*less-ness*. Every prospect of true life will vanish — consumed. Every hint of hope will be snuffed out without mercy — consumed (2 Thess. 1 and 2).

After reading an earlier draft of *Joyful Manifesto,* one committed Christian wrote me to say: "David, I have been so blessed to be one of your readers for this book. But when I finished reading your words on this page, I felt a sense of unspeakable sadness. I strongly sensed that I needed to get on my face before reading another word and cry out for all those — especially in my own family — who do not even know Jesus as their Savior and Lord." That's precisely the pain we are supposed to feel. Our desire for the New Heaven and Earth should increase in us a godly aching for those dearest to us who may never share in that happy day.

Yet that same vision of awful outcomes should empower Christians to press forward with greater anticipation, even while we bear our unceasing burden for the Lost. For we've inherited an alternate destiny. For all saints — those who have trusted Jesus, surrendered to Him, washed themselves with His blood, clothed themselves in His righteousness — the future calls for endless ages of thriving in union with Him as the glorious Sovereign of the Universe. He will become the unending passion of our lives forever. (The whole of chapter 5, *"Christ: The Consuming Passion of Christian Hope",* explores this in depth.)

QUOTABLE QUOTE

. . . from Jesus Christ — Loyal Witness, Firstborn from the dead, Ruler of all earthly kings. Glory and strength to Christ who loves us, who blood-washed our sins from our lives, who made us a Kingdom, Priests for his Father forever — and yes, he's on his way! Riding the clouds, he'll be seen by every eye, those who mocked and killed him will see him, people from all nations and all times will tear their clothes in lament, oh yes, the Master declares, 'I am A to Z. I am the God Who Is, the God Who Was, and the God About To Arrive. I'm the Sovereign-Strong.'

(REVELATION 1 — THE MESSAGE)

We will dwell in a Kingdom that abounds with hope-*filled*-ness, with promises realized and yet with much more to come. We will inhabit the Home of a Creator whose glory and grace remain eternally inexhaustible, yet always consumable. The Father has ordained for His Son to be the One we consume forevermore, just as Jesus invites us to do in John 6.

At the Marriage Supper (Rev. 19), lamb appears to be the main dish!

THINK WITH ME ...
Why does the *Consummation* project a
perfect portrait of our Lord Jesus?

Imagine an architect's enticing a client with blueprints for a prospective office complex. See her using a flip chart of transparencies, placing one design on top of another, gradually exposing how every window, gable, door and wall will finally fit together to form the desired structure. Eventually the presentation reveals her entire architectural scheme for the outside of the new building.

Similarly, as each of God's promises is fulfilled in Jesus, we could say each is superimposed one on top of the other. What will finally emerge, when all promises are gathered up in fullest revelation, will be the premiere picture of Christ Himself. *The Consummation will become God's grand eternal portrait masterpiece of His Son.*

When that day comes, surely all will be stunned the way John was in Revelation 1. The apostle had intimately followed Christ in the days of His flesh. Many years later on Patmos, however, he suddenly found himself utterly speechless before Him. Gazing on His ascended Savior in that hour, John was overwhelmed with fresh, unexpected, consummate dimensions of a greatness he had not previously known. He fell at Jesus' feet in bewildered, awe-inspired stillness, like a dead man. So taken back was he with what he saw, he could do nothing but silently surrender and wait. That day John literally saw his Lord as the Consummation up close and personal. It was right there in Christ's face (John wrote), shining like the sun with a baffling brilliance.

What this suggests is simply that Christ and the Consummation are forever "joined at the hip". To understand one is to expand our understanding of the other. There's genuine synergy here. Just as you cannot explain an acorn without somehow relating it to the oak tree from

---

QUOTABLE QUOTE

In the center the Son of Man, in a robe and gold breastplate, hair a blizzard of white, eyes pouring fire-blaze, both feet furnace-fired bronze, his voice a cataract, right-hand holding the Seven Stars, his mouth a sharp-biting sword, his face a perigee sun. I saw this and fainted dead at his feet. His right hand pulled me upright, his voice reassured me: 'Don't fear: I am First, I am Last, I am Alive. I died, but I came to life, and my life is now forever. See these keys in my hand? They open and lock Death's doors, they open and lock Hell's gates. Now write down everything you see: things that are, things about to be.

(REVELATION 1 — THE MESSAGE)

which it came, in a similar way you cannot explain the Consummation unless you relate it to the Christ who is its source and substance and song.

When the multitude of Bible prophecies has come to pass, we will find that the Consummation is simply all about *Him*. No wonder Paul exclaims, regarding the One "who is able to do immeasurably more than all we ask or imagine", that "to Him be the glory in the church and in Christ Jesus throughout all generations, for ever and ever" (Eph. 3)!

The Consummation Must Impact Our Daily Walk with Christ
(1 Thessalonians 1:2-10)

The visiting salesman knew how to make the pitch, so my parents ended up with a 12-volume children's illustrated Bible for their eleven-year-old son. A few nights later I picked up a volume to thumb through the pictures with little intention of actually reading anything. I chose the last one in the series. The moment I cracked it open, however, I found myself enthralled with a story I never knew was possible.

Colorful illustrations vividly captured some of the best known scenes from the Bible's final book, the Revelation of John. On page after page scenes of judgment, and Heaven, and fierce conflicts, and monsters, and angel choirs stretched before me. But it was the two-page spread picturing Revelation 19 — showing a Conqueror clothed in regal robes, seated on a white stallion, surrounded by armies of saints — that stunned my unsuspecting heart and seized my soul. Portrayed wearing a jeweled diadem, this incomparable King was piercing the clouds with the overwhelming radiance of His face, putting His earthly enemies to flight. This was a Jesus of whom I had never been told.

Before long on that winter evening, snuggled alone in a living room chair, I felt something like an electric shock that seemed to travel my body from head to foot. Although it was years later that I finally determined deeper meanings for what I experienced that night, there's no doubt that from that moment the reality of Christ's supremacy, waiting to be decisively displayed in the Final Battle, molded both my ambitions and my decisions.

Even in my darkest moments — even when I've wandered into selfishness and sin — it has been that vision of Christ that restored my soul. Introduced by a few elementary drawings but subsequently filled out for me by hundreds of Scriptures, His consummate glory continues to call me back daily to a wholehearted devotion to His Kingdom.

What I've come to understand, however, is that this is no private eccentricity. The fact is, the Bible calls all believers to order their steps *as if* we were already gathered about the Throne — to live *as if* we were already standing in the visible presence of our King. Because, in a very real way, our union with Christ makes this so.

THINK WITH ME ...
What if we acted as if the Consummation *was here and now?*

Think of it: Ascended on high, our Redeemer has, in one sense, already reached the climax of history. He got there ahead of us. The future can now be seen in Him with finality. In Christ the corrupted order of our existence — with its depravity, evil, sin and death — has been replaced with a new order, able to produce fruits of godliness, truth, love. In Him the *quality* of life expected in the Consummation, even if we don't yet have the quantity of it, has already been revealed for all to see ahead of schedule. "The life appeared; we have seen it and testify to it, and we proclaim to you the eternal life which was with the Father and has appeared to us" (1 Jn. 1).

True, the end is not yet. But every day we do worship Jesus exalted above, who shows us what the End is all about, preserving in Himself every guarantee that the End will come to pass as gloriously as it has been foretold (see Heb. 2). George Ladd reminds us again that Christ is "the presence of the future". He is the future for which the human race was created. As I like to say, at the Father's right hand the Son provides a "preview of coming attractions"!

What we've discovered in this chapter is that because of our union with such a Savior, the Christian is already abiding, *in principle,* in the Consummation. And that should change how we tackle each moment we live for Him.

Consider this: Outside the Kingdom humankind proceeds daily from the present into the future, with little sense (or hope) about what the future actually holds. What other choice do finite sinners have, separated from the living God? However, thriving under Christ's rule *the believer begins with the future and works its implications back into the present.* This places all decisions, ambitions, relations and missions in a totally different context.

Said another way, for the Christian the Consummation defines *in principle* how Jesus operates in our lives right now. It establishes guidelines about what He is willing to do for us daily, as well as how we ought to respond to Him daily. From the moment of new birth, every believer enters into a never-ending life, as comprehensive and as wonderful as the Savior Himself.

As the Puritans taught, Christians are never stuck with "half" a Christ as we labor in this present world. To the contrary, from the day of salvation we are immediately in union with the whole Christ — with the one who is the same yesterday, today and forever (Heb. 13). In other words, *when Christ comes at the end of the age, He will not have any more inherent glory than He has at this very moment.* What He is Lord of ultimately, He is Lord of *now.* Who He will be in the Consummation is who He is *now.* If the End is summed up in God's Son, then in a most amazing way the End is with us even now.

That's why we are invited to anticipate expressions of His supremacy today that resemble, in principle, what it will be like to live under His reign throughout the endless ages to come. This puts a whole new dynamic into discipleship!

THINK WITH ME ...
What if we acted as if the Consummation *could arrive soon?*

Of course, there's still much more to come. The full experience of the End awaits the return of Christ, which could happen at any time — literally. Little remains to unfold, most Bible scholars agree, before the Grand Finale makes its appearance. As the book of Revelation reminds us more than once, Jesus is coming "soon" or "suddenly" or "unexpectedly".

Even mission strategists agree that all the resources and manpower needed to complete the Great Commission in one generation are in place, assuming the Church is revived and empowered to finish the task. This is profoundly significant because Jesus taught: "This gospel of the Kingdom must be preached throughout the world as a witness to every people, and *then* the End will come" (Matt. 24).

This perspective can unleash new vitality into service to Christ now. This perspective can foster unwavering obedience in victorious living now. As Peter writes: "Since everything will be destroyed in this way, *what kind of people ought you to be?* You ought to live holy and godly lives as you look forward to the day of God and speed its coming.... We are looking forward to a new Heaven and a new Earth, the home of righteousness. So then, dear friends, since you are looking forward to this, *make every effort* to be found spotless, blameless and at peace with Him" (2 Peter 3, emphasis mine).

In chapter 12 of our *Joyful Manifesto* we explore many practical and exciting implications of this insight for an everyday walk with Jesus as Lord. There we redefine the Christian experience with a key phrase: *anticipatory discipleship.* Simply put, this refers to obeying Christ *in anticipation of* all that is to come. Both in immediate fulfillments of God's promises in Him as well as in the ultimate destiny held out to us in Him, Christians should seek to grow a life of discipleship that is *fully compatible* with all God has promised us in the unending reign of His Son. We should do so anticipating increased measures of His sovereign grace at every turn.

When the Final Hour does appear, one of two conclusions will transpire for every believer: Either the Consummation will reveal how much of this life was spent in indifference toward and even resistance to the reign of Christ; or, the Consummation will provide convincing confirmation that our commitment to Jesus was lived, even in this present age, in willing response to, and active pursuit of, His lordship in all things (Titus 2). One of these two outcomes will characterize our earthly pilgrimage. Either straw or gold will be found in our hands the day we enter the Throne Room, the value determined by the Lamb's holy fire (1 Cor. 3). There ought to be sufficient motivation in this fact to drive all of us back to Jesus with a consuming passion for His supremacy right now!

THAT DAY AND THIS DAY

Writing at the turn of the 20th century, A.B. Simpson thrilled over the growth of his own hope in Christ. Increasingly the worldwide advance of the Kingdom animated his ministry. Having founded a national alliance of Christians banded together to seek completion of the Great Commission in their generation, this Presbyterian clergy pastoring a New York City congregation was determined to find ways to re-mobilize his followers with even greater zeal for God's glory.

To do this, his preaching and writing frequently took aim at the Consummation. For him, above most other spiritual incentives, a vision of the Outcome had the compelling force needed to help the Church tackle its daunting task among the nations. These words are good medicine for mission-minded believers anytime, including those in the 21st century:

> Our little lives are too small to fit this magnificent hope.
> Let us make them larger, grander and more in keeping
> with the mighty, inspiring motive which comes
> from our expectations of that glorious day.
> ### *What a day it will be!*
> Gather together all the treasures of sight, all that is beautiful.
> Gather together all the treasures of sound, of sweet harmonies.
> Add to these all the treasures of the heart, of dear loves, holy friendships.
> Ransack the treasures of time.
> Pile them all in one.
> Then double them. Then triple them. Then quadruple them.
> Then multiply them a hundredfold. Then multiply them a thousand fold.
> Then multiply them by thousands of thousands.
> Then multiply them by all the arithmetic of all the ages.
> ### *What a day it will be!*

As it did for Simpson, pursuing Christ as the consummation of Christian hope will strike fatal blows against any current crisis of supremacy in the Church. That's because expanding our horizon this way gives us a fresh take on who Christ *really* is. It sharpens and reforms our Christology. It re-ignites our passions for His greater glory. It reinforces our resolve to carry out Kingdom ministries. It compels us to live as if we truly expected to walk with Christ as our supreme Lord not just for now but forever.

But despite all we've just uncovered in these past two chapters about our Lord Jesus Christ, the story of His glory is not over! The next two chapters take us further. They explore more fully the scope of the hope that cures the crisis of supremacy

Here's where we're headed next. Any reformation of contemporary Christology requires us also to re-visit Biblical teachings on approximations of the coming Kingdom to be experienced today — *approximations* of the Consummation, we might say. Such approximations define the normal Christian life under the Redeemer's rule. Regularly God wants to give us — as individuals and churches — introductory experiences of the Grand Finale. He invites us to enjoy firstfruits of His reign. He intends for us to delight in how the Spirit causes Christ's supremacy to invade our daily routines, or Christian fellowship, or times of worship, or Gospel missions at home and abroad. By injecting into the Church right now *preliminary installments* of Jesus' eternal reign, God desires to transform our fervency for intimacy with Jesus as Lord.

I can personally testify: Uncovering these "approximations" has changed my life. I would never want to go back to where I was before. I'm pretty confident it will do the same for you.

THE CONSUMMATION

The following "river of words" is a diagram which summarizes
how Christians throughout the centuries have defined the Consummation.
Each phrase also expands our hope in the supremacy of God's Son.

Zenith
Summit
Pinnacle
Culmination
Great Assize
Grand Finale
Denouement
End of the Age
Crowning Hour
Commencement
Eucatastrophe
Final Triumph
Total Vindication
Eternal Effulgence

The New Jerusalem

Cosmic Capitulation

Victorious Outcome

Ultimate Destination

Supreme Masterpiece

Mission Accomplished

Paragon of the Universe

New Heaven and Earth

Unqualified Perfection

Creation's Quintessence

Inexhaustible Celebration

Magnificent Consequences

Marriage Supper of the Lamb

Promised Fulfillment of All Things

Travail of the Cross Satisfied in Full

Universal Outpouring of the Spirit
Everlasting Habitation of the Father
All-Consuming Supremacy of the Son
Consummate Revelation of God's Glory

4

CHRIST SUPREME:

The *Approximation* of Christian Hope

Recover a Vision Shaped by the FULLNESS of His Supremacy

Over one hundred national prayer leaders gathered in Washington, D.C., the eve of the 1986 National Day of Prayer. On a warm May night we huddled in a church sanctuary to spend a season of prayer seeking God for spiritual awakening throughout America.

To begin our convocation then-Chaplain of the U.S. Senate Dr. Richard Halverson spoke to us for nearly an hour. He challenged us to re-examine our agenda in prayer for the evening. He pressed us with one major question: "How many of you are praying regularly for the Second Coming of Jesus Christ?" Not a single hand went up.

Gently he rebuked us: "If you pray for revival in our nation but don't pray for the Second Coming of the Lord, I must seriously question the legitimacy of your revival prayers." The audience sat in stunned silence. So he continued. "This is because, in a profound way, every revival involves a *coming* of Christ to His Church. In revival, as Scripture frequently documents, God shows up among His people to reveal to them more of His power and glory. In the final analysis *that's* what revives them.

"Now I wonder ... " he said as he paused to survey us over his wire-rimmed glasses. "How can we ask for God to fill us with a fresh sense of Christ's presence in revival and not, in the same breath, intercede just as earnestly for Christ's Kingdom to be manifested in its totality before the entire universe?"

He concluded his exhortation sounding this caution: "Only those who are regularly praying and looking for the *ultimate* Day of Glory will ever be able to sustain the necessary hope and resolve to keep praying for Christ to be glorified *today* by anything like a national revival."

The next morning as we met on Capitol Hill to intercede for America, I can assure you our requests took a decidedly new — and bolder — direction.

This respected Christian statesman had called us back to another awesome truth about the supremacy of Christ: He is not only the *summation* and *consummation* of Christian hope, but He is also the source of profound *approximations* of that hope poured out on His Church every day, in a host of ways this chapter will uncover. Among those blessings is one we sometimes call a "spiritual awakening". Whether with a congregation or a whole nation, every God-given revival is a *foretaste* of the "Final Revival", the one awaiting us at the very moment Christ openly returns to reign.

Halverson's perspective on prayer reminded me of other stirring words from the pen of the 17th century Scottish reformer, Samuel Rutherford. After years of persecution and imprisonment for preaching Christ's supremacy, he wrote from a jail cell that he still found it necessary to pray one major request for himself every day: *"Lord Jesus, come and conquer me!"* What did he mean by this?

Throughout his lifelong mission Rutherford knew one thing remained necessary for him to survive and thrive: He had to experience personal renewal in a manner similar to how Christ's kingship would one day renew all things. The magnitude of sacrifices this cleric had to make for his Scottish people demanded that Christ's supremacy constantly dominate his life. The reformer needed to be subdued daily to Christ Himself — conquered, as he put it — in a manner reflective of how His Lord would conquer the universe at the Resurrection, the Day when Rutherford's own ministry would finally reach its Grand and Glorious Conclusion.

Similar approximations await all who follow our Sovereign Savior. Rutherford's prayer must be answered for every believer. That experience should become a way of life! Paul models this when he writes: "I want to know Christ and the power of His resurrection.... and so somehow, to attain to the resurrection from the dead.... I press on to take hold of that for which Christ Jesus took hold of me.... Straining toward what is ahead, I press on toward the goal to win the prize for which God has called me heavenward in Christ Jesus.... And we eagerly await a Savior from there, the Lord Jesus Christ, who, by the power that enables Him to bring everything under His control, will transform our lowly bodies...." (Phil. 3).

Understanding what these approximations look like provides Christian discipleship its most dramatic dimensions. It also improves our ability to confront and cure any crisis of supremacy. It can empower us, like it did Rutherford's reformation movement, to carry out a Campaign of Hope for our own generation. So, let's investigate how Christ activates within His Church approximations of the Final Displays of His supremacy. These include:

- **A New Creation: The approximation of the consummate decree.**
- **The Holy Spirit: The approximation of the consummate life.**
- **The Church: The approximation of the consummate community.**
- **World Mission: The approximation of the consummate triumph.**
- **Revival: The approximation of the consummate awakening.**
- **Spiritual Warfare: The approximation of the consummate battle.**

We'll conclude the survey by looking at some ways His ultimate glory could transform the street where you live *today*.

The FULLNESS of His Supremacy
(Malachi 3:1-5, 16 - 4:3)

What's it like to spend an hour bird-watching with binoculars in hand? High-powered lenses allow an often unexplored world to open up magically. A blazing red cardinal sitting on top of a tall oak can seem so near to you.

You feel as though you could reach out and touch it. Binoculars allow you to watch its every move, even the ruffling of its feathers as it warbles its distinctive song. Though perched on the tip of a tree, the bird seems to be right on the branch next to you.

In the same sense, in our union with Christ we inherit more than just *future* ages of unceasing blessings. Like professional field glasses, Christ brings that future *near* to us. He magnifies it for us as He dwells among us. By virtue of who He is as Lord, He makes even our ultimate destiny — the Consummation — very *present* to us. By walking with Him daily we can experience the eternal dynamics of a Kingdom that is not yet fulfilled. Not only does God's Son grant us eternal life after death, but He also brings us into eternal life *before* death (Jn. 17:3). There's a *fullness* in Christ's reign meant for God's people to experience every day we breathe — a fullness derived from a supremacy that will transform everything on the Last Day.

THINK WITH ME ...
Why should Christ's supremacy feel like the future invading the present?

Have you ever had this happen to you? You're involved in a deeply meaning-ful time of prayer. Suddenly your heart swells with confidence about the results. It seems like God is about to act any moment. You "feel" as if the answers are already in hand. It's as good as done, you think! What triggers this unique experience? Here's what I think: The presence of Christ, tangibly touching us in a prayer meeting, reassures us that who He is, at the End of All Things, *is* the answer to all our prayers. As we draw near to Jesus in prayer we experience His promise: "Whatever you ask for in prayer, believe that you have received it, and it *will* be yours" (Mk. 11). The Spirit's witness of the glorious greatness of God's Son reassures us that, whether now or later, our prayers will be answered in such a way that there will be no disappointment with the outcome.

To be sure, *quantitatively* speaking we can never receive the full measure of answered prayers. That requires the Consummation. *Qualitatively* speaking, however, God intends for the Consummation to be a part of our daily walk with Christ, both in our prayers as well as in every other facet of discipleship. The glory of the Age-to-Come resides in Him. He resides in us. Therefore, all we could ever hope for is already *Christologically* near, we might say, even if *chronologically* it may not yet be near. In principle then, as Lord of all Christ makes Eternity *accessible* to us every moment.

That's why I like the phrase "approximations of the Consummation". Our Lord wants to give us foretastes of greater things ahead. He is (in the words of Steve Hawthorne) both *present* and *presiding* as King among His people right now. He is ready to share the *fullness* of His lordship with us right now.

We must never forget within every congregation on planet earth of 20 members or 20,000: The Lord Jesus is fully there. Not just a part of Him but ALL of Him. And He is supremely able, willing and ready to show us new facets of His reign each day. Therefore, just as He alone must culminate all of God's promises at the End, even so He alone can (and will) give us multiple *intermediate* experiences of those promises now.

Of course, approximations are still only that — *approximations*. They are not the ultimate reality for which we wait. Nor can foretastes of Eternity be compared with the glory that shall be revealed when Christ returns (Rom. 8 and 1 Jn. 3). Still, again and again God is willing to invade His frail, fickle, frequently frustrated people to re-awaken them once more to their destiny. He wants to unleash in us fresh works of Christ's Kingdom in a manner reflective of what, before long, His Everlasting Reign will unveil.

St. Catherine of Siena said it well: "All the way to heaven is heaven!" No matter how one interprets Biblical references to the Millennium (Christ's 1000-year reign as described in Rev. 20), we can all agree with this: To significant degrees an echo of Millennium-type blessings should resound within hearts and churches, here and now, because the Master of the Millennium dwells within us here and now. Scripture encourages us to sustain an attitude of constant watchfulness — not just for the Consummation but for approximations of the Consummation. Daily we are invited to anticipate increasing evidences of

> ## QUOTABLE QUOTE
>
> **Martha said, "Master, if you had been here, my brother wouldn't have died. Even now I know that whatever you ask God he will give you." Jesus said, "Your brother will be raised up.... You don't have to wait for the End. I am, right now, Resurrection and Life. The one who believes in me, even though he or she dies, will live. And everyone who lives believing in me does not ultimately die at all. Do you believe this?" "Yes, Master, all along I have believed that you are the Messiah, the Son of God, who comes into the world."**
>
> (JOHN 11 — THE MESSAGE)

Christ's supremacy among us. Daily we may look for His rule above to enrich our routines below. Daily we may expect to receive *fullness* of life from His Throne, drawing upon the quality of existence that will soon be ours when we are "revealed with Him in glory" (Col. 3). What could be more exciting than this? As we saw in chapter 3, the One who dwells among us is Himself the "presence of that future". He is our "preview of coming attractions".

As a major step toward confronting and curing the crisis of supremacy then, let's dig into six key approximations each of which magnifies the fullness of Christ's reign in the Church today. Each is also a foretaste of the Day when all promises are consummated in Him as Lord.

1. A New Creation:
Approximations of the Consummate *Decree*
(Titus 2:11-14; 3:4-7)

It's a curious thing. Throughout the book of Revelation each one of God's decisive judgments explodes onto the world scene amid hymns, doxologies and acts of worship. Singing and supremacy surface together. Believers, however, are invited into similar celebrations *every day*. That's because in union with the Son we have already passed through the Final Judgment. Already we stand victorious on the other side of His Reign of Fire. How did this happen?

THINK WITH ME ...
How has God applied the future to our
relationship with Christ today?

Despite the dramatic increase in life expectancy over the past one hundred years, no one has yet made claims to immortality — except One. Nonetheless, people in every culture continue to seek it. Some have their bodies frozen at death, ready to be reactivated when a cure for mortality is found. Others grasp for a place in eternity through mystical convergences with a Higher Power.

But to Christians Romans 5 declares that "just as sin reigned in death, so also grace might reign through righteousness, to bring eternal life, through

Jesus Christ our Lord" (vs. 20-21), meaning that even in this world believers are declared "immortal" and called to live like it! Throughout the New Testament Christians are identified as those currently dead, alive and ascended with Christ (Rom. 6; Eph. 2; Col. 3). It is as if we were already transported to the time of the Consummation, strolling through the New Jerusalem.

Something unusual has happened. It has to do with the *positioning* of believers before the Consummation. Surrendered to our Sovereign, entering into an intimate union with Him, we have a solidarity with Him that replaces forever our identity with fallen Adam and his race. The Old Creation has been disqualified. God decrees we now have an exclusive identity with His Son, allowing the Father to label us as His *new creation* (Rom. 5 and 2 Cor. 5).

> ## QUOTABLE QUOTE
>
> **He picked us up and set us down in highest heaven in company with Jesus, our Messiah. Now God has us where he wants us, with all the time in this world and the next to shower grace and kindness upon us in Christ Jesus.... It's God's gift from start to finish!**
>
> (EPHESIANS 2 — THE MESSAGE)

Christians aren't simply on a road to "the sweet by-and-by". Instead, the Bible invites Christians to *reckon* themselves ascended into Heaven, serving Christ in the power of His Spirit as re-created beings. God invites us to *act as if* we currently stand on the other side of Judgment Day. Jesus assured believers they will never come into judgment because they have already passed from death to life (Jn. 5 with 1 Jn. 3).

The moment I was born again (as a freshman in college) God decreed me to be eternally alive. *Christ's* future has become *my* future. The Father was free, in His justice, to treat me as if I were already raised and reigning in the Consummation. This was His *consummate decree*. As far as He was concerned, from that moment (and even long before that moment) I was not only foreknown, called and justified, but also glorified (Rom. 8). All of it was as good as done.

If I may borrow Luther's words: God created a "happy exchange". This placed me, in His eyes, within the Consummation drama as *if* it was unfolding here and now. This exchange transpired when Christ took upon Himself who I was in my sin and bestowed on me who He is in His righteousness. In response to the Gospel I was united to Christ by faith as both Savior and final Judge-of-all. Heaven's Supreme Court decreed that everything Christ is and has — as well as everything He experienced by His own death, burial, resurrection and ascension — was now transferred to me. From that hour the Father has treated me *as if* Christ is me and I am Christ.

Separated from Him eternally, dead to God in my sin, at one time I faced no other prospect but dreadful wrath. It rendered me hopeless. Only if *someone else* could bring me alive from the dead setting me free from the charges against me, could I ever hope to see my precarious condition reversed. No religion, no philosophy, no moral resolutions of my own could ever avail.

Then one day the Gospel came. I believed. Immediately from God's perspective I was raised with His Son from the dead. My destination became identical with His. God reckoned me to be crucified two thousand years ago with Jesus, at the very time He bore the judgment for my sin (and for all sin) on Calvary. The judgment my Lord experienced became *my* primary judgment, too.

Since I am permanently abiding in Him (Jn. 15), I can be disqualified only if Christ Himself could ever be disqualified from full participation in the Age-to-Come (which will never happen). There is no future judgment that will ever expel me from the glories of the New Jerusalem. In the most profound sense, my "day in court" has passed. The Cross was it. The Cross was final. The Cross put behind me the life-threatening consequences of my incalculable rebellions against the Almighty One.

Long before a New Heaven and Earth ever takes center stage, God has already decreed that I may walk before Him *as if* I were Christ Himself, and thus *as if* I were a fully resurrected inhabitant of eternity. Therefore, at no time should I ever be surprised that my life in Christ incorporates many other kinds of "approximations" of the impending Regeneration of the universe. Such foretastes may be preliminary, but they are substantial. They create genuine experiences of what it will be like when His supremacy has final sway.

Space will not allow us to explore key doctrines emphasized in Scripture (and by Christian theologians of all persuasions) that describe various dimensions of participation in this consummate decree of God.

Maybe you've heard some of the concepts, such as:

- Justification
- Acquittal
- Reconciliation
- Redemption
- Propitiation
- Remission
- Forgiveness
- Adoption

Lumped together, these terms constitute two great realities about our hope in Christ. They speak about our *destiny* in Christ. They speak about our *identity* in Christ. Consider:

Destiny refers to our future. One day soon we will stand vindicated with absolute confidence before a just and holy God. When the Consummation breaks upon us, we will face it unafraid, alive with every promise in Jesus, because *our* final judgment climaxed at the Cross long ago (Jude 1). That's our destination under His consummate decree. This is one expression of Christ's supremacy in our lives.

Identity, on the other hand, has to do with our current status before God's Throne. As we've just seen, believers can live as if the Day of Judgment had come and gone. Our sins have not simply been disregarded for the moment. They have been permanently eliminated by the blood of Jesus. God's wrath for us fell on Him instead. Because we abide in Him, from the moment of salvation forward God decrees us newly created. We provide a preview of how He will renovate creation at the Second Coming (Rev. 21). Now, all *we* need to do is take the initiative to reckon (decree) for ourselves what God proclaims (decrees) about us (Rom. 6). This, too, expresses how Christ's supremacy touches us everyday.

THINK WITH ME ...
What does the word "justification" tell us about the fullness of Christ's supremacy?

Let's use one of the more technical words listed above, *justification*, as one example. Theologians call justification a "forensic" work of God. This means that by divine *decree* (as described in His Word) God has thrust His decisions about our final fate into the present. He declares Himself fully satisfied with who we are in Jesus. He accepts us point blank as His own children.

Biblically speaking, the idea of being justified has always included the sense that God treats me *"just as if I'd"* [justified] already entered into the Consummation. To my utter amazement, Scripture teaches that the Father declares I have an intimate relationship with Him, right now, that mirrors what His eternal Son has enjoyed with Him from ages past and will enjoy for ages to come. This moment, He assures me unlimited, unhindered access into everything Christ has for me. On more than one level I can start enjoying many blessings of the Kingdom-That-Waits-To-Appear.

In the same way that the Father raises the dead and creates life, so does the Son. The Son gives life to anyone he chooses. Neither he nor the Father shuts anyone out. The Father hands all authority to judge over to the Son so that the Son will be honored equally with the Father. Anyone here who believes what I'm saying right now and aligns himself with the Father, and has in fact put me in charge, has at this very moment the real, lasting light and is no longer condemned to be an outsider. This person has taken a giant step from the world of the dead to the world of the living. It's urgent that you get this right: The time has arrived — I mean right now! — when dead men and women will hear the voice of the Son of God and hearing, will come to life.

(JOHN 5 — THE MESSAGE)

As Paul shows us in 1 Corinthians 1, we are not simply made wise or righteous or holy through Christ. Rather, Christ has been made *for us* all the wisdom, and righteousness, and holiness we will ever need. That means we do not just take His *help* for where we have failed. Rather, we take *Him* and all that He brings with Him. He encompasses the everlasting favor of God toward us. In Him the Father forgives our sins, sets aside His wrath and treats us brand new.

So it follows: *Justified*, I can rightfully claim to be liberated from all fear toward the Righteous Sovereign, released to start life all over again before His face. *Justified*, I can act as if there never was a reason for His holy fury, at least where I'm concerned. *Justified*, I am as fully vindicated as Christ was the day God raised Him from the dead. *Justified*, I remain accepted before the Judge of the universe forever because of my unassailable union with the Judge's Son — with Who He is and with all He inherits. *Justified*, I've become partaker of His holy nature (2 Pet. 1). This includes being incorporated into a people born again by His Spirit (Jn. 3). All of this is an *approximation* of the Consummation.

When the Last Day finally arrives with unquenchable fire for unrepentant sinners, it will be discovered that long ago Christians passed through the same examination. It happened when by faith we were decreed to have been crucified and buried with Christ, and then raised and ascended with Him. Our life in coming ages will essentially be the same life God invites believers to share in right now. At both points in time *the sum total of existence takes its cue from the person of our Savior, supremely sufficient for all the saints, "world without end"*. With Him as my hope the Father treats me "just as if I'd" exited the tomb and was currently walking the streets of gold! Talk about experiencing the fullness of His supremacy!

Oxford University theologian and author Alister McGrath puts it concisely for us when he concludes: "Justification language appears in Paul with reference to both the inauguration of the life of faith and also its final consummation. It anticipates the verdict of the final judgment, declaring in advance the verdict of ultimate acquittal. The believer's present justified experience is thus an anticipation, an advance participation of deliverance from the wrath to come, and an *assurance* in the present of the final eschatological verdict of acquittal" (Rom. 5:9-10).

That's a mouthful! But it deserves careful reflection. Are you a follower of Jesus? Is your hope in Him based on His supremacy over all things? Then McGrath is talking about *you*. He's describing one facet of the fullness of life that Christ's reign guarantees to you *today*.

2. The Holy Spirit:
Approximations of the Consummate *Life*
(2 Corinthians 4:16-5:5)

In his *New York Times* best-seller *The Power of Now: A Guide to Spiritual Enlightenment* Eckhart Tolle laid out for his readers a Zen-style message on achieving happiness. It comes about, he claims, by how one chooses to focus on the present, and only on the present. "In *The Now,* in the absence of time, all your problems dissolve," he wrote in a book that sold over a million copies. Claiming one can free oneself from the mind, and thus from one's most persistent fears, he offers his personal pilgrimage as proof, reviewing how he had used his "Now Therapy" to escape suicidal depression and achieve a breakthrough into what he called soul-centered bliss.

I'm pleased to announce that the Lord Jesus Christ offers a much more potent antidote to anxiety and despair! He provides the "power of *hope*", which means the power of the *future* brought into the "now". Biblically speaking, this distills down to the power of a *Person* who dwells within a Christian's very being: the Holy Spirit. The contrast between the ways of guru Tolle and the Spirit of God could not be greater.

THINK WITH ME ...

In what sense does the Spirit provide us the power of the future?

As Scripture teaches, the Holy Spirit unites us with our Sovereign (an intimacy without parallel — 1 Cor. 6), enabling us to take up residence within the totality of who Jesus is. Next He awakens our souls to more of the unsearchable riches found in Christ (Eph. 3), drawing us to embrace Him and enjoy Him wholeheartedly (Rom. 8). In fact, the greatest gift God's Spirit may impart to any believer is simply His sharing with us more of the Son and then teaching us how to receive Him better. He also sets our hearts aflame with Jesus' love for His people and for nations (Rom. 5), all of which flows out of our walking in the Spirit under the lordship of Jesus (Col. 2 with Gal. 6).

But that's not the finish. He also implants in us hope about greater things to come (Rom. 15). Just as the End can never be defined adequately apart from understanding the role of the third person of the Trinity, neither can the Spirit's mission in our lives right now be grasped without reference to the End. By the Spirit, the Father raised His Son from the dead and exalted Him on High (Rom. 8). By the Spirit, the Father sustains and spreads the impact of the Son's supremacy to the ends of the earth, to the end of time (Rev. 1, 4). By the Spirit, the Son activates His rule in the midst of the Church in ways that echo how He will do it for all ages to come (Acts 4-5). By the Spirit, God will faithfully deliver on every blessing promised to the heirs of eternal life (Acts 1, 2). The Spirit will be the Chief Architect — as well as the Defining Characteristic — of our very existence in the Age-to-Come. Even our resurrection bodies are called "spiritual bodies" in 1 Corinthians 15, meaning our whole being (body, soul, spirit) will eventually be animated and controlled by the Holy Spirit.

It should come as no surprise, then, that our life in Jesus right now is also defined Biblically as "life in the Spirit" (Rom. 8). The Holy Spirit "super-naturalizes" every aspect of our existence as Christians, doing so in ways that approximate how He will influence the entire universe when Christ returns.

When Scripture calls the physical body of a believer the "temple of the Holy Spirit" (1 Cor. 6), is there not the hint of something grand at work? Even before He reconstitutes Creation into a temple for the Lamb (Rev. 5, 21-22), the Spirit desires to make my piece of that universe — including my mortal dwelling — a "scale model" of what the finished product will look like. He wants to approximate the eternal Holy of Holies wherever *I* am standing at this very moment. What a witness to Jesus as Lord!

In addition, the Bible describes the Spirit as the Father's deposit (or down payment). This guarantees that all He has promised about our future with His Son — which we're sampling even now — will come to pass in glory — beyond a doubt. Dwelling within my being, the Spirit is the pledge or firstfruits of the full inheritance stored up for me in Heaven (Eph. 1; 2 Cor. 1). He puts Eternity into my heart and then walks me victoriously right into it.

No wonder Biblical word pictures for the Consummation find parallels in what we're taught about the Spirit's ministry to believers today. Jesus set the example when He chose the prophecy about the Spirit's End-Time ministry in Isaiah 61 to be His inaugural address in Nazareth (Lk. 4). That morning before the synagogue He claimed to fulfill the text that read "the Spirit of the Lord is on me, because he has anointed me...." Every promise made in Isaiah actually foreshadowed the blessings of the Eternal Kingdom He had come to secure (as the whole 61st chapter teaches):

- The anointing Spirit matches our poverty with God's riches.
- He sets free the spiritual captives among God's people.
- He confronts every kind of bondage to sin that cripples us.
- The Spirit opens our eyes to see more clearly God's glory.
- He lavishes upon us God's grace and peace in all circumstances.
- He opens up within us fountains of praise to God.

Now all of this stood among them because Jesus, full of the Spirit, stood among them. Ahead of the Climax, God's Anointing brought the fullness of the Son within reach of everyone that day.

THINK WITH ME ...
How does the filling of the Spirit connect us with Christ's supremacy?

To be *filled* with the Spirit (Eph. 5), therefore, means that everything Christ is and offers dwells in us right now — not in reduced supply but in all of its *fullness* (Eph. 3). So much so that the Spirit's indwelling presence can be boiled down to one phrase: *"Christ* in you" (Rom. 8 and Col. 1). Even in the darkest moments the Spirit is powerfully at work unleashing fresh expressions of the bounty of God's promises to us in Jesus. The Church has not received "half" a Savior. Wherever the Spirit abides, ALL of Jesus abides.

Of course, at times we do not see His fullness manifested in every believer, or in every congregation — at least not the way we would like. But if we seek Him, remain open to Him, stay alert to His presence and remain ready to receive His work among us; if we offer ourselves daily to Him to live at the center of who Christ is, where Christ is headed, what Christ imparts and how Christ is blessed, then the Spirit will make the Kingdom our theme. He will pour into us greater measures of Christ's fullness than we ever dared to dream possible (Eph. 3).

Maybe a few metaphors would help to clarify this connection. The Spirit is like an *alarm clock,* awakening us to Christ and fuller dimensions of His supremacy. He's like a pair of *eyeglasses,* enabling us to see Christ more clearly for who He really is. Again, He is like a *cell phone,* keeping us in constant communication with the Lord of life.

He serves us like a *fan belt* serves a car! He brings the future within our reach, in a way reminiscent of how the belt links up the radiator fan with the engine, bringing the power of internal combustion to bear on six little blades. To use another car metaphor: Less like fog lights that help navigate dark, bumpy roads, the Spirit is more like a *sunrise,* casting rays of everlasting glory all over us right now, enabling us to boldly travel into the full daylight of God's Kingdom purposes.

Here's one other picture: The Holy Spirit provides more than just a stunning *playbill,* describing for us the plot of future productions and revealing things to come (Jn. 16 with Rev. 1). In addition, He transforms daily obedience to Christ into active roles in Kingdom dramas that involve us in *dress rehearsals* foreshadowing the Final Episode. You might see such rehearsals played out, for example, when a Christian congressman fights for tax relief for the poor, or when a Christian high school student tries to keep sexually pure in the face of intense peer pressure, or when a missionary in India helps a Hindu renounce idolatry to embrace Jesus as Lord.

With whatever metaphor I choose one ultimate truth stands out: The Spirit unites me with Christ in a way that is *qualitatively* the way I can expect to abide in Him forever. The Spirit does not simply engrave God's promises on my heart; instead, He engraves on my heart the *Promise-giver* Himself! He wants me to remain consumed with Christ as my one great passion. He is at work to deposit in me a faith in Jesus that stirs me regularly to seek the benefits His reign produces. (Such insights leap from Jesus' upper room teaching on the ministry of the Holy Spirit — see Jn. 14 and 16.)

From Pentecost forward the Spirit has continued His work of introducing believers to "the powers of the age to come" (Heb. 6), causing those powers to operate within us in ways reflective of Jesus' own extraordinary earthly ministry (Heb. 2). Just as the miracles of Jesus were signs to His audience of what God would grant them at the Culmination of History, so those same powers function in believers today as precursors of the same destiny.

Physical miracles might be viewed also as *symbols* of the radical transformation promised for all creation when Jesus comes back. Healings (whenever God chooses to grant them) provide us *samplings*, if you will, of the Day all things will be delivered from their bondage to decay (Rom. 8). The Spirit uses miracles to *advertise* the Consummation and keep our hearts yearning for the fullness of our Savior's reign. Heaven's temporal signs and wonders are meant to provide the Church *appetizers,* making us hungry for even more of Christ's glory up ahead.

THINK WITH ME ...
How does the Spirit consecrate us for Christ's reign,
both present and future?

Despite His diverse ministries, the most comprehensive name Scripture gives Him is *Holy* Spirit. That's because at the deepest levels His mission is to impact the Church with Jesus' *holiness.*

One day, "the earth will be filled with the knowledge of the glory of the Lord as the waters cover the sea" (Habakkuk 2). In that day everything will be "Holy to the Lord" in heaven and earth (Isa. 6 with Rev. 4). Even so, the Spirit is concerned with sanctifying the saints ("the people who have been declared holy in Jesus") between now and then. It's a fulltime process. He's consecrating every true believer along three themes of holiness: from, unto and for. That is, He is separating us *from* sin, while separating us *unto* Christ, even as He is separating us *for* the purpose of glorifying Him forever.

To get the job done the Holy Spirit confronts and contests, in lives and churches, everything that falls short of Christ and His kingship. Just as He will do at the End, today the Spirit unleashes Christ's rule within every community of believers to refine them, purge them, reform them, revive them and empower them. He's the "fire" with which Jesus promised to baptize His people, incorporating them into one holy and happy society (Lk. 3 and Acts 1 with Rev. 4; also 1 Cor. 12).

His assignment involves more than simply helping us manage ungodly desires. Acting as our intercessor, helper, counselor and comforter (as Jesus spoke of Him), the Holy Spirit seeks to usher us *out of* anything that's incompatible with the Consummation, anything that would bring us shame when we stand before Christ at His appearing (1 Jn. 2). At the same time He intends to usher us *into* encounters with Christ reflective of what it will be like for us the Day we see Him face to face.

In the life of the Church, we might say, the Spirit provides an "interim" experience of how Christ's lordship will prevail in the Consummation. The Spirit imparts preliminary installments of God's pre-ordained plan to transform us into the image of His Son (Rom. 8). Paul tells us the Spirit transports us from glory to glory, in ever-unfolding engagements with the magnificence of the Son of God (2 Cor. 3).

Holiness and supremacy visibly converge within every saint as we become more thoroughly *Christ-like*. The Spirit's indwelling presence assures us that one day we will share a full measure of Christ-likeness.

The process is unceasing. The results are guaranteed. Reflecting on the intended impact of the Spirit's ministry, therefore, a good question for any Christian to keep in mind is this:

How does every longing, desire, ambition and passion
the Spirit stirs up within me
point me more fully toward Christ and enlarge my hope
in Him as Lord of all?

Helping you discover fresh and exciting answers to that question is one primary mission of the Breath of God.

QUOTABLE QUOTE

The created world itself can hardly wait for what's coming next. Everything in creation is being more or less held back. The joyful anticipation deepens. All around us we observe a pregnant creation. But it's not only around us; it's within US. The Spirit of God is arousing us within. We're also feeling the birth pangs. Waiting does not diminish us, any more than waiting diminishes a pregnant mother. We are enlarged in the waiting.

(ROMANS 8 — THE MESSAGE)

3. The Church:
Approximations of the Consummate *Community*
(Ephesians 3:14-21; 5:23-33)

In the founding generations of the American colonies the Puritans formed neighborhood prayer meetings where they sang, prayed, discussed recent sermons and took counsel on how to nurture their passion for Christ. One of their number, John Eliot (remembered as the "apostle to the Indians"), called the groups to walk together in such a way that "when thou comest to die, heaven will be no strange place to thee; no, because thou hast been there a thousand times before." God intends nothing less for any congregation. Each is meant to experience foretastes of the "consummate community" that will move into the Habitations of the Lord.

Between Christ's ascension and His coming again the Church not only receives God's promises, but is itself a *revelation* of those promises and how they work, for all peoples to see, and for even heavenly powers to marvel at (Eph. 3). As fully as possible the Church is called to be a preliminary demonstration of what God's Kingdom purposes in Christ will look like as expressed in *community* throughout eternity.

THINK WITH ME ...
What can happen when a congregation
sees itself gathered around the King?

During a time of heightened tensions, with a threat of unwanted schism, a local church near my home asked me to come and help. On the evening I shared my heart with them an unexpected breakthrough began the needed restoration.

At the outset I delivered a Biblical message on the supremacy of Christ. Then, I took the huge, gold trimmed, red velvet pulpit chair that was up on the platform, brought it down below and put it in the center of the group. Next, all the leaders of the congregation — elders, deacons, Sunday school teachers, youth ministry staff, the pastors — were invited forward to surround this throne-like structure. Crowded close-in, over forty elders were asked to get down on their knees, as if bowing before a king. In fact, they were asked to "envision" Christ Himself sitting on the chair in our midst. I encouraged everyone to extend their hands and touch some part of the "throne" as we held a spontaneous prayer meeting. After nearly fifteen minutes, I had them pray more specific prayers. I asked them to invite Christ to take up His full role among us once again as Head of the Church, Lord of their lives, and Ruler of their congregation. Repentant weeping could be heard among some. Expectant smiles dawned on the faces of others. There was newfound "peace among the brethren" for most.

Still circling the chair, we concluded by singing to our Redeemer the great hymn "Crown Him with Many Crowns, the Lamb upon His Throne". It became their public confession. This was how they expected to march forward as a Body. They wanted Him reigning unhindered at the center of their lives together. Many said afterwards they would never be the same again, nor look at Christ the same again, *nor* think about their congregation the same again.

The point made that night was simply this: Jesus is alive, presiding as King, universally available to His Church in the full extent of His supremacy. Therefore, He is able to give powerful expressions of His reign within any congregation whenever we allow Him to draw us together around Himself *in community*. He intends this to approximate how we will experience community life with Him at the Climax. From Him comes a fellowship not unlike what is promised and portrayed in the New Jerusalem. As the head of the Body Christ wants to nourish us now with the same *quality* of provisions for spiritual fellowship that He will have for us when we join Him at the Great Homecoming (Heb. 12).

Destined to inhabit eternal ages, among the nations this new society is already taking shape around our King. Barriers that separate human beings in this age — tradition, race, ethnicity, age, nationality, or cultural and social status — no longer define who Christians are, any more than these issues will define us in the Resurrection. Instead, Christ is our all, even as He dwells among us all (Eph. 2-3 with Col. 3). At the deepest level He unites His people in Himself right now, *exactly* the way He will when we visibly surround Him in the Consummation (Jn. 17).

THINK WITH ME ...
Why ought any church bear witness daily
to the climax of Christ's reign?

Ultimately, Christ's reign will transform the entire universe into all it was meant to be. No part of our existence will remain unaffected by His saving power. Yet even now He desires to manifest His supremacy through the company of His followers, doing so by our words and deeds and prayers.

Bible scholars point out that the Greek word for "church" — *ekklesia* — was used in New Testament times to describe an assembly of citizens gathered to hammer out policies for running the city government, or to elect leaders, or even to declare war. In other words, the original meaning of "church" highlighted the activity of "ruling". How appropriate to use the same term to designate a community of redeemed sinners invited to share with Christ in His glorious Kingdom initiatives right where they live.

There's a national church leadership training conference in the U.S. that regularly advertises the rationale for its program with this slogan: *"The Local Church Is the Hope of the World"*. But is that true? Isn't it the Lord Jesus Christ who is the great hope God gives to any generation? Of course. But we can still accept their motto by retaining this proviso: The Church is not just a rag-tag remnant trying to survive in a hostile world, "holding the fort" until Jesus returns. The Church offers itself as the hope for the world primarily because we are united in Christ and filled with His Spirit. Our community life consists of nothing less than the firstfruits of the consummation of all things! God's people hold out hope to others because we are the major manifestation of our Monarch's mighty reign in the world today. We are a reflection of what Christ's supremacy looks like when fleshed out in community. We embody hope.

Empowered by the Spirit to unveil the Kingdom of Christ before all peoples in advance of its Apocalyptic Climax, local churches could be called:

- *Advance teams* for the coming King.
- *Signposts and outposts* for the New Jerusalem.
- *Microcosms* of what God intends for the whole universe.

- *Pilot projects and prototypes* of the Eternal Age and its activities.

- *Bases of operation* by which Christ's future reign can invade the present.

As each description suggests, our very lives together bears inescapable testimony to the culmination of Christ's Kingdom. The Church is simultaneously a *herald* as well as a *harbinger* of the Consummation's chief characteristics. As imperfect as it may be, our life together can and should effectively declare our delights over Christ's denouement, right up until the moment He comes back as our conquering Hero.

To be sure, all that we share in as we walk together as believers — worship, prayer, strategizing for growth, burden-bearing, preaching, neighborhood evangelism, weekly discipleship groups, social reforms among the poor, world missionary outreach — produces a *preliminary* glory. But make no mistake: Preliminary glory is not pretense. It's a genuinely potent glory whenever it touches the nations because it remains Jesus' glory, the glory of His supremacy. And as such it will not fade (2 Cor. 3). That's what makes any local congregation "the hope of the world".

Philip Yancey recalls the drama that unfolded in the well-storied World War II Japanese-run prisoner camp in Burma, located by the River Kwai. After months of untold suffering the prisoners determined to form themselves into an "alternate community" — the opposite of what their tormentors exhibited — a band of brothers filled with joy, faith and compassion. This was their main strategy for survival. Despite the dehumanizing conditions around them they embraced a common hope that their lives would not end in a jungle prison. They anticipated a God-given day of total liberation. Then they cared for one another accordingly. Yancey observes:

QUOTABLE QUOTE

And I ask Him that with both feet planted firmly on love, you will be able to take in with all Christians the extravagant dimensions of Christ's love. Reach out and experience the breadth! Test its length! Plumb the depths! Rise to the heights! Live full lives, full in the fullness of God. God can do anything, you know — far more than you could ever imagine or guess or request in your wildest dreams. He does it not by pushing us around but by working within us, His Spirit deeply and gently within us. Glory to God in the Church! Glory to God in the Messiah, in Jesus! Glory down all the generations! Glory through all millennia! Oh, yes!

(EPHESIANS 3 — THE MESSAGE)

"Perhaps something similar to this was what Jesus had in mind as he turned again and again to his favorite topic: the Kingdom of God."

Without a doubt, in the jail house of this oppressively evil, deadly and chaotic world, Christ has called into existence a radically different fellowship, ordained to thrive while still remaining inside the prison of a fallen planet. It is made up of former prisoners, now liberated-in-heart. They are filled with a vision about the ultimate deliverance of all creation. Planted throughout the nations as "settlements-in-advance" of that coming reign, they seek to set other prisoners free. Because Christ fills His Church with sovereign grace and glory, many dimensions of the Final Liberation can break into the darkest moments. We can experience approximations of the Consummation, *together*. And so can those we touch.

The "Church Universal" — the undivided body of saints, from all ages, out of many nations, in heaven and on earth — can be celebrated even now as the "Church Militant" (theologians' term for the Body in terms of its current mission to the nations) because on earth it embodies *approximations* of the Consummation. Before very long it will rise up in the Last Day, once and for all, to become forever the "Church Triumphant", exhibiting the supreme sufficiency of Him "who fills everything in every way"(Eph. 1).

4. World Mission:
Approximations of the Consummate *Triumph*
(Acts 1:1-11)

William Carey, considered in some quarters the father of modern Protestant missions, had a good grasp on implications of the fullness of Christ's supremacy for world outreach. This was evidenced in his widely-acclaimed research published in 1792 on the state of unevangelized peoples. Titled *An Enquiry into the Obligation of Christians,* the volume drew on promises in Isaiah and other texts to argue the need for ongoing revival and missions. Shortly after its publication, at a district conference for his Baptist denomination Carey and his little prayer band challenged leaders to recover a Christ-exalting hope for the missionary cause. His arguments prevailed. With palpable zeal the current era in global evangelism ensued, eventually mobilizing the Church worldwide to unleash unprecedented approximations of the consummate triumph of the Kingdom.

THINK WITH ME ...
What was the vision behind the beginnings
of the modern missionary movement?

Many Biblical texts used by Carey as well as other missiologists of his day were actually focused much more on God's vision for the Consummation than on missionary activity per se. These leaders combined End-Time hopes with missiological demographics on unreached peoples, to appeal to the Church for a renewed Christology — for a vision of God's Son *big enough* to take on the nations and *big enough* to motivate the Church to reach them with the Gospel at any cost.

In the end it wasn't just statistics on global needs that roused God's servants. Much more, it was this overarching message of Christ's supremacy. Abounding expectations in Him broke the missionary logjam of indifference and unbelief in the 19th century, on both sides of the Atlantic. "Expect great things from God. Attempt great things for God," Carey preached to every believer. He was convinced foretastes of the Final Victory awaited *all* who would join Christ in the glorious enterprise of world missions.

The same was true of another breakthrough a few decades later. It surfaced at a unique young men's gathering in the summer of 1886. Nearly 200 university students from all over the Northeast met for a college Bible conference at Mount Hermon, Massachusetts, and were led by Dwight Moody (the Billy Graham of that day). One night in the final week of a month of meetings, after ten international students told about the needs of their homelands, the Spirit of God fell in a marvelous way upon those assembled. God harnessed their hearts with hope in Christ. Many of the youth spent the next hours walking alone under the stars to wrestle with God in prayer about His plan for their lives. This visitation climaxed the following day when exactly 100 volunteered for missionary service. That was the beginning of one of the greatest missionary recruitment movements in church history, known as The Student Volunteer Movement for Foreign Missions (or SVM).

Over the next 30 years nearly 20,000 new missionaries were launched into service from SVM chapters formed on campuses around the world, while another 75,000 formed the Laymen's Missionary Movement to send them. Beginning with the Concerts of Prayer that SVM chapters conducted to intercede for the advance of Christ's Kingdom, this extraordinary alliance sustained itself by its clear convictions about Christ's sovereign involvement in the outcome. In fact, they coined a motto under which the SVM marched for decades: "The Evangelization of the World in this Generation."

How did they become so boldly visionary? It happened as they fixed youthful spirits not only on Jesus as Lord but also on immediate possibilities for experiencing approximations of the Final Triumphs of His global cause. Anticipating God's promises, they were willing to "go" no matter what.

In the early years of the 21st century, many trends in world evangelization indicate that the hope of Carey and the SVMers is still utterly appropriate. University scholar Philip Jenkins, in his 2003 compendium *The Next Christendom,* used extensive research to fortify the perception that "Christianity exercises an overwhelming global appeal, which shows not the slightest sign of waning." He called today's Christian movement "an uncontrollable brush fire" extending into every nation.

The explosive growth of the Church outside the West has become a harbinger of a Christianity soon to be truly global in scope. In 1900, for instance, approximately 10 million Christians were in Africa. By 2000 there were 360 million. By 2025 conservative projections put the number at nearly 600 million. Similar studies suggest the number of Christians in Latin America in 2025 will be 640 million, and in Asia 460 million. All total, by 2050 we anticipate three billion Christians worldwide. That's one and a half times the number projected for Muslims. Studies show there will be nearly as many Pentecostal Christians at mid-century as the total of all Muslims today.

Even though much remains to be done — over *two billion* children, women and men have not yet heard of hope in Jesus — somewhere in these statistics are the unmistakable cadences of Christ's coming Consummate Reign currently breaking through among earth's peoples!

THINK WITH ME ...
How is missions an extension of Christ's hope-filled reign among nations?

According to Jesus the End cannot and will not occur apart from the completion of this missionary task. The End is contingent upon our obedience to finish that task (Matt. 24). The ends of the earth and the end of the age march together toward the consummation of all things.

No wonder virtually every traditional interpretation of the series of events related to the Last Days (no matter how much scholars may differ from one another on specific details) has had positive impact on the Church's motivation for global outreach. All prophetic traditions agree that the goal of history will be achieved preeminently by the summoning of peoples from every tongue and culture into a clear, decisive encounter with the Lord of History. The One who waits to come back wants to be *expected* among all peoples when He returns. Therefore He must be proclaimed throughout all the earth as the supreme hope for all peoples. Only then will the Climax come.

What I'm suggesting is that the mission of the Church is more than a *consequence* of Christ's dominion over the nations. It is equally a *manifestation* of it. World evangelization opens the way for fuller executions of His victorious reign. At this moment our Lord is bringing about unconditional surrender among all earth's peoples. He's doing so redemptively in a way characteristic of the fuller surrender of all creation to Him when He reappears in His glory. Thus, the Church's global mission should seek to influence *all* of life with the blessings of Jesus' lordship. We should do so in a manner commensurate with how we expect this to be experienced in the Kingdom-to-Come.

More and more Christians are replacing the idea of one's "work place" with the term *"life place"*. The shift is significant. It reminds us that all believers have been called and are sent by God to specific places and people as our assigned focus for outreach for Christ — in home, school, business, media, health care, factory, neighborhood, government. There in our "life places" we become the primary channels through whom Christ displays His saving power and transforming reign. Approximations of Christ's consummate triumph can happen right where we work or study or serve, simply because we are *there* in His name.

On the other hand world evangelization must always give *primacy* to the planting of churches among the thousands of unreached people groups worldwide. Mission leaders today talk about "a church for every people and the Gospel for every person". What a statement this is on Christ's rights as Redeemer King. For His sake we must be about the business of setting up bases of operation around the globe so that His hope-filled message can impact every culture. Through evangelism and missions the Church creates *possibilities* for a significant measure of Christ's consummate reign to break into the present among the lost. Every newly established congregation can serve as a dynamic *entry point* for His advancing Kingdom to have its impact.

Missiologists (those who research and plan for missionary advances) suggest that six million new churches are currently needed among over two billion non-Christians for the nations to be effectively reached for Christ and their cultures (and cities) transformed by His power. It is estimated, however, that this can only happen if an additional six hundred thousand intercultural workers are raised up to finish the task and are sent forth by the Holy Spirit from existing congregations on every continent. How do we motivate people to face such needs and tackle such a mission?

The answer is clear: First we must confront and cure the crisis of supremacy that paralyzes so much of the Church and its mission right now. Christians must re-embrace the consummate vision of our Lord's glory. Anything less will prove incapable of sustaining world outreach at the level at which it is required today. Anything less will fail to recruit the hosts of missionary personnel we so urgently need, as well as the army of supporters to send them.

THINK WITH ME ...
How can hope in Christ's supremacy impact earth's unreached poor?

National Geographic ran a banner headline in a 2004 article on Johannesburg, South Africa, that read: "Thank you, Father, for giving us freedom. Now, help us to hold onto our dreams." The quote was from the prayer of an Anglican social worker in Seweto (one of the poorest parts of the city) as she led a group of homeless Christians in worship one evening. Their cry expressed their dependency on the supremacy of God's Son, both to explain their blessings (His dismantling of Apartheid) and to secure their endurance (until hopes that come from Him turn into reality).

The fact is, over the centuries missionaries compelled by the hope of Christ's supremacy have been found rooting again and again for the oppressed, the disenfranchised, the unreached. With the Consummation as their touchstone these laborers have tackled down-to-earth realities even as they preached the Gospel of eternal life. They defended the poor. They fought for moral and social transformation. They opposed evils like slavery, widow burning and infanticide at every turn. They emerged as walking revolutions. They *themselves* became approximations of the Consummation. Why can't the same happen again in our generation?

Hope in the supremacy of Christ is the greatest gift we can bring to the poor and oppressed, whether Christian or non-Christian, anywhere we find them. We need to say so, without apology. The Gospel of the Kingdom heralds how Christ's reign will one day consume forever all economic poverty and human subjugation, along with injustice, illiteracy, tyranny, sickness and disease — and all spiritual darkness. The poor need to hear that and hear it now.

However, simply saying so is not sufficient. Our Message of Hope remains incomplete until we summon the poor into communities of disciples where they can experience preliminary installments of their Sovereign's liberation and begin to labor side by side with renewed confidence for increased justice and social reform where they live. The gospel encourages the poor to nurture exciting expectations and act on them. It incites them to pray for ample approximations of the Kingdom to transform the status quo around them. This is how Christ-exalting deliverance continues to unfold on earth, even in the face of brutal oppressions.

Recently my wife witnessed this truth firsthand in India when she visited with a particular sub-group of Dalits, the self-named Untouchables numbering nearly 200 million. Born into the occupation of "latrine cleaning", the Bhangi Dalits had no way out because of the Hindu caste system, that is, until the Gospel restored to many hope and dignity. Thousands have turned to Christ. They are experiencing His reign in the most practical ways — including education, hygiene, retraining and community transformation, along with worship and discipleship. Hundreds of new churches planted among them have sustained this wholesale spiritual and social people-movement. Even the Indian government has been forced to take notice of the significant benefits.

I've seen Christ's reign displayed in equal fashion through varieties of churches and Christian ministries working among some of earth's most destitute urban communities in places like Manila, Seweto, Calcutta and even New York City. Unquestionably, as God's people minister to them in the fullness of Christ's supremacy, the poor retain front row seats for redemptive dramas that mirror the Consummation. "Through a worldwide migration to the city God may be setting the stage for Christian mission's greatest and perhaps final hour", reflects urban scholar Roger Greenway.

At the close of the 20th century Christian statesman Billy Graham convened 10,000 itinerate evangelists in Amsterdam. The invitees were made up mostly of poorer Christians from the Two Thirds World. Dr. Graham's goal was to challenge and train them for the task up ahead. During his final address to the delegation this seasoned witness to the nations (for over fifty years) called them to look far enough beyond their poverty and seeming powerlessness to focus resolutely on their hope in the supremacy of God's Son. Listen in:

Let us light a fire
of renewed faith
to proclaim the Gospel of Jesus Christ
in the power of the Holy Spirit, to the ends of the earth.
Using every resource at our command
and with every ounce of our strength.
Let us light a fire in this generation
that, by God's grace, will never be put out.
Let us light a fire
that will guide men and women into tomorrow and eternity.
Let the Light of the World shine throughout the whole earth
until He comes again.

THINK WITH ME ...
Why should a vision for the future drive
our mission to the nations today?

It was recently estimated that 70% of all progress toward completing the Great Commission has taken place since 1900; that 70% of that has occurred since World War II; and that 70% of that came about toward the close of the 1990's. Missionary statesman Dr. Ralph Winter said it well: "We have before us the brightest set of hope-filled resources, the most extensive global network of eager believers in thousands of prayer cells and strategizing committees. We have never, ever had as many competent, sold-out soldiers for Jesus Christ. The job to be done is now dramatically smaller *in terms of our resources* than ever before." Even more encouraging, the "all authority in heaven and earth" that our Master claims (Mt. 28) gives us every reason to expect marvelous advances of His mission — because that authority guarantees His Consummate Triumph.

Dr. Luis Bush put it in a fascinating way. Formerly the international director of the *AD 2000 Movement,* Bush guided a global effort that created a coalition of thousands of leaders from mission agencies and churches in nearly 200 nations to accelerate the cause of world evangelization as we headed into the Third Millennium. Following that initiative he became the director of *World Inquiry* and was charged with conducting consultations in various countries to discuss increased global cooperation for the Great Commission. Having returned from a trip that convened hundreds of national mission leaders from a score of nations, Bush delivered a report to American Christians in which he said: "The Biblically-based goal of mission is the consummation of all things in Jesus Christ." He proceeded to quote from Ephesians 1:9-10: "And he made known to us the mystery of his will according to his good pleasure, which he purposed in Christ, to be put into effect when the times will have reached their fulfillment — to bring all things in heaven and on earth together under one head, even Christ." Then He concluded with this stunning statement: *"Christian mission is future-driven."*

And so it is. With Jesus as Lord the future is already upon us — and it *drives* our mission for Him. Daily the Church seeks to saturate the world with this future and its promise (Jer. 29) — with a Message of Hope shaped by Christ's glorious greatness. Our task as "World Christians" is, in fact, to infect people everywhere with desires that can only be fulfilled in Jesus, so that they turn to pursue Him with all their hearts. Our privilege is also to enlist lost ones — including the poor, and especially the poor — to participate with Him in God's future, laboring with His people toward the Final Victory.

As an approximation of the Consummation, mission outreach not only exposes people to the promises of God but summons them into a life of *readiness* for so much more (Rom. 5). While anticipating the royal return of God's Regent, the Church must also remain prepared, at any given moment, to experience greater displays of His dominion right now — to step into practical involvements with Him in the advance of His Kingdom right where they live as well as to the ends of the earth.

The reality of Christ's coming glory provides the healthiest heartbeat for Christ's global cause.

5. Revival:
Approximations of the Consummate Awakening
(Ezekiel 31:1-28)

One of history's most perceptive writers on the topic of revival was Jonathan Edwards. A brilliant New England pastor/scholar during the early to mid 1700's, Edwards argued that revival held a central place in the revealed purposes of God.

Here's how he reasoned: God's objective in creation is to prepare a Kingdom for His Son. All of God's providential activities, reinforced by Christ's coronation, are moving unhesitatingly toward the consummation of all things. Based on that fundamental theological non-negotiable, Edwards concluded, the *revival* of God's people must comprise one of Christ's most strategic activities between His Ascension and Return. In fact, the renewal of the Church is God's way of shepherding history and nations toward the inevitable culmination of Christ's Kingdom.

Edwards wrote: "Universal dominion is pledged to Christ. In the interim, the Father implements this pledge in part by successive outpourings of the Spirit [revival] which prove the reality of Christ's Kingdom to a skeptical world and serve to extend its bounds." Fortunately he had the privilege of observing revival firsthand across his own New England, and eventually in his own congregation (the largest outside Boston at the time). Scholars call the phenomenon "The First Great Awakening".

THINK WITH ME ...
Why does revival under Christ always ignite a *forward* look?

Revival was a shared experience by saints in both Old and New Testaments. There was a difference, however, between the two eras in how the experience played itself out. In the Old Testament the reviving of Israel is usually characterized by a look *back* as the nation sought to return to previous high-water marks in Israel's religious pilgrimage. For example, note how Elijah on Mt. Carmel challenged Israel to return to days of spiritual faithfulness before Baal worship had taken over (2 Kings 18); or recall how Hezekiah refurbished the time-worn temple and reinstituted the ancient Passover tradition, shaping the revival that emerged under his watch.

In the New Testament revival is characterized much more as a look *forward*. It is focused on fresh extensions of Christ's reign among His

QUOTABLE QUOTE

He has enriched your whole lives, from the words on your lips to the understanding in your hearts. And you have been eager to receive his gifts during this time of waiting for his final appearance. He will keep you steadfast in the faith to the end so that when his day comes you need fear no condemnation. God is utterly dependable, and it is he who has called you into fellowship with his Son, Jesus Christ, our Lord.

(1 CORINTHIANS 1 — PHILLIPS TRANSLATION)

people and into the world. Consider, as a case study, the prayer meeting of Acts 4: what they prayed; how God answered; the aftermath in the succeeding stories of missionary advance — all of which was forward looking.

In a Christ-dominated revival the Holy Spirit increases vision for what's *ahead*. He deepens our yearnings for greater approximations of the coming Kingdom. Because Christ in His supremacy dwells among His people, we should not be surprised that periods of renewal involve more than momentary "visitations" from God (an Old Testament concept). In New Testament-style revival, Christians are aroused to a reality of Christ's presence and power already theirs, but currently overlooked. They are summoned not only to recapture their first love for Him (Rev. 2) but also to discover a passion for Him that surpasses whatever they have known before (Eph. 3). Re-awakening us to greater dimensions of His glory, New Testament revival is ultimately about recovering and enlarging hope in Jesus as Lord.

That's why, as Edwards observed, revival is arguably the most dramatic display of Jesus' lordship in the present age. In no way depreciating God's "ordinary" work with us on a daily basis, these *exceptional* seasons of His "extraordinary" work accelerate every other foretaste of the Age-to-Come that God intends for His people. Let's study it in a little more detail

THINK WITH ME ...
What words help describe the hope in Christ
that revival brings?

Church historians have developed a variety of words to describe these unusual epochs, including:

- Reformation
- Restoration
- Renewal
- Renaissance
- Renovation
- Resuscitation

All these terms point to a similar phenomenon: In revival Christ sovereignly quickens and restores His Church in order to help Christians enter more fully into His reign. Using other modifiers, we might say that New Testament revival promises us wonderful seasons when the reign of Christ is:

- Amplified
- Clarified
- Sharpened
- Deepened
- Quickened

- Broadened
- Unleashed
- Extended
- Expanded

The Biblical phrase "outpourings of the Holy Spirit" (sometimes called "infusions") is an excellent picture of revival. The metaphor recalls the force of a monsoon. It represents God deluging His people so as to empower them to more fully engage His purposes in Christ. God floods His Church with fresh hope, passion, prayer and mission by refocusing us on Christ for ALL He really is. *Revival is a church saturated with the supremacy of Christ by the Spirit of Christ.*

Whatever term is most helpful to you, each one reminds us that revival is more than just an event in a church calendar. Inherently revival is an on-going *process*. When God re-energizes a community of Christians, He intends Kingdom results that last many years. Scholars' research verifies that, following each one of the four so-called "Great Awakenings" in American history (early 1700's, late 1700's, mid 1800's, early 1900's), decades of documented transformations took place both in churches and in society. God gave His people "fresh winds", not simply to fire up enthusiasm for spiritual things but also to extend further the reign of His Son within communities and nations through His Church.

THINK WITH ME ...
What does it look like when Christ rules
a people through revival?

Here's one story to demonstrate how revival can impact a whole nation for Christ's Kingdom. As you read it, ask yourself: "Is this the kind of 'approximation' I would like to experience where I live?"

At the close of the 20th century a wonderful move of God, with all the earmarks of the Consummation, came to the beleaguered nation of Uganda.

Once known as the "jewel of Africa", this beautiful land had become devastated, physically and spiritually, by multiple oppressive regimes headed by diabolical dictators. Economically Africa's bread-basket had become its worst "basket case". Most distressing, tens of thousands of Christians were martyred for their faith, many by unspeakable tortures.

As a result, in the late 1990's hundreds of thousands in the churches began to cry out to God for a spiritual awakening in their land. The believers grappled with the need for soul-searching repentance inside the Church. They confessed all the ways they were actually complicit in His judgments on Uganda as a whole. Broken in spirit, they pled for God's mercy. They faced their own unfaithfulness and indifference to the massive East African Revivals (as they were known) just a few short decades earlier. How quickly they had turned away from Christ's powerful work among them toward the beginning of the century!

Finally God answered their cries. Joyous confidence about Christ's Kingdom re-ignited their churches. Passion for the Promise-Giver once again marked thousands of congregations large and small. But this was just the beginning of revival.

At the same time ungodly strongmen were unexpectedly expelled. Corrupt structures of oppression were decisively dismantled. Political and religious prisoners were set free. Persecution of the Church came to an end. A devoutly righteous Christian leader became Uganda's president. He made his first official act a public re-dedication of the entire nation to Jesus Christ as its Lord!

Following that, to the amazement of all, significant economic recovery began. Far more importantly, in Uganda (once known as the African nation with the largest AIDS epidemic) a nationwide commitment to sexual abstinence turned back the plague. It rendered Uganda the country with the least threat of AIDS — all in just one decade! Some of the largest churches in Africa could now be found there, with one in Kampala growing from a few hundred to nearly 15,000 in five years. Fasting and prayer became a way of life for Ugandan Christians as they sought even deeper manifestations of Christ's reign in their generation.

To these African believers every change "felt" as if the Consummation had already broken in upon them. As a result Christians began to hunger for something greater, something beyond just national renovation. Their prayers became heart-sighs for nothing less than Christ's return to set up

His Kingdom in fullest measure among them, as well as throughout Africa and among the nations.

Stories like this are multiplying everywhere. A half-decade into the 21st century, one of Latin America's leading evangelists, addressing an all-night prayer vigil of 250,000 in Mexico City, declared: "Latin America is at the threshold of an enormous spiritual awakening!" The Argentine-born Alberto Mottesi continued: "I'm not speaking of a spiritual revival, but a spiritual awakening. This will bring forth revival in the economic, political and social arenas. It reminds me of what happened in Martin Luther's Reformation which became the preamble to the Renaissance, affecting the arts and culture. We are going to see something similar in Latin America."

Surely these are the kinds of stories God is willing to compose for His Son within churches and communities everywhere. Call it revival. Call it spiritual awakening. But call it, without a doubt, "approximations of the Consummation"!

THINK WITH ME ...
Why might "arrival" be the best metaphor to use for revival?

At the Last Day, in the consummate revival — the *Final Revival* — the entire universe will be awakened fully to all that Christ is. It will be summoned into full participation in His unconditional lordship. In every other revival, though on a lesser scale, God still wants to pursue a recovery of more comprehensive visions of His Son among His people.

Every other revival takes its cue from the Final Revival (see Halverson's words at the opening of this chapter). In hundreds of revival episodes the past twenty centuries we discover replays of the central themes of the Final Revival activated *in principle* by Christ each time He makes Himself known more powerfully tangible among His people.

Steve Hawthorne suggests revival might, therefore, be called *"arrival"*. It's as if Christ "shows up" in His Church afresh to re-capture us and re-conquer us. Isaiah 60, for example, suggests God's glory was *already* breaking over them like a sunrise, exposing many dimensions of His Kingdom purposes to them. Already the encounter had begun. What they needed to do was "rise and shine" and seize the day. That's why Biblical texts frequently use the motif of *encounter* to describe spiritual renewal. We find this in Isaiah's picture of a future when God would rend the heavens like a garment, visibly descending like a fire upon saints and nations alike (Isa. 64).

The Puritans coined a great phrase to define the "arrival" experience. They called such seasons *"the manifest presence of Christ"*. Here is how they reasoned. First, they said, there is Christ's *essential* presence. That is, Christ is everywhere present all the time. We are never far from Him, nor He from us. He is unavoidable. Second, they also talked about Christ's *cultivated* presence. Christians can enrich their sense of fellowship with Him as they abide in Him day by day, faithfully obeying Him. We may cultivate a deeper knowledge of the Lord through Bible study and prayer. As we do, Christ shows Himself to be much more present in our lives than we had realized.

The *manifest* presence of Christ was something else altogether. This was the Puritans' third term for those times when God reveals His Son to a new generation of His people. He does so in such dramatic fashion that it almost seems as if Christ has been hiding from us until that moment. Then suddenly He reinserts Himself among us. He arrives. This encounter cannot be cultivated. It is a *gift* from the living God. It is an "awakening" historians say. It must simply be received. Many promises of Scripture that describe Christ's coming in glory — His ultimate manifest presence — were applied *in principle* by the Puritans to any period of corporate spiritual awakening. The Puritans would most likely be comfortable in calling revival an "approximation of the Consummation".

THINK WITH ME ...
Why should Christ Himself form the central definition of revival?

One could almost say that revival is like a *coronation*. It leads believers to reaffirm their wholehearted devotion to the Lamb who sits on the Throne (Rev. 5). It reconnects them to His marching orders as their King. It serves as a powerful *sign* of the supremacy of Christ. The renewing reality of revival should be basically defined as this: Jesus expressing Himself more fully to His people *as Lord*.

In point of fact, one cannot think rightly about revival at all if one does not think rightly about the glory of God's Son. He is the criterion by which we measure both revival's legitimacy and its impact. The Final Revival will emerge from fresh in-breakings of Christ's sovereign dominion before every creature in heaven and earth. But we can taste of this Coming Climax in a *preliminary* fashion as the Spirit spreads abroad re-awakenings to Christ for ALL that He is.

Until the Consummation our Redeemer intends to continue invading His Church, extending His lordship among us, regaining the praise He rightfully deserves, and enlarging His mission through us among all earth's peoples. Edwards was on target: Revival is one of the most exciting expressions of Christ's supremacy any Christian can experience until He comes again.

When He does we will enter into an awakening of such unparalleled proportions that all the other awakenings will become, by comparison, like the faded memories of childhood adventures.

6. Spiritual Warfare:
Approximations of the Consummate *Battle*
(1 Peter 4:1-5, 13-19; 5:4, 6-11)

Along with promises of reviving grace, other passages sound forewarnings of retribution and wrath. For multitudes of mortals as well as droves of demons, the Great Judgment Hour looms ominously. The Judge has been appointed (Jn. 5). He has the supremacy in everything (Col. 1). He has all authority in heaven and earth (Mt. 28). He will carry out with finality every sentence handed down by Heaven's Court (Acts 17).

THINK WITH ME ...
Where around us do we see the judgments
of the Lord revealed already?

To *Christians* the judgments of the Lord bring significant comfort. The fulfillment of our destiny in Jesus desperately requires them. Caught up in a battle raging fiercely among the nations, this war remains beyond our meager abilities to resolve. The ages-long conflict must be — in fact, can *only* be — terminated by Messiah in His Reign of Righteousness when He visibly descends as Supreme Commander (2 Thess. 1 with Rev. 19). Only then will all sin be put away and all of Heaven's enemies defeated. What a gloriously awesome prospect of victory held out for every believer!

According to the prophets, however, disquieting spasms of the Final Battle can be felt already. Daily we experience initial engagements with Malignant Forces. Current combats with Dark Powers rock the nations and foreshadow a judgment that will soon shake the universe. Sometimes this takes the form of:

- Famines and natural disasters
- Plagues and epidemics
- Civil chaos and revolutions
- Wars and terrorism
- Financial collapses
- Dehumanizing poverty

From one perspective such tragedies are inevitable in a fallen world, separated as it is from its Creator. "The wages of sin is death" (Rom. 6). These eruptions bear witness that all humankind reaps what it sows (Gal. 6). Time and again in its hardhearted and treasonous rebellion, the world has sown the seeds of its own destruction.

From another perspective, however, such sorrows must be viewed as God's *preliminary punishments* of a rebel race. They are urgent wake-up calls extended to mortals everywhere. God is "shouting in the pain" (as C. S. Lewis put it), urging them to repent and seek the only hope they have, held out by a Redeemer who rules unrelentingly over every upheaval. Apart from Jesus' blood and righteousness, all peoples continue to dwell under the frown of the Almighty, facing only further installments of such cataclysms — precursors of the full fury of Christ that awaits the nations not long from now (Rev. 15-19).

In quite a different way God's righteous wrath is experienced daily and universally. It cannot be avoided. It is experienced in His overarching decision (according to Romans 1) to "give over" and "give up" the human race to its own devices. He permits earth's peoples to replace a passion for His glory with preoccupations, arrogant ambitions and idolatrous treasures. Apart from Christ's saving work no other option is left to sinners. They remain "without God and without hope in the world" (Eph. 2). One major way Christ exercises His sovereignty is simply by *withdrawing* the benefits of God's mercy from those who persistently reject His presence and piety and power.

That leaves nations and peoples to work out their destinies by themselves. But they must do so inside Enemy-occupied territory. This has been our lot since the fall of Adam. Our attempts are futile, and our efforts are fatal.

THINK WITH ME ...

How did you discover Christ's opposition to the unseen dark powers?

God's judgments, executed in the midst of raging combat, are *unseen* by most of us most of the time though the theater of this battle enlarges daily (Eph. 6). The acceleration of warfare is unavoidable. Solid advances of Christ's Kingdom (of which there are many!) can not be ignored by demonic hosts about to be crushed in His wake. In many ways, our hope hinges on how Christ's supremacy is expressed in the unseen dimensions. He must expel Satan and his subjects from the universe, and the Enemy knows it. By proclaiming His victory we rebuff counter-claims made by forces of evil.

Our testimony to the glory of Jesus, especially to fellow believers, helps expose the empty intimidations of Hell. It challenges the Devil's very legitimacy and calls him into question. Wherever hope in Christ is heralded and believed, a *limit* is automatically set on the deceptions of Evil. Whenever we help fellow Christians get a larger vision of Jesus, strongholds raised against His dominion inside the Church are torn down (2 Cor. 10). This hope exorcises the crisis of supremacy from *our* midst — which is always the prior step toward dislodging Satan among the nations.

In His earthly ministry when our Lord cast out demons, He defined such work as evidence that the Kingdom was near. It was the proof that His immediate, temporal victories approximated the triumphs at the End (Matt. 12). When, for example, He prepared to deliver a social outcast from a legion of demons, the evil spirits understood what His act foreshadowed. So they pleaded with Jesus to let them be temporarily spared the ultimate judgment (Matt. 8). When His disciples went on their first preaching expeditions, He interpreted their results the same way — apocalyptically. He explained that He saw Satan fall from Heaven as they ministered (Lk. 10).

QUOTABLE QUOTE

But if it's *God's* finger I'm pointing that sends the demons on their way, then God's Kingdom is here for sure. When a strong man, armed to the teeth, stands guard in his front yard, his property is safe and sound. But what if a stronger man comes along with superior weapons? Then he's beaten at his own game, the arsenal that gave him such confidence hauled off, and his precious possessions plundered. This is war, and there is no neutral ground. If you're not on my side, you're the enemy; if you're not helping, you're making things worse.

(LUKE 11 — THE MESSAGE)

Repeatedly the Bible records that Christ came into the world to destroy the works of the Devil (1 Jn. 3). He came to render Satan powerless, trouncing him under the feet of His followers (Heb. 2 and Rom. 16). He came to tear down every demonic device that defies the Gospel. He came to release captives from the Deceiver of the nations (Rev. 12) and to lead them into glorious service to Himself as the Delight of the saints.

At this very hour the Empire of the Son continues to advance — relentlessly — through His Church against Armies of Spiritual Destruction. Christ is displacing the works of Satan in every area of human experience. He is dethroning our adversary, one sphere after another. He's supporting sabotage against the dominions of darkness, liberating nations and peoples from enemy strangleholds. This is reminiscent of how He will conquer all Principalities in the day they flee His holy presence forever (Rev. 20).

Therefore, in Ephesians 6 Christians are urged to wear armor that's fully adequate to the intensity of spiritual warfare in which we're immersed. Properly clothed, the Church can foreshadow Christ's heavenly army in Revelation 19 as it descends with Him to do battle at the end of the Age. Since substantial installments of the Consummate Victory can be expected even today, *we should dress like it.* As Paul writes again: "The night is nearly over; the day is almost here. So let us put aside the deeds of darkness and put on the armor of light...., Christ" (Rom. 13). Attired accordingly, we can enter into Christ's End-Times triumphs *now* in ways that guarantee the outcome of the Final Battle *later.* Should this not encourage us to serve Him without reserve, and without fear?

It's impossible to know King Jesus and not celebrate daily both the exhaustiveness of His battle plans as well as our incorporation, right now, into His victory procession (2 Cor. 2). We march with Him against every barrier raised to defy our King among the nations. The hordes of hell have no way — they literally have no hope — of ever neutralizing the triumphs of Christ's Church as we continue to spread the Gospel throughout the earth. Our public confession of the Messiahship of our Master scatters darkness at every turn (Mt. 16).

THINK WITH ME ...
Why must preliminary installments of
Christ's victory often be so *costly* for us?

But let's not be surprised by how *costly* approximations can be (especially those recorded in this chapter). Every foretaste of glory invades enemy camps. Satan is not ignorant of how every victory displays Christ's grand intentions. Nor will he take such assaults lying down. To be involved in Christ's global cause will involve all of us in various forms of Christ's sufferings. This does not bring His supremacy into question, however. To the contrary, it confirms the glory of it even more.

Evil is not merely moral deficiency. Evil is a personal, heavily entrenched rebellion against the living God. Evil is not merely the absence of the good. Rather, it is an intentional and personal attack upon the good. *Warfare* is not too strong a term, therefore. We are fighting immense, depraved and malevolent beings. There will be temporary casualties among soldiers of the Cross.

As the Church embraces more of the approximations of the Consummation destined for our generation — and in so doing enters into more of the fullness of Christ's supremacy — we can expect this development to arouse the Anti-forces. It will push them into defensive action against us. The successful extension of Christ's reign, first into our congregations and then into our communities and nation, will inevitably whip up whirlpools of resistance in the invisible realm, created by the convergence of two diametrically opposed powers, only one of which is destined to prevail, and both of which know Who that will be.

We must match demonic death threats with fuller expressions of Christ's dominion, first in our lives and then in our churches. The glory of Christ's authority must be visibly and substantially manifested *in us* by the power of the Holy Spirit, dominating us in a manner equal to the intensity of the battle we fight. At the same time all expectations of prevailing in combat — of magnifying Christ's righteousness and love, as well as furthering His opposition to all ungodliness — depend directly on our willingness to lay down our lives when He asks for it. We must be willing, Jesus said, to *die* for the fame of His Name and for the spread of His claim (Mk. 8 with 2 Cor. 4).

This has been the pattern throughout Church history. Glorious Gospel conquests have normally been accompanied by persecution, even martyrdom. Not even Christ Himself could secure God's promises, or grapple effectively with the Powers opposed to them, without the shedding of His blood. Why should we assume He would not ask the same of us? In fact, the willingness of Christians to pay a price for the Gospel is testimony to their hope about its sure and certain triumph. It provides additional irrefutable evidence of the legitimacy of our vision of the supremacy of God's Son.

Maybe that's why the *World Christian Encyclopedia* records that the 20th century not only witnessed the most spectacular advances of church growth in history, but also recorded a march of martyrs that equaled the combined number from all previous nineteen centuries put together!

Each intensification of opposition forces should greatly encourage us. For all parties involved it verifies the undisputed status of Christ's throne. It is a strong indicator that His Kingdom is effectively *growing*. It proves that the Consummation is drawing nearer. The world's spiritual conflagrations, both the seen and the unseen, will culminate soon. This will take place when God's untempered judgments firmly and permanently dismantle Satan's domains, at the visible return of his Arch Enemy, the Lord Jesus Christ Himself.

One day, to our utter joy, the armies will confront each other in one grand Cosmic Conflict. This will usher in a New Heaven and Earth "in which righteousness will have its home" (2 Pet. 3). Then our hope in Christ will be vindicated once and for all, as we emerge as Overcomers (Rev. 2, 3) witnessed by angelic hosts shouting "Hallelujah!" before His Throne (Rev. 15).

Until then, we must wage spiritual war in Jesus' name. We must do so by the Word of God and prayer (Acts 6), confronting the Powers and loving the unredeemed, one skirmish after another. We can do this by advancing the hope of the Gospel in ways that approximate the War-to-End-All-Wars. In fact, God invites us to engage the Destroyer in such a fashion that our struggle not only prefigures the Final Battle, but actually contributes to *shaping* its glorious outcome.

APPROXIMATIONS ...
IN NEW YORK CITY AND WHERE YOU LIVE

Hundreds of pastors throughout New York City have banded together for many years in an unprecedented metropolitan prayer movement. Nearly seventeen hundred churches and 75,000 people have joined forces in hundreds of concerted prayer gatherings. I've had the privilege of watching much of it unfold firsthand.

The entire movement has been linked together by what is called "The New York Prayer Covenant". It is like a manifesto, a brief document that defines a four-fold agenda for all the praying. Despite extraordinary denominational and ethnic diversity among Christians in the Big Apple, all of us can pray enthusiastically about these four concerns. Called the "Four R's" they put our hope squarely on Christ's shoulders in four key areas:

- *Revival* in the Church
- *Reconciliation* among churches and races
- *Reformation* of society
- *Reaching* the lost

Increasingly God is answering our ambitious four-fold petition. As a result, many in New York have experienced meaningful "approximations of the Consummation". For example (to mention only four of them):

- Unprecedented unity and love among the city's pastors are visible to its citizens and openly honored by city officials (revival).

- Bridges of trust among churches have prevented bloodshed in neighborhoods during times of racial tensions (reconciliation).

- Extraordinary reduction in many types of crime in the city have amazed the watching nation (reformation).

- Some of the largest evangelistic outreaches ever sponsored in North America have been organized in New York over recent years (reaching).

But the prayer movement has refused to let itself become self-satisfied. Rather, the magnitude of previous answers has stirred us to seek God for a whole lot more. Christ's manifest presence in New York City, especially since the attacks of September 11, 2001, has actually renewed the determination of many to be more passionate in our prayers and witness. We have discovered an abounding hope for our city that draws on nothing less than a vision of the Consummation. Preliminary installments of that vision have made us doubly determined to keep on praying. Even as I write this paragraph, plans are underway for over 10,000 Christians to spend three days walking every street of the entire city next month, praying over every single residence and business and asking the Father to let the saving glory of Jesus be manifested in every place.

How about the street where *you* live? What approximations are waiting to unfold for you there?

All of us need to become like little children. We need to stand on tiptoe waiting for the parade of God's promises to round the corner and march straight into our churches and neighborhoods with the life-giving fullness of Jesus. You have every right to expect this. Resounding breakthroughs of His reign await you, here and now, even on the street where *you* live.

Until the moment all saints behold His splendor with joy unspeakable, none of us should grow weary in our pursuit of more of Christ's glory revealed *now*. This means we need to be about the business of confronting the crisis of supremacy wherever we find it (beginning in ourselves and in our churches). We also must be about the business of helping God's people give over their lives to the Savior in ways that transform us day by day, right where we dwell.

Which brings us to the issue of *passion*: As the Father pours out more of the fullness of Jesus on His people, what kind of passion for His Person should we show? Is there a special *fervency* Christ's supremacy ought to inspire in His followers? Is there a certain display of devotion for the dominion of His Son that God desires from us? Is there a measure of intensity He's looking for in our determination to experience the full extent of His lordship?

If we expect to overflow at the End with one *consuming passion* for our Redeemer — unbounded, unending and undistracted, inspired by ALL the hope He is for us — should we not strive to savor Him with similarly deepening affections right now? Does our Lord deserve any less than this?

Those are the right questions. And they bring us to one final chapter in **Volume I's** survey of the glory of the Son of God. Far more than the previous chapters, this next study will probably prove to be the most challenging for your *personal* experience of life under the lordship of Jesus.

QUOTABLE QUOTE

God's readiness to give and forgive is now public. This new life is starting right now, and is whetting our appetites for the glorious day when our great God and Savior, Jesus Christ, appears. Our Savior Jesus poured out new life so generously. God's gift has restored our relationship with him and given us back our lives. And there's more life to come — an eternity of life! You can count on this.

(TITUS 2 AND 3 — THE MESSAGE)

5

CHRIST SUPREME:

The *Consuming Passion* of Christian Hope

Recover a Vision Shaped by the FERVENCY of His Supremacy

At age 73 Lorin Maazel, long-time music director of the New York Philharmonic, reflected with keen insight on his years of conducting: "Great leaders elicit passion, not perfection. That's my main job — to energize people. If they grind it out and couldn't care less, then they wind up hating the conductor. Music without emotion is nothing. I'm never looking for a perfect performance. I'm looking for an *impassioned* performance."

If that's the sign of effective leadership, then surely it must mark the *greatest* Leader. By virtue of the hope He brings, Christ re-energizes Christian living. He elicits deeper desires for us to be His disciples. He impassions our pursuit of His greater glory. Our fervency for Him evidences to the world that His claims to supremacy must be taken seriously.

Although I have moved five times in the past twenty-five years from one coast to the other, each time I've prominently displayed a diploma-sized plaque on a wall of my office. It frames a favorite prayer from the African theologian and bishop, Augustine. It exposes his heart of *passion*, a passion fueled by a vision of Jesus as Lord. It has become a lifelong liturgy of longing for me. Maybe it represents your prayer, as well:

> You called, you cried,
> You shattered my deafness.
> You sparkled, you burned,
> You scattered my darkness.
> You shed forth your fragrance,
> And I drew in my breath.
> And I pant for you.

Using more contemporary phrases, psychologist Larry Crabb challenged Christians to respond with similar passion when he wrote the following (which I've formatted in blank verse style):

> To every cry from your passion-filled hearts,
> God replies, *"Christ."*
> Let your passion to explain
> become a passion to know Christ.
> Let your passion to be right
> become a passion to honor Christ.
> Let your passion to heal
> become a passion to give hope.
> Let your passion to connect
> become a passion to trust a sovereign Christ,
> who will do for you exactly what needs to be done.

Appeals, both ancient and modern, illustrate a key principle around which this chapter is built:

**A comprehensive vision of the supremacy of Christ
will always transform our hope in Christ
into a consuming passion for Christ.**

Since Christ is the heir of every promise God has given us — since He is the summation, consummation and approximation of all Christian hope — how could any commitment to Him require any less than *consuming* passion? Very unlike the deadly fate of a moth drawn to the warmth and beauty of a candle flame, the closer we get to our Radiant Redeemer the greater our joys, the more energized our labors, the more enticing our prospects — the more *alive* we will feel! Paul urges us in Romans 12: "Never be lacking in zeal, keep your spiritual fervor, serving the Lord. Be joyful in hope" — which echoes Proverbs 23: "Always be zealous for the fear of the Lord. There is surely a future hope for you, and your hope will not be cut off."

In this chapter we'll explore the glory of Jesus' kingship on one additional front: the *fervency* due His supremacy and inspired by it. We'll discover that:

- **Passion for Christ is a chief evidence of a strong hope in Him.**

- **The best definition of our passion for Jesus is found in His passion for us.**

- **The best reason for our passion for Jesus is the Father's passion for His Son.**

- **Fervency requires Christian disciples to be *consuming* Christ.**

- **Fervency requires Christian disciples to be *consumed with* Christ.**

- **There are simple ways to test the state of your passion so you can let it grow.**

The FERVENCY of His Supremacy
(Haggai 2:1-9)

I regret not reading from the classic King James Version of the Scriptures more often. Its lofty language remains unparalleled in literature. Take, for example, its rendering of that wonderful verse in Haggai 2:8 (sung regularly in Handel's *Messiah*): "The Desire of all nations will come". It implies that Christ's Second Coming will satisfy all the aspirations of human hearts. I like that. However, modern versions like the New International Version suggest the better translation of the Hebrew should actually say "the *desired*" of all nations will come, meaning the "treasures" of earth's peoples will be offered up when multitudes worship God in the Consummation. They will honor the reign of His Son by laying their wealth at Jesus' feet. (Rev. 21 expands on the same vision.)

And yet, to be quite honest, I think the King James was not far off by translating the Hebrew as "the *Desire* of all nations". On That Day all peoples will have to acknowledge that every spiritual thirst we sought to satisfy with earthly refreshment was only quenchable by His glorious presence. From the beginning *all* of humankind's heart-desires have been for *Him*, whether they understood this or not. Augustine's "My heart is restless until it rests in Thee" speaks for all of us. That's what makes our Lord Jesus the "desire" of all nations! That's what makes fervency for His supremacy our destiny.

THINK WITH ME ...
Where do you see evidences of consuming passion today?

So it makes sense to ask: In *this* life should our desire for Him be similarly "all or nothing"? Is it reasonable to pursue undiluted passion for Him *now*? Can His glorious greatness compel an all-out devotion equal in some measure to how we'll love Him at the End?

A recent gathering of nearly three million teenagers answered with a resounding "Yes!" With groups forming on thousands of high school campuses at public flagpoles to pray, *See You at the Pole* celebrated its 15th annual event with this particular year's theme word *"Consumed!"* Sponsored by a national network of hundreds of youth ministries, the promotional literature asked young people: "Do you want the fire of God to fall on your campus and in your community? Do you *really*? You must realize that when fire falls, it consumes *everything* that is unholy and ungodly. The fire of God purifies lives, melts hearts and devours sin. How desperately do you want the fire of God?" By the millions they rallied to their Savior that September day. They asked *Him* to be the fire in their lives, to *impassion* their outreach to the world. Many continued asking for this in organized daily prayer meetings the rest of the year. *Consumed*!

This event was followed four months later with another national convocation of nearly 20,000 university students to form what one delegate called "the world's largest Christian missions academy". News headlines proclaimed "a new generation of college students is making plans to transfer its passion for Jesus Christ from the campus to the mission field". At the close nearly 10,000 committed in writing to short and long-term mission assignments. Surveying their zeal, the director of InterVarsity

Christian Fellowship's URBANA Conference stated unequivocally: "Students in the 21st century will be the greatest missionary force the world has ever seen."

None of this should catch us by surprise. From the beginning our Father created all of us, young and old alike — body, soul, spirit, will, intellect, emotions — to be passionate for His Son. We must never be afraid to give ourselves up to Him with unqualified abandon. Nothing about the Christian life can ever be dubbed as dull while following a Master who marched out of a graveyard to ascend the Throne of the Universe.

Listen to how Jesus fosters fervency for His supremacy: "If anyone would come after me, he must deny himself and take up his cross and follow me. For whoever ... loses his life for me and for the gospel will save it" [consuming passion] (Mk 8). "If anyone comes to me and does not hate his father and mother, his wife and children, his brothers and sisters — yes, even his own life — he cannot be my disciple.... Any of you who does not give up everything he has cannot be my disciple" (Lk. 14) [consuming passion]. "Anyone who loves his father or mother more than me is not worthy of me; anyone who loves his son or daughter more than me is not worthy of me.... Whoever loses his life for my sake will find it" (Mt. 10) [consuming passion].

THINK WITH ME ...
How can passion for Christ *right now* reflect what it will *ultimately* become?

In chapter 3 we learned that one day Christ will assert Himself openly as the center and circumference of everything, for everyone, for all time to come. Unchallenged He will continue to be what He has always been, though manifested to an infinitely greater degree: namely, supreme.

But Christ has not procrastinated on securing this reputation. From Acts 1 onward, long before the Climax, He has been actively pursuing preeminence in every believer's life as well as among the nations. He's not content to postpone inflaming our love for Him until some hour when He returns in glory. He wants to be engaged as Lord of All by the hearts of believers right now. *At this moment* He longs to incite increased homage toward Himself to intensify our daily obedience to His purposes.

In Christ, God's supremacy is on display for us — *today*. Therefore, our best response back is to put more of our affections for Him on display —

today. We're not to relegate such devotion until after He returns in triumph. We must offer Him now the ardent affection He will rightfully command then.

At the end of the Age the reality of Christ's supremacy will secure one of two permanent reactions from every human who has ever lived: Some will reject it and despise it, only to shrink back in terror. Others will put their hope in Him more completely as (to borrow Augustine's phrase) they "pant for Him" even more. God gives His creation no other options but these two. For the redeemed the Son's unparalleled, unsurpassable, unending *royalty* will instigate unconditional, unwavering, unabated *loyalty* — not just during a millennium but throughout eternity. Why not encourage such passion to become the primary goal for every Christian along the way from here to there?

THINK WITH ME ...
What does our passion reveal about the *content* of our Christology?

The dictionary matches "passion" with these words:

- Enthusiasm
- Unquenchable zeal
- Fervent longing or craving
- Intense, driving emotions
- Ardent affection
- Strong devotion to an activity, person or object

Passion comes in many forms. It can be heard in a child's cry to be held by caring parents. It may take the shape of wholesale campaigns among the nations — like the environmentalists' "green revolution", or the United Nation's fight against AIDS. It can be seen among millions of Hindus who gather at the Ganges to wash away their sins in the river goddess. A world currently at war with fanatical Islamists promoting calls for Jihad has discovered a diabolical form of passion — a deadly combustible religious zealotry that blows up innocents.

Clearly, then, Christians have no edge on passion. The truth is, everyone is passionate about *something*. Whoever and whatever we consistently pursue — that is, what we turn to in order to find ultimate happiness or purpose in life — defines our preeminent passion.

Neil Postman in his book *The End of Education* maps out all the ways modern technology incites pseudo-religious fervor among Americans. With promises of a better future technology compels people to rely on it, then celebrate it, stand in awe of its mysteries, scorn those who reject it, feel bereft when denied access to it, and gladly alter our relationships, habits, lifestyles, schedules, goals and dreams to accommodate it. That's one form of consuming passion experienced by much of modern society.

There's a reason I share this with you. Note that every one of the main verbs in the preceding paragraph could be used equally to describe the kind of devotion the Father desires His children to give to their Lord. Passion is no stranger to Americans.

So let me ask you, dear Christian reader: In what sense are you a person of passion toward *Christ*? If I could observe its expression, what would the outward evidence of passion suggest about your convictions regarding His lordship? What would it show me about the extent of your hope in Him? What would your displays of devotion for God's Son tell me about the *magnitude* of your vision of Him as Redeemer of all?

It was his Christology that infected the ministry of Francis of Assisi, the great 13th century missionary leader whose initiatives changed the face of Europe. One biographer wrote: "Francis was always occupied with Jesus — Jesus in his heart, Jesus in his mouth, Jesus in his ears, Jesus in his eyes, Jesus in his hands, Jesus in the rest of his members." That sounds pretty radical, to be sure. But since such fervor is our destiny at the Great Day when Christ appears, should we not anticipate at least hearty foretastes of it even now?

Francis did. For him, as for multitudes of saints in every age, to be "alive in Christ" meant to go hard after as much of the revelation of His glory as one could possibly embrace. In his case a whole army of humbly devoted messengers called Friars imitated him as they proclaimed the preeminence of Christ for generations throughout the Church.

THINK WITH ME ...
Why does greater hope in Christ help increase
 passion for His Kingdom?

In its final form our conversion to Christ will climax with nothing less than a full and final *180-degree turn,* a face-on encounter with the Redeemer in glory. In that hour we will be perfectly "pivoted" in the right direction. Christ will totally, thoroughly and forever occupy our attention, our affections and our allegiance.

Which is to say whether here or in Heaven, passion must concern itself with this — the *direction* of our lives. Christ wants us to *face Him.* He also wants us to face the same *future* He faces. Furthermore, He wants us to *follow* Him into that future — to head out with Him as far as He intends to go, both to the ends of the earth and the End of Time. The uniqueness of Christian passion lies in its response to an *eternal Person* as well as to an *eternal hope* guaranteed and encompassed in that Person.

The "direction of affection" — This comes out clearly in two important confessions all Christians must make: First we confess what we do *not* have. This is the passion to *flee from* our own emptiness and bankruptcy into the finished work of Christ. But our second response is to confess what we *need.* This is the passion to *pursue more* of everything Christ is and offers. Fervency for His supremacy makes us want to lay hold of Him more firmly.

Jeremiah (called "the weeping prophet") provides a great case study of the impact of hope on passion. It is found in his book, *Lamentations* (a pretty passionate word in itself). Despite all the judgments and sufferings he and Jerusalem were forced to endure, the promises of God gripped his soul. Time and again in that one little volume, Jeremiah exudes burning zeal for God's eternal purposes with Israel. He exhibits passion for the promised reign of God. Listen: "I call this to mind and therefore I have hope: His compassions never fail, they are new every morning. Great is your faithfulness. I say to myself: The Lord is my portion, therefore I will wait for him. The Lord is good to those who hope in him, to the one who seeks him. Though He brings grief, he will show compassion, so great is his unfailing love" (see Lamentations 3:17 3: 17-23, 24-29, 36-58).

How much more, therefore, should I as a *Christian* exhibit passion for the One in whom God's never-failing compassion has permanently enveloped me — King Jesus? Consider some examples of a grace that's new for us every morning:

- God promises to usher Christians into eternal blessings in heavenly realms with Christ Jesus (Eph. 1). How could we not be passionate for the *gifts* that come through Christ alone?

- God promises to bring every facet of Christian existence under the redeeming control of Christ Jesus (Heb. 1). How could we not be passionate for the *reign* found in Christ alone?

- God promises to conform every believer to Christ's image so that who He is now is what we're about to become (Rom. 8). How could we not be passionate for the *beauty* of Christ alone?

- God promises to magnify His Son's glory among the nations, using disciples like us to do it (Acts 1). How could we not be passionate for the *mission* of Christ alone?

- God promises to move Christians forward victoriously with His Son, consummating the journey in His Day of Glory (Phil. 3). How could we not be passionate for the *praises* of Christ alone?

Every God-given expectation we treasure, drawn from thousands of promises throughout Scripture, was designed to nurture in us deep affections for the One who secures and embodies such hope. He is the key to the future — to *our* future. We can never think too highly of God's Son, nor put too much stock in Him, nor grow too deeply in love with Him. As some traditions sing:

> Standing on the promises of Christ my King,
>   through eternal ages let His praises ring;
> glory in the highest we will shout and sing —
>   standing on the promises of God.

THINK WITH ME ...
What does sagging passion for Christ
tell me about my relationship to Him?

On the other hand, a feeble (rather than fervent) passion for Christ ought to suggest one's outlook is seriously lacking in Kingdom-sized hope. Complacency may indicate we've lost (or, maybe never had) wholehearted convictions about who Christ is, where He leads and what He imparts.

Sometimes our passion founders because we simply never think enough about eternal realities to get very excited about them in the first place. Many forget to stoke heart-fires for the Final Day when every creature throughout all creation will confess the truth that the Jesus who is *our* Lord is also Lord of ALL (Phil. 2).

C.S. Lewis understood. In one of his most oft-quoted sentences he observed: "Indeed, if we consider the unblushing promises of reward and the staggering nature of the rewards promised in the Gospels, it would seem that our Lord finds our desires, not too strong, but *too weak.*" Once we do grasp the *grandeur* of God's promises in Christ, it is impossible to remain neutral or dispassionate toward Him for very long.

As Christ's disciples we ought to live with such holy ambitions for His praises that our lives are inexplicable apart from the great truth of Christ and His supremacy (1 Pet. 3). Hope in Christ ought to *possess* our hearts with zeal for Him as Lord. At the same time this hope ought to *dispossess* us of every other affection outside of our love for Him (2 Pet. 3).

Thus, my thesis for this chapter remains solid:

A comprehensive vision of the supremacy of Christ
will always transform our hope in Christ
into a consuming passion for Christ.

THINK WITH ME ...
What kind of passion is owed to Jesus
as our Supreme Commander?

When an armored division is ready to attack, cautious timidity must not be tolerated among the troops. Reticence at that point indicates either fuzziness of objectives or fear of failure. In either case, if left unchecked it could seal a platoon's doom. Once the order to advance is given, every muscle must engage with full resolve. Every soldier must act as if victory is certain. To waver not only confirms lack of confidence about the outcome but can also permit self-fulfilling prophecy ending in disaster. Hope and passion are intertwined with victory.

In like manner the commanding confirmations of Christ's supremacy — His irrepressible grace, irresistible glory and irrefutable purpose — should be enough to compel each of us to rally to Him for battle without hesitation. He is our Commander-in-Chief. He deserves unconditional trust and undying allegiance (2 Tim 2).

The book of Ephesians, itself a "fireworks" of phenomenal promises in Christ, concludes by enlisting every reader into an army. Our assignment is to hold the ground as we "wrestle with spiritual rulers in Heavenly realms" who oppose the fulfillment of God's purposes in Christ. But what armor are we to wear? The answer Paul gives: *Christ Himself!* We're to don His strength inside us, the breastplate of His righteousness to cover us, His salvation as a helmet to secure us. We're to let our faith in Him serve as a shield to fend off Satanic arrows, while our message about Him equips us for action like boots equip a soldier (Eph. 6).

Talk about being fervent for someone — even obsessed with someone! Paul calls us to engage the battle not only by following Christ as our Leader, but actually by *wearing* Him as both protection and weapon. The radical nature of this intimacy should not surprise us. After all, in every spiritual conflagration, with His Kingdom at stake, He alone is our future, our destiny, our supply, our strategy, our refuge, our commander, and our guarantee that we'll prevail. Why should He not also be our armor? Why should His power and presence not be "all over us"?

St. Patrick certainly thought this was the way to go. The Christian leader exhibited what Brennan Manning terms "magnificent monotony" — a single-minded preoccupation with the majesty of the Lord he loved. In the midst of extraordinary 6th century missionary work in Ireland, Patrick wrote a hymn to capsulate how he turned his hope in Christ into a passion for Christ:

> Christ be with me, Christ within me,
> Christ behind me, Christ before me,
> Christ beside me, Christ to win me,
> Christ beneath me, Christ above me,
> Christ in quiet, Christ in danger,
> Christ in hearts of all that love me,
> Christ in mouth of friend and stranger.

Everywhere Patrick looked Christ held full-orbed fascination for him. To describe what this meant he employed words that one might normally expect a Christian to use if he or she were standing directly before Christ at the Eternal Throne. What does this tell us? Simply put, Patrick's Christology required him to respond to Jesus as his Commander right now, the way he expected the whole universe to respond before long. Surely this good Celtic missionary would endorse the basic thesis of our chapter:

A comprehensive vision of the supremacy of Christ
will always transform our hope in Christ
into a consuming passion for Christ.

So how can the rest of us experience the kind of passion Patrick had? Let's take a look.

Our Passion Defined by Heaven's Passion
(Hebrews 12:1-4)

One of America's best-known worship leaders recently confided to me a personal heartache he faced repeatedly in churches where he ministered: "Often it feels to me as if, for many of our people, singing praise songs and hymns on a Sunday morning has turned into an *affair* with Christ." I was stunned by his imagery. But I was curious.

He continued: "Too many of us are far more passionate about lesser, temporal concerns such as getting ahead at the office, finding personal happiness in a hobby, driving a new car, beefing up homeland security, or rearing well-balanced children. But we rarely ever get that excited about Christ Himself, at least on any consistent basis. Except when we enter a sanctuary on a Sunday. Then for awhile we end up sort of '*swooning*' (he said) over Christ with feel-good music and heart-stirring prayers — only to return to the daily grind of secular seductions to which, for all practical purposes, we're thoroughly '*married*'."

He concluded, "Christ is more like a '*mistress*' to us. He's someone with whom we have these periodic affairs to reinvigorate our spirits so we can return, refreshed, to engage all the other agendas that dominate us most of the time."

Frankly, his insights hit where it hurts! Let's admit it: Our affections for Christ can prove pretty anemic! How frequently infatuation with His exaltation turns fickle and fades! Then where do we go? How do we rehabilitate frail fervency? How do we get our passion back to the level where it needs to be? — where He deserves for it to be?

There are answers. They require us to go back to the *source* of every legitimate passion any of us will ever experience: *Christ's passion for us.*

THINK WITH ME ...
How passionate was the King about you from the beginning?

I made a fascinating discovery the other day. In my *Webster's New Collegiate Dictionary*. Along with a half dozen synonyms for "passion" (like those mentioned above) I found to my amazement that the very first definition it offered read: *"Passion: Christ's sufferings from the Last Supper to His death on the cross."*

Amazing, I thought! A standard secular dictionary is perceptive enough to highlight Christ's unique moment of agony as the measure for human passion — and rightly so. I wonder how many Christians would make the same connection? How many even know why we call our Lord's final days "Passion Week"?

Actually the English word comes from the Latin "passus" meaning "having undergone suffering". In other words, Jesus loved us so much it hurt. He thought He would die — and then He did. He "loved me and gave Himself for me" (Gal. 2). In 2004 many got an eye-full of the extent of His suffering with the release into theaters worldwide of Mel Gibson's graphic but Biblically sensitive portrayal *"The Passion of the Christ"*. Reports were legion about viewers sitting in their seats weeping uncontrollably at the end.

Renowned American pastor Dr. John Piper wrote: "The closer you get to what makes Christianity ghastly, the closer you get to what makes it glorious." That's why we are able to recover consuming passion for Christ (and renounce periodic "affairs" with Him) to the degree we learn to cherish His *Cross.*

The Cross radiates billboard-like the full extent of the passionate heart of the Lord Jesus for all the world to see. This is precisely what the Greek word translated *"portrayed"* means (literally "like a large sign") when Galatians 3:1 states: "Before your very eyes Christ Jesus was clearly portrayed as crucified." Paul called the Cross a marquee advertising Christ's unfathomable love for the Elect — hung before the nations, unavoidable, irrefutable, beyond doubt. Like a jumbotron (the word Paul might use today) in a cosmic stadium, the Cross witnesses to the everlasting costliness of the King's compassion for His subjects, a truth that will be explored and shouted by them forever.

In a very real sense, on the Cross *Christ* was consumed with passion for *me*. He was consumed with His vision for my destiny to display His glory. I thrive in the wake of the Suffering Servant who, with heart-and-soul, embraced to His own demise the totality of my desperate plight in order to rescue me from oblivion (Isa. 53). Because of "the joy set before Him" (Heb. 12) — that is, because of His own great hope about the wonders God would perform for you and me through His death — He willingly bore my sin on the Tree. All eternally bright prospects, all promises in God's Word, were sealed by the Son's "passion" for me — by a substitutionary death that was for me.

So what is to be my response to His deep devotion to me? Answer: I must be willing to experience the same kind of consuming passion *for Him*. I must be willing to value wholeheartedly the same joy He embraced, the same glory for God He died to vindicate, and the same Kingdom advance over which He reigns as the Lamb slain. I must enter into all of that not just for my sake but for *His* sake.

James Caviezel, who played Jesus in Gibson's movie, described in a *Newsweek* interview that he endured quite a bit of personal pain while making the epic — from accidents during the flogging scenes, to hanging on the cross for day after day of filming, to being struck by lightning during one mountainside episode, to dislocating his shoulder while carrying the cross in another scene. When the interviewer asked "Did playing Christ deepen your faith?", Caviezel (already a strongly committed Catholic believer) responded: "I love Jesus now more than I ever knew possible. I love him more than my wife, my family. There were times up there on the cross when I could barely speak because the continual hypothermia was so excruciating. But it was there that I connected with Him where I could have never, ever gone otherwise. I don't want people to see me. All I want them to see is Jesus Christ."

This same passion burned in 18th century German Moravian missionaries as they circled the globe laying down their lives for the Gospel in foreign fields. They marched to the beat of their memorable motto: "The Lamb has conquered. Let us follow Him!" How can Christians choose to advance under any lesser banner? About the year the Moravian movement rallied around the Lamb, Isaac Watts expanded on their vision this way:

> When I survey the wondrous cross
> on which the Prince of Glory died,
> all the vain things that charmed me most,
> I sacrifice them to His blood.

> Were the whole realm of nature mine,
> that were a present far too small;
> love so amazing, so divine,
> demands my soul, my life, my all.

THINK WITH ME ...
Why must the Father's passion for His Son deepen ours?

The full measure of our passion draws upon something else equally profound: How the Father responds in love for His Son. The Father is *also* consumed with infinite love for Him. The Father finds deepest fulfillment (if we might say it that way) in their relationship. He has for all eternity. He too is thoroughly caught up in promoting among the redeemed the adoration His Son deserves. This is the Father's active agenda — past, present, future.

The Father *boasts* in His Son – both in His superior life and in His sacrificial death. The Father celebrates Jesus *glorified*. He holds dear Jesus *crucified*. This is at the core of the Father's passions. Toward His Son His affections display their full measure.

To use human terms the Father is "sold out" to everything Jesus is passionate about. Above all that includes the Savior's unquenchable commitment *to us*. The Father longs to lavish on *us* fervent affections that originally He reserved for His Son. "In love, he predestined us to be adopted as his sons through Jesus Christ, to the praise of his glorious grace, which he has freely given us in the One he loves" (Eph. 1). "Behold, what manner of love the Father has for us, that we should be called the children of God. And such we are. It does not yet appear what we shall be, but we know that when Christ appears we shall be like Him for we will see Him as He is. Those who have this hope in Christ purify themselves, even as He is pure" (1 Jn. 3).

Talk about the zeal of love! "Consuming" does not appear to be too strong a term when applied to the passions found around the Throne. Clearly, mere "infatuation" for the Son has no home in the heart of the Father! So we should not expect Him to allow it among the saints who surround Him with praise.

But there's more. The *Spirit* gets involved in this "love fest".

As the Spirit inhabits believers, He makes it possible for us to experience the unbounded affection shared within the Godhead. Daily the Comforter shapes our vision of the preeminence of the Son so that it corresponds to how the Father sees Him. The nearer He brings us to Christ the larger our King and His dominion appears to us. The larger Jesus appears the more we find ourselves compelled by what we see to keep drawing nearer to Him. Let's call this unending encounter — this Spirit-induced spectacle — hope's *magnificent obsession*. It will be the sole celebration at the Grand Finale just ahead of us (2 Thess. 1). Passion is embedded wherever the Holy Spirit enflames a revived heart. We simply need to learn how to let this love loose in us! Writing about this in the midst of the Fourth Great Awakening, Bessie Head said it well: "O Breath of Love, come breathe within us, renewing thought and will and heart. Come, Love of Christ, afresh to win us. Revive Thy church in every part."

Consuming and Consumed With
(Revelation 5:1-14)

Some may consider phrases like "consuming passion" as little more than stained-glass rhetoric designed by Christian activists to make the rest of us feel guilty about how much we lack. For me the phrase does just the opposite. It *inspires me!* Here's why.

As noted in chapter 3, the word "Consummation" has the word "consume" at its center. That should alert us, we concluded, to two prevailing expressions of any Christ-dominated hope, whether for saints in heaven or on earth, whether in this age or the age to come: (1) *consuming Christ* is one, and (2) *consumed with Christ* is the other. As Paul puts it in 2 Thess. 1:

"On the day He comes to be glorified in his holy people [consuming] and to be marveled at among all those who have believed [consumed with] ... so that the name of our Lord Jesus may be glorified in you [consuming], and you in him [consumed with], according to the grace of our God and the Lord Jesus Christ." Let me apply this perspective specifically to our experiences of loving Jesus right now.

THINK WITH ME ...
How do we go about *consuming*
God's Son day by day?

Augustine's prayer, you'll recall, is filled with palpably earthy images — seeing, smelling, hearing, then *tasting*. Biblical metaphors often describe our relationship to Christ specifically in terms of eating: panting for Him like a thirsty deer does for a stream; feasting on the bounties of heaven; drinking-in His presence, savoring Him like fine wine; supping at a banquet table set in the Kingdom of God.

This brings to mind the Old Testament sacrifices. Offered at the Temple altar, whether sheep or wheat, they were literally to be eaten on the spot, either by a priest or by the worshippers themselves. The very animals whose blood provided temporary atonement for the Israelites' souls doubled as nourishment for their bodies. Eating was an inseparable part of making sacrifice to Jehovah, a demonstration of their true passion for God's glory.

Which brings us to the Eucharist (or Lord's Supper): When we take the cup and bread, the Bible says we "proclaim the Lord's death *until He comes*" (1 Cor. 11). The sacrament announces future triumphs in Christ even as it recalls His ancient agonies. We act out this testimony with others in a very graphic way: eating and drinking. In so doing, we dramatize how we must spiritually "consume" Christ and His finished work on the Cross.

"Consuming Christ" expresses quite well, I think, what Luther meant by a Christian's "sweet desire" for the Savior. It speaks of intense, hope-filled

> **QUOTABLE QUOTE**
>
> How changed are my ambitions! Now I long to know Christ and the power shown by his resurrection: now I long to share his sufferings, even to die as he died, so that I might perhaps attain, as he did, the resurrection from the dead. I keep going on, grasping ever more firmly that purpose for which Christ Jesus grasped me. I leave the past behind and with hands outstretched to whatever lies ahead, I go straight for the gold — my reward the honor of my high calling by God in Christ Jesus.
>
> (PHILIPPIANS 3 —
> PHILLIPS TRANSLATION)

longings that never go away, and are never fully quenched in this life. It is the opposite of the complacency that makes a heart temporarily satiated by the world's deceptive delicacies. Rather, consuming Christ leads to *increased* hunger to see, seek and savor more of Him and His blessings upon our lives. A passion to consume Christ renders us dissatisfied with anything short of Him. It keeps us "greedy for God", as it were — desperate (like starving beggars) for God's promises to become reality in our walk with Jesus.

When I consume a meal, my body ingests the food on my plate to provide power for physical activities. A noontime sandwich is "sacrificed", in a sense, in order to keep me going at the office. This is no less true with the passion to "feed" on Christ daily. In fact Christ is called our Passover feast, a meal we're to munch-on habitually (1 Cor. 5). In John 6 Jesus actually urges us to persist at eating His body and drinking His blood, spiritually speaking, infusing us with eternal life now, so He can finally raise us up to banquet forever at The Marriage Supper of the Lamb (Rev. 19).

From another angle, in Revelation 3 He knocks at the heart-doors of disciples, asking full entrance for the express purpose of sharing a meal with them in intimate conversation. Solomon pictures this poetically: "He brings me into His banqueting hall, and His banner over me is love" (Song of Solomon 2). Again God appeals through Isaiah: "Come, all you who are thirsty, come to the waters; and you who have no money, come, buy and eat!" (Isa. 55)

In the imagery of one New Testament parable, the Father sends out invitations to come and dine with His Son saying: "Come to the table, for everything is now ready" (Lk. 14). The Kingdom of God knows nothing of a McDonald's-style fast food, drive-thru window. Ours is a sit down banquet with an unlimited menu set before us now ("in the presence of my enemies" says Psalm 23) as well as in Eternity. Christ comes to us as "appetizer, entrée and dessert" combined! He permits us to make Himself the main course for now, just as He will be our only necessary provision in the Consummation when it comes (Lk. 13). Supremacy means Jesus is totally sufficient to feed the hunger of God's holy people forever. No wonder Peter writes: "Like newborn babies, crave pure spiritual milk, so that by it you may grow up in your salvation, now that you have tasted that the Lord is good" (1 Pet. 2).

Theologian Jonathan Edwards preached this truth one Sunday in 1742 to his Massachusetts congregation, concluding: "There is an admirable conjunction of diverse excellencies in Jesus Christ." His sermon proceeded to lay out how justice and grace, glory and humility, majesty and meekness, obedience and dominion, resignation and sovereignty all converge in an infinite display of Christ's sovereignty. Then he described candidly for his people his own zeal for such a vision: "The excellency of Jesus Christ is suitable food of the rational soul. The soul that comes to Christ feeds on this, and lives on this. It is impossible for those who have tasted this fountain, and know the sweetness of it, ever to forsake it."

In *The Weight of Glory* C.S. Lewis concurred, modifying the metaphor. He likened this experience to the transfixing beauty of a sunset and then described how the viewer lingers, trying to absorb every fading ray of its splendor. Similarly (to paraphrase Lewis): We do not want merely to see the beauty of Christ. We want to be united with the Christ we see, to pass into Him, to receive Him into ourselves, to bathe in Him, to become part of all He is. That's the passion to consume Him. It's one major step toward the cure of the crisis of supremacy.

THINK WITH ME ...
How do we go about being *consumed with* God's Son day by day?

Most of us have heard how believers were hounded by their enemies during the opening centuries of the Christian era. As countless martyrs perished in Roman arenas, they showed a holy boldness that spectators could not refute. With fierce hope in their own resurrection Christians bore testimony to all tormentors of their unwavering conviction that the Lord of Life had power to reclaim His people by giving them victory over the grave. So potent was this witness that Roman officials often would burn the martyrs' remains after the spectacle and scatter the ashes in an attempt to remove all possibility of being raised from the dead. But pagan defiance of Christian passion proved utterly futile in turning back the advance of the Gospel. The persecuted were consumed *with* Christ which meant, at times, they were consumed *for* Him — literally.

Consumed *with* Christ — this is the other side of a passion incited by our hope in His Kingdom. But what does this mean? Here are two metaphors that have helped me understand.

In order to consummate a *business transaction* a contract needs to be signed. Financial investments are committed in writing. Legally, once that happens there is no turning back no matter how costly the agreement becomes later on. It is legally binding. We have "consummated the deal", we say. Our resources are now consumed with the projections spelled-out in the contract.

In the same way, Christians become so confident about Jesus — about all He promises us and His ability to carry it off — that we invest everything we have into who He is and what His Kingdom is all about. *No turning back* no matter what the cost. Hope in God stirs in us courage to press on without reservation to make Christ and His Kingdom our singular venture. Our contract with Him is *consummated*. We are *consumed with* Him and all He offers.

Or consider how a man and woman consummate *a marriage*. Though they exchange their vows in front of many witnesses, they seal those vows privately in a most profoundly meaningful way by sexual union in the honeymoon suite. It involves an unforgettable exchange. There is nearly total abandon of two bodies and souls to each other — an unconditional giving of everything that's precious, with no holding back. They "consummate their love", we say. With vigorous affection they are *consumed with* the promises they bring to each other as lovers.

For Christians there must be *no holding back* either. We must consummate our commitment to the Lord Jesus Christ. We must allow ourselves to be increasingly enraptured with Him, to become more intimately involved with Him. We must desire to be thoroughly abandoned to the destiny He offers us as His beloved ones. Daily we must embrace Christ as our bridegroom, abandoned to every hope of glory He holds out to us. In this way our relationship with Him is consummated. Increasingly we can be *consumed with* our love for Him.

Both illustrations reinforce how fervency for Christ's supremacy renounces any reservations. Neither implies reckless enthusiasm or uncontrollable compulsions. Rather, both involve two sobering realizations: As happens in consummating investments or marriages, our hope in the Lord Jesus requires that there be *no turning back* and *no holding back*. We are saved to be consumed with Him!

We may use eight hours a day for sleep, eight for work. The rest may be given to prayer and service, for friends and family, or in recreation. But all 24 hours are claimed for *eternity* as far as God is concerned! In God's eyes every day is designed for the Kingdom of His dear Son. He wants every moment to be consumed with Jesus. After all, "our God is a consuming fire"

(Heb. 12) — which means He never stops burning! Why then should we?

If the Consummation could be defined as Christ-obsession *universalized*, then daily discipleship should be defined as Christ-obsession *personalized*. We're to become obsessed, utterly preoccupied with what's on His heart — *fanatics* for His glory (from the Latin "fanum" meaning "temple dweller", referring to a Roman so in love with his deity that he never left the idol's presence day or night).

"Decisive devotion" — that's my all-time favorite description for practical daily heart-felt zeal for our Living Lord. "Decisive devotion" reminds us that Christ-obsession will always call Christians to a *purpose* — a purpose beyond themselves. It will point to a passion for God's promises that takes us somewhere, that results in strategic (decisive) action to advance the work of Christ's Kingdom. "Decisive devotion" suggests that affections for the Savior must become *ruthless*. We must resolve to eliminate everything in our lives not compatible with the focus, fulfillment, fullness and fervency of His supremacy.

> ## QUOTABLE QUOTE
>
> **If anyone would come after me, he must deny himself and take up his cross and follow me ... whoever loses his life for me and for the gospel will save it.**
>
> (MARK 8:34-3)
>
> **No one who has left home or wife or brothers or parents or children for the sake of the kingdom of God will fail to receive many times as much in this age and, in the age to come, eternal life.**
>
> (LUKE 18: 29-30)

In another well known prayer Augustine expressed the same radical love for Jesus:

> He loves too little
> who loves anything together with Thee
> which he loves not for Thy sake.

THINK WITH ME ...
What might a congregation look like
if it was controlled by consuming passion?

As we visited in his office, the senior pastor of the world's largest church shared with me a most fascinating answer to a question I'd held for a long time: "Is there one Biblical text that summarizes how the explosion of Christ's work in your congregation came about?" He responded: "One passage defines better than most others the kind of people that make up many of our 700,000 members" (as well as the 40,000 elders who serve them!). He read to me Matthew 11:12: "The Kingdom of God is forcefully advancing, and people of force are laying hold of it."

"Mirroring God's forceful efforts to promote His Son's glory," he said, "true seekers of God's purposes display a similarly aggressive spirit toward the cause of Christ. Seizing God's Kingdom mission, they grab onto His sovereign initiatives and go with *Him*. Within my own city this passion has taken the form of thousands of cell groups. They operate on virtually every city block. They pray for, and reach out to, nearby friends and neighbors to bring them to Christ. That's how we've grown from 100 to nearly three quarters of a million in just 40 years!"

The good news is that every congregation has been redeemed for this same kind of adventure, not necessarily in terms of numbers but certainly in terms of dynamics. Local churches everywhere are invited to pursue the advancement of the Kingdom by prayerful dependence on, and righteous cooperation with, our Lord. I've met such seekers all over the world. I've found them not only in mega-churches in Korea and Brazil but also in unassuming house churches, like those that blanket so much of China. They are abiding in Christ, fervently bearing the abundant fruit He has promised (Jn. 15).

Such passionate churches are not necessarily more spiritual. They are simply more *restless*. They sense impending breakthroughs. They are convinced that since Jesus reigns, God is always ready to unveil exciting expressions of His promises in Christ for those "laying hold" of His global cause. They have moved beyond curious fascinations with the Savior to insatiable hunger for more of His Kingdom. More often than not such churches are filled with Messengers of Hope, Prisoners of Hope and Vanguards of Hope — terms which we will discuss in the final chapters of *Joyful Manifesto*. Each term implies that in many different ways every Christian can express a consuming passion for Christ and His glory.

THINK WITH ME ...
How did Paul exhibit the consuming passion
we can all experience?

Writing at times from dismal dungeons, Paul referred to himself as "a *prisoner* of Christ Jesus". But there was so much more to Paul's fanaticism than sitting hostage in dank Roman cells. He was chained to a triumphant vision, the vision of Christ's cause spreading worldwide. For him it was a blessed bondage!

Looking at God's grand designs up ahead for which Christ laid hold of him, Paul made an extraordinary choice. He discounted everything about himself that the world prizes in order to seize the opposite. As he put it, he wanted to "be found in Christ" so as to "know Him, in the power of His resurrection and the fellowship of His sufferings" and then to "press on to win the prize for which God has called [me] heavenward in Christ Jesus." Furthermore, he reassured the Philippians, all maturing believers should expect God to teach them to be equally passionate in hope (Phil. 3).

In fact he went so far as to present himself as "Exhibit # 1" of the devotion *every* Christian was meant to display: " ... whatever you do, do all for the glory of God.... For I am not seeking my own good but the good of many, so that they may be saved. Follow my example, as I follow the example of Christ" (1 Cor. 10:30-11:1).

More concisely than anywhere else Paul outlines in Colossians 1:24-29 (see the accompanying "Quotable Quote") the consuming nature of his hope in Christ — the vision that captivated him, the desire that drove his whole mission — the fervency for Christ's supremacy that God wants burning in all of us.

THINK WITH ME ...

How do you respond to these probes on passion?

Maybe it would be helpful for you (or your small group) to pause right here to reflect on a few questions most of us have never been asked before. They might help pinpoint where your passion for Christ needs to grow stronger in order to confront and cure the crisis of supremacy in your life or the life of your church.

QUOTABLE QUOTE

Now I rejoice in what was suffered for you, and I fill up in my flesh what is still lacking in regard to Christ's afflictions for the sake of his body, which is the Church. I have become its servant by the commission God gave me to present to you the Word of God in its fullness — the mystery that has been kept hidden for ages and generations, but is now disclosed to the saints. To them God has chosen to make known among the Gentiles the glorious riches of this mystery, which is Christ in you, the hope of glory. We proclaim him, admonishing and teaching everyone with all wisdom, so that we may present everyone perfect in Christ. To this end I labor, struggling with all his energy, which so powerfully works in me.

(COLOSSIANS 1:24-29)

1. What usually absorbs my affections on a daily basis? What genuinely preoccupies me? What are my main obsessions?

2. What challenges arouse my interest? What causes inspire my commitment? Where do my true ambitions lie?

3. What do I consider to be the pinnacle of my life-purpose — the reason I was created and redeemed in the first place?

4. In what ways has a vision of the glory of God's Son and the hope this guarantees ignited in me fervency for His supremacy?

5. How has Christ's passion for me ennobled all my passions and desires toward Him?

6. How has the Father's passion for His Son stirred up my own desire to love Christ so much more?

7. Do I ever fear being labeled as one who has become too fanatical about Jesus or too radical for Him? Why is that? What is it I really fear?

8. How do I intend to increase a life of decisive devotion toward my Redeemer — a passion that makes a difference in what I say (as a messenger), how I grow (as a prisoner) and what I show (as a vanguard)?

9. Am I prepared like Paul to pour out my life for an awakening in the Church to Jesus for *all* that He is? How will I confront the crisis of supremacy in my life or my church so that Jesus might receive the greater praise He deserves? What might this cost me?

Come! and Come!
(2 Corinthians 11:1-6; 13:5)

In Revelation 22 Scripture concludes with two invitations (almost commands) related to a Christian's life of passion. Interestingly, both invitations involve the word *"Come"*:

- **COME!** (vs. 17) ... One voice urging us is spoken by *Christ* to believers. He invites us to enter His presence in order to *consume* Him. He invites us to drink deeply of all He has to offer of the Water of Life which He actually is for us. It is a call to embrace His *centrality* in our lives and churches.

- **COME!** (vs. 20) ... The second invitation is issued back to Christ from *believers*. We welcome Him to invade us so fully that we are *consumed with* the splendors of the revelation of His righteous rule over Heaven and earth. It is a longing for richer experiences of His *supremacy* in our lives and churches.

Consuming passion — whether expressed by God's Son or God's people — cries out in unison with God's Spirit: *"Come!"* Both cries draw directly from the breadth and depth of ALL Jesus is. Both cries rise from a largeness of vision for God's Son — from joy in His centrality, but most of all from passion for His supremacy. It is the only response that matches the magnitude of the hope His Kingdom inspires.

If that's the destiny to which Scripture points us, should our personal, daily walk with Jesus be shaped by anything less than a desire for the same two "comings" — our coming to Him (consuming Him) and His coming to us (consumed with Him)?

Come! In this one-word invitation the streams of centrality, supremacy, hope and passion converge.

As we bring **Volume One** to a close, I don't know about you, but personally, *I feel like shouting!* These past chapters have drawn us to mountain peaks of Jesus' majesty many have never climbed before. What a view! And the trek is not over. There's more to come. **Volumes Two and Three** will continue to help us recover all the hope we are meant to have in Him.

Before we press on, maybe it's time for all of us *to shout!* As one familiar chorus puts it: "Shout to the Lord all the earth, let us sing. Power and majesty, praise to the King. Mountains bow down and the seas rejoice at the sound of Your voice ... Nothing compares to the promise I have in You!"

To help you "shout" I've developed a little reading called ***Interlude I: Hope-Filled Christians Arise!*** I suggest you take time to reflect on it right now. (You may find it works best if you read it aloud.)

After that, please join me in **Volume Two.** There we will begin to unpack more fully *"The Crisis of Supremacy"* that forms the greatest challenge the Christian movement faces in this hour — the key culprit in the curtailing of a consuming passion for Christ.

INTERLUDE I

Hope-Filled Christians, ARISE!

Hope-filled Christians can arise within any nation, from any race, at any age, out of any denomination. They are first of all *Christians* — that is, "Christ's ones" — preeminently committed to Christ Himself. He sets the devotion, the direction and the destiny for their lives, and they know it. At the same time these Christians are *full of hope*, hope in the supremacy of God's Son.

WILL YOU ARISE to be a Hope-filled Christian?

Those who do arise can't help but delight in the supremacy of God's Son because:

- He **sums up** before them the heights of God's promises, for now and forever. Therefore, they prize the *focus* of His supremacy.

- He **consummates** for them the breadths of God's promises, for now and forever. Therefore, they profess the *fulfillment* of His supremacy.

- He **approximates** within them the depths of God's promises, for now and forever. Therefore, they pray for the *fullness* of His supremacy.

- He **consumes** them with a passion for God's promises, for now and forever. Therefore, they pursue the *fervency* of His supremacy.

- His lordship acts as a sharp lens for **refocusing their vision on Him.** (Focus)

- His lordship creates a launch pad for **releasing their mission for Him.** (Fulfillment)

- His lordship opens up healing streams for **renewing their life in Him.** (Fullness)

- His lordship forms a firebrand for **re-igniting their love toward Him.** (Fervency)

WILL YOU ARISE to be a Hope-filled Christian?

For those who do arise it means:

- **They intend** for Jesus to be known as "all in all" for themselves and every believer — all they see, all they hope in, all they love and live for, all they wait and long for, all they pursue, all they worship and praise, all they share with each other as well as with the nations.

- **They believe** that God is ready to act, not intending for His people to remain indefinitely unaware of all Christ is, or to remain deficient in hope and passion toward the glorious greatness of His Son.

- **They are praying** for God's Redeemer, King of Heaven, to revisit His people in power, to reveal to them greater dimensions of the Father's promises, in order to re-engage them passionately with who *He* is, where *He's* headed, what *He's* doing and how *He's* blessed.

- **They are preparing** themselves and others, with great expectations, for the wonderful awakening to the Lord Jesus Christ that's coming to the Church in answer to many prayers.

- **They are willing** to reshape their daily discipleship, so that it becomes *Person*-driven — dominated by God's Son for ALL that He is and for ALL that He promises.

- **They are committed** to speak about His supremacy at every opportunity, as part of a Campaign of Hope where they live. They are convinced this is strategic for the re-awakening of the Church to Jesus as Lord as well as the restoration of its hope and passion toward Him.

WILL YOU ARISE to be a Hope-filled Christian?

Those who do arise want to join in a Campaign of Hope because they realize:

- A *deficient vision* for Christ's glory plagues today's Church.

- A *desperate loss of hope* in Christ's glory exhausts today's Church.

- A *pervasive loss of passion* toward Christ's glory weakens today's Church.

- A *diminished worship* of Christ's glory impoverishes today's Church.

- A *debilitated pursuit* of Christ's glory shames today's Church.

WILL YOU ARISE to be a Hope-filled Christian?

Those who do arise will join in a Campaign of Hope designed to:

- *Re-convert* God's people back to Christ and to the full extent of His supremacy.

- *Re-awaken* God's people to the hope shaped by the glory of Christ's supremacy.

- *Re-deploy* "Messengers of Hope" who proclaim to God's people the hope found in Christ's supremacy.

- *Re-capture* "Prisoners of Hope" who devote themselves to living in the light of Christ's supremacy.

- *Re-activate* "Vanguards of Hope" who prepare themselves to get strategically involved in increased manifestations of Christ's supremacy in churches, communities and among the nations.

WILL YOU ARISE to be a Hope-filled Christian?

If so, from here on out:

- *Hope in Christ's supremacy* will become the dominating perspective of your life.

- *Passion for Christ's supremacy* will become the driving motivation of your life.

- *A Campaign of Hope* will become the decisive ministry of your life, as you help fellow Christians recover all the hope and passion that Christ's supremacy is meant to inspire for them.

VOLUME TWO

THE CRISIS OF SUPREMACY

Where Is The Hope We Must Recover?

"My hope is built on nothing less
than Jesus blood and righteousness ...
On Christ the solid rock I stand
all other ground is sinking sand.

When all around my soul gives way,
He then is all my hope and stay ...
On Christ the solid rock I stand
all other ground is sinking sand.

In every high and stormy gale,
My anchor holds within the veil ...
On Christ the solid rock I stand
All other ground is sinking sand.

When darkness veils His lovely face,
I rest on His unchanging grace ...
On Christ the solid rock I stand
All other ground is sinking sand."

— *Edward Mote*

6

THE GREATEST CRISIS OF ALL

How Did We Come to This?

Some crises can break a heart. Some crises can stun a nation. Some crises can alter the course of a whole generation.

We live in an age of crises. I had no doubt of this as I stood near my home on a mountain crest called Washington Rock Park. From this vantage point in 1777 George Washington monitored the movements of British troops in the New Jersey valley. From this rock one can see the entire skyline of New York City just 20 miles away. On this September 11 evening what I saw, however, recalled funeral pyres I'd witnessed along India's Ganges River. Smoke billowed to blanket the horizon from the steel tomb *TIME* magazine called "The Twin Terrors".

In the fall of 2001 a whole nation gazed at a crisis unlike anything we had ever seen before. It was a crisis both global and personal — one that has permanently changed the outlook of millions worldwide. As a result, noted U.S. foreign policy scholar Walter Russell Mead predicted for *TIME* that he now believes the 21st century will be remembered as the "Age of Apocalypse". He wrote: "People feel that the veil of normal, secular reality is lifting, and we can see behind the scenes, see where God and the devil, good and evil are fighting to control the future. They believe history is accelerating, that ancient prophecies are being fulfilled in real time." In the rise of global terrorism our nation now faces a crisis of apocalyptic proportions.

There's another crisis looming before us that outweighs all others. It is not unrelated however. But it carries far more sobering Biblical consequences than all others. This second "ground zero" is more sobering, potentially more catastrophic than collapsing towers in lower Manhattan. It is more decisive as far as eternity is concerned. It is the crisis this chapter (and this whole manifesto) is commissioned to address head on, as we:

- **Define why our greatest crisis must be identified as a "crisis of supremacy".**

- **Review how the crisis of supremacy has manifested itself the past 2000 years.**

- **Survey some of the ways the crisis is unfolding inside the Church today.**

- **Look at the impact the crisis may be having on *your* congregation.**

- **Revisit the contrast between a Monarch and a mascot.**

- **Describe how the Ascension gives us leverage to confront the crisis.**

Our Greatest Crisis in an Age of Crises
(1 John 2: 18-19; 4:1-6)

The crisis of which I speak is not, first of all, among unbelievers. It is found *inside* the Church of Jesus Christ. More ruthless than attacks on New York City and Washington, D.C., this crucible carries repercussions for an entire generation of God's people. It impacts ultimate issues touching the Kingdom of God and its advance among the nations. It affects *believers* at the heart level. Its ominous overtones echo the Battle of Ages.

Have I stated the issue too strongly? I don't think so. Before the close of this chapter I think you'll agree.

THINK WITH ME ...
What should we call the overarching crisis
we face inside the Church?

Some have called it a "crisis of *Christology*." As mentioned in the opening chapter, I prefer to call it "a crisis of *supremacy*". Either way, the challenge has everything to do with how fully Christians serve the claims of God's Son. And that, in turn, has everything to do with how effectively we minister to the nations in the face of every other threat, including "Terrorism, Inc."

As we started to explore in chapter 1, the "crisis of supremacy" rises inside the Church wherever Christians are paralyzed by a significant shortfall in the way they understand the person of the Son of God, His leadership in the Purposes of God, His distribution of the Resources of God and His honor from the People of God.

This disquieting discrepancy has blindsided far too many believers around us. It has sabotaged a host of unsuspecting disciples. It has preempted the vitality of our worship, prayer, community life and ministry outreach. In too many cases it has numbed our daily walk with our Redeemer. Above all, it has robbed God of His rightful praise through His people among all peoples.

More terrifying than Muslim extremists on the path of Jihad or the proliferation of weapons of mass destruction, the world's most precarious danger is actually manifested in many churches as a lack of adequate vision for the Lord of Glory. Every other crisis faced by the nations impinges, directly or indirectly, on how *Christians* deal with the primary one, the one *we* face, the crisis within our own ranks.

> **QUOTABLE QUOTE**
>
> **The erosion of Christ-centered faith threatens to undermine the identity of evangelical Christianity ... real revival and genuine reformation will not be built on flimsy foundations.**
>
> (DR. TIMOTHY GEORGE)

John tells us: "Anyone who runs ahead and does not continue in the teaching about Christ does not have God" (2 John). Period. No exceptions. Could anything be more debilitating for the global cause of Christ than this verdict? Even *Christians* can come up short on how they view and value the supremacy of God's Son. They can also renege on living out before the world the implications of His supremacy.

This shortfall is as old as the first Easter morning. Recall Mary Magdalene's despair before the empty tomb. Weeping over a Master she thought had been reduced to a stolen corpse, she stood paralyzed with fear and confusion and hopelessness. Her "crisis" sprang from doubts about His promise of ultimate power over the grave. Suddenly ... Jesus — alive and well! — confronted her, probing her: *"Who are you looking for?"* (Jn. 20). That's the right question to put to any believer, any time. It can be asked in a variety of ways, of course. For example, on that same Easter other disciples struggling with similar despair were approached by angels challenging them: "Why do you seek the living among the dead? He is not here; he has risen" (Lk. 24). It was like saying: "Do you really know *who* it is you are seeking?"

Surely, no more incisive inquiries confront the global Christian community in the 21st century than these: *Who* really is the Christ you are seeking? Do you know *why* you are seeking Him? And do you know for sure *how* and *where* to find Him?

Let's lay it on the table. How many Christians do you know who are fully alert to God's Son for ALL He is in the glory of His supremacy? How many Christians in your congregation may require, in fact, a *re-introduction* to Him on a number of fronts? Drawing from the last four chapters, how regularly do we worship Him as our:

- Sovereign Son of the Father, reigning at His right hand forever and ever?

- Triumphant Victor over every foe — sin, death, Hades?

- Glorious Conqueror, the dominating personality for all ages to come?

- Unequivocal Commander of heaven's hosts, ready to obey His every word?

- Indisputable Judge of peoples and nations, to whom all must give an account?

- Undeniable Ruler of history, overseeing its path and its outcome from beginning to end?

- Incomparable King of an Empire that will ultimately fill creation with His power and piety?

- Irreplaceable Head and Heart of a people whom He has bought with His own blood?

- Reigning Redeemer of a Church universal, militant and triumphant, sending His salvation to the ends of the earth?

- Supreme Lord in this moment just as fully as He will be Supreme Lord at the End of Time?

If our churches are experiencing the "crisis of supremacy", we must not run from it. It's far too critical. We must expose the ambivalence God's people harbor regarding *who* we seek, *why* we seek Him, and *how* and *where* we expect to find Him. Let's confront the crisis and cure it!

THINK WITH ME ...
In what sense might the Church suffer an "identity crisis"?

Many in today's Church wrestle with the ultimate *"identity crisis"*. It's not so much a misunderstanding about our own identity (although in the end this is also affected). Rather, it is a disturbing confusion about *Christ's* identity. It is our blindness to the glory of the One we claim as Lord. Many in our congregations suffer needlessly from insufficient exposure to the Grand Hope we are meant to have in God's Son. Too few disciples are growing in their knowledge of "Christ in you, the hope of glory" (Col. 1) — Christ as the summation, consummation, approximation and consuming passion of Christian hope (the way **Volume I** presents Him).

Here's my observation from years of traveling the evangelical movement: Many in our ranks need to heed something akin to the angelic announcement that shook the disciples on Resurrection Day. To paraphrase the Gospel record:

> Why are you seeking the Living One in all the wrong places?
> The Christ you claim to follow is not to be found
> where you have been looking.
> Great news: He's so much more than you thought He was!
> He's risen. He's Lord. He's going ahead of you.
> He's the hope of all the victories to come!
> Open your eyes to His *truest* identity
> (and, find your own in the process).

The Church's "identity crisis" over Jesus surfaced dramatically following the attacks of 9/11. Initially, national polls revealed a groundswell of renewed interest in the Gospel of Christ that fall. Attendance in churches rose significantly. In some places the increase was as much as 50% in one month. People gathered to pray, sometimes filling whole stadiums. Sobered by predictions of more attacks to come, multitudes were attentive to Scripture like never before.

QUOTABLE QUOTE

Since September 11, 2001 I have seen more clearly than ever how essential it is to exalt explicitly in the excellence of Christ crucified for sinners and risen from the dead. Christ must be explicit in all our God-talk. It will not do, in this day of pluralism, to talk about the glory of God in vague ways. God without Christ is no God. God-in-Christ is the only true God and the only path to joy. If we would see and savor the glory of God, we must see and savor Christ.

(Dr. John Piper)

And yet, a year after the 2001 Al Queda invasion the long-term impact of 9/11 on the spiritual condition of Americans was negligible. Research revealed that church attendance actually declined to levels lower than before that September day. One pollster concluded that 95% of Americans had not been permanently affected for Christ at all. Apathy toward evangelism prevailed in most quarters. Giving to all charities, especially outreach ministries, was significantly down. Divisiveness among churches did not abate. On one survey over half of our fellow citizens concluded a year later that the message of Christ was decreasing in its influence. Far too often seekers looking for answers felt themselves unwelcomed when they brought their shattered hearts to local congregations. As one Biblical scholar put it, instead of helping spawn a culture-wide awakening to Christ, after 9/11 most Christians ended up simply "reshuffling the chairs on what felt like a sinking ship".

But this story is only a tip of the troubling truth. The hour has come to wake up fully to Christ. *There's urgency to this emergency!* We must take up the challenge with all the resolve and courage the Holy Spirit inspires within us. Everything precious to us and our churches is at stake. The very advance of Christ's mission in this generation is on the line.

THINK WITH ME ...
What is our most strategic response to the "crisis of supremacy"?

The crisis of supremacy is so intractable and so pervasive that it will never be cured with half-hearted measures. It requires nothing short of a new kind of *reformation* — a re-forming, if you will, of vision about the *whole* Christ throughout the *whole* Church that helps us embrace *whole*-heartedly the *whole* extent of His glorious reign for the *whole* world.

Increasing numbers of Christian leaders have sensed the need for such dramatic changes. At a gut level many suspect reformation is precisely what the Spirit is moving the Church toward, on many fronts. All that really remains to trigger a fresh stirring to action may be nothing more than a clarion call — a *manifesto* — to unleash among us (what I have chosen in this book to term) *"A Campaign Of Hope"*.

Such a summons will have little impact, however, unless it spreads far and wide. The message must be delivered by an ardent army of heralds inside the Church. A "Campaign of Hope" must enlist Christians like you and me who care whether Christ receives the glory He deserves among His people. It is we who must proclaim a larger vision of the King throughout the Body, holding nothing back as we do. In fact, that's precisely what *this* manifesto envisions: A magnif-icent movement of messengers — a Church flooded with Christ-proclaimers!

Stated simply, my premise is this: There's nothing more strategic that any of us could choose to do at this moment, for the advance of the Kingdom of God's dear Son before the nations, than to promote a vision for the full extent of Christ's lordship among each other as believers.

QUOTABLE QUOTE

Jesus, King of Kings, I am yearning for the day your kingdom comes in power, for even momentary impressions of your dominion leave me breathless. My mouth cannot keep silent — I must tell of your mighty acts and make known the glory of your kingdom. We need your reign. Nothing else will do.

(TRICIA RHODES)

Each of us must begin right now to make a decisive difference in our churches by what we say about the Savior to disciples who sit with us every Sunday. We must call *Christians* to re-engage with our Sovereign around the grand scope of the hope His supremacy secures.

Be encouraged about this. The potential for renewal is unparalleled. God's miracle-working grace has already preceded such a campaign. Already the Spirit has rekindled countless Christians waiting in the wings, hungry for a fresh message about the greatness of God's Son, eager to band with us to exalt Him in new ways. Already, God is raising up a multitude of willing proclaimers poised for action. I've met with thousands of them around the world the past two decades. And there are literally millions more.

These "change agents" must be mobilized as quickly as possible. First, they must be recruited as *Messengers of Hope*, equipped to present to fellow

Christians a more dynamic vision of Jesus that calls them to be re-converted to Him for ALL that He is. Second, they must discover the thrill of growing as *Prisoners of Hope* as they seek to live out the promises Jesus secures for them. Third, they must form *Vanguards of Hope,* working together to overthrow the spiritual lethargy that plagues so many of our people along with showing other believers how to serve Christ in anticipation of Kingdom breakthroughs. These three steps toward mobilization comprise the "Campaign of Hope" I'm calling for. (Chapters 9-12 look at them in depth.)

Before we take on a cause with such monumental consequences, however, we need to investigate more thoroughly the source and nature of this crisis. Because ... it has haunted God's people for a very long time.

A Crisis Resurfacing Across the Ages
(Colossians 1:22-2:10)

Let's stake out some historical background to understand better what's happening today. The concept of a crisis of supremacy is not a novel notion. Every generation has had its own versions. As is well known, for example, Thomas Jefferson so fully rejected Christ's claims to divinity and lordship that, while serving as our third President, he sat down one night with razor in hand to create his own Bible. He literally cut out of the pages of the Gospels everything he found offensive about the greatness of the Savior until he arrived at a version he called "The Philosophy of Jesus of Nazareth". Jefferson's was certainly one form of the "crisis of supremacy"!

The need to restore the Church's vision for the kingship of Jesus has been perennial. Through the centuries Christians have been challenged repeatedly to think about and respond to God's Son in fresh, new ways. As a case in point, in the 2nd century of the second millennium, two major armies of hope-filled proclaimers surfaced in Europe to confront the crisis. First came the Franciscans. Coupling a life of simplicity with their message of hope, they brought a fresh vision of Christ into the cities of Europe. Close behind arose the Dominicans whose whole religious order was formed for the express purpose of preaching renewal in Jesus throughout the Church. Eventually thousands of these "mendicants" (Latin for "beggars") were traveling across the Continent and beyond, pursuing one ambition: to bring Christians back to Christ through a vigorous message of His supremacy. One might differ over certain aspects of their interpretations of Scripture, but there's no arguing with their conclusion: Whenever there's a crisis in how God's people relate to His Son, it's time to send forth heralds of hope to re-awaken believers to Him for ALL that He is.

> ## QUOTABLE QUOTE
>
> **Christology is the true hub round which the wheel of theology revolves, and to which its separate spokes must each be correctly anchored if the wheel is not to get bent.**
>
> (DR. J.I. PACKER)

Franklin Graham, son of the famed evangelist, assumed a similar posture. For years he consistently counseled the Church not to back off from making the deity and lordship of Christ a primary issue everywhere, and at all times. Then in 2001 while praying the inaugural prayer for President George W. Bush before an august body assembled on the Capitol steps, he "dared" to close his petition by saying "in the name of Jesus Christ". Those six little words ignited a firestorm of controversy. Finally, Graham answered his critics by publishing a bestseller titled simply *The Name*. In it he made his case for the uniqueness and greatness of the Lord Jesus and for a Christian's obligation to confess His lordship at every opportunity.

Graham held common cause with the two preaching societies of the Middle Ages, realizing that a failure to proclaim Christ for *all* that He is, especially among His people, debilitates Christian worship and witness and in turn discourages vision for His mission to the nations. That same "power failure" has become, once again, the greatest crisis of *our* times.

But the waxing-and-waning of vision for our Lord is not an inevitable cycle of history. Understanding past and present struggles can help us uncover effective, more enduring cures for the crisis in the 21st century. History's insights can strengthen our resolve to pass on to the next generation a panorama on the glory of God's Son that's more thoroughly Biblically consistently.

THINK WITH ME ...
What are some ways that the crisis has manifested itself over the ages?

Right from the get-go the Gospels record a variety of occasions when every one of the first disciples, not just Mary, stumbled over their Master's true identity. They doubted Him, challenged Him, denied Him, betrayed Him, abandoned Him, gave up on Him. Following His resurrection, however, they were *reconverted* back to Him as their victor. They found in Him a Kingdom-sized hope that looked, ever after, with expectancy toward the end of the earth and the End of Time (compare Lk. 22 and 24 with Acts 1).

This revolution didn't stop with the Twelve, fortunately. A Pharisee from Tarsus wrestled with his own crisis about the Messiah. This led him to hunt down and imprison early believers. Then came his life-changing Damascus road encounter when Paul asked Heaven's Highness: "Who are you, Lord? ... What would You have me do?" (Acts 9). The vision of God's Son, along with the answers to his questions, seized him and became the catalyst for most of his epistles, spanning three decades.

Paul challenged legalists at the Jerusalem council who argued that Christ alone was not adequate for salvation (Acts 15). He confronted Peter's compromising retreat from Gentiles in Galatia because it raised suspicions about the sufficiency of God's Son (Gal. 2.) He exposed Gnostic enticements that invaded the little church in Colossae because they suggested that Jesus was merely a stepping stone into larger mysteries. He patiently nurtured naive new believers in Rome who desperately needed to understand the radical nature of their union with Christ. In all these situations the Apostle found himself caught up in a marvelous mission — restoring *Christians* to a higher view of the supremacy of the person and work of the Messiah.

In its opening centuries the Church tackled numerous other Christological heresies, such as Athanasius' refutation of the Arians' claim that Christ was created and not eternally God. Some early confrontations were precipitated by the desire of *all* parties, interestingly enough, to preserve for God's Son in their own ways the highest possible honor as Lord of all. This can be seen in the 2nd century controversy with Marcion over his teaching that Christ was *too* exalted as God (!) to ever become fully human. It took the councils like Nicea (A.D. 325) to resolve many of these tensions. Fourth century bishops concluded that if Christ were not both fully human and fully God at the same time, He could not be the supreme revelation of God to us — which would mean that to worship Him as supreme Lord would be nothing short of blasphemy. Dealing with these arguments often resulted in major Confessions and Creeds that still serve us well today, such as the Apostles Creed or the Nicene Creed, each of which reaffirmed an exalted view of the Savior.

Challenges to the supremacy of Christ resurfaced frequently over ensuing centuries. These ranged from Constantine's pragmatic co-opting of the cross symbol in A.D. 324 to solidify his empire; to multiple bloody Crusades bent on reclaiming the Holy Land for the name of Jesus; to Medieval "passion plays" that incited violence against Jews more than love for the Lamb; through a variety of demoralizing papacies in the Middle Ages; to the deadly veneer of a politicized Christianity in post-Reformation Europe; on to the existential appeals of 18th century Unitarianism in New England; and to the emergence of Christo-paganism among scores of African tribal groups in the 19th century; up to the current Jesus Seminar whose regular dissertations, media blitzes and mass-marketing savvy has recast Christ for millions as a mere mortal at best. These and a file full of other "winds of doctrine" (as Ephesians 4 describes them) have mocked the truth about God's reigning all-righteous Regent. Spiritually, they have paralyzed the Church in one generation after another.

The 20th century, it should be noted, saw its share of assaults on the supremacy of Christ. Take the writings of theologians like Germany's Bultmann. The professor reasoned that most of what we know about Christ is based on myths of human concoction. Dismissing any appeal to the uniqueness of God's Son, he undermined confidence about the ministry for thousands of clergy. To this add what some called the "Anglican Unitarians", so preoccupied with Christ's humanity that they were forced to discount His deity. Next, from Latin America emerged "Liberation Theologians". They convinced multitudes of impoverished Christians to champion Jesus as their ultimate "freedom fighter". Characterizing Jesus as one of the world's outcasts — abused and powerless — this camp intended for Him to inspire the poor everywhere to liberate themselves from oppression (if necessary, through armed revolution).

QUOTABLE QUOTE

The Church has become uncertain of Jesus, even uncomfortable with Him. We instinctually sense that the foundation of salvation is in trouble. And it is. Church history is sadly replete with a tendency to forsake Christ. The Church has a long history of discomfort with Christ. The maneuvering of Christ to the margins of our culture — and to the margins of many of our churches — may diminish the status of Christianity (Christendom). At the same time, it also puts believers in a position to experience the transforming power of the gospel in new ways, for the gospel is most empowered when it is least encumbered.

(DR. JAMES R. EDWARDS)

THINK WITH ME ...
Who is Jesus in America, and how much
hope do Americans place in Him?

This quick overview hasn't even begun to unwrap the crisis of supremacy as it has evolved within U.S. culture. Boston University professor Stephen Prothero in his *American Jesus,* revisited a pantheon of Christ-images that Americans have concocted over the past two centuries, including (what he calls) the Enlightened Sage, the Laughing Jesus (life-affirmer), the Sweet Savior (feminine-like and intimate), the Manly Redeemer (muscular Christianity), Superstar, Elder Brother, Black Moses, and Oriental Christ (a Dali Lama personage). All of these, as Prothero documents, have transformed the Son of God into what he calls a "national icon", ubiquitous throughout popular culture. He's "the man nobody hates", allowing Americans of all religious persuasions to "embrace whichever Jesus fulfills their wishes". Dr. Robert Orsi of Harvard University concurs, stating that in American life "imagining and re-imagining Jesus has been one way men and women have engaged the challenges of their times".

Americans live in what sociologists conclude is the world's most religiously diverse nation, ever. Although the United States houses more Christians than any other country in human history, recent statistics show our country currently is home to more than 2,000 mosques and 600 Hindu congregations, with at least 200 Buddhist centers in Los Angeles alone. In many ways the Church here finds itself enveloped by a post-Christian world where Buddhism, Hinduism, Islam and Christianity have been blended into a religious "stew" from which everyone is welcome to sup. This has profound implications for how Jesus is ultimately perceived, even by believers.

How well, do you think, is the testimony of our Master prevailing within the pantheon of gurus offered on the *BeliefNet* website? What is the future for a growing movement in some quarters called "The Christ Myth", insisting that Jesus is merely a Xerox copy of one primitive pagan god that became the primary model of all other gods — Egyptian, East Indian and Christian? Is it even "politically correct" anymore to propose in public that Jesus is Lord, triumphant over all other faiths and the only hope of the universe?

Published within a few months of Prothero's book, a professor from Yale University issued a complementary treatise: *Jesus in America.* Richard Fox confirmed Prothero's critique in his subtitle: "Personal Savior, Cultural

Hero, National Obsession". Fox wrote (based on broad surveys): "Jesus, for most Americans, is the God-man who offers forgiveness, succor, and hope ... he makes them feel better by loving them and he makes them feel worse by reminding them of their failure to love him and their neighbors." It appeared that Jesus exists to meet *our* needs. Such a Jesus has retained "multiple identities" throughout our land, Fox concluded. He is frequently "liberalized into a God of pure love" by those rejecting old-fashioned constraints to boundless freedom. Though the majority of our citizens indicate to pollsters they believe Jesus is God, was born of a virgin and was raised from the dead (nearly 70%), "he is so pervasive culturally that some representations of him have no apparent religious reference at all". Maybe you've noticed that crucifixes have become the new hip fashion statement.

Returning a moment to *American Jesus* (borrowing words from its subtitle), we need to ask ourselves: How did the Son of God became "a national icon"? Though Americans may never reach consensus on who Jesus really is, Prothero found that in a country divided by race, ethnicity, gender, class and religion, Jesus mattered to most because He functions as our "common cultural coin". In a recent Presidential debate one candidate actually named Jesus as his favorite "philosopher". Unfortunately, Prothero admits, "this cultural Jesus is only a *shadow* of the Biblical Son of God".

It came as no surprise, frankly, when a Pulitzer Prize winning ex-Jesuit priest authored a best-selling book with the disturbing title: *Christ: A Crisis in the Life of God*. In it, to critical acclaim, he reasoned that at the opening of the 1st century "God was under extreme duress", weary with eons of ineffective restraints over His enemies. So, He came up with the last-ditch idea of Jesus to try to salvage His reputation. In His failed effort to defeat His foes, He used Jesus to implement a new strategy: co-opt their rebellion with sacrificial love. "Jesus" resolved God's crisis over His own *impotency* (is the claim). Jesus was God's final stab at effecting some kind of meaningful change in the world.

Jack Miles' book simply highlights the ages-long struggle for the soul of the Church. Do we have a crisis in the life of *God?* Not at all! Rather, the Church regularly hosts deadly disturbances in

> QUOTABLE QUOTE
>
> **The bottom line here is that Jesus of Nazareth saw himself as the Son of God. Whatever we do afterwards, we must first decide what to do with this. If he was correct, we must fall down and worship him. If he was not correct, we must crucify him.**
>
> (DR. DONALD MACLEOD)

the life of *God's people*. It is a crisis over how we define the supremacy of God's Son. It shapes how we see Him and seek Him — and finally, how we speak of Him.

The Same Crisis Infects Today's Church
(Luke 19:37-45)

We were forewarned by Jesus long ago to expect this tug-of-war: "For many will come in my name claiming 'I am the Christ' and deceive many" (Matt. 24). Decades later the Apostle John gave the same alert when he wrote: "This is the last hour; and as you have heard that the antichrist is coming, even now many antichrists have come" (1 John 2). (Hint: For "antichrists" think "antacid", as in tablets. These teachers tried, often subtly, to *neutralize* the impact of the glorious greatness of God's Son.)

Well, the crisis of past ages has returned with a fury! And it may be manifesting itself *inside* the Church more than anywhere else.

Not long ago at an annual national gathering of Christian leaders, a furor erupted when one pastor stood to challenge the convention with the question "So, what's the big deal about Jesus?", suggesting there may be many other avenues for salvation. His question highlighted the fundamental struggle among God's people as we plunge into the 21st century. The Church is once again facing an insidious dismantling of Biblical Christology across the board. Once-settled certainties about Christ and His preeminence in the universe are receding, even among evangelicals. And the outcome of the trend is not at all certain.

THINK WITH ME ...
What are some ways this crisis is making
its appearance inside the Church?

Surveys suggest that on many Sundays sermons heard across the evangelical spectrum major more on helping parishioners grapple with challenges in daily living than on grabbing hold of the hope Jesus brings. Emphases on the pragmatics of spiritual survival can gut unwittingly the impact of Christ's lordship. Too often we've encouraged each other to incorporate

Christ into our lives when and where *we* feel the need for Him. We mimic Him to mold ourselves into more caring communities. We invite Him to enhance the fulfillment of self and family. We run to Him to sustain our sanity in a dog-eat-dog world. But more often than not, for all practical purposes, God's Son finds Himself discounted when it comes to expectations regarding direct and decisive displays of His dominion over our everyday experiences.

Even among Bible-based Christians there is evidence of a significant rise in the number of "nominal" or "vague" evangelicals. Many in our churches have a *form* of evangelicalism (they can recite the date they were "born again", let's say) but deny the primacy of the One who presides over them. Though active in Gospel-minded churches, many have found ways to bypass the fuller implications of Jesus' claims. Compared to other kinds of lukewarm Christians, nominal evangelicals may be in double jeopardy: Why? Because, according to Jesus, those who profess to "see" but really don't, end up twice as blind (Matt. 13 and Jn. 9).

Among the emerging generation of younger American Christians, researchers have uncovered a shift from rational, logical, systematic outlooks on spiritual realities to longings for experiential, mystical engagements with the "divine". In the words of Dan Kimball, consultant on post-modern evangelism, "personal preferences have replaced predetermined truth". Diminishing discoveries about Christ's dominion have often led by default to a more "me-centered" approach to Christianity. Therefore, steeped in modern religious pluralism, a significant number of Christian young people have succumbed to the culture around them. In a recent finding superficial faith among youth from evangelical families has left only 35% claiming to be "absolutely committed" to Christ as *supreme* Lord and Savior. In fact, most research indicates that the percentage of those who profess faith in Christ in North America, 30 years and under, is smaller (3% to 6%) than at any time in our nation's history. Such trends raise serious implications for dealing with the wider spiritual emergency our churches face.

QUOTABLE QUOTE

In the United States, Jesus is widely hailed as the "King of Kings." But it is a strange sort of sovereign who is so slavishly responsive to his subjects…The American Jesus is more a pawn than a king, pushed around in a complex game of cultural (and countercultural) chess, sacrificed here for this cause and there for another.

(Dr. Stephen Prothero)

The crisis of supremacy embroils whole denominations as well. Even as I write, some are debating the doctrine of Christ's nature and role as Lord. One of the largest denominations just acquitted its head bishop of heresy — for the fourth time! — even though he openly denies Christ's divinity, atonement and resurrection. More radical feminists, promoting a movement called "Re-Imagining God", have encouraged us to pray to a feminine Jesus whom they call "Christa". Uneasiness about the uniqueness and exclusivity of Jesus also dominates the front lines of world evangelization. Numbers in the missionary community are rethinking the primacy of the Savior due to the onslaught of fierce resistance from the ancient faiths of Islam, Hinduism and Buddhism. *Time, Newsweek,* and the *U.S. News* have regularly weighed in with front-cover reports on these painful religious controversies.

In his book *Surveying the Religious Landscape* George Gallup, Jr. concluded his research on contemporary religious culture by suggesting that the main shift taking place is not so much an aggressive resurgence of base paganism. Rather, he identified a subtler surrender to what he called "syncretism". In short, many inside our churches are attempting to combine a Biblical faith with neo-pagan trappings. They are mixing their seeming devotion to Christ with various superstitious practices, or Eastern religion rituals, or false doctrines like reincarnation. Maybe that helps explain the popularity of *Religion for Dummies*. Compiled by a priest and a rabbi, it offers "a spiritual buffet" (as they put it) to help their readers "sample faiths from all over the world".

So, which Lord *do* we worship when all is said and done? In a nation "infatuated with Jesus" (in Fox's words) — actually with many "Jesuses" distilled from a rainbow of cultural impressions, including African American, Latino American, Korean American, Anglo American, Irish American, Native American, Italian American, Chinese American — is the *real* Son of God the one most Christians follow here? Our historically unprecedented religious diversity has tempted far too many U.S. believers to "pick and choose" from a spiritual smorgasbord piled high with Christian and non-Christian delicacies. In the end, I fear, many have unconsciously pieced together a deity that's a far cry from the Biblical Sovereign whose name "is above every other name" and before whom "every knee shall bow and every tongue confess that 'Jesus Christ is Lord' " (Eph. 1 and Phil. 2).

Is the evangelical movement infatuated with the *real* Redeemer — with a Jesus who claims to be "all"? Let me ask it another way: Throughout the land how regularly do we publicly, intentionally and consistently proclaim the supremacy and glory of our Lord, confessing Him boldly as the One who has trumped every other form of spirituality Americans embrace. Do we even talk this way about Him among *ourselves?*

THINK WITH ME ...
What are other tangible ways to measure the crisis among us?

It should be no surprise that Western Christendom is experiencing a precipitous drop in new recruits for ministry. This is due, in many cases, to the private doubts of millions inside our churches about the *finality* of Christ's lordship over all things human or divine, both at home and abroad. What does it say about modern evangelical Christology when it is statistically verifiable in America that there is an epidemic of people in pastoral leadership who are living in quiet desperation? Every month 1,400 clergy leave the ministry. Every week 53,000 parishioners forsake the Church never to return. According to the National Network of Men's Ministries, nearly 70 million American men never darken a church door. However, 85% of *those* men have chosen to leave a church they once attended! And consistent church attendance continues its disturbing decline among the 27 million men who remain members.

Over 80% of U.S. congregations are either stagnant or dying. With every passing year there are approximately 3,000 fewer churches in America than there were the year before, with so many closing their doors. In proportion to population there are fewer than half as many churches today as there were only a century ago. In fact, the United States is considered by some to be one of the largest unchurched nations in the world, in a class with China, India, Indonesia and Japan. According to the book *Lost In America,* some studies suggest that the United States is so extensively unchurched that if the non-Christians in our land were to form a nation by themselves, it would become the largest mission field in the English-speaking world, the fifth largest among all nations.

Should not such facts send forth strong warnings? Shouldn't these developments challenge us, at the very least, to re-examine in what ways the glory of Christ Himself is currently *mis*-understood and *mis*-communicated *inside* the Church by those who claim His name?

Tragically, countless Christians live in a theological fog. Biblical illiteracy in many churches is confirmed consistently by national polls. A Barna Research survey found that only 4% of Americans come at life with anything

QUOTABLE QUOTE

In Jesus Christ the reality of God entered into the reality of this world.... Henceforth one can speak neither of God nor of the world without speaking of Jesus Christ. All concepts of reality which do not take account of Him are abstractions.

(DIETRICH BONHOEFFER)

comparable to a Biblical worldview, with nearly half of the nation's pastors exhibiting the same deficiency (while other research confirms that 40% of clergy admit they are addicted to another topic: pornography!). Barna reflected: "The most important point is that you can't give people something you don't have."

This may help explain why millions of Americans who declare themselves as Christ-followers also concede, when surveyed, that Jesus struggled with sin like the rest of us. When it came to temptation He suffered defeats like every other human. Another national survey found that only 41% of those who call themselves "born again" believe God's Son is the one true way for salvation. This dissipation of delight in our Lord's exclusive rule as Earth's Redeemer reinforces Charles Colson's conclusion: The Church is "dumbing-down" its message, moving from a Word-driven vision of Christ to one that is image-driven and emotion-driven.

On one other front we need to ask: How truly adored is the Head of the Church when, in some parts of Christendom, multi-millions of dollars in lawsuits have been brought against predator pastors? Thousands — both Catholic and Protestant — have sexually abused a multitude of children under their care — and done so while their superiors often stood by in silence. The *Boston Globe* reported, as one example, on the court appearance of a 73-year-old priest. He protested that for years his sodomizing of young boys was merely an attempt "to show them that Christ is human." He went on: "I felt that by having this little bit of intimacy with them it would make them feel like they were being with Jesus." When whole segments of the Church start declaring financial bankruptcy due to the magnitude of court-mandated monetary penalties, maybe it is time for all of us to ask ourselves: What has *really* become "bankrupt" here? Our coffers? Or our *Christology*?

All this upheaval is happening despite the fact U.S. churches have spent over $500 billion *on ourselves* the past ten years, primarily to shore-up the internal commitment to Christ of our parish members. What does *that* suggest about our crisis of supremacy?

Sociologist Thomas Wolfe gives one answer in his ground-breaking volume *The Transformation of American Religion*. In it he concludes that although Americans are still a pervasively religious people, our form of godliness is neither culture-shaping nor life-arresting. He finds little in evangelical churches that's different from the world around us. Wolfe refers to this as the *"toothlessness* of evangelicalism", suggesting this condition is due to how we have "ignored doctrines, reinvented traditions, switched denominations, redefined morality" even as we have allowed our call to verbal witness to be downgraded to a non-intrusive lifestyle, at best. This conclusion was reinforced in 2004 by a Family Research Council report. In it blame for much of the downward slide of American culture was laid on congregations' lack of passion for the Kingdom, which rendered them mute and uninvolved in combating "depravity run rampant".

Coming back to Wolfe's thesis, theologian John Armstrong adds: "Truly we evangelicals have created a religion for dummies." Unfortunately, the story elsewhere in the world has proved equally discouraging sometimes. There are additional warning signals we must not ignore.

THINK WITH ME ...
In what ways does this crisis manifest itself
in the Church worldwide?

According to mission statistician David Barrett, 91% of what we think of as global Christian outreach to the totally unevangelized does not target non-Christians at all. Frequently missionaries are forced to minister within nominally Christian populations, desperately trying to re-convert them from a waffling, superficial devotion to Christ as Lord which our own efforts reproduced.

This tragic condition is especially evident in "Christianized" Europe. In some nations fewer than 3% attend any church. It would be difficult to separate the relationship between these dramatic downsizings and the rampant deficiency of vision for Christ and His Kingdom. Recent surveys of clergy in Great Britian, where church attendance is at an all-time low, verified that over 50% of these leaders don't believe in Jesus' supernatural birth, with fully one third actually denying He rose from the dead! One of the marks of Pope John Paul II's final years has been his repeated sharp warnings of the "loss of Europe's Christian memory and heritage", of a growing secularism and indifference that "rules as out of order" any references to Christ. "This has sown widely," he observed, "a growing fear of the future." According to Greater Europe Mission, 14 of 27 countries are less than 1% Christian. Things are actually so spiritually "burned over" that more Christ-followers can be found in Islamic countries than in Europe today.

The Church in many parts of the Two Thirds World, though clearly more dynamic than the Church in the West, at times fares little better. The World Evangelical Alliance concluded that Asian, African and Latin American churches face what WEA called a "crisis of cultural evangelical-ism". Multiplied congregations have retained only a residue of vibrant hope in a sovereign Savior. Christian leaders in Latin America and the Caribbean, for example, suggested that among the 53 million that claim to be evangelicals, there are signs of serious "decline and defection". Recent research indicated that significant numbers are forsaking Christ altogether. Said one leading Latin missiologist: "Defection has been higher than most leaders ever thought it would be." In many cases a pastoral strategy devoted to meeting people's material needs, he said, has left them hungry for more of Christ, making them vulnerable to any other teaching that claims to fill that longing.

What about China, where glowing reports on church growth have thrilled us in recent decades? Without question the spiritual harvest there has been unprecedented over the past half century, for which we must praise God. There may be as many as 100 million there who claim to be Christian. Yet we must be circumspect about these apparently amazing results. A senior China research specialist at the U.S. Department of State for 25 years and a deeply committed Christian scholar, warned recently in a publication from the U.S. Center for World Mission: "This revival looks statistically incredible, but it is spiritually vulnerable." From personal observations, she suggested that millions of Chinese Christians may be "just one unanswered prayer away from moving on to another religion". Why? Some mass conversion methods, she notes, have left a shallow faith for many. Efforts for "quick results" and "short cuts" have created a revival movement that she describes as possibly "a mile wide and an inch deep". Many, it appears, may need to discover a fuller vision of the glory of Christ's true greatness if the momentum is to continue. Even in the midst of a Chinese "harvest" a crisis of supremacy threatens.

THINK WITH ME ...

Where do you see the crisis manifesting itself in your church?

I don't need to multiply statistics and stories to convince you about the challenge we face, however. It is quite *self-evident* when you come right down to it. To see what I mean, try this experiment.

For the next 30 days monitor the conversations that go on among your Christian friends. Listen as well to what you hear taught in Sunday school or in your small group Bible study. Ask yourself two questions: (1) How often do I hear the name of the Lord Jesus mentioned *at all* (apart from quoting one of His sayings, or a phrase at the end of a prayer, perhaps)? (2) And whenever I hear His name, if I do, are the things said about Him intended in any way to magnify more clearly His glory as God's Son? — or to celebrate more fully the advances in His global cause?

In other words, do the Christians around you ever spend time talking to each other about the *supremacy* of God's Son (by whatever terms they use)? If so, do they speak in ways that indicate a desire to deposit with each other *larger* visions of who He is and how He reigns? Whether conversing between worship services, or in a weekly home Bible study, or at a Saturday men's breakfast — do the Christians you know seek to promote among themselves greater *hope* in Christ and His Kingdom? Do they freely talk about issues that draw on Biblical teachings regarding the focus, or fulfillment, or fullness or fervency of His supremacy (see chapter 1)?

After one month if your congregation is like the vast majority where I've applied this test, I think you'll be stunned by what you hear (or, shall I say, by what you *don't* hear). Jesus taught that words reveal what's in a person's heart. So your findings will provide "proof enough" there *is* a disturbing drought of Biblical vision and passion for the Lord Jesus among the Lord's followers. It is real. It is serious. It is spiritually debilitating. And it is *now*!

The Divine Conquest by A.W. Tozer raised a sobering speculation. The author viewed the mid-20th century evangelical movement with this question: "May not the inadequacy of much of our spiritual experience be traced back to our habit of skipping through the corridors of the Kingdom like children in the market place, chattering about everything, but pausing to learn the value of nothing?"

Good question! Let me slightly re-phrase Tozer's probing to ask a similar question of the Church in the 21st century:

May not the Church's loss of hope and passion toward Christ

be traced back to how we chatter on about everything else,
but rarely pause to draw one another into the larger vision
of the supremacy of God's Son?

THINK WITH ME ...
What is the crux of the evangelical movement's "identity crisis"?

In his popular book *And The Angels Were Silent* pastor/author Max Lucado
discussed his concerns over what he called a "computerized Christianity" in
which God has become the "ultimate desktop", with the Bible as the maintenance manual, the Holy Spirit as the floppy disk and Jesus as the 1-800
service number! When we replace the glorious greatness of God's Son —
when we ignore the focus, fulfillment, fullness and fervency that His
supremacy sets before the whole universe — we can end up with "computerized" forms of discipleship. Push the right buttons, insert correct data, format
rituals and (Voila!) print out spiritual success. He concluded: "God hates it. It
crushes his people. It contaminates his leaders. It corrupts his children." Max
Lucado has captured the crux of our identity crisis. It's a predisposition that
should set off alarm bells inside every congregation in the country.

Lucado's comments remind me of the intriguing metaphor we discussed
at the opening of chapter 1. There I describe my most disturbing observation
while traveling the evangelical movement: In many parts of the Church
Christ has become our *mascot*.

For me this one metaphor represents more effectively than any other the
damage that's been inflicted by the current crisis of supremacy. What's so
deceptive about the image of a mascot is that it seems to encourage us, at
first. It suggests excitement, strategies, camaraderie, celebration, victories.
It promises a form of discipleship richly appealing in our event-oriented
churches. But it is utterly counterfeit. It promotes the *opposite* of what our
Lord's supremacy actually means for His people. Eventually this deceptively
subtle shift — moving from Christ as our Monarch to Christ as our mascot —
diverts our hearts from Him. It diminishes our hope toward Him. It depletes
our passion for Him. It destroys our effectiveness in His global cause.

We call Him "Lord", but do we end up *welcoming* Him as Lord? When
you get right down to it: Do we give Him much more honor than what is
expressed by Europeans for national royalty? In Denmark, Norway, Great
Britain, for all practical purposes, kings and queens are treated more as
highly favored figureheads, kept around for ceremonial purposes, to

embellish philanthropic events, or to lend dignity to national celebrations. But they have no final authority over day-to-day activities in government or marketplace. Similarly, Jesus gets feted Sunday after Sunday — highly praised and cheered. Displays of devotion toward Him rarely linger into Monday, however. Though we may return to Him at moments when the demands of the week become too much for us, we engage Him too seldom on a daily basis as the One on whom depends the destiny of all nations – not to mention our very own future — and before whom every life stands or falls.

How about *you:* Are you captivated by His Royal Highness? Or, for all practical purposes has He evolved in your thinking into someone much more akin to a figurehead? Observing your daily walk with Him, what would a fellow believer conclude? Which model of our Lord's role — Monarch or mascot — would they find at work in your life? None of us should be too quick to answer. Let me tell you why.

For most of us the crux of this Christ-related identity crisis boils down to our misunderstanding of His *supremacy* in contrast to His *centrality* (discussed in chapter 1). Clearly both concepts are Biblical truths. Both speak to the glory of God's Son and His place in the universe. Both fill out the true meaning of this manifesto's title *"Christ is all"*. However, "centrality" when isolated from "supremacy" can unintentionally relegate Jesus' place in a Christian's life to the "mascot" position. When my commitment is *only* to keep Him at the center of who I am, where I'm headed, what I'm doing and how I'm blessed, I'm just a few steps removed from assuming He is there primarily for *me*. That perspective, if left to stand alone and taken to its logical conclusion, will eventually recast Him as my "mascot" — the "ultimate desktop" (as Lucado says) ready to print out my demands.

"Supremacy", on the other hand, incorporates the idea of "centrality". Then it lifts things to a higher level. It has "Monarch" written all over it. To profess my Savior as preeminent automatically requires that I see myself caught up in who He is as the Son of God, where He's headed in the

> ## QUOTABLE QUOTE
>
> **Unbelievers do not see Christ as their greatest treasure. *Neither do most believers.* We live as blind people, chasing after the light we can see — the satisfaction that blessings bring — and not valuing the light we cannot see — the glory of Christ. More is available to us in Christ than we dare imagine. We settle for so much less. We taste Him so little.**
>
> (Dr. Larry Crabb)

Purposes of God, how He's imparting the Resources of God and what He receives from the People of God. Without qualification, the truth of Jesus' reign demands that my eternal existence remains all about *Him*!

But, a special blessing awaits me if I am willing to make Him my Monarch, not my mascot. My *own* "identity crisis" gets resolved. I am united with the Lamb-on-the-Throne. I have an unspeakably hope-filled destiny, not only because I'm wrapped *around* Him (centrality) but also because I'm wrapped up *in* Him (supremacy). Peter, you may recall, vividly describes this: "(God) has given us new birth into a living hope through the resurrection of Jesus Christ from the dead, and into an inheritance that can never perish ... (sufferings come so that your faith) may be proved genuine and may result in praise, glory and honor when Jesus Christ is revealed ... Therefore, prepare your minds for action; be self-controlled; set your hope fully on the grace to be given you when Jesus Christ is revealed" (1 Pet. 1). With such promises tied to the Monarch of millennia, why would any of us ever settle for a mascot?

THINK WITH ME ...
Why is the *Ascension* key to rebuilding our vision of Christ as our *Monarch?*

Someone has said that the most neglected holy day in the Church calendar is Ascension Day. Think about it. Multitudes celebrate Christmas, Lent, Good Friday, Easter, Pentecost, plus a host of dates dedicated to key saints (like St. Patrick). But most of our congregations have given little, if any, thought to the one event when Christ was crowned King of the Universe — that moment, 40 days after His resurrection (Acts 1), when He ascended into Heaven to vindicate His supremacy once and for all. Yes, there really was a day, like today is a day, when He was bestowed a Name above every name before which all nations, demons and angels must bow (Eph. 1; Phil. 1; Rev. 5). Can you remember any specific Sunday when your church commemorated the coronation of our Savior?

Why is this question so important? Quite simply, it strikes at the very heart of the short survey we've just conducted. It explains the critical nature of the 2,000-year-old battle over the true parameters of Christ's sovereign glory. What we've discovered is that frequently from its inception — and especially in recent decades — the Church has been required to choose between two radically different perspectives on God's

Son. Evangelical theologians describe it as a choice between a "Christology from *below*" versus a "Christology from *above*". Each time the choice was made, the outcome shaped a generation's message about Him and service to Him.

Think of it this way: We must, of course, embrace the truths about the humanness — the Incarnation — of Jesus (this is the "below" perspective). But the "above" approach attempts to filter every facet of our vision of the Redeemer (including the Incarnation) through one primary lens: *Who He is, at this very hour, seated upon the Throne of Heaven.* It invites us to see Him as "God of God" — exalted to the Father's right hand, incomparable in authority and majesty, reigning over earth and Heaven — and to regard everything else in this light: worship, prayer, service, fellowship, the gifts of the Spirit, evangelism and missions, lifestyle choices, applications of Scripture, our struggles with sin, as well as the macro "sea-changes" (political, religious, economic and otherwise) among the nations.

The four Gospels, it must be remembered, were written just a few short decades after Jesus' ascension. Their take on the life of Jesus was selected, arranged and composed in a climate where the universal lordship of Jesus had become the daily diet of discipleship. Matthew, Mark, Luke, John — they reflected on Jesus' earthly life and teachings as those who (with all believers) had already been raised up with Him, seated with Him on His throne, invested with His authority and living for Him in realms of glory. (Compare passages like Romans 6 with Ephesians 1 and 2.) As vital as the "below" vision of Christ's earthly ministry was (and is), the Incarnation was not the final word for New Testament Christians. Even His atoning sacrifice was viewed through the lens of who He is *now*, the Anointed One (Christ) to be honored "above".

Even so today, whether studying Scripture, singing Sunday praises, witnessing to neighbors, serving Christian relief works or sharing the Gospel with unreached peoples, the scope of the Son's sovereignty — His person, His position, His purposes, His praise — must dictate what we think and feel and seek and choose and do. Ultimately, above all else and before all else, it must define how we *hope*.

Sometimes I call this springboard for living "*super*-spective" (a word coined by Ralph Winter). The Ascension helps Christians put everything into its *proper* perspective. Our Sovereign longs to fill our horizons with a view of Himself that is *super* — overflowing with the realities of His wonder, greatness and grandeur as Lord of all. To do this, He invites us to interpret all of existence, ours and creation's, perched on the footstool of His throne. The opening chapters of *Joyful Manifesto* **(Volume I)** help you regain this vantage point — this *super*-spective — as it lifts you from one mountain range of His glory to the next, from one promise of His Kingdom onto another.

Personally, I'm looking for the time when throughout every Christian tradition we will annually celebrate Ascension Sunday, making as much out of that day as we do out of Christmas, or Good Friday, or Easter. Only because of *that* day does Jesus' incarnation, crucifixion, and resurrection have any permanent redeeming impact.

I envision Ascension Sunday as not only a day of "pomp and praise" but also as a sacred season of *repentance* — a time for turning from specific ways we have reverted (individually and corporately) to treating Jesus as a mascot; a time for calling the Church to be re-converted back to Him as our Monarch and, in the process, to recover all the hope in Him we are meant to have.

QUOTABLE QUOTE

We need a Jesus who can explain the Christ of faith: one big enough to account for Jewish hostility and Roman fear; one big enough to explain why he became the subject of such a book as the Gospel of John; one who made such an impression that people easily believed that he had risen from the dead; such a colossus that within a few years of his death those who had known him best were identifying him with Yahweh and laying down their lives rather than refrain from worshipping him; a figure of such universality that his church has had a multi-ethnic, multi-cultural appeal without precedent in the history of religion. What manner of man was he: able to overcome the scandal of his crucifixion and exert such an influence on human history that to this day scholars eagerly discuss his impact not only on religion but on art and science, politics and literature? (He alone) renders Christianity explicable.

(Dr. Donald MacLeod)

Looking Ahead: The Elephant or the Flies?

The crisis of supremacy — we've just begun to expose it for what it really is. The next two chapters expand on the theme in two directions. They study the crippling effect it has on a Christian's loss of *hope* and loss of *passion*.

Before you turn the page, however, let me make you a promise:

Standing in front of an elephant cage at the zoo, one can choose to look at the elephant. Or, one might simply study the size of the flies buzzing around it. Similarly, as we dig deeper into the crisis — even when our findings are thick with flies, so to speak — I intend to keep all eyes on the *elephant*. The "bugs" uncovered in chapters 7 and 8 may appear to be fairly ominous. But in the end, compared to the One who never ceases to dominate every crisis with Himself they are *only flies*. Reading on, you'll discover that our Lord Jesus Christ (the "elephant in the room") remains at the forefront — as well He should, since the crisis is about Him and the cure is in Him! The goal of this manifesto is nothing less than the restoration of a giant-sized portrait of Christ for ALL that He is — a picture to help put everything else, including every other crisis, in proper perspective.

Not long ago Os Guinness related a story about one person's desire to see the "Elephant". It took place in a weekly Bible study on Capitol Hill involving a number of Senators. When asked to open a session in prayer, one of the newest believers among them caught everyone by surprise. In childlike faith he said: "Father, may all the Hindus confess that Jesus Christ is Lord. May all the Muslims confess that Jesus Christ is Lord. May all the Jews confess that Jesus Christ is Lord." Then he ended: "And, may all the *Christians* confess that Jesus Christ is Lord!"

Said a thousand different ways, that brief petition summarizes the chief agenda I've heard expressed all across the land, in all sizes of prayer gatherings for church renewal. It's the prayer *Joyful Manifesto* is designed to help answer. Each of us needs to plead: "May all *Christians* confess — and ultimately *proclaim* — Jesus Christ as Lord, the *supreme* Lord of His Church!"

When that prayer is answered, something wonderful will happen! A re-awakening of fresh hope and passion toward Christ will be released throughout all parts of His Body. Believers will once again engage with Him, not only as Lord over global concerns but as the One who is *their* "all in all" — as the One supreme over *them* forever.

The greatest crisis of all will be dealt a fateful blow when the "Elephant" re-takes the room and rules!

7

WHY DON'T WE HOPE?

The Crisis of Supremacy
and
Our Loss of *Hope*

On New Year's Eve 1999 a multitude gathered in St. Peter's Square to welcome the Third Millennium. Pope John Paul II challenged the pilgrims to enter the 21st century determined to "conquer fear" and "rediscover the Spirit of hope". At the same time near my home, in Times Square the Millennium Ball made of Waterford crystal and dubbed the "Star of Hope" descended the pole at the stroke of midnight. Thousands of revelers cheered the future while a billion others watched by television across the globe. Millennium celebrations everywhere — in Beijing, at the Pyramids, on the Thames — unanimously emphasized similar anticipation about the coming decades.

> QUOTABLE QUOTE
>
> **Behind the debris of our self-styled, sullen supermen, there stands the gigantic figure of one person, because of whom, by whom, in whom, and through whom alone mankind might still have hope: the person of Jesus Christ.**
>
> (G. K. CHESTERTON)

Instinctively every human being knows hope is what both individuals and civilizations need to survive and flourish. In the same sense hope is key to the vitality and impact of Christians in any generation.

However, if not grounded in a comprehensive vision of Christ — if not shaped by everything He is, seated on His throne — every promising outlook we profess can quickly dissolve into uninvited *crises* of hope. Our one reliable refuge against every onslaught of hopelessness and despair is our bedrock conviction about the inexhaustible riches of His supremacy (Eph. 3). Whenever diminished hope overtakes a believer, it is usually a sign of a far greater challenge: *the crisis of supremacy.*

But there's also good news each time hope is shaken! The experience can bring a blessing *if* the setback drives Christians to re-examine what we really believe about the glory of God's Son — and *if* in turn this wakes us up to all the hope we are meant to have because Jesus is Lord.

So, what is the state of hope in the Church today? Let's find out by surveying four vital topics:

- **Everyone's critical need for hope and its role in our survival.**

- **The loss of hope within our generation and how this impacts Christians.**

- **The loss of hope *inside* today's Church and three major sources of it.**

- **The need for Christians to take seriously this struggle for the soul of the Church.**

Everyone's Critical Need for Hope
(Psalm 102:1-22)

Philosophers suggest there are at least three seminal issues everyone must confront to find deeper meaning for their lives:

- What must I *know*?

- What ought I to *do*?

- What may I *hope*?

In many ways, our answer to the third question precludes our response to the other two. It is *hope* that sets the agenda for both our "knowing" and our "doing". Life's priorities are determined mostly by what lies ahead, where we believe we are going and how we expect to get there.

THINK WITH ME …
What is the relationship between hope and human survival?

When coalition forces liberated Iraq from the brutal tyranny of Saddam Hussein, they found millions of traumatized people debilitated by years of ruthless indoctrination, fearful of severest reprisals, paralyzed by a reign of terror involving death squads and unspeakable tortures, and ground down by abject poverty. Without hope many Iraqis initially were unable to act rationally much of the time, or to care about others' needs, or to respect others' property. *U.S. News* concluded a special report with an insight that, frankly, applies to all peoples: "In the end, the ultimate therapy for a traumatized nation is a hopeful personal vision of the future."

History teaches that not only in Iraq but in every nation the ability to believe in the future separates growing civilizations from dying ones. Only where hope exists can meaningful life be sustained, whether for nations or for individuals. Without hope one can lapse into everything from lethargy to bitterness to mind-numbing gloom. There's a predisposition in human nature that demands we anticipate something better to come. We all need something to look forward to, something that holds promise of more than we have yet experienced. This is no less true for every *Christian*.

Thoreau wrote that humans "live lives of quiet desperation" where hints of happy expectations quickly fade. Agnostic philosopher Bertrand Russell cynically concluded shortly before his death: "There is a darkness without. And when I die there will be darkness within. There is no splendor, no vastness anywhere, only triviality for a moment, and then nothing." Jean-Paul Sarte confessed the same despair: "I've discovered I'm alive, and the thought of it sickens me." How many of *us* at one time or another hear ourselves asking: "Is this all there is to life? Is this as good as it will get?"

By comparison Viktor Frankl, who studied Jewish prisoners in German concentration camps, wrote *A Man's Search for Meaning*. In it he documents the resilient power of "*hope-fullness*". What made the difference between those who survived and those who perished, he found, was often the degree of hope they nourished. Those who prevailed through horrible trials did so primarily because they were convinced there was "something beyond the barbed wire to live for, something to look forward to, something to go home to."

Many times followers of Jesus face the same tug of war between hope and disillusionment. In determining the outcome for *us* the magnitude of our vision of the Sovereign Savior proves most decisive.

This was clearly the case with Russia's brilliant 19th century novelist, Leo Tolstoy. As much as anyone he exhibited how spiritual survival for Christians requires a good dose of hope. His writings were acclaimed far and wide. He was lavished with the trappings of fame. But through it all Tolstoy endured a secret nightmare of depression. More than once he threatened suicide. At one point he imagined himself abandoned in relentless confusion — someone lost in a forbidding forest who must forever wander, with no way out. His personal crisis of hope came down to one unavoidable question, as he put it: *"What's next?"* He agonized about whether any larger purpose for life could transcend his fleeting accomplishments.

Finally the years of torment began to lift as he turned back to his Christian roots. He rediscovered that all along, deep inside, one truth had preserved him from total despair. From childhood he had clung to a deep-seated conviction that God was "there". This gave Tolstoy an unshakable prospect: If he chose to seek the Lord, the Lord would be found. He did not postpone the seeking. He encountered his Savior afresh. He began again with Jesus as Lord. This hope led to his survival on every level. And subsequent generations have benefited from the spiritual insights of his later writings.

So, if we need hope to survive, what does that tell us about the condition of the current generation?

The Loss of Hope for Our Generation
(Ephesians 2:1-3, 12)

Probably no previous generation has been as preoccupied with the future as citizens of the 21st century. "Future shock" has become the normal experience of those caught up in the advance of unfettered technological innovations. NASA's space explorations tease the imagination with images of "Star Wars" adventures just ahead. The promise of impending medical breakthroughs, leading to increased quality and longevity of life, keeps us dreaming of healthier tomorrows.

However, buoyancy over breakthroughs bogs down for many who face fruitless attempts to fulfill cherished expectations. A vague dread descends upon us, a fear of pursuing dreams that will ultimately deceive and disappoint. Shakespeare's Macbeth said it well for both Elizabethans and multitudes of moderns: "Tomorrow, and tomorrow, and tomorrow creeps in its petty pace from day to day.... It is a tale told by an idiot, full of sound and fury, signifying nothing."

THINK WITH ME ...
What is responsible for today's disappearance of hope?

Above every other explanation, the Bible is clear that humankind is deprived of lasting hope simply because we are *dead* in sin and *dead* to God (Eph. 2). Psalm 7 recognizes that "he who is pregnant with evil and conceives trouble gives birth to disillusionment" — to shattered dreams. And yet it is often the nature of sin to keep us defiant, seeking self-made solutions with an arrogance that God critiques like this: "You were wearied by all your ways, but you would not say, 'It is hopeless' " (Isa. 57).

Depraved at heart, corrupt in affections, self-seeking in relationships, fearful over death, enslaved to forces of darkness and candidates for God's everlasting wrath — this is the pitiful pit from which humankind cannot extract itself. If, as psychologists tell us, "melancholy" overtakes people who've lost the ability to imagine a better future, who suspect that life is absurd and will never meet their deepest longings, then *all* of us must succumb eventually.

> QUOTABLE QUOTE
>
> **How does one dare to propose the way of trust [or hope] in the face of raw, undifferentiated heartache, cosmic disorder and the terror of history?**
>
> (BRENNAN MANNING)

Adding to the universal plagues of spiritual lostness, unprecedented adversities have ambushed the last few generations, piercing hope to its core. The 20th century witnessed the crumbling of a host of novel "pseudo-hopes" — extraordinary projections masquerading as whole new beginnings for the human race. Instead of finding promised foretastes of "Paradise

Reclaimed", however, the 1900's regularly descended into battlegrounds over deceptive, humanistic utopias. Deficient, even demonic, worldviews competed with one another for the allegiance of nations: communism, socialism, fascism, totalitarianism, along with scientism, secularism, fanatical Hinduism, radical Islam. Each deadly dream unraveled in tragic ways, not the least of which took the form of two World Wars followed by a paralyzing Cold War standoff. In the words of Alexandar Solzhenitsyn, the 20th century became "what previous generations would have called '*Apocalypse*' ".

False fulfillments embedded in alluring Western materialism left many people ambivalent. A *New York Times* best-seller *Affluenza* called rampant consumption an "all-consuming epidemic" negatively affecting health, wealth, economy and environment and monopolizing our citizens with elusive promises that never seemed to match their hype. Not a few found that a sense of super-abundance fostered unanticipated *fear* — fear over how material blessings of such a magnitude simply could not last much longer.

QUOTABLE QUOTES

Hopelessness is hell — literally. God made us creatures for whom hope is life, and whose lives become living deaths when we have nothing good to look forward to.

(J. I. PACKER)

Christians, unfortunately, have not escaped these forces unscathed. Hope has taken a beating for us as well. Many believers, though prosperous, remain inwardly empty and confused. "We're so *blessed* we're *stressed!*" someone put it. Overwhelmed, overcommitted, oversold, overextended, overactive. Clearly it is hard for disciples to anticipate greater Kingdom advances when they can hardly see past the relentless demands of daily routines.

On the flip side, multitudes of others have succumbed to hopelessness in the midst of *want* — poverty, misfortune, disease, violence, oppression. Many could identify with the sign over the inferno in Dante's *Divine Comedy*. Written across every facet of their deplorable circumstances were the words: "Abandon all hope, all ye who enter here." A friend of mine attending a Yankees game in the Bronx saw near a main gate a homeless man holding up a large cardboard sign as fans filed past. He wasn't asking for a handout. The scrawled message simply said, "I have no hope." These past decades countless others like him — an estimated 40 million poor residing in the US alone, *many of whom are also our brothers and sisters in Christ* — have been stripped of dignity and diminished by demons of doom day after day.

Our world is being slashed to pieces by waves of injustice, brutality, terrorism, poverty, racism, phantom affluence, perversion, epidemics and illusionary utopias. How do we convince people imprisoned in a canyon full of broken dreams to risk believing that some form of concrete, lasting hope still exists? Instead many say, "Eat and drink and be merry, for tomorrow we die," reminiscent of Paul's quote about pagans who lacked confidence about a victory over the grave (1 Cor. 15).

What does this have to do with the Church's crisis of supremacy? For the moment recall this: Paul wrote 1 Corinthians 15, the great "resurrection chapter", to challenge *Christians*, some of whom had bought into the fatalism of the wider culture around them. Would he need to address the same concern to modern-day American congregations? As we saw in chapter 6, there seems every chance he would.

THINK WITH ME ...
How does hopelessness hit us at the heart level?

When you get right down to it, every modern expression of insufficient hope — whether for believers or unbelievers — hits at the heart level. The struggle may mask itself with a host of unsavory feelings that every human, including every *Christian*, knows all too well:

• Loneliness	• Panic	• Grief	• Fear
• Isolation	• Guilt	• Anger	• Anxiety

Gordon MacDonald reminds us that even Christians can lose personal hope due to the basic heartaches of life, such as when:

- marriages go sour.

- investments go "south".

- catastrophic illnesses overtake us.

- friends betray us or abandon us.

- youthful ambitions hit the wall of midlife limitations.

- someone we deeply love dies.

- our own mortality threatens us.

Such setbacks can crush any of us at any moment. Without warning we can find ourselves anxious over irreversible results of past actions; or bewildered with the disintegration of once-close family relationships; or despairing over unbearable disappointments on the job; or disillusioned when life's circumstances cut off our best efforts to pursue long-held goals. This can hook a Christian's heart as well, challenging at the core what we say we believe about Christ's supremacy.

It should be no shock, therefore, that in a land inhabited by over 140 million citizens with *no* church participation whatsoever, swamped with pluralistic babblings about the divine, many have lost confidence. They doubt life holds any paramount purpose for them to pursue. Around us reside friends and neighbors who are, in the words of Eph. 2:12 "without God and without hope". As C.S. Lewis noted, "futility" is the legacy for those who have lost a sense of personal "utility". Hopelessness is all that remains for those to whom a divinely orchestrated destiny appears to be permanently impossible.

THINK WITH ME …
Why do the world's crises of hope impact *Christians* even harder?

At the end of the day, every heart-level crisis of hope is fundamentally *spiritual* in nature. That's why Christians, despite a saving relationship with God's Son, can't expect to remain immune to feelings of "perplexity" (2 Cor. 4), or times when we also "despair of life" (2 Cor. 1). This world of our pilgrimage is a mine field of disillusionments. As they do every other human being, attacks of angst can threaten the believer.

On top of this, Jesus' followers frequently find themselves taunted with *additional* misgivings uniquely experienced by saints — troubling questions pagans would never even think to ask. For starters, in the midst of every difficult challenge the world faces, Christians must come back to founda-tional issues of faith, such as: Does God's Word promise tangible triumphs through His Son that I can anticipate at this moment with *confidence*? Even if it does, is Christ ready to deliver on those promises any time *soon*? Is He actively shaping my future right now, or just watching it unfold? Will He empower me to prevail and sail, even when the storms of life overwhelm me? Will His supremacy make any *practical* differences in the midst of my most despairing circumstances?

Now I ask you: What Muslim, or Hindu, or hedonist do you know who feels it necessary to address at this level such personal questions about hopefulness?

When it comes to dispersing disillusionments, the answers given by too many Christians may ring just as hollow as that of unbelievers. Buying into the same futile fears that plague our whole generation, many disciples approach uncertain futures exhibiting little noticeable contrast with the response of secularists, New-Agers or Buddhists. We may be credited as "survivors" but still retain little testimony as "thrivers". Too many of us hear the daily news, cast its pessimistic resignations with stained-glass language, and bring it *inside* the Church, into our daily walk with Christ, only to undermine both our personal confidence toward God as well as our message of hope to each other.

1 Peter 3 puts it this way: "But in your hearts set apart Christ as Lord. Always be prepared to give an answer to everyone who asks you to give the reason for the hope that you have." Even pagans should be so impressed with the boldness of our forward-looking faith in Jesus that they regularly require us to define it for them. The compelling courage they observe in us should intrigue them to beg us to explain how we keep going.

> ## QUOTABLE QUOTE
>
> **You can't read the number of Puritan sermons I've read and not confront the central question of those sermons: *your mortality*. The Puritans knew that this life doesn't go on forever, and that you need to live your life in the shadow of eternity. It's frightening to confront your own mortality. Studying the Puritans made me confront what we try so hard to avoid in this society. But it confirmed in me the sense that there needs to be an eternal hope.**
>
> (Dr. Harry S. Stout)

The implications of this are huge. Any *loss* of hope inside the Church wounds our witness outside the Church. It guts the credibility of our claims to a deeper spirituality. It significantly paralyzes our mission to neighbors and nations. It reveals to the world that our vision of God's Son is too small. In turn, our message about the Kingdom unravels into little more than meaningless mutterings.

But it's the demise of hope originating inside the Church that creates our greatest challenge.

The Loss of Hope *Inside* the Church
(Hebrews 3:1-8, 12-14)

Christian demographers such as Ray Bakke tell us that of all the major barriers to reaching the world's cities for Christ, ninety percent are found *inside* our churches, not outside. These hindrances include such things as lack of holiness, Biblical illiteracy, avarice and disunity. At the top of the list is what Bakke calls a *spirit of hopelessness* often originating from the pastors themselves (documented in studies of congregations in hundreds of cities on all continents).

The results of such studies indicate that urban challenges can seem too formidable for the Gospel to handle. Malignant forces — poor housing, injustice, addictions, crime — appear virtually unstoppable. Many Christians conclude incorrectly that few tangible evidences exist where the lordship of Jesus effectively turned the tide. His reign seems inadequate for the pressures city-dwellers confront, including gangs, drugs, pollution, noise, racism, substandard health care, inadequate housing and injustice. Cut-and-run becomes much easier as we pull back turtle-like and say to one another, in essence, "Let's just try to hold the fort until Jesus comes back again!"

This spirit of hopelessness reinforces other internal impediments to God's work in the city. Disunity among local churches is often the result of a vision of Christ's kingship so introverted that leaders become embroiled in debates over secondary concerns like worship styles or spiritual gifts. Controversies like these cripple our ability to find ways to serve Christ together to further His triumphant mission within our communities.

THINK WITH ME ...
How does a spirit of hopelessness show
itself as *spiritual paralysis*?

Harassments of hopelessness aren't unique to the urban Christian experience, however. One poll documented that pessimism about the future of the Christian faith in America was expressed by over 80% of all U.S. pastors. Not a few clergy indicated anxiety that non-Christian religions and New Age spirituality would increasingly dominate national life. Even more disturbing, one of America's largest Protestant denominations verified by its own studies that *depression* is the biggest problem among its pastors — a more debilitating challenge than church conflicts or marital difficulties. And most of these leaders were found in *suburban* churches.

As all of this illustrates, Christians who lose hopeful hearts inherit a huge handicap — a kind of *spiritual* paralysis. When part of a person's physical body is paralyzed, that individual may have commendable ambitions, but often to little avail. The common frustration of paralytics is that they feel trapped by an inability to do with their bodies what their minds can visualize and what their hearts desire. Future options seem greatly limited. In the same way spiritual paralysis is a good diagnosis of a church's deadly disabilities caused by despair.

Paralysis takes hold when Christians, feeling powerless before the darkness in our culture, grow awkward about proclaiming Christ's kingdom where they live. Having experienced persistent times of barrenness and frustration, not infrequently through a variety of failed Christianly enterprises, we doubt things will ever improve. Dreams of meaningful service to Christ elude us. For many it is not so much an issue of being *unwilling* to overcome previous heartbreaks but rather a sense of being *unable*. Tim Stafford calls some believers "the walking wounded". They are unhappy ghost-like disciples composed of the abused, the neglected, the lonely and the guilt-laden whose endless neediness leaves them with empty hearts that nothing seems to fill.

QUOTABLE QUOTE

When I stand to welcome the people to worship on Sunday morning, there are spouses who can barely talk. There are sullen teenagers living double lives at home and school. There are widows who still feel the amputation of a fifty-year partner. There are single people who have not been hugged for twenty years. There are men in the prime of their lives with cancer ... There are soldiers of the Cross who have risked all for Jesus and bear the scars ... What they need is a kind of joyful earnestness that makes the broken heart feel hopeful and helps ones who are drunk with trifles sober up for greater joys.

(Dr. John Piper)

Reduced to spiritual paralytics, we may dream big dreams of what we'd like to do for the glory of Christ. But little — personally or corporately — seems to cooperate. Our strength feels unequal to the needs and opportunities around us. Grappling with the same disheartening challenges unbelieving neighbors experience, we pull back from the clear light of Scripture's teaching on the reign of Christ. We refuse to allow His bold claims to form our final interpretation on this "veil of tears".

To understand this phenomenon better let's explore three widely shared experiences of paralysis inside the Church: Busyness and fatigue, confusion over Christ's unfinished mission and disconcerting disappointments with Christ Himself. Ultimately all three boil down to a loss of Kingdom perspective rising from a crisis of supremacy.

THINK WITH ME ...
How does the evangelical "rat race" exhaust our hope in Christ?

Let's be totally candid with each other. Too many times we evangelicals abandon persistent pursuits of Christ and His power to entertain the opposite — a frenetic, over-extended pace in church-related meetings, reflected in the plethora of announcements in last Sunday morning's bulletin. (Everything performed, of course, in Jesus' name!)

It's really quite disturbing. A closer look indicates we've constructed ministry schedules that actually pull us away from the joy of Christ-focused obedience to which Scripture calls us. Our calendars of churchly events have drained the vitality out of whatever sense of Christ's presence we once knew. Tempted to sample from the abundance of religious options around us, we have inflicted ourselves with spiritual exhaustion. As crazy as it sounds, we have depleted our enthusiasm for glorifying God's Son by how we've tried to *serve* God's Son. Then we wonder why church members protest a lack of time and energy to handle one more personal investment in the advance of His Kingdom.

It's all so tragic! Pressures from pious programming block us from a restorative rest in God. Christianly routines and rituals deflect us from pursuing the deeper implications of the promises Christ offers us. We allow this even though we know His word points toward the life-changing renewal for which we so desperately long. Instead we attempt to make up by our own efforts for blessings in Christ that *seem* no longer relevant, or adequate, or dependable, or workable — at least in our own experiences.

Too quickly we fall into the same trap that stifled 1ˢᵗ century Christians in Galatia province. Having begun in the Spirit, they ended up *trying* to perfect God's work by their own desperate activities for Christ, called "the flesh" by Paul. (Look at Gal. 3:1-5.) As a result they no longer embraced their Savior for who He really is, or for what He imparts, or where He leads. By self-sufficiency and self-reliance they denied the hope Christ's supremacy offered them. Consequently, Paul confessed he was "in travail" until Christ would be formed in them again (Gal. 4). Paul's labors to rally them back to the preeminence of Jesus caused him great personal pain (both physical and spiritual). But he knew otherwise they would miss out on God's Kingdom blessings.

I hear Christian leaders everywhere groaning under this wearisome burden, the oppression of over-busyness. They are desperate to escape playing the role of "chaplaincy to the rat race" (as Richard Lovelace describes it). Research indicates most pastors in America are asked to function in as many as 17 different roles to fulfill parishioners' expectations — from teacher, to counselor, to mediator, to business manager, to fund-raiser, to cheerleader, to promoter!

Where did these mounting demands come from? Primarily, I suggest to you, from hope-starved parishioners. Lacking solid confidence that Christ is supremely sufficient to meet their needs, they have turned to their leaders demanding that *they* make up the difference. Yet none of us were ever meant to take over Christ's role as the sovereign in other saints' lives. Help bear their burdens? Yes. Eliminate their burdens? Impossible.

No wonder even clergy, wrestling with congregational frustrations and stresses, gradually lose hope in Christ for themselves. Eventually they succumb to disillusionment with the ministry, which evolves into a "hardness of heart" as a form of self-protection. In private conversations over the years scores have shared with me this sad outcome. Frankly, I've had to deal with the same battle in my own life more

QUOTABLE QUOTE

The Church is born of hope and it is necessary to rekindle it *today* if we want to give new impetus to faith and make it able to conquer the world again. Nothing can be done without hope. When a person reaches the point of having no hope in anything, it's as if he were dead. To give hope to someone is the most beautiful gift that can be offered.

(DR. RANIERO CANTALAMESSA)

than once and for the same reasons.

Recall the three foundational questions at the opening of this chapter:

- What can I know?

- What ought I to do?

- What may I hope?

Normally, activist-oriented Christians boast impressive answers to the first two questions. Most of us are confident about what Christians should *think* (our doctrinal positions are well-honed) and what they ought to *do* (our extensive curricula for discipleship bear witness to this). But do we have significant answers for the *third* and most important question? Are we abundantly clear about what and in whom our people may *hope*? Or about how *fully* they may hope in Him as Lord of all?

Furthermore, do we *consistently* feed those convictions to fellow believers? Do our Sunday schools and sermons and Bible study groups — as well as our counseling sessions, committee meetings, youth rallies and hospital visitations — *major* on making hope in Christ a prime issue? Are we doing everything we can to foster the fullest possible answers to "What may I hope?" for all whom we serve?

And are those answers faithfully magnifying the supremacy of the One in whom their hope must rest?

THINK WITH ME ...
How has our hope in Christ been paralyzed
by the magnitude of the task?

World renowned mission strategist Ralph Winter speaks for thousands of hope-filled Christians when he exclaims that the Church is in "the final era of world missions". Favorable facts seem to substantiate his encouraging outlook. For the first time in history, based on resources and manpower alone, the task of planting the Christian movement within every remaining unreached nation and people group could be completed in one lifetime. In many places around the globe the Church is exploding numerically.

Yet despite such prospects, a major reason for loss of hope — again, a reason unique among Christians — relates to the task God has given us. Many are disabled with hopelessness because of their erroneous perception that world evangelization has *failed*. Numbers of believers are unsettled over what seems like overwhelming, inexplicable gaps — disturbing discrepancies between what the Church claims about the outcome of Christ's mission to the world and what has actually been accomplished so far. Equally, they are stymied by the magnitude of what remains to be done.

After two thousand years of massive, sacrificial efforts, why does it seem we still have so far to go? Despite bold beginnings in the book of Acts, why have 67% of all humans from A.D. 30 to the present day never heard the name of Jesus (as documented by the *World Christian Encyclopedia*)? Where's the bright tomorrow for God's Kingdom in *that*? — or, by extension, for our *own* destiny? Quite honestly, it is hard to sustain hope in Christ and His supremacy for *personal* challenges when we conclude that the immensity and complexity of the larger mission is still too elusive.

Billions still have no one like them, near them, to tell them about the Lord Jesus. Should we not feel compelled to ask: Where has our King been the past two millennia? What are the evidences of His lordship in the face of what seems like so little advance? Where are signs that His Kingdom is triumphantly advancing among the nations? — or, for that matter, even in our own neighborhoods?

To put it in perspective, there are more unevangelized people in our world right now, literally, than the number of times an average human heart beats from the day of birth to age 75. The nations are teeming with multitudes yet untouched by the hope held out in the Gospel. We might wonder: What does that say in the end about the hope Christ offers *us*? Does this picture really inspire the kind of unshakable confidence in Jesus on which to build *our* future? If we were brutally honest, many would have to respond "No".

Based on the phenomenal opportunities, strategies, laborers and treasures at the Church's disposal the previous twenty centuries, recent missions research by demographer Dr. David Barrett and others has confirmed that the world should have been evangelized *a thousand times over* by now. Instead, there's so much left to be done. Satan seems to have retained the upper hand. But here's the kicker: What does this say about the dependability of God's promises *to us*? What does this say about the conclusiveness of Christ's supremacy for any of our own congregations?

QUOTABLE QUOTE

Many suffer with an unperceived smugness that drugs the soul with the notion that our present boundaries of understanding God are the permanent boundaries of His readiness to reveal Himself to us.

(Dr. Jack Hayford)

   This crisis of hope (and supremacy) haunts us yet another way. During the past one hundred years there have been more Christians worldwide martyred for their faith than in all the rest of Church history. In the Sudan, for example, hundreds of thousands of our brothers and sisters have been intentionally and systematically starved, slaughtered or sold into slavery by an oppressive Muslim government. What may *those* believers hope about a Christ who conquers amidst suffering? Where are the manifestations of His Kingdom for *them*? And what does this say about God's promises to lead any of us in Christ Jesus' victory procession (2 Cor. 2)?

   What feels like a string of dashed expectations for outreach among the nations now haunts the *local* mission of our churches, as well. Surveys suggest that in the last 20 years 80% of American churches have been identified as either stagnant or dying in membership. This failure disheartens the very community that professes to follow the King of Heaven's Armies. It mocks the people who aim to proclaim the claims of the One called "the assurance of all the glorious things to come" (Col. 1:27, *Phillips*). Make no mistake: *This is merely the crisis of supremacy in different "clothes"*.

THINK WITH ME ...
How have we lost hope due to personal disappointments with Christ?

Hopelessness sneaks up on many of us in much subtler ways than we've explored so far. It multiplies within the murky pools of hidden disillusionments with God's promises. The most disabling form of despair any Christian can experience is this: *Our personal, secret disappointments with Christ Himself*.

   Frankly, this tragedy is more prevalent in our churches than most care to confess. Many have concluded privately that they will never consistently experience what the Bible says an abundant life in Christ looks like. They've not been transformed into genuine Christlikeness — they know this. The victorious Christian life has not unfolded the way they thought it was supposed to work, and they're deeply confounded by this fact. Despite a few encouraging exceptions on a broad range of moral issues, current research by Barna and Gallup verifies there's little measurable difference between the quality of character found in Christians versus the life-ways of non-Christians in America. Why has Jesus made so little difference in us?

Unmet longings for promised spiritual advances, in heart and hearth, suggest that Christ somehow has *failed* us. He has not brought to pass what we have every right to expect from Someone who declares to utterly love us while at the same time holding sway over an entire creation. If truth were told, you and I have probably backlogged a bushelful of prayers for help and healing that inexplicably still remain unanswered.

On the surface we may teach and sing about God's mighty acts in Scripture. But in more reflective moments most of us are needled with nagging doubts about the whole story. Will the outpourings of God's blessings — Jesus' resurrection power that we've been told can conquer, above all, our battles with sin — ever become tangible *reality* in our lives?

As psychologist John Eldredge reminds us, such doubts can unleash "the most poisonous" lies in Satan's arsenal. Using them to intensify every other form of hopelessness, the Tempter whispers: "For you personally, *things will never, ever change!*" Once we buy into that definition of our destiny, expectations toward the King fizzle for sure.

If what I've described feels familiar, remember *you are not alone.* Take a look at the smiling saints around you politely perched in their pews while singing God's praises on a Sunday morning. Scores harbor secret sorrows just as you do. Their horizons are confined to the same fog of fleeting dreams we all experience from time to time. They assume that once Sunday service is over, the coming week will leave the sighings of their souls still unsatisfied by the Savior.

Instead of pressing into God's promises many of us nurture inwardly what I call a *"tentative spirit"* toward the Lord Jesus Christ. Like the state motto of Missouri "Show Me", we bargain with God. It's as if we say, "From now on, God, I'll believe your promises in Christ only when You *show* me!" We might not verbalize it quite that way, but the attitude lurks deep inside.

QUOTABLE QUOTE

If for all practical purposes we believe that this life is our best shot at happiness ... if this is as good as it gets, we will live as desperate, demanding, and eventually despairing men and women.... All our addictions and depressions, the rage that simmers just beneath the surface of our Christian façade, and the deadness that characterizes so much of our lives has a common root: We think this is as good as it gets. Take away the hope of arrival and our journey becomes the Battan death march. The best human life is unspeakably sad.

(DR. JOHN ELDREDGE)

We simply can't forget the times it seemed God did not come through for us even after we pleaded with Him for deliverance. When the pastor's sermon mentions miracles from Heaven, quiet suspicions nurture a suffocating cynicism inside our souls.

With reticence we wonder if we'll ever know consistency in how God fulfills the possibilities proclaimed from the pulpit. In the words of Brennan Manning, loss of confidence in the overarching dominion of God's Son causes "incalculable harm to Christian spirituality", leaving in its wake "the flotsam of distrustful, cynical Christians, angry at a capricious God".

We just never say so aloud.

THINK WITH ME ...
What happens if we don't get to debrief our disappointments with Christ?

It's regrettable that no forum exists in most churches today where Christians may openly confess their disillusions. There's no spiritual "emergency room" where we might join others to diagnose and treat our struggles. We have no place to debrief the soul's pain, no "safe haven" to explore troubled hearts, no mutually supportive ways to dismantle crises of hope. Instead many practice what Dallas Willard calls a "conspiracy of silence" by covering up the ways our lives contradict the claims of Biblical promises. In other words, *we live in denial.*

Things deteriorate further as we stand aloof from signs of new beginnings. We're alarmed whenever God appears to be urging us to trust His Son "just one more time" for prospects that seem either too good to be true or have appeared elusive in the past. We tremble at the thought that if renewed reliance on Christ evaporates, it may permanently shatter our ability to trust Him for anything enduring, especially an eternity with the saints in glory. I mean, how can we ever dare risk finding out that Christ *Himself* may not be totally dependable — that He may be somehow neither sufficient nor supreme?

Finally something inside of us starts to *die.* Disappointments that lead to fear petrify eventu-

QUOTABLE QUOTE

Spiritual strongholds in the Church are the mindset impregnated with hopelessness that causes the believer to accept as unchangeable something that he or she knows is contrary to the will of God.

(DR. ED SILVOSO)

ally into a hidden *hardness of heart,* formed mostly for our own protection to help us avoid ever experiencing again the trauma of disillusionment with the Son of God. We garrison our feelings to fend off the pain of future betrayals. We forego any expectations toward Christ that might be dashed as before.

Does any of this sound familiar to you? As I'm sure you've suspected by now, I'm speaking out of my own pilgrimage here. I have waged the battle with hopelessness at a level that even the pagan world never faces! Why? Because, as I said earlier, for all believers any loss of hope *mocks* our main message that God's Son is Ruler over our total existence. It challenges our claims to the victory that defines the destination for which we trust in Him. If the promises of God seem to fail *us,* then as believers we are doubly doomed. Paul speaks to this when he concludes in 1 Corinthians 15: "If only for *this* life we have hope in Christ, we are to be pitied more than all men."

A diminished vision of Christ leaves Christians functioning more like *mirrors* than *windows.* We tend to reflect the hopelessness of unbelievers around us instead of providing them ways to gaze out upon the wide-open spaces of Kingdom promises. We shrink from inviting our friends to look through our eyes at the wonders of the Son of God because we ourselves need our own sight restored.

There's far more to this drama than bearing up under individual heartaches. At stake is the potency of our vision for the future of God's Kingdom. At stake is the breadth of the belief that will dominate the Church and its mission throughout the 21st century. *What I have just explored with you in this chapter is the ugly underside of the crisis of supremacy.*

THINK WITH ME ...
How is all this paralysis evidenced in the Church's prayerlessness?

Without question one of the most pervasive manifestations of paralysis is the phenomenon of *prayerlessness.* It is far more prevalent throughout the Christian community than most care to admit. Too many churches and ministries today hobble along with a painfully persistent "prayer vacuum". For many, weekly prayer meetings are literally non-existent. Those scheduled are attended at best by just a handful of stalwart saints.

Prayerlessness in the Body of Christ is not only a *reason* for our frequent feelings of impotence before life's challenges. Prayerlessness is also the *sign* of a deeply-rooted (often unsuspected) paralysis already upon us. It rises from our busyness, our self-reliant service to Christ, our feelings of frustration over the failures of Christ's mission and our heartaches over a host of disappointments with Christ. But in the final analysis prayerlessness is really evidence of a pre-existing shortfall in our vision of the glory of Jesus. It bears witness to our shriveled sense of His supremacy. No believer or church is moved very often to pray Kingdom-sized prayers when faith is crippled by impoverished understandings of His claims. Who wants to pray if he or she assumes people or situations are beyond experiencing divinely-orchestrated breakthroughs?

For all practical purposes prayerlessness is like slamming the door in the face of Jesus. When we reject the possibility that God might be able, willing and ready to do something extraordinary on behalf of those who call on Him in the name of His Son, we function less like apostles and more like *agnostics*! Think of it: Christian agnosticism. It is the attitude expressed by believers who lack the courage to believe; who doubt the possibilities of tangible spiritual successes anytime soon; who live with a gnawing fear of further failures just around the bend; who have disqualified themselves from ever experiencing a Redeemer who accomplishes in them and through them that which is exceedingly, abundantly above and beyond all they might ask or think by His power at work within them (Eph. 3).

Some suggest we call this form of Christian hopelessness "*ig*-nosticism" because it ultimately rises out of our ignorance of key dimensions of Christ's dominion. If this is so, nothing short of a spiritual awakening to God's Son may ever reverse the curse.

The Battle for Hope is a Struggle for the Soul of the Church
(Luke 1:26-38, 46-59, 76-79)

Former first lady of the Soviet Union Raisa Gorbachev observed shortly before her death in 1992: "There is a struggle going on in my nation for the soul of my nation. It is a struggle between good and evil, between truth and treachery, *between hope and disillusionment."*

For me her observation reaches beyond the political landscape in Russia. What I mean is this: Christians everywhere are embroiled in a similarly sobering struggle, a struggle for the heart of our worship before Heaven and for the health of our witness to the nations. It is a battle not only for the soul of a country but for the life-breath of the Church in the current generation.

As we've seen in this chapter, the issue ends up being a very *personal* struggle. It's a tug-of-war between hope and disillusionment inside our own hearts. We wrestle with competing visions. The truth of the greatness of God's Son fights to reverse uncertainties that, left unchecked, paralyze our obedience to Him. We need to hear again about the hope His suremacy can bring. It is *this* hope we've been called to proclaim to one another. It is *this* hope for which we must campaign among the churches. Because it is *this* hope that can lead believers out of the crisis and back into an experience of everlasting triumphs through Him who sits at the Father's right hand.

More than a few Christians have prevailed in the battle, however. For many the crisis of supremacy has been substantially confronted and cured. In light of what we just discussed above, it is no small thing that millions of them are exhibiting this fresh "awakening to Christ" by the fact that they *are* praying like never before and are praying for fellow believers to be re-awakened at the same time.

In travels to many nations I have met personally with ordinary Christians who are not only praying but also changing the world around them in marvelous ways *because* they were restored to triumphant hope in Jesus ... and then acted on it.

I'll always remember sitting with Mother Theresa many years ago in her tiny, sparsely-furnished stucco office in Calcutta. We were talking about the far-flung ministries of her Missionaries of Charity founded decades earlier. Behind her was a weathered, hand-drawn map of the world with inked lines radiating out of one of India's most desolate cities and flowing to cities all over the globe. The poster indicated the extent of the nuns' outreach. Across the top was printed their motto. It went something like this: "Ministering to the poorest of the poor, we will preach the Gospel of Jesus Christ to all the nations of the world."

That day with delicate animation Mother Theresa told me of great expectations toward God that propelled her in her work. But she affirmed this could be sustained only as she spent the first hours of each day in prayer, re-devoting her life to the lordship of Christ. A short while later as we toured her "Home for the Dying", I had an extraordinary sense that Jesus was present among us revealing a measure of His victory over death. I could see Him at work in the destitute men and women lying on cots before me as He filled them with Heaven's hope — the very same hope that sent her missionaries back into the streets to rescue others like them, day after day after day.

That one afternoon permanently spoiled me for anything less for my own life. In her little corner of Calcutta I was challenged on the shallowness of my own service to Christ. I became desperate for deliverance from my own poverty of *spirit* — from every shortfall of hope that might cripple involvement in Christ's global cause. Haven't you ever sensed the same need to be re-awakened to hope in the supremacy of God's Son?

THINK WITH ME ...
How much do *Christians* need to be re-awakened to a larger hope in Christ?

One Sunday in church not too long ago just after the opening prayer our congregation recited the *Nicene Creed* in unison. As we did, I reflected on the eternal truths contained within. Regarded as one of the premiere documents of Church history, the creed was developed by an all-church council in the 4th century. As we spoke it aloud line by line, I wondered to myself: How many of these insights on Christ determine my daily outlook on life's challenges? What practical impact do these characteristics of my Redeemer have on the anxieties that drive so many of my daily decisions? How should this confession help me develop a greater hope — a more *sustainable* hope — beyond what any non-Christian could ever experience? How often, I wondered as we came to the last line, do I respond to life in a way that does justice to this glorious 4th century acclamation?

That morning we confessed:

- One Lord Jesus Christ
- Only begotten Son of God
- Begotten of the Father before all worlds

- God of God
- Light of light
- Very God of very God
- For our salvation came down from Heaven
- Incarnate by the Holy Spirit
- Ascended into Heaven
- Sits on the right hand of the Father
- Will come again with glory to judge the living and the dead
- Whose kingdom shall have no end
- To be worshipped and glorified with the Father and the Spirit

Mentally, of course, we would all assent to each truth spoken in unison. How could we do otherwise? Each rings out the glories of our Lord. But when I get right down to it, I must admit that this confession does not always provoke me on any practical level to re-shape my day-to-day activities as His disciple. Too rarely do these truths set the tone for weekly worship with my church family. Too rarely do they inspire me to sacrificial giving to missions. Too rarely do they incite in me trust in God for tomorrow's demands at the office.

Unfortunately, I'm not alone. Many have not yet reclaimed the kind of comprehensive Christology we need for a restoration of enduring hope throughout the Church. Too few are convinced, at the moment anyway, that a crisis of supremacy has overtaken us (by whatever name we choose to call it). Fewer still are ready to engage it with urgency as if our lives depended on it – which they do!

THINK WITH ME ...
How is *passion* affected by the battle for hope?

For the moment some readers might remain hesitant or unconvinced about the current struggle for the soul of the Church. It may be helpful to examine the *second* fallout from the crisis of supremacy, our increasing loss of *passion*. We will do just that in chapter 8.

Why does the issue of passion need equal consideration? Let me illustrate. In his 12th volume of oral history *Hope Dies Last* Studs Terkel focused on the theme of how people get on top of hard times. He uncovered

a number of personal stories from activists who changed the world —
people of passion — from union organizers to war protestors to civil rights
leaders. When asked, "What trait do most activists share?" he responded:
"They have hope, and they imbue others with hope." Hope and passion walk
together. As Terkel's research confirmed, the quality of one's passion for
something springs from the degree of enduring hope that surrounds it.

This has powerful implications for the Church. Vision of the King of
Kings (or our lack of it) pretty much determines the strength of
our heart-felt zeal for His Kingdom. If hope in Him dies, the death of
passion will not be far behind. One can't exist without the other because the
one always quickens the other. Plummeting passion among God's people is
one of the chief characteristics of the absence of Christ-exalting messages in
the Church. Deflated desire provides indispensable insight into the serious
nature of the crisis of supremacy. It is part of the struggle for the soul of the
Church.

The way I see it, when it comes to confronting the crisis and finding its
cure, the next chapter — *Why Don't We Care?* — may be precisely what the
"Doctor" ordered!

Author's Extra Curricular Activity

Please feel free to skip this final section and go straight to chapter 8: *Why Don't We Care?*

However, if you would like to work though some of the themes of chapter 7 — if you would like to explore a little more the potential loss of hope in your own life — the following questions may prove helpful. At least they have been for me. They can help you pinpoint where *your* vision of Christ and His supremacy still needs to grow larger. They might guide you toward more of the hope you and I are meant to have.

But I suggest you reflect on these questions not only as they relate to yourself. Think as well about the Christians you fellowship with regularly. How do you think *they* would answer these questions? What might that tell you about the nature of their own struggle to sustain a vibrant hope in Jesus as Lord?

- **Who really is the Christ to whom you were converted in the first place? In what kind of Lord did you seek to place your eternal hope at the beginning? Did you knowingly receive Him for who He is as the Son of God, full of majesty and authority? Even more importantly, do you sense that He truly *conquered* your heart that day, the way a King of Kings has every right to do? Do you sense that as reigning Lord He *still* maintains full sway over you right now? How would you describe this relationship? What do your answers tell you about the "state of hope" for your life? (Or for your congregation?)**

- **Are you *convinced* all the promises of God are really and truly summed up in His Son? Or do you still struggle with hopelessness? For you, are His promises as sure as the fact that He's alive from the dead? Do you view God's promises as *totally available* to you in Christ Jesus? Do you know Him as trustworthy, as the One on whom you can depend without reservation? Do you expect Him always to be sovereign and sufficient for you? Do you expect Him to back His claims that He will ultimately overrule with victory in every challenge you confront? If so, how do you exhibit such convictions? What kinds of practical differences does this make in your daily walk with Him? Do you consider**

Him able, willing and ready as the reigning Lord to minister increased blessings to your life? How do you show it?

- How has He, to any depth, become *experientially* what Paul meant by "Christ in you, the hope of glory" (Col. 1:27)? Are you fully relying on Him to be to you increasingly everything God's Word promises Him to be? Do you daily expect Him to work in you above and beyond what you have received from Him thus far? Do you harbor any *tentativeness* about this happening for you? What do your answers tell you about the "state of hope" in you? (Or in your congregation?)

- In light of the pervasive loss of hope in the Church — fostered from both outside and inside — how might the Church be *flooded* again with the Bible's magnificent message about the full extent of Christ's supremacy? What do you think you should do about it? Why should any serious Christian make His supremacy her or his premiere proclamation to other *Christians?* Why ought we to consider at least a *"Campaign of Hope"* throughout the Church bent on restoring to *believers* a fresh vision of hope in God's Son for ALL that He is? Can there be any more strategic step for any of us to undertake than the mission to awaken God's people to our glorious destiny in Jesus? We take this step so that in turn they might join us in taking this vision to neighbors and nations. If this seems right, what does this mean for your own sense of mission for Christ? (Or for your congregation?)

8

WHY DON'T WE CARE?

The Crisis of Supremacy
and
the Loss of *Passion*

Before Christopher Columbus set sail from Spain in 1492, his country's national motto was "Ne Plus Ultra", meaning "There is nothing beyond". In one sense this was a boast. Spain considered itself superior to other European nations. In another sense it was a vision. In its own estimation Spain occupied the very ends of the earth. Geographically speaking, Spain was as far as any traveler would ever dare to go.

After the explorer returned with glowing reports of bountiful lands, the motto was revised to "Plus Ultra" meaning "There is something beyond". Spain's confession? "There is something more waiting for you across the Atlantic. There are promised treasures beyond what our nation can give you." Intriguing, global-sized prospects turned Spain (and later a whole continent) toward the pursuit of New World wonders. We might say that hope "converted" them. It moved them beyond their shores. It incited in them a *passion* that resulted in centuries of adventures and discoveries.

There's no place for "Ne Plus Ultra" in our union with Christ, either. There's no reason to settle for dreary, truncated visions of Kingdom prospects. We must refuse to set boundaries on what we expect Jesus to be for us or to do through us. We must cease acting like "flat-landers" and venture forth to become "round-earthers" (like Columbus) living by faith and not by sight (2 Cor. 5), focused on which others may not yet see: the consummation of all things in Him. God's great salvation inspires us to pursue possibilities beyond the horizon of human heartaches. It invites us to go after eternal treasures surpassing even our current experiences of the Kingdom. Daily we need to ask God to reveal to us through His Word "great and unsearchable things which you have not yet known" (Jer. 33). Our cry should be: Lord Jesus, take us with you on the jubilant journey that explores blessings "exceedingly above and beyond all that we ask or even imagine" (Eph. 3).

The supremacy of Christ promises every disciple "Plus Ultra!" It calls us to renounce "pea-sized" expectations toward Him as well as "down-sized" affections for Him. Soren Kierkegaard said it well: "Hope [in Christ] becomes a passion for the possible."

In the last chapter we asked a question every human being must face: "What may I hope?" What really lies beyond the horizon? In this chapter we examine struggles to "set sail". More specifically: What does it take to increase a passion to pursue the full extent of Christ's supremacy? And above all: Why do so many in the Church seem to care so little about the glory of God's Son or the advance of His Kingdom, especially by what they seek (pray) and what they speak?

We'll consider:

- **The relationship between conversion, hope and passion.**

- **Four ways passion for Christ loses its punch for many of us.**

- **Why the loss of passion is often due to short-sighted messages about Christ.**

- **How facing this loss can help us effectively confront and cure the crisis of supremacy.**

- **The possibilities for recovering passion for Christ through a "Campaign of Hope".**

Conversion and Passion
(Acts 26:15-19)

Conversion turns sinners into "round-earthers". Conversion involves *a turning from* everything false and illusionary while *turning toward* Christ and the dependable promises His supremacy offers. In fact, what lies *outside* ourselves forms the main motivation for every Christian's commitment to Christ. *Outside* we are welcomed into intimate encounters with His redeeming reign, on many fronts. *Outside* we are beckoned by Him into victories so vital we must reject anything that might deflect, defy, or diminish the Victor's role in our lives. More specifically, *outside* there awaits us (as outlined in chapter 1) the sum total of His glory — the focus (who He is), fulfillment (where He leads), fullness (how He imparts), and fervency (what He receives) of His supremacy.

> ## QUOTABLE QUOTE
>
> **The Person of Christ appeared ineffably excellent with an excellency great enough to swallow up all thought and conception.... I felt an ardency of soul to be what I know not otherwise how to express: emptied and annihilated; to lie in the dust, and to be full of Christ alone .**
>
> (JONATHAN EDWARDS)

We mustn't confuse conversion with the Biblical doctrine of *regeneration*. Regeneration is a sovereign work of the Holy Spirit (Titus 3) exercised even when we are dead in our sin (Eph. 2). By contrast conversion marks our *response* to God's regenerating work in us. It answers the question: "How does hope express itself primarily?" You could say conversion is hope in action. Conversion is how I cultivate and nurture the hope in Christ the Spirit has already placed within me. Conversion is "hope with a passion". Passion describes how we care about that hope. Passion causes us to "set sail".

THINK WITH ME ...
What three essential choices in conversion are fundamental to Christian passion?

Allow me to be personal for a moment. My new life with God's Son began the year I turned eighteen. The Spirit tapped a couple of zealous Christian students in my dorm at college to take me on. So for three months during my freshman year they shared the Gospel with me almost daily. Of course, I made sure to show them little outward interest. But gradually they got through. On autumn afternoons I would retreat to a graveyard near campus to wander and wonder. I challenged God earnestly (even out loud, at times) about His Word — about His promises in Christ and their implications for me. Instinctively I dreaded the direction those truths might take me. I feared the future they might foster for me. I resented the passion they might require of me. Finally the Scriptures overcame the stranglehold of my prideful unbelief. The Spirit by the Word convinced me that life in Jesus, as offered in the Gospel, held out infinitely more than life without Him.

That's when it happened. As I sat on the edge of a tombstone in a 200-year-old cemetery to watch the sun set one November afternoon, it was *hope* — the offer of an eternal hope anchored in a supreme Savior — that converted me. There among the graves I not only entered the Empire of the Son but also the *future* of the Son! Peter affirms that I was "born again into a living hope by the resurrection of Jesus Christ from the dead" (1 Pet. 1). I sometimes say to people: "I came alive among the dead!"

That afternoon conversion required of me three simultaneous choices (which I only vaguely understood at the time). Each choice continues to stoke the fires of devotion for my Savior:

> QUOTABLE QUOTE
>
> **Without a doubt there comes to many of us the choice between a life of contraction and one of expansion; a life of small dimensions and one of widening horizons and larger visions and plans; a life of self-satisfaction or self seeking, or one of unselfish or truly Christ-like sharing.**
>
> (DR. JOHN R. MOTT)

1) *I chose to turn from sin and self as my identity and my destiny.* From that day and forever I would never, ever again define myself apart from Christ. I refused then — and do so now — to stay inside myself separated from the God who made me, doomed to everlasting death (Rom. 6). I ceased justifying my need for any *identity* based on my own goodness and righteousness. I ceased orchestrating a *destiny* ordered by my own ingenuity, my control on events, my self-absorbed dreams and plans, my assumed abilities to fulfill them or my persuasive powers of positive thinking. The Spirit convinced me that left to myself I could anticipate nothing but the "same-old/same-old": forever falling short of the glory of God and the promises of His Kingdom (Rom. 3). I wanted no part of that scenario any longer. And I still don't.

2) *I chose, at the same time, to turn toward Christ as my identity.* This meant that in breaking free of sin and self I would forever seek to define myself in four primary ways: The grandeur of Christ's glory, the testimony of His triumphs, the riches of His grace and my service to His Kingdom. My life became forever interpreted by who Christ is as God's Son (focus), where He leads in God's purposes (fulfillment), how He imparts God's resources (fullness) and what He receives from the God's people (fervency).

3) *At the same time, I turned to Christ as my destiny.* My future became eternally wrapped up in His risen life at the right hand of the Father. Now, every prospect I could claim would spring from His righteousness, His wisdom, His plans, His abilities, His Kingdom, as well as His designs on the future and His powers to get us there together. I chose that day — and each day since — to follow the One who alone guarantees for me all of God's promises. He is my assurance about glorious things to come (Col. 1 and 3). I can truly say at that momentous hour I was converted *in* hope and *by* hope.

This isn't just my story. Whether or not one can fully grasp all its dimensions, the moment Christian conversion takes place this is how salvation unfolds — incorporating these three choices — for every believer, including you.

As for you it was for me: That first moment of decision wasn't the last time I faced these issues. Conversion is more than a once-in-a-lifetime experience. Conversion is an all-through-your-life adventure where we constantly choose to build our lives on an identity and a destiny rooted in the hope that Christ and His Kingdom gives us. Since I first emerged from that graveyard, conversion has remained a *process*, a daily embrace of God's promises about my identity and destiny. Conversion ushers me into a life of constant *caring* about the supremacy of God's Son as I give "my utmost for His highest", to use Oswald Chambers' phrase.

> ## QUOTABLE QUOTE
>
> **The Gospel-centered community continually encounters and celebrates Christ. Thus, the heart of the Church's evangelistic ministry is its own *continuing conversion* to the fullness of Christ and His mission. The continual conversion of the Church happens as the congregation hears, responds to and obeys the Gospel of Jesus Christ in ever-new and more comprehensive ways.**
>
> (Dr. Darrell Guder)

THINK WITH ME ...
Why does a life of *continual* conversion prevent a loss of passion?

Let's remind ourselves that even the Protestant Reformation emphasized the need to see conversion as a process. It stated that the Church, once reformed, must *keep on being reformed* by the message of Christ. In a similar vein Luther spoke of *repentance* (forsaking sin and choosing to return to Christ as our only hope) as a *practice*, as a way to follow the Lord faithfully every single day. As 17th century Puritans emphasized, we must be both "converted and *always converting*".

Followers of the Savior understand that conversion involves more than adopting proper doctrinal codes. It also implies on-going growth in one's affections for Him as well as allegiance to His Kingdom, all based on God's promises to us in Christ. That kind of Gospel inflames attitudes, motivations, relationships, priorities — above all, our worship of the living God. It becomes a *prelude* to consistent zeal for Jesus' glory that lasts long after initial commitments are made.

Even Timothy, Paul's protégé, needed from time to time to "fan into flame" God's call on his life (2 Tim. 1). The apostle pressed this dedicated pastor to intensify his hope-filled ambitions for the work of the Lord. Paul taught Timothy to be more like a soldier concentrating on victory in battle; or an athlete set on winning a race; or a farmer energetically tending his field in full assurance of harvest (2 Tim. 2). At the same time, he challenged him to proclaim this same hope to other believers, especially when faced with their indifference or opposition (2 Tim. 4). Paul urged Timothy to stay vigilant about maintaining his own passion for Christ, never falling short of what God's promises were meant to inspire in him, while keeping his hearers looking upward and outward as well (2 Tim. 4).

Timothy is not an isolated case. From time to time all Christians need to be re-awakened to our identity and destiny in Christ and His glorious reign.

We all need to re-ignite the passion that hope deserves. A process of *continuous* conversion must mark us if we're to help cure the current crisis of supremacy.

THINK WITH ME ...
How would John Wesley confront a loss of passion?

In 2003, 30 million Methodists worldwide celebrated the 300th birthday of John Wesley, a prime spark in the First and Second Great Awakenings in the 1700's. In 1739 Wesley took to the open fields in Bristol, England, to preach to multitudes of "churched" Anglicans about their need to be re-converted to Christ. Then he formed them into support groups called "classes" to hammer-out their new found life in His Kingdom.

Wesley never let up. During four decades on over 70 mission trips he crisscrossed the whole of England, Ireland and Scotland by horseback. In the process he lobbied for the poor and used profits from the sale of his many books to support various charitable causes such as health clinics. He translated works from Greek and Hebrew, wrote a history of the Church, produced a library of Biblical commentaries, compiled an English dictionary and published 23 collections of hymns. His *Journals* still are read eagerly worldwide. Eventually Wesley's efforts resulted in a revival movement that has now penetrated nearly every nation on earth. The hope he proclaimed (about which his brother Charles wrote hundreds of hymns) ignited new levels of passion for God's Son, not among pagans first of all but rather among struggling *believers*.

As Wesley understood, at its heart every God-given revival, whether personal or corporate, starts with the *re*-evangelization of God's people. Christians are invited into fresh encounters with the Christ of the gospel. They are encouraged to re-engage with Him once again around the full implications of His lordship. So to speak, revival is a "re-conversion". The Holy Spirit persuades us to get passionate all over again about God's Son and the great hope of our salvation. We start to care again about the issues that touch His supremacy in our lives and among the nations.

Frequently, when the Spirit resurrects fresh zeal for the Savior, an equally useful phrase to describe the phenomenon is *spiritual awakening* (the response that Wesley's hearers vividly illustrated). Isaiah invites believers to "Arise, shine, for your light has come, and the glory of the Lord rises upon you.... Nations will come to your light, and kings to the brightness of your dawn" (Isa. 60). Christians are admonished in Scripture to "Wake up, O sleeper, rise from the dead, and Christ will shine on you" (Eph. 5). It was the church in Rome that required Paul's exhortation: "The hour has come for you to wake up from your slumber, because our salvation is nearer now than when we first believed" (Rom. 13). More recently George MacDonald caught the essence of such verses when he wrote: "We must wake our souls unnumbered times a day and urge ourselves to live with a holy greed ... athirst and empty, for God's breath to fill."

When Christians wake up to the glory of Christ, important changes ensue. We shake off the soothing slumber of the status quo. We rise up once more to pursue wholeheartedly Christ and His global cause in the full light of His Day. Dispelling fears of fanaticism, we foster a fervency toward Christ for *all* that He is and *all* that He is up to. We start to care about Him.

When Passion Loses Its Punch
(Luke 24:13-32)

The Church's perennial need for spiritual awakening warns us, however, that passion for Christ's Kingdom can peter out. Like chewing gum, it can lose its flavor. Like an airplane in the midst of a steep climb, it can stall. Not just sometimes. Frankly, too many times. This can become the experience of His most devoted followers. It's a daily battle for all of us.

THINK WITH ME ...
How do life experiences fight against our fervency for Christ?

In the most surprising ways we may find ourselves reflected in the mood of the disciples walking the road to Emmaus (Lk. 24). Just as the crucifixion weighed on their spirits, circumstances beyond our control as well as life's disappointing outcomes can unsettle us. To our dismay we feel helpless and hopeless, desperate to reclaim the devotion we once held toward our Lord. There seems to be nowhere to turn. We wonder how to rekindle the fervor. We fret over how to care more deeply about God's eternal purposes in Jesus. Setbacks tempt us to replace passion with resignation.

Not long ago a nationally respected Christian leader, someone who for years has incited wholehearted obedience to God's Son among thousands, faced the hopeless prospects of aggressive cancer. After months of gradual and painful physical decline, discouragement began to overwhelm him. Writing to his many prayer partners, he confessed: "I have never experienced a mental battle like what I've lived through these last months. It becomes easier to give up with each passing day. To those who ask about my health, I can so quickly give in to reciting a litany of my physical afflictions." Then, his letter urged readers to pray for him what Jesus prayed for Peter in a time of trial: "I pray for you that your faith will not fail" (Lk 22). Although the Holy Spirit had kept my friend in "forward motion" most of his life, now he was tempted to procrastinate pursuing a relationship with the Lord Jesus any further. He found himself protesting to God, "Not right now. Later. I'll seek You again when I feel better. Let me wait until I'm back on my feet."

I'm grateful for his candor. For any Christian inexplicable suffering can cut into our caring about the Kingdom. In seasons of sickness especially, fervency for Christ's supremacy can fade long before the body does. But it need not be so. Listen to this godly leader as he concluded his letter:

"But in the midst of this battle, my wonderful Lord challenged me with these words: 'Now is the time. You have a choice to choose. Without any immediate feelings of glorious rapture for Me, you can choose right now to proclaim My wonders anyway, instead of focusing on your sufferings.'" This insight was the turning point for my friend. His letter was the first step toward embracing Christ wholeheartedly once again. As a result, passion of a more profound sort unlike anything he had ever known began to penetrate his heart. That's why he wrapped up his report with stirring words from 2 Timothy (written, as we know, by another who chose proclaiming over complaining): "The Lord stood at my side and gave me strength for the sake of the message of Christ" (4:17). Like Paul, this disciple had found true victory.

Of course, it isn't always suffering that dampens enthusiasm for the King. Brennan Manning tells of a Stanford University professor's confession that the pressures of her job on campus seemed to "conspire to deplete any passion for Christ". As she put it to one friend: "Once the fire of Christ burned inside of me. But slowly, almost imperceptibly, I stopped sitting at the fireplace. Instead, my job became all-consuming. I'm like Mary Magdalene in the garden, crying: 'Where has my Beloved gone?' "

Very few American Christians have experienced a sense of spiritual brokenness that compelled them to beg God for His mercy and acceptance through the love of Christ. We have a nation of "Christians" who took the best offer, but relatively few who were so humiliated and hopeless before a holy and omnipotent God that they cried out for undeserved compassion. That helps to explain why in practical terms it's hard to tell the difference between those who have beliefs that characterize them as born again and those who don't.

(DR. GEORGE BARNA)

It appears she is not alone. Many of us are similarly depleted. Looking in all the wrong places, our search for success frequently deflates devotion for the One whose dominion alone can assure success the way God measures it. A poll by the Barna Research Group asked Americans what they believed was necessary for them to have a successful life. Health? Happy children? Occupational achievements? Only one out of every fourteen adults said that anything related to spirituality or faith in Christ would help achieve what they might term "success". Is it any wonder many Christians have lost their passion for Him?

There are additional fronts in the fight to find renewed fervency for God's Son. Each reflects the impact of a prior shortage of hope in Christ for ALL that He is. Four are so critical we need to examine them right here.

THINK WITH ME ...
How does sin suffocate passion
for Christ and His supremacy?

At its core every sin is an act of rebellion. No sin is insignificant because all sin is measured by the sovereignty of the One it offends. His dignity determines that our depravity is nothing less than *treason*. Whether overt or covert, sin is an attempt to dethrone the Lord of Glory and enthrone ourselves in His place as masters of our fate. This is just as true of sin in a believer as it is in an unbeliever.

Some sins consist of a "yes" to God's "no" — our attempt to breach the boundaries He set for the subjects of the King as we assert our own invalid rights "to rule". Even more damaging, many sins, especially for a believer, consist of our "no" to God's "yes" — our refusal to receive the riches of His

grace because that might require us to crown the
Son in a submission we're not ready to give Him.

When *unbelievers* set their passions on
temporal things; when they withhold their
affections from the God who made them; when
they embrace darkness over Light while dismissing
the supreme rights of the One who alone can save
them (Jn. 3), in His just wrath the Lord of Heaven
and earth gives them over to "sinful desires". He
allows them to be possessed with "shameful lusts"
that ultimately destroy any capacity they may have
to worship and adore the King of the Universe
(Rom. 1).

It should come as no surprise, then, that sin
exacts no small toll on a *believer's* heart as well.

> ### QUOTABLE QUOTE
>
> **I must surrender my fascination with myself to a more worthy pre-occupation with the character and purposes of Christ. I am not the point. He is. I exist for Him. He does not exist for me. Is there a passion to be consumed with the work of Christ, a passion to know Him as Lord?**
>
> (DR. LARRY CRABB)

Maybe we're *refusing* Him. Maybe we're *using* Him. But every sin results in
defusing Him as it waters down a disciple's vision of who He really is and
causes zeal for Him to lose its zip and zest.

Simply put: Fleshly sin and godly passions cannot peacefully co-exist in
a redeemed soul. The flesh and the Spirit are always at war (Gal. 5).
Christians are sowing either to the Spirit or to the flesh (Gal. 6). The
primary role of the Holy Spirit is to make Christ more glorious to His
followers (John 16; Eph 1 and 3); to manifest His lordship through our
lives (Acts 1 and 2; Romans 8); to empower our acts of love for Him (1
Cor. 12; 1 Thess. 1); and to increase our hope in Him (Rom. 15; 1 Jn. 3).
Since the effect of sin in a Christian's life is to grieve the Spirit (Eph. 5), and
quench the Spirit (1 Thess. 5), and resist the Spirit (Acts 7), and insult the
Spirit (Heb. 10), then it follows necessarily: Sin suffocates a Spirit-ignited
savoring of the Son every time. Knowing this, Paul urges: "Have nothing to
do with the fruitless deeds of darkness.... Understand what the Lord's will is.
Do not get drunk on wine, which leads to debauchery. Instead, be filled with
the Spirit. Speak to one another with psalms, hymns and spiritual songs ... in
the name of the Lord Jesus Christ" (Eph 5).

There is one sin in particular that soundly destroys devotion for Jesus
among believers: It's the spiritual scourge of *presumption*. Presumption
involves a self-congratulatory, self-absorbed approach to discipleship that
concludes what we already have is all there is, or at least all we really need.

The church in Sardis boasted a reputation of being alive, but Jesus told them "you are dead" and in need to "wake up and strengthen what remains" (Rev. 3). The church in Laodicea (Rev. 3) protested, "I am rich; I have acquired wealth and do not need a thing". Their self-deception ignored the truth of how "wretched, pitiful, poor, blind and naked" they truly were, especially compared to the One confronting them as "the Amen, the faithful and true witness, the ruler of God's creation" (all titles of royalty, by the way). In their self-enclosed smugness they discounted the supremacy of their Savior. They ignored Him while at the same time they trumpeted their own supposed accomplishments for Him. Standing outside their feeble fellowship, Jesus warned them: "You are neither cold nor hot. I wish you were either one or the other! You are *lukewarm*! Therefore, I am about to spit you out of my mouth."

Wherever arrogance arises among the saints, ardor atrophies. The only path back to spiritual fervor, Jesus told these two congregations, was to "hear what the Spirit says to the churches" about His eschatological glory (the theme of the entire book of Revelation). So it is in every generation: Christ's knock lands on doors shut tightly by self-satisfaction. With urgency He invites us to open up, to gaze on Him again for *all* that He is, to awaken to more of what He could be in us and through us, so that we might join Him back on His throne (which, hopefully, some in Laodicea finally did — see the last verses of Rev. 3). He wants us *"hot"* for the honor of His Highness and inflamed to serve the full implications of His everlasting reign.

When because of its perceived benefits preoccupation with maintaining the status quo distracts our delight in the Beneficiary; when the proliferation of religious achievements becomes more alluring than the Promised One in whom the Father has accomplished everything for us; when our churchly goals are less for Christ's acclaim than for the reputation of our own denominational name, we are in trouble. Hearts burning for "things above where Christ sits" (Col. 3) soon give way to lukewarm love for the Lord, a condition for which He has no more use than you or I have for tepid soup (Rev. 3).

> ### QUOTABLE QUOTE
> **Jesus is my God, Jesus is my Spouse, Jesus is my Life. Jesus is my only Love, Jesus is my All, Jesus is my Everything. Because of this I am never afraid. I am doing my work with Jesus. I am doing it for Jesus. I'm doing it to Jesus; therefore, the results are His, not mine.**
>
> (MOTHER THERESA)

THINK WITH ME ...

Why would Christians *fear* a passion for Christ's supremacy?

The presumption found in "religious flesh" isn't the only culprit that suffocates Christian passion. For others it may be *fear* — a "dis-ease" about opening the door and letting His lordship have the full run of the house.

Not long ago a major Christian consulting firm was asked to research the level of spiritual growth within one of the larger evangelical churches in America. Using an exhaustive questionnaire plus in-depth interviews with elders and teachers, the consultants uncovered significant shortfalls in the vision of many members. Later, after reading the report, one of the elders said, "I am in tears."

What was discovered? The primary reason members gave for attending this body was to find *safety* from the negative influences of the larger culture. They demanded refuge from the ungodly forces threatening their families. But they confessed something else: Despite how much they enjoyed increasing their intellectual grasp on the Bible, surprisingly *they admitted to a prevailing fear of intimacy with the Christ of the Bible.* They dreaded the "risk" of getting too personal with Him. A majority said they wanted to be cared for and provided for by God — and that they were grateful for all Jesus had done for them. But they indicated significant discomfort with the idea of God taking them deeper in their walk with the Savior.

> ## QUOTABLE QUOTE
>
> **Overall, Christian ministry is stuck in a deep rut. Too many Christians and churches in America have traded in spiritual passion for empty rituals, clever methods and mindless practices. The challenge to today's Church is not methodological. It is a challenge to resuscitate the spiritual passion and fervor of the nation's Christians.**
>
> (DR. GEORGE BARNA)

This is evidence of the greater tragedy: That congregation was suffering one form of the crisis of supremacy. Many members needed to be re-introduced to the *real* Jesus for *all* that He is. It is unfortunate that this is typical of thousands of other churches involving millions of believers. How many of us, in fact, rest easy with Biblical prospects of on-going encounters with our Savior as all-consuming Lord of Hosts? How many of us are secretly apprehensive about ever beholding His regal glory *up close* and *personal?*

We can find some comfort, at least, in knowing even the apostle John had to face a similar fear. John's original love for his Master was so intensely intimate that he concluded his Gospel by suggesting that were he to write down everything he personally knew about Him, the libraries of the world might not be able to contain all the books (Jn. 21). Yet, this very same John froze with fear when Jesus displayed to him a much fuller revelation of His supremacy on the Island of Patmos. Beholding Him enveloped in eschatological brilliance, the disciple lost every ounce of courage. He fell prostrate on the ground, barely able to breathe. For a moment even John experienced a "crisis of supremacy".

Instantly, however, his Savior reassured him with words conveying great hope. In essence He said to him (paraphrased): "There's no reason for fear. Get up. Gaze unhesitatingly at My magnificence. Take stock of the death I've defeated, the keys of power I hold, the vision for the future I embody. Then write it all down so that every other believer can see what you see. They too can triumph over fear with the wonder of *all* that I Am." As the rest of Revelation confirms, John was immediately back in the business of serving His Lord with a sense of destiny he had not known before.

THINK WITH ME ...

What primary fears often restrict passion for Christ and His supremacy?

Fears can provide faithful barometers on how seriously we have disconnected from the truth about God's grace and glory in Jesus. For myself there are three major fears I've had to confront. Time and time again they have resurfaced in my struggles to rebuild a more passion-driven (rather than panic-driven) discipleship:

1) *The fear that He WON'T.*
This is the fear that Christ will *not* want to break through for me in the ways His supremacy promises, thus leaving me confused, or disillusioned, or heavy-hearted, or ashamed. *I fear the potential failure* of ever experiencing His supremacy in *my* life.

2) *The fear that He WILL.*

This is the opposite fear, that Christ *will* want to break through for me in the ways His supremacy promises. The whole idea of intimate encounters with Him feels unpredictable, disruptive, uncomfortable and, most of all, costly. What if, when He draws near, He exposes me for who I really am? What if He takes me where I've never gone before? *I fear the potential success* of His supremacy manifested in my life.

3) *The fear that I CAN'T.*

No matter how powerfully or prosperously Christ's supremacy may break through for me, I dread the level of obedience He will expect of me as a result. I'm apprehensive that the action steps this will require of me will go beyond my ability to please Him. *I fear the potential demands* His supremacy will make of my life, because I feel impotent to respond as fully as my King deserves.

However, there's good news for all who struggle with such fears. What God did for John (and more recently has brought to bear on my life) He is willing to do for any Christian. Grace can effectively challenge every "crisis of supremacy" (exhibited in part by each fear above) as the Spirit unveils more of the *truth* in Jesus. We rise with renewed expectations and holy ambitions toward our King. As He did for John, the Spirit can convince us that every promise of Jesus' reign will be accomplished without fail; that every demonstration of His reign will apply only God's best to us; that every demand of His reign will be underwritten by His power and resources.

The Father wants us to revel daily in the preeminence of His Son. He invites us to do so right now in ways reflective of how we will celebrate Him in the blaze of His Eternal Dominion. In light of a *full expectation* of that Final Moment, He urges us in this present moment to abandon ourselves wholeheartedly to obedience to Christ. In the Day of Glory all believers (including John) will prostrate themselves before the Throne, not from terror but out of sheer unbounded adoration for the Lamb, we will

QUOTABLE QUOTE

If, therefore, all things are put under Christ with the exception of Him who put them under Him, the Son is Lord of all, and the Father is Lord of Him. There is one God, to whom all things are made subject together with Christ, to whom the Father has made all things subject—with the exception of Himself.

(HIPPOLYTUS — CHURCH FATHER AND MARTYR, C. 205)

be filled forever with unfettered fervency for His magnificent supremacy (Rev. 5). In greater measure than we have yet known that experience can become much more ours even today.

Passion is God's gift to us. Any child of His can become passion-driven to the degree he allows himself to be *Person*-driven, reassured by a hope shaped around Christ for *all* that He is.

THINK WITH ME ...
In what sense is a loss of passion a result of "spiritual warfare"?

Even those already on fire for Christ are not quite out of the woods, however. Passion untouched by sin or fear can still come under siege from another camp. Our enemy prowls near every believer who is motivated by a righteous resolve to follow the Redeemer. This opponent is diametrically opposed to Christ's message of hope and the passion it inspires in us. He is ready to devour any who would embrace either (1 Pet. 5).

At the minimum Satan is determined to *distract* us from God's promises by *diverting* whatever hope we have in Christ into a myriad of empty enticements. He wants to *diffuse* our affections for the Son, to *douse* any flicker of passion he uncovers that might move us to pursue God's Son more intentionally (2 Pet. 2, 3).

But the conflict goes deeper. Forces of darkness love to fabricate thick barriers against fresh revelations of the character and Kingdom of Jesus. Inside the church in Corinth, for example, Paul identified "strongholds" of deception that obscured their growth in the knowledge of God's glory. False teachers had discouraged the believers' surrender to Jesus as exclusive Lord (2 Cor. 10). Paul claimed this activity was a result of Satan's doing everything he could to draw Christians away from pure, undistracted devotion to Jesus. Satan's goal was to enslave them to counterfeit gospels, creating in them a crisis of supremacy. In turn it was the believers' duty — one of their most effective tactics — to stay on the alert. They needed to be ready to oppose the enemy with the truth about the Lord at every opportunity, "bringing every thought into obedience to Christ" (2 Cor. 11)

Mark this clearly (because the Devil does!): The capstone of the Consummation just ahead of us will involve a chorus of consuming passion for Christ, swelling forever from the saints in Glory. Therefore it follows: If we intend to conquer for the Lamb in *this* world, between now and then our ardent affections for Him, amplified with pulsating praises, must increasingly dominate us each day we walk with Him. Our passion for Jesus (which actually starts, as we saw in chapter 5, with *His* passion for *us*) is where all evil powers will firmly and fully meet their demise at the End. We can be thankful that to significant measure this can happen even now as we make His supremacy our identity (compare Eph. 6:10-20 with Rev. 19:11-16).

THINK WITH ME …

What overriding *disconnect* often triggers our loss of passion?

But there's one more reason for the depletion of passion for Christ among evangelicals: *the profound disconnect between the Biblical vision of Christ and that which is promoted in many of our churches.*

This phenomenon helps explain how sin and fear and Satan can get footholds in our lives and sabotage our zeal. For many of us the disconnect began the very hour of our initial conversion. It was in the DNA of the kind of gospel that came to us. The initial truth we believed too often lacked much of what this *Joyful Manifesto* has sought to recover. The full extent of Christ's gracious reign was somehow never heard — maybe never spoken.

Here's my point: Current inabilities to sustain fervency for Christ and His Kingdom are due more often than not to the *impoverished content* of the good news that brought us to Him in the first place. It simply was not comprehensive enough. Self-serving proclamations, however well-intended, diminished our view of the fuller implications of His lordship. Shortsighted testimonies about His Kingdom distorted our view of, and dampened enthusiasm for, the role we must play to advance His cause among the nations.

To restore passion to multitudes of Christians, it's time for spiritual leaders to tackle head on the deficiencies in our teachings about hope in Jesus. It's time to develop effective ways to get the *caring* back into our *calling* as God's people. We

---

QUOTABLE QUOTE

My view of the work of Christ was severely limited. It wasn't that I didn't believe the right truth. I simply didn't understand how far-reaching and all-inclusive the work of Christ really was. When I discovered the universal and cosmic nature of the work of Christ, it was like being born again. I was given a key to a Christian way of viewing the whole world, a key that unlocked the door to a rich storehouse of spiritual treasures, treasures that I am still handling in sheer amazement.

(DR. ROBERT WEBBER)

must not delay. Otherwise, the impoverished vision of Him we suffer will continue to sap vitality out of the Church's fervency for His supremacy.

A Loss of Passion Due to
Shortsighted Messages about Christ
(2 Timothy 4:1-5)

Reviewing recent reports by Gallup, Barna and others on Christian perspectives in America, one could argue easily that a loss of passion has overtaken millions of believers. The truth about Christ and His supremacy is simply not getting through to us. A case in point: 20% who call themselves "born again" still believe in reincarnation, as do 26% in astrology, 45% in human potential for getting into heaven and 25% in communicating with the dead. Chuck Colson describes this as "salad-bar Christianity", mixing up so many other agendas with the lordship of Christ that many are no longer moved by Jesus' call to follow Him exclusively. Their passions are set on other things besides the glory of God's Son.

Looking at this current condition, some have proposed (humorously) that we rename great old hymns of the Church to reflect our trivialization of the Glad Tidings. For example: "I Surrender Some", "Fill My Spoon, Lord", "Take My Life and Let Me Be", "I Love To Talk About Telling The Story", or (my favorite) "Oh, How I *Like* Jesus".

If you ask Christians, "How *strong* is your passion for Christ?" primarily you are asking, "How compelling was the *message* of Christ you first heard and received?" That is parallel to asking them, "How *big* was the hope in Christ to which that message pointed you?"

Did the message you heard at the beginning of your walk with Jesus captivate you with the righteous reign of Jesus, both for you and for nations? Or was it more about the possibilities of personal fulfillment through the addition of a Savior to your life? Was the message primarily focused on *Kingdom* prospects, or more on enhancing *immediate* prospects? Did it announce to you a supreme Lord in whom everything in Heaven and on earth is to be consummated, who therefore has every right to consummate your life in Himself and His purposes? Or was the offer more akin to exciting news about a good God who was ready to help you get a good life with Christ available where needed?

For many the message seemed only to promise: *"God loves you and has a wonderful plan for your life in Jesus"* — which is a genuinely happy hope! And entirely true! But this offer that speaks more to the *centrality* of Jesus must be incorporated into a grander invitation, one that addresses the *supremacy* of Jesus. An attending announcement might sound something like this:

> *God has a wonderful plan to sum up all*
> *things under His Son as Lord*
> *and to glorify His name among the*
> *nations for all ages to come.*
> *And, He loves you enough to give*
> *you a strategic place in it.*

The first offer (improperly interpreted by many as a "me-centered" message) has been separated too often from the second (which is overwhelmingly, unavoidably a message about the preeminence of Someone Else). Plainly, the first offer is not the final word God intends for us. Unless it is coupled with the second, it can end up inadvertently fostering both a hope that is hollow and a passion that is shallow.

Tragically, the Gospel embraced by a multitude of Christians today appears to have been truncated ("dumbed-down" some have said) in order to make it more palatable, less demanding, more manageable, less costly, more pragmatic for meeting daily needs. Why don't we *care* about the things of Christ as the New Testament calls us to do? Here's a big part of the answer.

QUOTABLE QUOTE

At heart, Boomers are consumers. The way we presented Christ to most Boomers struck a resonant chord with them from that mindset. We told them all they had to do was say a prayer admitting they made some mistakes, they're sorry and they want to be forgiven. Boomers weighed the downside — which really amounted to nothing more than a one-time admission of imperfection and weakness in return for permanent peace with God — and figured it was a no-brainer, a can't-lose transaction. The consequence has been millions of Boomers who said the prayer, asked for forgiveness and went on with their life, with virtually nothing changed.

(DR. GEORGE BARNA)

THINK WITH ME ...
How *need*-centered is the message about Christ most Christians have heard?

A colleague recently related that a pastor friend of his, anxious to reach a widely unchurched community, set about advertising a series of sermons with catchy titles like "Making A Living or A Life?"; "Redefining Success On The Job"; "How Much Is Enough?"; and "How To Have A Happy Marriage". This pastor justified his subject matter as a way to appeal to people's search for happiness so that he could show them how "finding Christ brings true happiness" (which is true, of course, as far as it goes). Then my friend, who is a published theologian and was involved in parish ministry for 20 years, made this thought-provoking observation: "He's not actually preaching *Christ* in the best sense. He's got the *message* we're to bring confused with the *fruits* it's supposed to produce. Unwittingly he's delivering sermons bent toward what Dietrich Bonhoeffer once called 'cheap grace'. We must never forget [my friend concluded] that the message you use to *win them* is the same message you then must use to *keep them*."

Studies estimate that nearly every Sunday morning a majority of sermons heard across America are centered on daily survival issues rather than Christ's Kingdom issues. Too frequently we evangelicals propagate among ourselves a gospel that fails to get beyond immediate remedies for hurting hearts, or failing families, or troubled communities. Too infrequently do our messages summon hearers to passionately pursue Christ Himself for all He is worth, making a greater revelation of Him the primary goal of the Sunday sermon experience.

Such an outlook eventually produces spiritual hypochondriacs. Christians demand a regimen of churchly remedies to make life more bearable —

guaranteeing the enhancement of personal relationships, the development of human potential, or the healing of the "inner child". These believers settle for spiritual sedatives that never can ignite a pursuit of Christ for who He is, what's on His heart, and where He is headed.

Others term this trend the *"privatization"* of the gospel. The Good News has been reshaped to emphasize answers for *personal* hopes about success in marriage and family life, or satisfying emotional longings, or advancing career ambitions. Another insight from Charles Colson: The Gospel has been transformed into a commodity, with the local church acting as the retail outlet, while members are seen as customers. Naïvely perhaps, we've marketed a "smorgasbord Christianity" that encourages us to pick and choose according to personal needs and tastes!

I have no intention of throwing stones here. Certainly none of this analysis is meant to single out clergy. I, too, have shortchanged the Gospel in my own ministry. Sometimes I, too, struggle with a loss of passion by entertaining meager messages about my Monarch.

As horrifying as the following questions may sound we need to ponder: Is the message spread by the evangelical church actually arousing *inordinate affections* in our hearers? Does it cause people to treasure the blessings of the Christian enterprise more than they treasure Christ *as the Prize?* Do we encourage people to want the *things* of Christ more than they want Christ *Himself?* Do we foster a vision among our people that makes the Lord Jesus a *means* to self-determined ends rather than the *End* for which we exist?

And when we invite people to Christ, do we inadvertently imply that they need only come to Him as far as *they* feel the need to come? In other words (and I shudder even to think it might be so!), do our offers of God's grace unwittingly encourage others to *exploit* Christ for their own agendas? To attempt to *manipulate* Him to enhance their lives? To interpret Him essentially as someone at *their* disposal for their own benefit?

The answers can tell us a lot about the kind of gospel that occupies the hearts of many church members. Those answers can unmask a variety of "trite Christologies" that explain disconnections between claims about faith in Jesus and the depth (or lack thereof) of actual devotion to Him.

THINK WITH ME ...
What are some forms which "trite Christologies" take inside today's Church?

Sad to say, some church members appear to be more motivated to attend potluck suppers in Parish Hall than to prepare their souls for (or even to think about preparing for) the Marriage Supper of the Lamb (Rev. 19). How can that be?

How can it be that every week thousands of worshippers in Sunday services, convened to praise the Savior, find themselves embroiled in what observers call "worship wars"? We fuss so much over choosing correct choruses for our gatherings it's hard to remain fascinated with the majesty of the Master we've come to adore. Some can become so passionate about styles or methods that they fail to get excited about the excellencies of the Son whose glories they celebrate. We're intent on how the music meets our emotional needs; or how the rituals preserve our cherished traditions; or how our singing and prayers provide dynamic spiritual experiences. But, what kind of Savior have we proclaimed that allows such attitudes to arise among us in the first place?

When I encourage someone to "invite Jesus into your heart", is it possible that in doing so I actually create a personal crisis of supremacy for her or him? What if a person unconsciously concludes from this phrase: "Jesus in my heart makes Him more readily available to me, as required to meet my needs, under my supervision so things don't get out of hand"? No one would ever admit this out loud, of course. But for all practical purposes many have settled for a safer Savior, a manageable one, downgraded by theological formulas designed to make Him easier to cope with. Basically we have rendered Him *auxiliary* to our Christian experience. (The Bible might choose to call this *idolatry!*)

We have *trifled* with the Son of God! For all practical purposes our self-serving messages about Him have *domesticated* Him in our own eyes. We have *marginalized* Him among His own people. We have *sanitized* the Son of God! We've settled for sleepy, sentimental, scaled-down versions of the One who reigns supreme. We seldom see Him as Lord over creation, over history, over the Church and over all the ages to come. Seldom do our hearts and minds get intrigued with *Him* above everything else.

May Heaven forgive us! Trite Christologies haunt the evangelical movement. We're plagued with a whole spectrum of self-serving messages that gut the greatness of our hope in God while putting out the fire of our passion for Jesus. To name just a few, we've redefined the Lord Jesus Christ as:

- Our *"handyman"* — seen as a source of "quick fixes", to deal with our adversities by providing instant solutions on command.

- Our *"interior decorator"* — contracted to embellish and enhance everything we do in the arena of churchly activities, giving it that "extra something" that always makes our efforts feel so special.

- Our *"EMT"* (emergency medical technician) — poised on standby, ready to be brought in at those points where we have finally exhausted our own ingenuity and resources, especially in our determination to do something important for God.

- Our *"personal trainer"* — kept on retainer, the way we depend on our favorite golf coach, to provide practical pointers from time to time so we can play the game of life a little more successfully.

- Our *"pharmacist"* — dispensing liberating self-discoveries, or putting healing balm on hurting hearts, or prescribing salves for the suffering that life throws at us.

This is just a starter list. I'm sure you could come up with a number of other metaphors. But there's one more I'd like to suggest. It's the one I've observed most often in my years of travel in Christian circles — the one developed in chapter 1:

- Our *"mascot"*
  This may be the most descriptive (and most disturbing) of all the self-serving visions of our Lord. We welcome Him among us to cheer us on, to inspire our efforts, to give us confidence about the outcome of the contest. But in the end the "game" is really about us, not about Him. We call the plays, organize the team, execute the strategies, pile up the points and achieve the wins. Most of the time Jesus is relegated to the sidelines as our figurehead — the "name" by which we take the field, the definition of all we aspire to, the one we call on when we get behind. Our cheers may be for Him, but our victories are for us. Rarely does it cross our minds that the *supremacy* of Christ means that He *is* the game in the final analysis. He coaches the players, calls the strategies, quarterbacks the plays, achieves the touchdowns, wins the game, and gets the "write up" next day. The

team has no existence and no reason to exist apart from Him. From Him, through Him, for Him, under Him, in Him and to Him are all things. And every fan in the stadium must bow at His feet before they dare to cheer in His name.

Each of these trite Christologies holds an element of truth, to be sure. Of course, Jesus is available for emergencies. Of course, He can transform everything we do for the Father into something beautiful. Of course, He trains, and cures, and inspires. Yet each of these taken alone betrays the scope of the hope God gives us in Christ's glorious greatness. How can heartfelt passion be ignited by trite Christologies like these? In fact, if this is all that He is — handyman, pharmacist, mascot — where's there any *need* for heartfelt passion to start with?

Clearly none of these "lesser lords" can ever begin to express the wonder of our original definition of Christ's supremacy (see chapter 1). None of them by themselves could ever begin to encourage an enthusiasm for Him that matches *Heaven's* celebration of ...

Who He is as the Son of God
   (the summation of hope — the focus of His supremacy).

Where He leads in the Purposes of God
   (the consummation of hope — the fulfillment of His supremacy).

How He imparts the Resources of God
   (the approximation of hope — the fullness of His supremacy).

What He receives from the People of God
   (the consuming passion of hope — the fervency of His supremacy).

May I be personal with you for a moment? For all practical purposes, what would the visible intensity of *your* passion as a disciple tell others about the "Christology" that empowers in your daily walk with the Son?

THINK WITH ME ...
What is the greatest tragedy shortsighted messages create?

Above every other concern this chapter has addressed regarding self-serving, shortsighted messages of Christ, surely the most grievous is this: *The Cross itself gets trivialized by every one of them.* Every superficial Christology distorts the testimony of Calvary. Our witness to each other about the wounds of Jesus ends up being weakened and wounded itself, rendered ineffective.

This same danger hounded 1ˢᵗ century Christians, too. That's why Paul composed such a dramatic close to his epistle to the Galatians. He knew they were susceptible to the seduction of shrunken gospels. So he wrote "God forbid that I should boast [a form of passion] except in the cross of our Lord Jesus Christ [the focus of passion], by which the world is crucified to me and I to the world [both displays of Christ's supremacy, keeping our passion alive]" (Gal. 6). No apologies here. These words exude confidence — not in a physical cross but in the One who hung there. The greatest power and most profound wisdom God would ever share — the fullest revelation of the magnitude of the Son's majesty — was manifested in the "powerlessness" and "simplicity" of Jesus as He died for all (1 Cor. 1 and 2).

So we, too, must return to the message of the Cross — to the passion of the Christ — if we're ever to restore *our* passion for Him and reaffirm our hope in Him for ALL that He is. Describing one form of his own zeal for his Lord, Paul exclaimed: "I have been crucified with Christ and I no longer live, but Christ lives in me. The life I live in the body, I live by faith in the Son of God, who loved me and gave himself for me" (Gal. 2). For him the Cross was inseparable from heart-and-soul *fervency* for Christ's supremacy!

THINK WITH ME ...
How did Jesus confront "trite Christologies" in His own ministry?

Our triflings with Jesus are not that much different from what we read in John 6. The crowd's goal, you'll recall, was to make Him their king. At first glance His supremacy seemed to have captured their hearts. But in point of fact they were simply clamoring for another round of miracle bread to satisfy their pressing lack of lunch. Jesus would have no part of the sham coronation. He rebuked them for ignoring the heavenly feast He had come to spread before them. His intended focus for them was not on His miracles but on *Himself*.

So, He presented them with an alternative — the opportunity to enter into a thoroughly exclusive, all-consuming relationship with Him as Lord. He described it in graphic terms using the

QUOTABLE QUOTE

In the midst of all gatherings of Thy people may there be the downfall of holy fire. May the Lord Jesus Christ be exalted in the midst of His church. Bring many to His feet, we pray. Work, Lord, work mightily! Thy church cries to Thee. Oh, leave us not! Lord Jesus, in Thee all fullness dwells. Thou dost fill heaven. Thou wilt surely fill all things. Fill us, oh! fill us today with all the fullness of God, and make Thy people joyful and strong and heavenly!

(CHARLES SPURGEON)

metaphor of *cannibalism*! He invited them to ingest His redeeming work by faith. (Now that represents passion!) The result, He promised, would be a totally resurrected life for any who engaged Him wholeheartedly and settle for nothing less.

To His sorrow, as John 6 records, most of Jesus' disciples walked away. It seems the parameters He set on passion were too comprehensive and demanding. Yet, paradoxically, they were also too narrow, too limiting, too exclusive. Fortunately, a remaining few concluded: "Where else can we go? You alone have the words of eternal life!" In that hour their prior choice to wrap up their identity and destiny in Him was re-affirmed. Having already experienced firsthand eternal hope defined by His very presence, all but Judas determined Jesus would remain the love of their lives forever.

As the New Testament record testifies, their dedication to His exaltation stood the test of time. All the disciples labored tirelessly for the Kingdom out of devotion to their Lord until their earthy ministries ended, for many in martyrdom.

When Our Losses Become God's Gains
(Isaiah 54:1-8)

Hope and passion go together. Loss of hope in the Church normally results in loss of passion. Both shortfalls are usually the bitter fruit of a much greater deficiency: the crisis of supremacy. But this need not be the end of our story. God's Kingdom abounds with fresh opportunities.

Crisis and opportunity — quite a combination. The mix can be explosive when we belong to Jesus! No crisis of supremacy should ever be seen as irreversible. Proper repentance over trite Christologies holds the promise of *re-converting* us back to Christ for all that He is; *recommitting* us to His unrivaled dominion in our lives; *re-engaging* us with Him in the light of His incomparable glory and unshakeable purposes; *replacing* self-serving messages about Him with a hope set on "things above, where Christ sits at God's right hand" — in order to walk once again in the triumphs of His grace.

THINK WITH ME ...
Why might Chinese and Hebrew words
for "crisis" encourage us?

The Chinese word for crisis combines two characters: One for "danger" and the other for "opportunity". Mandarin speakers correctly conclude that a crisis not only alerts us to imminent danger but also opens us to previously unexploited opportunities. The same is true for the crisis of supremacy with its attendant loss of hope and passion. Left unchecked the crisis is spiritually threatening. But it can also become God's tool to help us write a dynamic new chapter in the history of the Christian movement. It can become His prod. It can incite in us far deeper explorations of the King's heart, far richer experiences of the King's dominion.

Interestingly, the Hebrew word for crisis carries much the same idea as the Chinese characters. The term literally means a "birthing stool". It refers to a piece of furniture upon which a Jewish woman would position herself in Old Testament times to aid in delivery of her baby. To be sure, the stool was a place of pain and trauma. A woman in labor might feel as if she were being swallowed up in the contractions. But at the end travail gave way to the marvelous moment of motherhood. Agony turned to fulfillment. At the foot of the stool emerged a new life, a new beginning. In the same way a spiritual crisis can actually "midwife" a whole new set of blessings as our desperation pushes us back into the arms of the Son of God.

Speaking for myself, I know it's time for *me* to face straight-on any remaining crises of supremacy in my own life. Each one establishes a unique opportunity to say once again:

I affirm:
In light of all Christ is, there is far *more* of Him to know
than I've yet discovered.
Therefore, I must be passionate to know Him much more than I am.
And I must draw near to Him with far more hope in Him than ever before.

I also affirm:
There is much *more* God longs for the Church to discover
about His Son.
I must, therefore, proclaim Him to Christians more fully than I ever have.
Considering the full extent of hope believers share in Christ's supremacy,
I must never fear praying for or proclaiming His glory too much.

Do these affirmations reflect desires of your heart, too? If so, I invite you to come with me into *Volume III: A Campaign of Hope.* It is the best next step we can take together. Let me show you why.

THINK WITH ME ...
Are you willing to join me in a *Campaign of Hope?*

Even as I write, zeal for our Triumphant Lord is being stirred afresh in thousands of Christian young people around the world who are affirming their willingness to follow Christ at any cost. They share a common conviction: "God is preparing to give our generation a mighty revelation of the glory of His Son for the sake of the nations, and we want to be part of it!"

Theirs is a Campaign of Hope. They are inviting others to join them. Over the past two decades I've walked among movements of young people worldwide who care deeply about Christ and His global cause, such as: Youth with a Mission, Operation Mobilization, Marches for Jesus, Mission Korea, Europe Hope, Teen Mania, Acquire The Fire, Caleb Project, The Call, Campus Renewal, Sold Out, along with the tried-and-true works of Campus Crusade for Christ and InterVarsity Christian Fellowship.

One such movement actually incorporated itself recently with the word *"Passion"!* Then teams of students were sent to university campuses across America to raise up communities of worshippers-doubling-as-evangelists. Sponsoring annual national gatherings, they recruited thousands to commit to 24 hours of fasting and prayer while camping out in open farm fields. The events, called "One Day", were designed to return young people to schools and churches with one resolve: To glorify Christ and help fulfill His purposes for earth's unreached peoples.

The common thread that runs through all of these examples? Passion for Christ and His Kingdom. His youthful followers are inflamed by hope in His supremacy. But this is a movement open to young and old alike. Campaigns of similar design (even if the particulars are quite different) must become a lifestyle for all of us who want to confront and cure the crisis of supremacy inside the Church. **Volume Three** explores many practical strategies for getting a Campaign of Hope off the ground where you live.

First, we tackle the priority question: "What must such a campaign proclaim?" (This is answered in *chapter 9.*) The right message at the right moment has the power to restore vision and re-ignite passion toward Christ, unleashing a Christ-awakening in one life or in one church. Proclaiming among *Christians* a fuller vision of Jesus and His reign not only recaptures hearts for Him but ultimately empowers many to proclaim the same message among the nations. We're on our way to seize new ground for His mission among the lost.

Then *chapters 10-12* unpack three major applications of that message to be used wherever it is proclaimed to God's people. Each fills in the "job description" for those whom God uses to help the Church recover the *hope* in Jesus we are meant to have. I call them Messengers of *Hope*, Prisoners of *Hope* and Vanguards of *Hope*.

Ponder the egg! In *Mere Christianity* C.S. Lewis, speaking of Christian conversion, warned that eggs (believers) must either "hatch or go bad". The chick can't stay inside the shell indefinitely and expect to thrive. In the same way, unless Campaigns of Hope begin to unfold inside many of our churches, a whole lot of "chicks" may never break free of their "shells". They may never discover the richness of following Jesus without limits.

"Hatch or go bad." Isn't it time for a host of heralds to invade the "chicken coop" and set some captives free?

QUOTABLE QUOTE

What is at stake in pastoral admonition and in preaching is not merely the Church's progress in sanctification but its perseverance in final salvation. There is no standing still in the Christian life. Either we are advancing toward salvation, or we are drifting away to destruction. Drifting is mortal danger (Heb. 2:1). If we do not point our people to the inexhaustible riches of Christ so as to stir them up to go forward into more of God, then we encourage drifting downstream where they will make shipwreck of their faith. (1 Tim. 1:19)

(Dr. John Piper)

Before exploring the campaign, however, experience a "pause that refreshes". Set aside the next five minutes for *Interlude II: A Prayer over the Crisis of Supremacy.* Use it to confess the crux of our crisis to the Father. Recite it to declare your desire for deeper devotion to the Son. Let it be your cry to the Spirit to restore the hope all of us so desperately need.

Try reading it aloud. Make it your own. See if it does not touch what really matters to you at this moment. See if it does not express to God a little of what you are feeling right now.

INTERLUDE II

A Prayer Over
the Crisis

*(To be read responsively where possible, using alternate
dark and light print)*

We press into Your heart this day, glorious God and Father of our Lord
Jesus Christ.

**We celebrate all that Your precious Son is — who He is to us, and
for us, over us, and within us, through us, and before us, and
upon us.**

Before all Heaven we proclaim:

- **Christ is supreme!** — He is sovereign, superior, sufficient and
  totally satisfying!

- **Christ is our hope!** — He is the summation of all Your promises,
  the source of all Your riches, more and more and more, for now and
  forever!

- **Christ is our glory!** — He is Alpha & Omega, the consummation of all Your purposes, for all creation, for all peoples, for all the Ages to come! In Him our life is hidden with You, until the hour He returns in the final triumphs of grace and truth.

- **Christ is among us!** — He is accessible to us now, in all of His riches. He stands with us now, willing, able and ready to act for us, in us, and through us to magnify ALL that He is, before us and before all nations!

[SELAH: Pause for silent reflection]

Therefore, we REPENT — individually and on behalf of all your people:

- **We repent ... for how we have *diminished* your Son,** regarding Him more as our mascot than our Monarch.

- **We repent ... for how we have *manipulated* your Son,** coming to Him to use Him, as far as we think we need Him — that far and no more.

- **We repent ... for how we have *hoarded* your Son,** seeking His blessings for ourselves, with little thought about bringing those blessings to others. **We've assumed that He was there only for us.** We've acted as if He was not Lord of neighbors and nations.

- **We repent ... for how we have *resisted* your Son,** withholding our affections from Him because we were afraid of what it would cost us to draw near to Him — and thus we denied His lordship over all.

- **WE repent ... for how we've *replaced* your Son...**with creeds, and programs, and organizations, and causes performed in His name — **but without the consuming passion He deserves as the Center and Circumference of everything for us and all peoples everywhere.**

[SELAH: Pause for silent reflection]

Confront our crisis of supremacy. **O Lamb of God.** *Cast out* our crisis of supremacy. **O Lamb of God.** *Cure* our crisis of supremacy. **O Lamb of God.**

Forgive us! **Cleans us!** Purify us! **Resurrect us!** Re-convert us! **Restore us!** Refill us! **Re-commission us!** By your blood. By Your mercy. O Lamb of God. **O Lamb of God.**

We are *ready* — **ready! ...** to revolutionize mind and action with new hope in the promises of your Word ... **ready! ...** to embrace the full extent of Christ's glorious reign for us and all peoples ... **ready! ...** to walk with Him in passionate obedience ... **ready! ...** to be wrapped up in Him and His global cause ... **ready!...** for this...**and nothing less!**

Together in hope, with brokenness mixed with great joy — **O God of our salvation, we cry out for all to hear:** *"Lord Jesus, **Come and conquer us!** Lord Jesus, **Come and conquer us!** Lord Jesus, **Come and conquer us!"***

[SELAH: Pause for silent reflection]

Holy Father, in this decisive moment, by Your Spirit, we adore Your Son using the words of Saint Augustine:

"Redeemer of the ends of the earth:
You called, You cried, You shattered our deafness.
You sparkled, You burned, You drove away our blindness.
You shed your fragrance, and we drew in our breath.
Therefore, from now on, we will pant for YOU alone."

To that end, Father, awaken us — **awaken us to see ALL that the Lord Jesus Christ is:** to see who He is as the Son of God ... **to see where He is leading in the Purposes of God** ... to see how He imparts the Resources of God ... **and to see what He must receive from the People of God.** Quicken us to pursue Your magnificent promises which are wonderfully defined by His supremacy! **Help us recover ALL the hope we are meant to have in our Sovereign Savior.** Do this for the revelation of Your glory in Him, throughout this nation — **and among all the nations** — beginning in this hour and in this place. **Hallelujah! AMEN!** Amen! **It shall be done!** It *shall* be done.

Volume Three

A CAMPAIGN OF HOPE

Recovering the Hope We Are Meant to Have!

Rise up, O saints of God!
From vain ambitions turn;
Christ rose triumphant that your hearts
with nobler zeal might burn.

Commit your hearts to seek
the paths which Christ has trod;
and quickened by the Spirit's power,
rise up, O saints of God!

Speak out, O saints of God!
Despair engulfs earth's frame;
as heirs of God's baptismal grace,
HIS WORD OF HOPE PROCLAIM.

— *Norman Forness*

9

WHAT MUST THIS CAMPAIGN PROCLAIM?

His Supremacy Is Our *Message of Hope* to the Church

"Please give me my *special thing!*" came the appeal of each child from the bedroom.

All through their growing up years, one by one Robyne and I would tuck in our children by whispering to each a single sentence — one simple benediction uniquely designed for each child. "My special thing" they liked to call it. Built on the root meaning of their first and middle names, each blessing reflects our sense of their destiny as followers of Christ. How I cherished my nightly "daddy" routine with Adam, Bethany and Benjamin, each adopted from India.

Benjamin (which is Hebrew for "son of the right hand"), for example, has the middle name of "Dheeraj" (Hindi for "prince of courage"). Putting them together formed my special thing for him. Snuggling up close, I would say: "God is making you to be a courageous follower of the Son at His right hand."

Thus, every day ended for them with a *message of hope* — a promise personalized for each child, anticipating a tomorrow shaped by nothing less than Christ's supremacy. Night after night we encouraged our little ones to delight in their calling in Jesus which is now how they approach life as adults. (Today, incidentally, Benjamin is doing urban missionary work, courageously sharing the Son every day with others.)

Surely, planting hope toward the Lord Jesus within another human being is one of the greatest ministries we can ever have, beginning with our children.

On a grander scale throughout the ages God Himself has spoken a myriad of "special things" to His children. As suggested earlier there may be as many as 7,000 separate promises in the Word of God. Each one is focused on establishing the preeminence of God's Son. Accordingly, each promise can help to "color in" any full-orbed message about Christ, not only for unbelievers but for Christians as well. That message will be the central contribution of the "Campaign of Hope" discussed in the next four chapters. This campaign is one mission desperately needed *inside* the Church.

This chapter catalogs some of the unparalleled "special things" God invites us to share with each other — a vision that can cure any crisis of supremacy. We will:

- **Survey the makeup of the "Message of Hope" we're called to proclaim to each other.**

- **Identify the impact such a message can have on our hope and passion toward Christ.**

- **Apply our findings to a Campaign of Hope throughout the Church.**

- **Uncover characteristics of people who actively promote this message.**

- **Explore how you can know if you are ready to serve in a Campaign of Hope.**

- **Show why we must do so in *prayer* — first of all and through it all.**

Proclaiming Christ: Our Message of Hope
(2 Thessalonians 1:5-12)

Listen to a widow of September 11 as she addressed a national conference in Philadelphia shortly after her young husband died in a Pennsylvania field on

Flight 93: "After the hijacking I was left with a choice: Either living with fear or living with hope. As a follower of Christ I could only choose hope, hope in Him." Despite unspeakable tragedy this sorrowing saint offered to other believers a message about an "abounding hope by the power of the Holy Spirit" (Rom. 15). She proclaimed to Christians that hope does not just fix its sights on the next few days or years, as important as that is. In the final analysis true Biblical hope encompasses a *Person*. It exalts in the triumphant consummation of all things in Him, when death itself will be swallowed up in victory (1 Cor. 15).

While multitudes may see only a hopeless end to their existence, Christians proclaim *an endless hope*. We become a people *alive* in hope. For us the true meaning of current events (even tragic ones) lies largely in the Grand Finale and in the Son of God who will reign undisputed at the End.

That's why our message about the Lord Jesus Christ, especially to each other as believers, must remain indelibly marked by a spirit of *hope-filledness*. It should exalt the One whose role is to rule in the Church as "Christ in you, the hope of glory" (Col. 1), so that we become a people passionate for "Christ Jesus, our hope" (1 Tim. 1).

The instincts of this 9/11 victim (and of others, like my friend Lori) were to reach out to fellow believers to help them exchange *their* burdens of hopelessness with a life-restoring vision of hope in Christ. That day her love for Christ caused her to take up her own Campaign of Hope. She forced the issue of the supremacy of Christ to come to the forefront for her hearers to help them grow into disciples gripped by hope in Christ.

All of us are called to this same mission. Christians not only *pray as if* all God's promises were true; we not only *obey as if* greater triumphs in Jesus are yet to come; but we also can *speak as if* our Message of Hope is the greatest gift we can offer another believer. To fully love the saints is to take them captive to the same hope in Christ that grips ourselves. Only to the degree the Church first is flooded with proclaimers of Biblical hope will we, in turn, truly feel compelled to share it with unsaved neighbors and unreached nations.

QUOTABLE QUOTE

The world dreams of progress, power and of the future. Disciples meditate on the End, the last judgment and the coming Kingdom. To such heights the world cannot rise.

(DIETRICH BONHOEFFER)

THINK WITH ME ...
How does our message stack up against other "hopes" the world talks about?

At the opening of the 21st century the nations witnessed a barrage of pre-meditated massacres of epoch proportions. Muslim extremists sought to annihilate resistance to their radical Islamic utopia. In doing so they were willing, for Allah's sake, to become martyrs — "suicide bombers" – and take a host of innocents with them.

By contrast, a very different vision occupies center-stage in the Church's mission to the nations. The hope the Gospel unleashes can feel *wild* sometimes (as Tom Sine suggests) — provocative, unfathomable, unpredictable, uncontainable — reflecting characteristics of the One who encompasses hope on both personal and cosmic levels. Biblical promises boast blessed benefits that Mohammed's followers never dreamed of. Our message is not about utopian revolutions of human fabrication. It is, instead, about a life-giving, liberating *Person* who is destined to consummate the whole universe *in Himself.*

To be sure, our hope — like theirs — is based on blood. But it is not the blood of fanatical martyrs out to destroy the enemy at any price. Ours is the blood of a Surrendered Servant whose fanaticism (if we may call it that) was displayed by His substitutionary *sacrifice,* given to spare and redeem His enemies. Suffering, not violence, provides the irrefutable argument for *His right to rule.* The Bible testifies: " ... that in everything He might have the supremacy. For God was pleased to have all his fullness dwell in him, and through him to reconcile to himself all things, things in heaven and on earth, making peace through his blood, shed on the cross" (Col. 1).

None of the Bible's "big picture" talk of hope makes any sense apart from the *Cross* of Christ. As we noted earlier, hope in Christ's supremacy is empty apart from hope in His sacrifice. Every message we proclaim to one another as Christians as well as to earth's unreached peoples must retain

QUOTABLE QUOTE

Does Islam — or any other faith besides Christianity — cherish the crucifixion of the God-Man, Jesus Christ, as the only ground of our acceptance with God? The answer is no. Only Christians "follow the Lamb" who was "slain" as the one and only Redeemer who sits on the "throne" of God (Rev. 14:4; 5:6; 7:17) ... The closer you get to what makes Christianity ghastly, the closer you get to what makes it glorious.

(DR. JOHN PIPER)

the Cross at its heart to remain a legitimate heralding of *hope*, or to boast any lasting effect in raising up a people of hope. The entire book of Revelation is superintended by the *Lamb* of God (Rev. 5 onward). The Cross has become for all time the greatest display of Christ's supremacy we will ever experience! That's why it always dominated the New Testament's "Message of Hope" even when — and especially when — delivered to believers.

In his memorial eulogy for seven astronauts lost in the 1986 explosion of the space shuttle Challenger, President Ronald Reagan suggested that even in dying they had "broken the bounds of earth" and "touched the face of God". Then he went on to say of their sacrifice: "The Challenger crew was pulling us into the future, and we will continue to follow them." In a similar way every facet of who Christ is pulls us onward. To adapt the President's words, Christ *is*, in Himself, the Face of God. He is also the One to whom belongs a future of phenomenal blessings. Because of His willingness to *die* to get us there the lives of Christians are saturated with the promises and purposes of God.

Christianity is *"good* news" — even more, it is the *best* news! — because it is *great* news about a great *future* shaped by God's everlasting purposes through a great Savior. The major difference between Islam (or any other world religion) and true Christianity impinges on this scope of the hope Christians claim and proclaim. In Christ God offers believers every possibility intended for His creation. In Christ every degree of "newness" designed to last forever has been brought to us, fully. Christ encompasses in His very being everything we long to receive *from* God as well as everything we long to become *for* God. Both. All the Father's promises are stamped with one resounding "Yes!" to us because the Father has appointed a person — His Son — to bring them to completion *for* us (2 Cor. 1). He alone inhabits, and then happily shares, His inheritance with those who surrender by faith to Him as Lord of all (Eph. 1).

This is a "Message of Hope" the world can't possibly match.

THINK WITH ME ...
How did Paul proclaim Christ as the great "Message of Hope" for every Christian?

A few years ago the Bryants relocated to metropolitan New York City. Within a week families living around us welcomed us to the neighborhood with a party. The whole group was quite intriguing. Scores of their members moved into the area 20 years earlier from other parts of the Northeast to establish proximity with each other as members of a denominational renewal community. They call their fellowship the "People of HOPE". As they reached out to us, we observed something quite unusual about their ministry to fellow Christians. Theirs was not a "hope so" approach to life, nor just a "hope for" vision for renewal. Rather, it was a "hope in" relationship with Jesus. For them hope was a noun far more than a verb! For them hope was a *Person* dwelling in their midst. Loving us in very tangible ways, they made Him that much more personal for us as our hope, too.

Where did this vision come from? For them and for all Christians the apostle Paul is a key source. His writings on Christ take us to the pinnacle of Christian hope and give us the heart of every "Message of Hope". No other Bible author does a better job of capturing the supremacy of God's Son. Harnessing dozens of superlative phrases, Paul describes God's Son with a cascade of choice characteristics. Consider a few:

- "everything under His feet"
- "above and beyond"
- "fulfillment of the times"
- "fullness of the Godhead"
- "surpassing glory"
- "every spiritual blessing"
- "above all rule and authority"
- "Him who fills all in all"
- "all things summed up in Christ"
- "the power to bring everything into subjection to Himself"
- "in Him be all glory, throughout all generations, forever and ever"
- "when He comes to be glorified in His saints"
- "brought life and immortality to light"
- "firstfruits of those who sleep"
- "every tongue shall confess that Jesus Christ is Lord"
- "the Blessed Hope and glorious appearing of our great God and Savior, Jesus Christ"

Can you imagine someone being foolish enough to nominate any other name in all of history or from any nation to receive the praises these phrases require we give except the name of our Lord Jesus Christ?

Can you imagine any figures of renown, whether historic or mythological, coming close to matching the person painted in Paul's great Christological texts? I'm thinking of Ephesians 1, Colossians 1, Philippians 2, Romans 8, Galatians 3, and I Thessalonians 4, among others. What a collage of claims. What a panorama of promises. What other personality in the universe, past or present, could ever begin to compete with the Kingdom role Paul attributes to the Lord Jesus Christ? Not even founders of great world religions would dare to compare themselves with the picture penned in such passages.

After studying Paul's take on Christ over many years, I never cease to be amazed at the regal rainbow of truths he uses to exalt our Lord. He does it in a way unparalleled in any other literature, secular or Christian. Each phrase explodes even for *Christians* (Paul's primary readership) the borders of their preconceived notions about what lies ahead. Each phrase pushes *Christians* into new frontiers of expectations toward Christ. Each phrase leaves no doubt that because Jesus reigns, God has much more for His people than we have yet experienced. As Paul puts it in Ephesians 3, by the power of Christ in His Church God will do "exceedingly, abundantly, above and beyond all that we dare to ask, or even think ... throughout all generations, forever and ever. Amen."

A Biblical vision of God's Son, not only from Paul but from the rest of the New Testament (see *Appendix V),* results in a "Message of Hope" that is both *abounding and apocalyptic.* Understanding these two dimensions of our message can help us appreciate why proclaiming the supremacy of Christ to one another must become our central strategy for confronting and curing the crisis of supremacy. So, let's look at each one for a moment.

QUOTABLE QUOTE

To moderns drowning in hopelessness, disappointed, disillusioned, despairing, emotionally isolated, bitter and aching inside, Bible truth comes as a lifeline, for it is future-oriented and hope-centered throughout. The hope that the Scriptures brings us arrests and reverses the drowning experience here and now, generating inward vitality and renewed joy, and banishing forever the sense of having the life choked out of us as the waves break over us. The Bible throughout is a book of Hope.

(Dr. J. I. Packer)

THINK WITH ME ...
Why should our message about Christ point
Christians to an *abounding* hope?

Because it is embodied so fully in God's risen Son, Biblical hope is automatically "abounding", as noted in Paul's benediction over the Church at Rome (Rom. 15): "Now may the God of hope fill you with all joy and peace as you trust in Christ, so that you may *abound* in hope by the power of the Holy Spirit" (vs. 13).

Abounding hope means we rejoice over blessings still waiting to be unleashed even before we see them (Rom. 5). Our hearts are so possessed with God's love for us that we renounce the fear He might somehow fail to fulfill what He has promised us (vs. 5). We celebrate a God who longs to empower us in Jesus way beyond our boldest prayerful projections (Eph. 3:20-21). He wants to surprise us with awesome deeds of righteousness that become, at the same time, hope for all the ends of the earth (Ps. 65:5). He offers to show us great and unsearchable things which we have never seen before (Jer. 33:3). He wants us to experience times when he does "awesome things that we did not expect" because "no eye has seen any God besides you, who acts on behalf of those who wait for him" (Isa. 64). So we pray for the understanding of this hope to grow and enlarge throughout the whole Church (Col. 1:3-6, 23).

According to 1 Peter, abounding hope is God's gift to everyone born again into a *living* hope by Jesus' resurrection from the dead (1 Pet. 1:3). Abounding hope is possible only when there's resurrection hope. Abounding hope sets its sights on promises of even greater grace up ahead (vs. 13). Hope abounds because the life we now share with our Lord constitutes only the beginnings of a harvest of cosmic proportions just before us! Abounding hope anticipates a future as bright and bold as the coming Day of Triumph itself. The Bible says it is by this very hope we are saved, hope in Christ and His ultimate victories (see Rom. 8:24 in its context). Urged on by the Spirit's prayerful groanings for the consummation of everything, Christians join all creation in its "eager expectation" of liberation "from its bondage to decay [as it is] brought into the glorious freedom of the children of God" (Rom. 8:19-21).

Peter assumes that such hope will become so visibly compelling — so *obviously* abounding — that non-believers will eventually become curious enough about it to actually ask us about it (1 Pet. 3:15-16)!

Abounding hope comprised the 18th century life-motto of William Carey, the father of modern Christian missions. Before leaving England to serve the cause of Christ for 40 years in India, he coined his motto one afternoon in 1792 while exhorting a delegation of Baptist leaders in Northhampton, England. Speaking before the crowd of weary clergy, the young man shared a vision of the Lord Jesus taken from one of Carey's favorite prophecies, Isaiah 54:

> Enlarge the place of your tent ... do not hold back ...
> You will spread out to the right and to the left;
> Your descendants will dispossess nations ...
> For your maker is your husband —
> the Lord Almighty is his name ...
> He is called the God of all the earth.

Coupling Isaiah's vision with similar passages from other prophets, Carey preached to his elders about a Lord whose reign must extend to the ends of the earth as well as to the End of time. His treatise proclaimed an exalted Christology, which he restated on the spot into a motto to justify his bold mission vision.

> *Expect great things from God.*
> *Attempt great things for God.*

A new British missionary society grew up around William Carey's motto. Organized then and there by some of the leaders who heard him that day, the society sent him on his way and in subsequent decades launched many others to pursue "great things" for Christ around the world. Scores of other societies followed in its wake.

But here's the rest of the story. Carey's vision for the victorious reign of Christ never ceased restoring ministry resolve. Abounding hope gripped his heart, pressing him forward in outreach through four physically draining decades in the withering heat of Calcutta. It sustained him even when three of his children died of tropical diseases; when his wife went insane, requiring years of endless care-giving; when his financial support in England disappeared over minor disputes about missionary policies; even when fire destroyed his printing press outside Calcutta along with nearly twenty years of Bible translation work.

And this same hope, based on a vision for the greatness of Christ's Kingdom, revolutionized the mindset of Carey's contemporaries, too. In fact, before he died in Serampore, India, in 1834, Carey's high view of the Redeemer effectively inspired hundreds of Christian young people from many nations to volunteer for service in Christ's global cause. What an abounding, reproductive, life-giving hope was his!

Standing one afternoon in quiet meditation by William Carey's overgrown gravesite just outside Calcutta, I reflected on his story. It struck me that over four decades of extraordinary missionary service his accomplishments could be explained only by his vision of Christ (as his writings affirm). Carey saw Christ as *superior* to every hope he held dear (worth more than all of God's promises put together). He saw Christ as *sufficient for* every hope he held tight (ensuring the outcome of all of God's purposes). Christ was *sovereign over* every hope Carey could name (shepherding God's kingdom to perfect fulfillment). Christ was the *summation of* every hope Carey could claim (reigning over God's eternal plan until someday it reaches culmination). Therefore, Christ was Carey's *supreme* Message of Hope to the Church (and to Hindus as well). Carey's was an *abounding* hope throughout his life and ministry.

QUOTABLE QUOTE

So then, God has not abandoned man to a meaningless prolongation of his existence on the earth. History makes sense. By announcing the good news of the End, we are calling people to prepare for the climax of history, when God's judgments will be poured out on all of us.

(DR. ARTHUR GLASSER)

THINK WITH ME ...

Why should our message of Christ also point Christians to an *apocalyptic* hope?

Scholars call certain sections of the Bible, such as Isaiah 2 or Joel 3 or Malachi 4, *apocalyptic*. This is especially true of whole books like Ezekiel, Daniel, and Revelation which dramatize radical, though at points enigmatic, visions of the future. Each seer addressed a people caught in hope-draining circumstances. Ezekiel spoke to war captives, Daniel to fearful exiles, John to persecuted Christians. Apocalyptic messages were meant to expose God's people in graphic detail to ways God's sovereignty guaranteed the fulfillment of God's purposes for them.

The very word *apocalypse* is taken from the Greek word translated as the title of the Bible's concluding book: Revelation. It means to *unveil* in wholesale fashion, to *reveal* dramatically or to *dazzle* by open displays of

God's power and glory. What a rousing vision the writers delivered to hurting hearers then, and to an anxious generation now! Lifting up key universal themes about God's Kingdom, they took believers to the Throne of Heaven. By painting word pictures with "apocalyptic" colors the prophets shared striking snapshots that, on our side of the Ascension, take us straight to Christ as our hope.

One of these "Messages of Hope" adorns a main wall in the United Nations headquarters in New York City. Inscribed there is the dramatic reversal of despair proclaimed by the prophet Isaiah, chapter 2:

> They will beat their swords into plowshares and
> their spears into pruning hooks.
> Nation will not take up sword against nation,
> nor will they train for war anymore.

Isn't it curious that even the remote prospect of an era of international "shalom" has galvanized ambassadors from every part of the world to labor for global peace? If only they would recognize and embrace the supreme Uniter-of-Nations who alone can bring Isaiah's vision to pass. If only they knew that already Christ is in charge — King over the UN, King over the G8, King over NATO, King over the International Monetary Fund, King over the Arab League. If only they realized that already He has ascended on high, the Lamb slain and crowned to be the one and only *hope* of individuals and nations. If only they understood that one day the promise of Isaiah 2 (and hundreds of other verses about the consummate hope) will be brought to pass when every tongue confesses in unison that God's Son is supreme over all, for ever and ever (Phil. 2). The language of Isaiah 2 only makes sense in the light of Christ's supremacy. It will never come to pass amidst the clamor of General Assembly debates or UN peace-keeping forces. Isaiah's anticipated outcomes require the Regency of Jesus, the primary theme throughout most of his other prophecies.

What about us as *Christians,* though? What if *we* lived daily with such apocalyptic visions? What difference would it make for the Church as well as the nations? If *Christians* would urge each other to expect *foretastes* of the Kingdom to come, what glories of the Son might God reveal afresh to our

---

QUOTABLE QUOTE

All of us need to be aware of how Christ is moving in the midst of His Church toward the end of all things, and equally aware of our deep and immediate intimacy with Him. The one who dwells in the midst of His church is bringing closure to our present age. We cannot help but have a strong sense of living at the edge of the final consummation. We breathe the very air of the impending Kingdom.

(DONALD MOSTROM)

cities and communities? If Christians would start proclaiming to each other a Biblical vision of victory in Jesus — stirring up inside our churches a determination to live for nothing less than the Empire of the Son — would not the task of world evangelization take major strides forward?

THINK WITH ME ...
How did Jesus transform churches with a message about abounding, apocalyptic hope?

Pressing for abounding hope — and, above all, apocalyptic hope — was how our Lord Jesus ministered to struggling churches in chapters 2 and 3 of John's Revelation. We studied this in another chapter, but notice again: He focused on seven local congregations scattered across Asia Minor (modern day Turkey) that were struggling, each in its own way, with a true crisis of supremacy — whether due to heresy, or persecution, or lethargy, or pride. They all needed a fresh Message of Hope to cure their crisis. And that's what the Savior came to give them.

First, He invited them to sample an "appetizer" of the climax of God's purposes by reintroducing them to *Himself*. He walked among them (as the seven letters from John record) revealing that He was heir to the Throne, center of the universe, ruler over creation and keeper of keys to the outcome of history. His message to them was not so much about "last things" as it was about "*ultimate* things". Jesus let the seven churches glimpse previews of His coming glory, of how they would see Him in the Consummation. They did not have to wait for the End. They could start benefiting from the impact of the End already — they could become what He called "overcomers".

Despite differing circumstances, each congregation had the same basic need: a Message of Hope to renew resolve to live for His glory, no matter what. In the rest of John's masterpiece Jesus amplified that message. Chapter by chapter our Lord revealed to them waves of wonders, confirming all that His supremacy held out to them not just later but *now* — and yet in ways, right now, that foreshadowed what *would* come later.

Does Jesus have any less of a Message of Hope for His Church today? Do we inherit any less certainty about His supremacy than what He gave to the Christian movement in 1ˢᵗ century Asia Minor? Can *our* churches presume to adequately serve Him unless this all-consuming, apocalyptic vision of our Lord possesses us, too? Should the Message of Hope we spread among our own people be any less bold and visionary regarding the preeminence of our Redeemer than what He gave to Ephesus, Smyrna, Sardis or Philadelphia?

THINK WITH ME ...
How often do our churches hear a message
about Christ that sounds like *this?*

Reflecting over the last few pages, ponder these questions: Is *this* the truth about Jesus to which most of our contemporaries have been converted? Is *this* the magnitude of the work of God's Son we hear consistently proclaimed in our churches? Are *these* the marvels of the person of Christ we talk about with each other every chance we get? Is *this* the majesty of our Redeemer by which we summon each other to pour out our lives with increasing devotion to Him? In other words: Is this the Message of Hope proclaimed inside the Church?

In all honesty, and with broken hearts, we must confess that far too often it is not.

Thankfully, more and more Christian leaders are discovering the shortfall, willing to admit how many of our people do not know Christ in these fuller terms. They sense a major catastrophe in the making. Lately I've heard an increasing number warning us: A failure to resume proclaiming a more comprehensive Christology to one another as *Christians* will only allow the crisis to infect more of what we're doing.

We must no longer postpone mobilizing this "movement of messengers". Christians must choose to commit to bringing a fresh message of Christ and His supremacy to other Christians right where they live. The tragedy is this (as church history verifies): If we don't act, the gulf that currently exists — the one between the majesty of God's Son and the evangelical church's loss of hope and passion toward Him — will only grow wider and more ominous.

To our everlasting encouragement, however, I hasten to add: Among a significant core of disciples, especially within the younger generation, has appeared renewed hunger to feast on deeper Biblical teaching about the glorious greatness of Jesus. More than ever I hear the cry of Christians to be mentored by leaders who refuse to settle for shallow solutions to the crisis. Many are asking to be led into fuller encounters with Christ's glory. They also want to be equipped to proclaim the wonders of His reign to others.

Which brings me back to my original recommendation: The time is at hand to mount a campaign within the Church to reconvert the people of God back to the Son of God for all He's worth — to recover all the hope we are meant to have in Him. Frankly, there is no other choice.

A "Campaign of Hope"
That Proclaims a "Message of Hope"
(Psalm 68:1-3, 11, 18, 34-35)

I'm talking here about a genuine, all-out campaign — a campaign for the glory of Christ; a campaign to restore hope and passion toward Christ; a campaign that involves each of us as *proclaimers*. We must set about the task of delivering to *fellow Christians* a radically reformed (though thoroughly Biblical) Message of Hope. And we must do so without delay.

Consider how a campaign started to unfold when the Son of God walked among us.

THINK WITH ME ...
How did the supreme Proclaimer of hope
shape His "campaign"?

The Gospels document extensively how Jesus carried out His own version of a Campaign of Hope. From the moment He went public He ministered as a "Messenger of Hope" to multitudes who followed Him.

I'm thinking, for example, of the day He preached His inaugural sermon at the synagogue at Nazareth (Luke 4). This was clearly a defining moment for

Him. He set the course for His public ministry with promises taken from Isaiah 61 with its heavy emphasis on *proclamation* by the coming Messiah. Let me quote from the Phillips translation in Lk. 4:

> The Spirit of the Lord is upon me,
> because he anointed me
> to PREACH good tidings to the poor;
> He has sent me to PROCLAIM release to the captives ...
> to PROCLAIM the acceptable year of the Lord.
> (emphasis mine)

Notice Luke's choice of words: "good tidings ... release to captives ... acceptable year ... good news of the Kingdom." Hope, glorious hope, was Christ's central theme from the day He set out. A short time later in that same chapter Jesus added: "I must *tell the good news of the Kingdom of God* to other towns as well. That is my mission ..." about which Luke comments: "And he continued *proclaiming* his message" (all from Luke 4, emphasis mine).

Maybe no passage captures for us Jesus' life-message — the "manifesto" of His campaign — better than Mark 1:15. One might call this text "marching orders" for any Campaign of Hope. His proclamation can be boiled down to four dynamic declarations, each encouraging extraordinary expectations in the hearts of His hearers:

(1) "The time is fulfilled."

Jesus gathered to Himself all Old Testament promises focused on Messiah. In essence, His manifesto called everyone to get ready because God was prepared to act on His promises in order to revive, restore and re-deploy God's people for His purposes, according to His power through His Messiah. A new day had dawned with fresh hope for them ... and for us.

(2) "The kingdom is at hand."

Jesus announced that God alone in His sovereignty would carry out these promises for His people. Through Messiah's coming reign in their midst as well as among the nations God was poised to intervene in kingly power. He would do for them what they could never do for themselves. Jesus' manifesto announced the awesome expectation of a full manifestation of His supremacy. It continues to do so for us today.

(3) "Repent!"

Then, Jesus extended a call for conversion. The impending, extraordinary new work of God demanded it. His hearers were to renounce their best efforts to do God's work in their own strength. They were to *turn from* all sin, all unbelief, all false hopes. Theirs was to be an unhindered involvement in what God was ready to do. In addition, He invited them to *turn toward* what was coming — to turn to the God of the future as well as to the future God held out to them. This remains the priority response to every Messiah-shaped Message of Hope today.

(4) "Believe this good news!"

Finally, conversion not only involved a turning toward God and His promises. It also included a response of proactive believing — more like seizing the Kingdom-hope for daily life and eternal destiny. Jesus encouraged *passion*. His followers must stake their very existence on this reality. Not only must they wrap their lives around Messiah and the good news of His supremacy. They also must be wrapped up in pursuing the full extent of Messiah's reign. This same opportunity belongs to Christians everywhere right now.

Jesus' campaign continued to unfold throughout the Gospels. Repeatedly He urged His hearers to embrace the joy of soon-coming displays of His Kingship, and to act accordingly. For example, two verses later in Mark 1 He spelled out to an audience of fishermen what a proper response would be to His message: "Come, follow me [passion], and I will make you [supremacy] to be fishers of men [hope]".

QUOTABLE QUOTE

Jesus Christ, by coming into this world, has changed the sunsets of time into the sunrises of eternity.

(CLEMENT OF ALEXANDRA —
3RD CENTURY)

Later He invited His disciples to something else — something more: to join Him in the very same Campaign of Hope. We see this on at least two occasions when He sent them out two by two (first the 12, and then the 70) to preach "The Kingdom is at hand". Limiting their audience to "the lost sheep of the house of Israel", the campaign targeted those who considered themselves inside the family of the redeemed. He defined these hungry believers as a "harvest" waiting to be reaped, and as scattered "sheep" waiting to be rallied back to the Chief Shepherd (Matt. 9 and 10). On Resurrection evening one of His initial encouragements to disheartened believers was His promise: "As the Father has sent me, so I send you" (Jn. 20). Then, forty days later, just moments before His coronation in glory, Jesus told the same group (along with as many as 120 others) that they would become His witnesses, beginning in Jerusalem. Ascended to His universal honor as Redeemer King, He commissioned them to proclaim the fame of His name, not only to the ends of the earth (the unreached), but — first of all — to those who called themselves the people of God (Jerusalem and Judea, as well as the splinter sect in Samaria).

Would he not desire a similar movement and message unleashed inside the Church today? Over the past 2,000 years, in fact, Campaigns of Hope shaped by the same priorities have arisen innumerable times. Let's look at a few examples.

THINK WITH ME ...
How have multiple campaigns in the past impacted the advance of Christ's Kingdom?

Why is the Christian movement currently eighty-three million times larger than when it began? What has turned the outward progress of the Gospel into the longest sustained human endeavor in history? One answer is that consistently God raised up a people full of Christ-exalting hope, and they wouldn't stop talking about it — *first of all to each other*.

The Bible catalogs a veritable Who's Who of promise-primed proclaimers to God's people. The Old Testament sets before us Noah, Abraham, Moses, Joshua, Deborah, Hannah and Samuel, Elijah and Elisha, David, Isaiah and Hosea, to name a few. The New Testament highlights Mary, Simeon and Anna, John the Baptist and John on Patmos, Priscilla and Aquila, Apollos, Peter, Paul and Timothy, among others. *All* were "Messengers of Hope", trumpeting testimonies about bold breakthroughs from God as well as promised new beginnings in His Kingdom. Appealing to fellow believers to prepare for fabulous futures (especially in the least promising of times), they preached for saints to wake up to the power of God's grace and the wonders of His ways. The goal was to set their hearts on both things above and things to come. But this kind of ministry didn't end with the close of the New Testament.

As much as any church historian, Yale professor Kenneth Scott Latourette in his massive seven volumes on *A History of Christianity* detailed the impact of Biblical hope on the expansion of the Christian movement worldwide. The pattern he uncovered reminded Latourette of waves crashing toward the shore with the incoming tide. Despite eras of spiritual recession, he noted, it would only be a matter of time before other "Messengers of Hope" surfaced in some segment of the Church to lead their own Campaigns of Hope in reinvigorating Christians with passion for Christ's greatness and glory. Each time such efforts ushered in new epochs of Gospel advance among unbelievers.

In seasons of recession, Latourette noted, *hopelessness* would envelop parts of the Church, such as: when initial persecution drove believers into the Catacombs; when Christianized Rome was sacked by barbarians in 410; when the Black Death obliterated European churches in the 14th century, decimating whole congregations; when 20th century Christians endured a Cold War that threatened the very future of Christ's mission with nuclear Armageddon. Yet in the midst of such times, hope in Christ continued to grip a host of believers. Their vision for His Kingdom moved them to action even in the darkest hours. As a result they transformed the course of nations for God's glory. Sometimes these movements consisted of multitudes; sometimes of remnants.

But it wasn't the size of the campaign that made the difference; it was the size of vision for their Savior in the midst of the campaign. Therefore, when persecuted Christians testified openly before pagans in the coliseums, many listeners came to faith. When Rome was sacked, the disaster provided the backdrop for Augustine's revolutionary theology on the City of God, a work that permanently changed how much of the Church viewed Christ's supremacy. During the plague when they faced death willingly in order to comfort the diseased, thousands of priests in the Middle Ages ended up winning many to the Gospel. And, despite the specter of atomic holocaust, the 20th century saw the greatest numerical growth of the Church in 2,000 years as the word of Christ spread widely among the nations. These seasons of advance, took

QUOTABLE QUOTE

Hail, gladdening light, of his pure glory poured

Who is the immortal Father, heavenly, blest,

Holiest of Holies, Jesus Christ our Lord.

Worthiest art thou at all times to be sung,

With undefiled tongue, Son of our God, giver of life, alone!

Therefore in all the world thy glories, Lord, they own.

— OLDEST COMPLETE HYMN IN EXISTENCE, FROM THE 3RD CENTURY, USED WHEN FAMILIES LIT LAMPS AT EVENING place because truths about Christ and His Kingdom were freshly proclaimed. The message of His supremacy was heard again *inside* the Church. This resurgence of messengers ignited wholesale hope and passion toward the Lord expressed in movements of united prayer, waves of revival and renewal, sweeping social reforms and sacrificial missionary outreach.

The monastic orders that rose up during the opening centuries of the second millennium come to mind. Sufficiently convinced about Christ's ultimate triumphs, monks throughout Europe took redemptive action in education, medicine, ethics and the environment along with worship and evangelism. Similarly, a Kingdom-concerned message fueled the spread of the Reformation across a whole continent and beyond. This message re-appeared to inspire the tireless labors of William Wilberforce and the Abolition movement in 19th century England. It was a vision for transformation of prophetic proportions that invigorated the early days of the Civil Rights movement in America. In the midst of battling to secure Biblical justice for his people in the early 1960's Rev. Martin Luther King reminded fellow believers (and all of us with them): "At times, we must accept finite disappointments. But we must never lose the infinite hope God gives us in Jesus!"

Today, taken captive to the same Message of Hope, multitudes of Christians in Africa and Asia and Latin America have spawned some of the largest congregations in the world (such as a 700,000 member church in Seoul, Korea). Believers have sparked rapid church planting initiatives (like the thousands springing up across Indonesia) and fostered nationwide spiritual awakenings (as in the Fiji Islands where currently most political leaders are active confessing Christians), and propelled evangelistic movements unparalleled in church history (like the millions reportedly coming to Christ within the house church movement in China).

The current missionary-sending endeavors from Third World churches may be the greatest confirmation yet of the impact of Christ-saturated vision among God's people. From these churches thousands of laborers are being sent out by believers who live, in many cases, in abject poverty. Yet the missionaries' confidence in the supremacy of God's Son compels them to take risks for advancing the Gospel that most Christians in the West know nothing about. In India, for example, I've met with members of indigenous movements that have mobilized tens of thousands into prayer bands. Made up of individuals barely surviving on the equivalent of $500 a year, these groups fast and pray all night once a week for their missionaries as they give sacrificially to send them out to preach. Full of hope in Jesus, they are committed to evangelize unreached castes and tribes in other parts of their nation no matter what the cost. Many have told me personally they do so with an unhesitant conviction that, in the words of Habakkuk 2:14, India will soon "be covered with the knowledge of the glory of the Lord as the waters cover the sea".

All of these case studies bring us back to the one key theme: When believers hear afresh God's "exceedingly great and precious promises" in Christ Jesus (2 Pet. 1), many will find themselves *converted* to live in view of Eternity; *captivated* to pursue Jesus' triumphs among the nations; *consumed* with passion for the praises of the Son; and *commissioned* to proclaim hope in Jesus at every opportunity, both inside and outside the Church. This pattern — converted, captivated, consumed and commissioned — can be replicated within any congregation where the supremacy of God's Son is the Message of Hope they give to each other.

THINK WITH ME ...
Is it time for you to join in with a movement of proclaimers?

Restoring hope about Christ's glory within the Church is a holy mission. God invites us to announce, declare, cry out, broadcast, trumpet, herald and publish abroad (all synonyms of "proclaim") the wonderful person, purposes and promises of His Son *inside* the community of Jesus' followers. Each believer can re-engage God's original call on our lives: to become a community of *prophets* (compare Acts 2 with 1 Cor. 12, 14). Once more a movement of Christ-proclaimers can arise, spreading hope among one another and confronting the crisis that impedes spiritual growth and witness.

The stakes are high, especially in our witness for Christ to neighbors and nations. Only as we carry out a Campaign of Hope successfully *inside* our churches will Christians be able and willing to embrace wholeheartedly our mission to earth's unreached peoples outside our churches (compare Isa. 60 with 1 Thess. 1). Paul writes: "Faith comes from hearing the message, and the message is heard through the word of Christ" (Rom. 10). These words are the goal not only in missionary outreach. They are also God's goal among His own people. He knows we can help the *world* really "get it" about His Son only to the degree that first *we ourselves* really "get it".

Considering all that hangs in the balance, you might want to take a moment right here to ask yourself: Do I personally know Christ *well enough* to present Him to other Christians *fully enough* to help them come back to Him for all that He is? Do I know how to speak to other believers about a vision of Christ that's *grand enough* to start healing their disappointments from the past and delivering them from daunting fears about the future? Am I so confident about Christ's total sufficiency for the heart-cries of the human soul that I am willing to exalt Him to fellow Christians without apologies every chance I get?

And, have I ever offered myself to the Father for this primary purpose: To be re-awakened by His Spirit to the greater glory of His Son so that in turn I can effectively invite other Christians to recover hope in Christ's supremacy and rediscover fresh passion for His Kingdom?

If this is the direction you're headed, eventually you may want to go back over chapters 1-5 where a lot of the "meat of the message" can be found for you to share with fellow believers. Also, plan to press ahead into chapters 10-12 where specific strategies for delivering the Message of Hope effectively are laid out. However, there is a *prior* step you need to consider. It is essential for all the rest: creating a Campaign of Hope based in a movement of *prayer*.

THINK WITH ME ...
Why do *pray-ers* of the hope often become the best *proclaimers* of the hope?

Unprecedented in Church history, across the Body of Christ today a prayer movement is exploding. Working with it over 25 years, I've come to one exciting conclusion: *This host of intercessors comprises potentially one of the most powerful armies of Christ-proclaimers the Church has ever known*. It certainly provides a prime recruiting ground for any Campaign of Hope.

Recent research indicates that nearly 200 million Christians worldwide are committed to praying for the advancement of Christ's Kingdom as a daily spiritual discipline. Over 40 million of these meet to do so in small weekly prayer groups. In other words, already many are waking up enough to our magnificent hope in Christ to set themselves in the pursuit of His purposes with determined desire for God to work. They have banded together, faithfully appealing to Heaven for major manifestations of Christ's supremacy in our generation.

In the process they are learning to *proclaim* their hope in Christ. They do so every time they *pray* their hope in Christ. For them a Campaign of Hope has already begun — not on earth but in *Heaven*. Their requests are often reflective of the prayers in Paul's epistles, such as his petitions for the Ephesians (consider both chapters 1 and 3). Paul, you'll notice, hammered out some of his loftiest descriptions of Christ's supremacy *as he prayed!* Similarly, as the 21st century army of intercessors starts proclaiming to fellow Christians the hope they've been praying about so persistently, the transformation will unfold quite naturally. Stepping from Throne Room into living rooms, they will be able to speak authentically to believers about a grander vision of Jesus because it was *that* vision — and their longing for a wide-scale awakening to that vision — that drove them to prayer in the first place.

Hundreds of praying Christians I know are already making this transition. In them the kaleidoscope of strategies outlined in the next three chapters — becoming Messengers of Hope, Prisoners of Hope and Vanguards of Hope — has begun to take shape. I can sense it every time they seek and speak about their hope in the supremacy of Christ. That's why I suggest even a local prayer meeting may be the best starting point for a Campaign of Hope in your congregation or community. Let me end by illustrating from a personal experience.

THINK WITH ME ...
How might a prayer meeting become a
starting point for a Campaign of Hope?

For years I was involved in one of three regular "prayer meetings" in my town. One meeting was made up of people caught up in Eastern religion — New Agers, often reciting monosyllabic mantras as they sat in a lotus position on the floor. Their goal? "Harmonic convergence" with the universe they called it. Another gathering consisted of hundreds of Muslim university students who convened at the local mosque every Friday, flat on their faces while reciting Koranic meditations (often Arabic prayers which I suspect most of them did not understand). Their goal? To reaffirm a worldwide Islamic brotherhood and to ensure continued favor in the eyes of Allah.

The third group, however, was profoundly different. This prayer meeting made up of a couple dozen Christians from twenty churches, assembled month to month, rotating from church to church. The way we prayed would have confused New Agers and offended Muslims. And it would probably have baffled not a few fellow Christians if they had heard us.

You see, we had bought into Paul's superlatives. We agreed with what he taught about who Christ is as the Son of God, where He leads in the purposes of God and what He imparts as the Regent of God. In other words, we pursued God's Kingdom fervently. We learned how to pray back to the living God the hope recorded in His Word.

Gradually, praying like this started to reform our view of Christ. With increasing boldness we invited our Father to unleash Christ's reign more vividly in our lives, in the residents of our city (including Muslims and New Agers) and beyond. We prayed for revival throughout the Church and for the fulfillment of the Great Commission. Our prayers incorporated expansive visions at times, but the requests were always rooted in the magnificence of our Monarch. Our prayers were rampant with great expectations. Our eyes were fixed on victories that would eventually transform Heaven and earth, but which had implications for our lives right now. Over years we prayed in anticipation of substantial interventions from Heaven — breakthroughs in our situations that would foreshadow the Consummation itself.

And we were not disappointed. We saw amazing answers — from personal spiritual renewal; to physical healings; to increased visible unity among believers in our town; to outreach to poor families of our community; to newly sent missionaries from our churches into other nations; to city-wide evangelism efforts that brought many to Christ.

Spoken in a thousand different ways, every prayer we offered was really one prayer. It echoed the last prayer of the Bible (Rev. 22). In all our gatherings one great heart-cry prevailed: *"Lord Jesus, come and reign among us."* If I could tie up those hundreds of hours of prayer into one concise bundle of requests, here's a taste of what Heaven heard:

Come, Lord Jesus!

Come, ultimately, in the triumphs of Your victorious return.

But until then come with similarly transforming power

even now, right where we live.

Pour out preliminary experiences of Your supremacy.

Give us foretastes of what will some day fill Heaven and earth.

Focus us on Your worthiness as the Son of God.

Fill us with Your resources as the Regent of God.

Fulfill through us Your mission in the Purposes of God.

Fire us with Your zeal for the Glory of God.

By Your power, transform our lives, our churches and our city.

Let Your people here become a showcase of your majesty

before the nations.

Do all of this in a way that approximates how Your supremacy

will be gloriously manifested when You are fully revealed

at the consummation of all things!   AMEN!

Three prayer meetings. Two were driven by empty superstitions and routine obligations. The third was driven by great expectations, mobilized around a Message of Hope defined by a Person who claims to be Lord of all.

But there was another demonstration of His lordship among us. Just as significant as the resulting answers to our prayers was what happened inside of each of us as we prayed — including what happened inside of *me*. Those wonderful years of hope-filled intercession profoundly *liberated* my whole walk with Jesus. They *fused* my heart with hope in Jesus. They enriched my passion for the Kingdom of Jesus. They *reanimated* daily discipleship with promises anchored in the majesty of Jesus.

Those seasons of prayer also recruited me to action for Jesus. They turned me into a Messenger of Hope. They motivated me to launch my own personal Campaign of Hope. How could I do otherwise? How could one pray like that — with such undeniable prospects for the revelation of Christ's glory — and not begin to proclaim to others a fresh Message of Hope in Him at every opportunity?

Eventually such prayers crafted in me a desire to spread the very vision of God's Son I was praying *about*, especially among those I was praying *for*. After all, Christians' waking up to Jesus for all that He is, is the ultimate answer to everything I ever sought from the Lord anyway. Offering myself to the Father to be a Christ-proclaimer gave me a way to help prepare Christian friends for the awakening when God grants it.

To this very hour I continue to keep both emphases together — praying and proclaiming, seeking and speaking. I pray my hope in Christ *to* God. Then I proclaim my hope in Christ *for* God.

Where We're Headed

Having watched her husband chart our nation's course through the stormy seas of World War II, First Lady Eleanor Roosevelt once observed: "The most important word in the English language is 'hope' ". A half century later, looking back on his role in liberating his country from Soviet domination in the 1990's, Vaclav Havel, the first president of the Czech Republic, penned a similar conclusion: "I cannot imagine that I could strive for something like this if I did not carry hope within me. Life without hope is an empty, boring, useless life for sure." Both leaders discovered the revolutionary impact *any* message of hope can have on the course of men and nations. How much more should Christ's disciples expect radical results from proclaiming among God's people the greatest hope of all — the hope of Christ's supremacy!

Chapter 10 explores how to do this. It begins unpacking the strategies for a Campaign of Hope. How do we fashion and deliver a life-changing the Message of Hope inside the Church? What does it take to be a Messenger of Hope? I think the answers in the next few pages will encourage you a great deal.

10

BECOMING MESSENGERS OF HOPE

How to Re-inspire the Church with the Supremacy of God's Son

During World War I, I'm told, the U.S. government unleashed throughout America a massive public speaking campaign known as *The Four-Minute Men*. In an 18-month period, in order to promote patriotism and commitment to the war effort, nearly 75,000 were recruited and trained to deliver four-minute talks at every opportunity. Their missions took them to sporting events, movie theaters or just standing on the sidewalks of major cities. In less than two years more than seven million speeches were delivered to an aggregate audience estimated to be 300 million. As a result intensified hope about the outcome of the war bathed America.

In much the same way, it's time to flood our churches with Christians alert to another kind of speaking assignment. Let's raise up a battalion of heralds — "Messengers of Hope" — determined to speak to Christians about the glory of Christ and the greatness of the Biblical promises based on His supremacy. In every kind of setting and at every opportunity these proclaimers must be ready to testify single-mindedly for their cause — like "fanatics", in the sense Mark Twain defined the term: "A fanatic is someone who won't change his mind and won't change the subject!"

More to the point, they should assume a role similar to John the Baptizer in his "campaign" down by the Jordan. John defined himself as just *"a voice"*, one standing inside a spiritual wilderness crying out to God's people, "Prepare a way for the Lord". He knew if they "cleared a path" by repentance and faith toward their coming Redeemer, "all flesh shall see the glory of God" (Isa. 40 and Luke 4). To encourage a people who were weary, discouraged, harassed and helpless, he proclaimed: " ... the Kingdom of God is at hand", adding "One more powerful than I will come ... He will baptize you with the Holy Spirit and with fire", leaving the crowds "waiting expectantly" (Lk. 3). Declaring his Message of Hope, John became a friend of both "bride" and Bridegroom (Jn. 2). His vision brought the two together. Then he stepped aside to give Jesus the preeminence in many hearts not only for his generation but for ours.

In our last chapter we concluded that a Campaign of Hope is our most strategic step for curing the crisis of supremacy. Following John's example our initiative must call for repentance, we must confront head-on a collapse of commitment among the saints and re-establish a vision of Christ's glorious greatness for those who claim His name. We must call for the re-conversion of God's people back to Christ for ALL that He is. In the words of Dallas Willard, we must strive to "gain a fresh hearing for Christ" throughout the Church.

This chapter looks at the first of three major strategies for this campaign: becoming Messengers of Hope. In it we'll discuss:

- **Why sharing a Message of Hope with the Church is such a powerful ministry.**

- **What the chief characteristics are of every effective Messenger of Hope.**

- **How the Bible is a "book of hope", revealing Christ's supremacy throughout.**

- **How to employ a four-part strategy for spreading a Message of Hope.**

- **What the ultimate measure of success is for any Messenger of Hope.**

Messengers on a Mission

(Isaiah 40:1-11, 21-23, 27-31)

Larry King once asked Billy Graham what the most exciting part of his ministry might be. Was it speaking to millions? Being a best-selling author? Having the respect and love of leaders worldwide? Billy's instant response was this: "The most satisfying moment in my ministry comes when I know I have received a word from God and fully delivered it."

As we've explored throughout this *Joyful Manifesto,* there is a word from Heaven to believers everywhere. It speaks of joyous promises ratified by the reign of the Son of God. It calls the Church to celebrate the coronation of the Christ and to prepare for greater involvement in His eternal plan for the nations. Once this message gets inside a believer's heart, that person cannot

> ## QUOTABLE QUOTE
>
> **The greatest need in our churches is for men and women who can envision the better future God wills for His people; who will motivate people to action; who will create intelligent plans for positive change; and who will spearhead the implementation of those plans, for the enduring glory of God.**
>
> (DR. GEORGE BARNA)

keep quiet. He or she can be satisfied only by fully "delivering" it to other believers, spreading the vision inside the Church to build up the Body. In doing so Messengers of Hope become one of God's greatest tools for mobilizing His people to reach the nations.

As someone has said, only two things last forever: (1) the *promises* of God, and (2) the *people* for whom those promises were intended. Every Christian must accept as his or her first order of business, therefore, the task of getting God's promises more fully *into* God's people. Heralding to each other the glory of Christ solidifies and deepens our cooperation with the redemptive reign of Christ. As we noted in chapter 9, this effort can produce the prime impetus for new waves of revival, evangelism, social reform and missions.

Is there anyone who has more power and influence in the Church than a believer, or a coalition of believers, who can make other believers *feel the reality* of the supremacy of Christ and the unparalleled possibilities of His Kingdom? What greater contribution could any Christian make than to help fellow Christians deepen their delight over the reign of God's Son and thereby renew their desire to serve Him? This mission is especially significant when taken up by pastors and ministry leaders who already carry primary responsibility for teaching God's Word in order to lead others into "the fullness of the stature of Christ" by helping them "grow up into Him who is the Head" (Eph. 4).

THINK WITH ME ...
How does Paul demonstrate the strategic mission of a "Messenger of Hope"?

Colossians 1:24-29, to which we've turned often in this manifesto, defines so well Paul's lifelong goal. He presents himself first of all as a commissioned proclaimer, not to unreached peoples but — and this is the specific application of the passage — to those *inside the* early Church. Here's my paraphrase of what I hear Paul saying about himself through this text:

> *My commission is to help you Christians fully grasp God's message. This word is all about Christ Himself — the One I just described as having the supremacy in everything — the One who also dwells in your midst. He alone guarantees for you, forever, all the glorious promises God offers you. That's why I proclaim Christ in the marvelous ways I do, everywhere I go and in everything I write, including this epistle. In doing this, I labor with all the strength God gives me to bring you to a full understanding of who Christ really is, so you will live in a way consistent with His glory.*

However, Paul wanted *all* of God's people to become "Messengers of Hope". He made this point to the Colossians in chapter 3 when he summoned them to a ministry like his. He actually employed the exact same words that he had first applied to himself: "Let the word of Christ dwell in you richly as you *teach* and *admonish* one another with all wisdom" (Col. 3). *Every* Christian was meant to be a Paul-like proclaimer of Christ to fellow believers.

In Ephesians 4 Paul outlines *key communication gifts* embedded in local congregations, each of which indicates Christ's active reign in Heaven. He writes: "He who descended is the very one who ascended higher than all the heavens, in order to fill the whole universe. It was he who gave some to be apostles, some to be prophets, some to be evangelists, and some to be pastors and teachers, to prepare God's people.... " (vs. 10-12). Assigned by our exalted Head in order to build up His Body, all five gifts require the recipient to be a messenger, primarily *to the Church.*

In context even an "evangelist" may not mean, first of all, someone sent to win pagans to Jesus (though he or she can and should). The Greek word for "evangelist" may imply "good-news-ing" the *Christian* community by making sure *they* have a more comprehensive grasp of the Gospel of God's Son for their own lives. There's a strategic reason for casting Gospel vision inside the Church. Whenever believers are enthralled with the greatness of their Redeemer's finished work they will become, in turn, passionate about sharing Him with outsiders. They will want to proclaim Him to the unevangelized of their generation.

> QUOTABLE QUOTE
>
> This is my life work: helping people understand and respond to this Message.... Here I am, preaching and writing about things that are way over my head, the inexhaustible riches and generosity of Christ. My task is to bring out in the open and make plain what God, who created all this in the first place, has been doing in secret and behind the scenes all along.... All this is proceeding along lines planned all along by God and then executed in Christ Jesus.
>
> (EPHESIANS 3 — THE MESSAGE)

Let's take a closer look at what the work of sharing Christ *inside* the Church really means, starting with two key New Testament words for every messenger's work: *proclaim* and *witness.*

THINK WITH ME ...
What does it mean to be a *proclaimer* of Christ inside the Church?

In 1st century Rome, when a son was born to the emperor, a manifesto was published announcing the auspicious event. The document clarified implications of the birth for the future well-being of every citizen and the empire as a whole. Technically called a *proclamation*, the news was carried into public squares, announced for all to hear and then nailed up to be read afterwards. As they traveled from one community to the next, official messengers delivered the same proclamation time and time again. When related to more urgent matters Rome's proclamations were actually royal *decrees,* such as: "Pay your tribute!" "Worship the Emperor!" "Prepare for war!" Once issued, citizens had no alternatives. Debate was suspended. Action was expected. The Sovereign had spoken, period.

The New Testament writers borrowed this dynamic word ("proclaim") to describe the activity sometimes translated as "preaching". We could say that in the Bible the Greek word "proclaim" meant: "We appeal for others to join the King in celebrating his good fortune. We publicize important news about Empire-shaking developments. We sound a note of triumphant outcomes just ahead." In addition, every Gospel spokesman on behalf of Heaven defined appropriate responses to impending threats or unexpected blessings. Those with ears to hear were commanded to reorder plans and priorities around the goals of the Empire of the Son.

Doesn't that sound like the kind of ministry that, if carried out intentionally *inside* the Church, could begin to cure a crisis of supremacy? The first priority of New Testament-style proclaimers is to sharpen, strengthen, deepen and intensify for believers the great news of who Christ is for them as King. Magnifying God's Son to each other, we bank on the principle in Romans 10: "Faith comes by hearing, and what must be heard is the message of Christ." *We count on our Lord Jesus to be most fully at work where He is most fully proclaimed.* As disciples grow to appreciate greater dimensions of His lordship, He will reveal Himself increasingly to us in ways comparable to His person and power.

QUOTABLE QUOTE

One of the most fascinating of all the preacher's tasks is to explore both the emptiness of fallen man and the fullness of Jesus Christ in order then to demonstrate how He can fill our emptiness, lighten our darkness, enrich our poverty and bring our human aspirations to fulfillment. To encounter Christ is to touch reality and experience transcendence.

(DR. JOHN R. STOTT)

THINK WITH ME ...

What does it mean to be a *witness* to Christ inside the Church?

Drawing its meaning from the legal sphere the purpose of a "witness" in a court of law is to contribute toward a *verdict* from the hearers. At a trial a witness steps to the stand, raises her or his right hand and swears to "tell the truth, the whole truth and nothing but the truth". A witness is called upon to help a lawyer sway the decision of the jury by an honest recitation of firsthand observations. Witnesses do not call attention to themselves but point to something far more important. Witnesses testify to what they have seen and heard, as Peter and John claimed to do before the Sanhedrin (Acts 4).

As Messengers of Hope we should bear witness first of all to other Christians, eventually inviting them to render fresh a *verdict* about the supremacy of Christ: Is He *really* who He claims to be? Is He *all* that He claims to be?

In this analogy a witness is never asked to play the role of an attorney. A witness is not *pleading* a case for Christ's supremacy with their hearers. That's the role of the Holy Spirit, and He advocates well (Jn. 16). The "courtroom" (the Body of Christ) should sense, however, that the witness wants to *influence* the jury (his fellow believers) with his or her Message of Hope. The witness is intent on persuading them to "rule in favor of" the truth about who Christ is as the Son of God, where He leads in the Purposes of God, how He imparts the Resources of God and what He receives from the People of God (the four components of our original definition of supremacy). Our first job as witnesses remains persuasion by life and lip, leading believers to exalt in God's Son for *all* that He is. The contemporary collapse of Christology in our churches requires this.

> QUOTABLE QUOTE
>
> **You need neither fear their threats nor worry about them; simply concentrate on being completely devoted to Christ in your hearts. Be ready at any time to give a quiet and reverent answer to any man who wants a reason for the hope that you have within you.**
>
> (1 PETER 3 — PHILLIPS TRANSLATION)

The Church also must witness to unbelievers by word and deed in our neighborhoods as well as among unreached peoples throughout the nations. In no way do I depreciate the critical need for many more evangelistic outreaches everywhere. But our top priority is clear: In compelling ways we must bear witness to Christ to each other as believers. We must challenge one another to live out the fuller implications of His supremacy day by day. God's Word is our portfolio. It can stir up holy expectations toward Jesus that transform all areas of discipleship and evangelism.

Otherwise, considering the significant loss of Christ-inspired hope and passion in the Church (as we saw in **Volume II**), I ask you: How else will a revived spirit of evangelism surface among us? Where else will the hundreds of thousands of new missionaries come from, so urgently needed at this moment to complete the Great Commission?

This was Jesus' game-plan in Acts 1. Providing His disciples with convincing proofs of the Resurrection, Jesus stayed on after Easter for an additional *forty days*! Why that long? After three years of disciple-making what was still missing in His ministry to them? What could possibly require so much additional input? A study of Luke 24 and Acts 1 strongly suggests He stayed behind to better prepare His disciples to be Messengers of Hope. According to Acts 1 He did so by exposing them to unexplored dimensions of His Kingdom purposes. He spent time convincing them that now that He had prevailed as sole conqueror of death for the entire universe, His very person was the "linchpin" of that Kingdom. Prior to this season with Him in post-Easter dramas, how could they have grasped such awesome truths?

QUOTABLE QUOTE

Unrolling the scroll He found the place where it was written, "God's spirit is on me. He has chosen me to preach the Message of good news to the poor, sent me to announce pardon to prisoners and recovery of sight to the blind, to set the burdened and battered free, to announce 'This is God's year to act!' ... Then He started in, 'You've just heard Scripture make history. It came true, just now, in this place.' "

(LUKE 4 — THE MESSAGE)

Finally, Jesus concluded His 40-day tutorial by commissioning them to be witnesses of all they had seen of the vastness of His victories. "Witness" wasn't what they were to *do*. "Witness" was what they had *already become* by dwelling in His presence and beholding His risen glory.

Ten days after His Ascension the disciples rose up to speak about Him with a level of boldness never seen in them before. They testified to His coronation at the Father's right hand. They broadcast promises guaranteed by His position on the Throne. But notice — their ministry began in Jerusalem and then spread to Judea, moving on to Samaria. Only then were they to go to the ends of the earth — to unreached peoples. In other words, *their first assignment was to testify to the people of God*, many of whom gathered at Pentecost to hear them.

The emerging 1st century church maintained the pattern of Acts 1. Throughout the rest of the book, planting and growing a Message of Hope always began with insiders first. It focused on those who regarded themselves as the Chosen of God so that *they* might discover the new life that God's Kingdom (and King) offered His people. In turn *they* could become a blessing to the families of the earth. (See the conclusion of Peter's sermon to insiders in Acts 3.) As Paul put it, the witness was always "to the Jew first" (Rom. 1) — to the insider first.

There's no less of a need for this kind of consistent witness inside the Church to the people of God today.

If we are serious about a reformation of Christology, we must recommit to the diligent practice of being Messengers of Hope *to each other*, starting with our gatherings every Sunday morning. We must aim also to get Christ back into the conversation at the dinner table with our families as well as in everyday exchanges with Christian friends.

THINK WITH ME ...
What topics are people talking about these days in your congregation?

Is this witness — from Christian to Christian — actually happening in our churches? If it isn't happening there, can we honestly expect it to grow among the pagans? To get at the answer try the experiment suggested in chapter 1: Next Sunday morning listen to the conversations that go on in your church. Stand in the narthex outside your sanctuary, or linger in the fellowship hall where people enjoy coffee between services. What do you hear them talking about? Reflect on what church members discuss in the course of a Sunday school class or at a weekly home Bible study group you attend. In all such cases, ask yourself:

- How often do I even hear the name of Jesus mentioned in these conversations?

- When (or if) I do hear His name, do Christians speak of Him to each other with words that expand their hearers' vision about who He really is? Does their "witness" to each other magnify some dimension of His supremacy for others to delight in? Are the Christians in my church seeking to persuade each other to exercise greater hope in God's promises, in light of all Jesus is?

Chances are you will come away disappointed over what you find. In many churches members make meager efforts to serve each other as Messengers of Hope. While leading numerous pastoral seminars I've heard from leaders how very few believers are acting as witnesses unto Christ and His glory *inside* our congregations. There are few attempts on any significant level to help each other lay hold of greater expectations toward God's Son and then live accordingly.

Now consider this: If we fail out of ignorance, indifference or self-consciousness to speak about the great glories of our Lord Jesus Christ among ourselves as Christians, *why should we be surprised so few of us ever dare to speak about Him to the unbelievers around us?* We've had so little practice doing it with each other! Little effort has been made inside our churches to proclaim Jesus' majesty in order to increase a vision for His preeminence among ourselves.

We need not despair, however. At this very hour Messengers of Hope are rising up everywhere to meet the challenge. Each place I visit I find Christ-proclaimers emerging inside all kinds of congregations and Christian ministries. These witnesses are key both to revival in the Body of Christ as well as to a worldwide acceleration of the Gospel of Christ. *Is it possible that you are among them?* How would you know for sure? To start with, you might like to re-read **Interlude I** and see how well it reflects what God doing in your own heart. Beyond that, let's examine what a Messenger of Hope usually looks like.

Describing a Messenger of Hope
(Isaiah 61)

In truth, every person is already a messenger of some kind, to some people, somewhere, about something. This is simply unavoidable — even more so for Christians. Two fundamental questions need to be asked, therefore:

- What *type* of messenger am I?
- And what will be my *message*?

The second question — about the message itself — is what **Volume I** tackled. So let me address the first question here. After years of traversing

the diversity of the Body of Christ — denominational, ethnic, cultural — I have pinpointed
thirteen characteristics evident in almost
every Christ-proclaimer I've met. No single
messenger may exhibit all thirteen at any one
time. But most effective messengers in Scripture,
as well as many from Church history, displayed
most of them. Numerous 21st century Christians
bear the very same marks. Such marks can be
reproduced in any believer by the power of the
Spirit. Here's a quick survey of all thirteen.

> ### QUOTABLE QUOTE
>
> **Preach Christ, always and everywhere. He is the whole Gospel. His person, His offices and work must be our one great, all-comprehending theme.**
>
> (CHARLES SPURGEON)

THINK WITH ME ...

Which of these 13 characteristics are already found in your life?

A Messenger of Hope tends to be:

- **SINGLE-MINDED** ... Messengers of Hope determine to make Christ and His supremacy their primary message. They accommodate and shape their service to Christ around their message rather than the other way around. For them Christ is truly *all*.

- **VISIONARY** ... Messengers of Hope look at everything through the "lens" of thousands of Biblical promises summed up in Him in order to help Christians interpret every facet of life from the perspective of Christ's all-encompassing dominion. These messengers encourage the Church to see everything about Christ and His Kingdom from the vantage point of the Ascension (what this manifesto calls "superspective").

- **CONSISTENT** ... Walking out practical lifestyles of hope-*filled*-ness, Messengers of Hope give Christ a daily obedience compatible with their identity and destiny in Him. At all times they work at pursuing a hope and passion toward Him for ALL that He is, and then they turn the life-experiences this produces into the vision to be shared with others.

- **PRAYERFUL** ... They "seek" before they "speak". Interceding for measurable demonstrations of God's promises in Jesus, they seek Him not only for church renewal and missionary advance but also for the Consummation itself. Messengers of Hope pray, too, that their Messages of Hope will help re-convert believers back to Christ and His supremacy. They seek to gather others to pray with them in the same directions.

- *COMPASSIONATE* ... Hope-givers and Christ-givers are also *care-givers* sent to Christians in the grip of despair and disillusionment to minister a fresh vision of Jesus' glory through word and deed. Sacrificing time and energy, they do so with patience and gentleness. Messengers of Hope are motivated by mercy toward "prisoners of waterless pits" (Zech. 9). Sensitive to the heartbreaks and disappointments of fellow believers, messengers know this is due, more often than not, to a crisis of supremacy in their lives. They gently restore hurting believers to a Biblical Christology to help them recover all the hope they are meant to have.

- *REASONABLE* ... Giving adequate justification for fresh hope toward Christ, they help disciples become "prisoners of hope" (Zech. 9) captivated with the greatness of Christ and His Kingdom purposes. By providing Biblical rationales for living with abounding hope in God, Messengers of Hope seek to convince their hearers to make Christ their "all in all" (Col. 3). They accomplish this by: firing Christians' imaginations about victories ahead; challenging them to envision God's promises fulfilled; telling them stories of previous advances of Christ's Kingdom; and stirring up holy expectations toward God's Son for their own lives.

- *HUMBLE* ... Christ-proclaimers have no desire to promote themselves. Their message is not about their own vision. It is all about God's vision for His Son. They refuse to take credit for the impact of their witness on other disciples. Readily they confess that even their own hearts of hope are a gift from God. Serving in a spirit of brokenness before the Lord, they desire to be Christ-proclaimers with "clean hands and a pure heart", depending on promises like Zephaniah 3:9: "Then will I purify the lips of the people that all of them may call on the name of the Lord and serve him shoulder to shoulder.... "

- *FORETELLER* ... Joyfully alerting believers to issues of Kingdom hope, these messengers make the climax of God's purposes – with the grand culmination of Christ's global cause – a major factor in how they help believers develop in discipleship. Urging Christians to recognize that the Consummation is always Christologically near (even as it may be chronologically near), they get them to begin right now praying and preparing for the End. Their Message of Hope keeps before the Church the truth that what Jesus will be Lord of ultimately, He is Lord of even now. At the same time, they challenge them to anticipate approximations of the ultimate dominion of Christ — substantial fulfillments and preliminary installments — by how He manifests His Everlasting Reign among them right now in the power of the Holy Spirit.

- *FORTH-TELLER* ... They study and teach God's Word for what it really is, a "book of hope". They help disciples get a good grasp on the four dimensions of Christ's supremacy: Focus, Fulfillment, Fullness, Fervency — and all the ways God's Word applies those dimensions to life and mission for Christ. Like Philip with the Ethiopian (Acts 8), they employ promises and prophecies that speak of Jesus' glories to arouse greater expectations in their hearers. At the same time, they summon believers to join them in promoting the reformation of Biblical Christology so desperately needed in this hour. As hope-filled witnesses they inspire others to confront the crisis of supremacy and speak out clearly about the full extent of Christ and His Kingdom.

- *DECISIVE* ... Exercising tough love, they challenge God's people to face their own crises of supremacy, to confront their own deficiencies in vision of Jesus and His Kingdom, and to own-up to the shortfall of hope and passion toward Christ they experience every day. Messengers of Hope campaign for life-changing responses to their comprehensive message by encouraging the re-conversion of Christians back to Christ for *all* that He is. They appeal for verdicts. They urge their churches to be intentionally involved in His current reign by serving the advance of His cause among the nations.

- *MOBILIZER* ... Messengers of Hope are proactive. They call for, seek out and rally "Prisoners of Hope" to grow together; to deepen their Christology together; to sharpen their knowledge of the promises together; and to pray and take creative action together as agents of renewal. Their goal is the development of *Vanguards of*

Hope who can model what a community shaped by the glory of Jesus looks like, and who help confront and cure the crises of supremacy inside the Church. Messengers of Hope want to flood the Church with Campaigns of Hope.

- **EXPECTANT** ... Messengers of Hope are confident the ultimate outcome of their efforts to stir up "Prisoners of Hope" and galvanize "Vanguards of Hope" rests with God. They know He alone can re-convert His people back to His Son. They're equally sure He will not fail to act somehow, someway. Filled with vibrant hope as big as the Kingdom, they persist as Christ-proclaimers even when results are not immediately apparent. They depend on the Holy Spirit to take their vision of Christ and His supremacy and plant it supernaturally in the hearts of fellow Christians. The Spirit empowers His messengers to persevere *in hope* until the awakening comes.

- **CO-PROCLAIMER** ... Throughout their mission messengers never lose sight of how Christ ultimately heralds hope by His Spirit through their faithful witness to His Kingdom. As the Father's final Spokesman, even now Jesus sustains all reality by His powerful word (Heb. 1). Only His voice, by the Spirit, can penetrate hearts like a sharp sword (Rev. 1). Christ-proclaimers make their appeal on *His* behalf as if He were appealing through them (2 Cor. 5). Jesus joins them to preach the Kingdom not only to those "far away" but also to those who are "near" (Eph. 2), at times verifying their message with signs and wonders (Heb. 2). He actually preaches through them (2 Cor. 13), right in the midst of the congregation (Heb. 2), so that in every proclamation of God's promises not one voice heard, but rather *two*.

How many of these characteristics do you find at the forefront of your service to Christ already? Where do you want to grow?

The Bible in the Hands of a Messenger of Hope

(1 Timothy 3:16-4:8)

Beyond question, every Messenger of Hope is a card-carrying communicator of God's Word. That is top priority. For this reason Christ-proclaimers aim to study and teach God's Word for all it is worth!

Of course, our Message of Hope will need to be personalized, designed in unique ways based on the scope of our *own* hope in the Master. But for all of us Scripture must remain the *source* of every vision we share. Although there are many effective methods of communication we can use (using music, visual images, humor and drama, lecture, dialog or PowerPoint), our fundamental gift to God's people is always the same: God's truth about the supremacy of His Son and the hope this inspires.

There's a tension here, however. On the one hand by keeping God's Word at the forefront we won't *incapacitate* fellow believers by promoting unrealistic expectations about the advance of the Kingdom, thus setting them up for unnecessary disappointments. Messengers of Hope must be careful to share God's promises in their proper Biblical context, for example. We must strive to keep bringing our hearers back to what the Son of God has *said,* what He has *done,* and above all who He *is,* by anchoring every promise of God in Him.

> ### QUOTABLE QUOTE
>
> **We ought to read the Scriptures with the express design of finding Christ in them. Whoever shall turn aside from this object, though he may weary himself throughout his whole life in learning, will never attain the knowledge of the truth: for what wisdom can we have without the wisdom of God?**
>
> (JOHN CALVIN)

On the other hand we want to spread our Message of Hope in such a way that it encourages believers to open their eyes and *stretch* their outlook on Christ. We want to prod them to view Him as comprehensively as the Bible does. By feeding them a feast of Scripture promises, we want to enthrall them with larger dreams for serving the Kingdom. We want to help them gain and retain a horizon on the future that is nothing short of Christ's climactic Kingship, with everything this implies not only for later but also for now. This effort will demand a wholesale reordering of how most churches study the Bible — whether in preaching, or Sunday School, or Bible study classes, or one's own personal devotions.

Making such changes won't prove to be overly complicated, however, because practical approaches have been developed that can transform in exciting ways any Christian's ministry of God's Word to God's people. Let's look at some.

THINK WITH ME ...
How would you deliver to *Christians* God's Word on the supremacy of His Son?

It goes without saying, Christ-proclaimers talk about a *Person* above all. We rehearse the Bible's story not only of what He has done and is doing but, just as much, of what He is getting ready to do. Proclaiming Christ requires tracing back *every* topic we tackle back to the larger hope in Christ related to the Focus, Fulfillment, Fullness or Fervency of His supremacy. As Messengers of Hope we should gear our teaching to confront every form of *counterfeit* hope in a believer's life with God's promise. This can create exciting, fulfilling ministries of encouragement and renewal.

Let's assume you've been given an opportunity to take a few Christians through a small group study of a particular Scripture text. As a Messenger of Hope what would you do with the members? How would you help them study the Bible in such a way that it becomes a "book of hope" for them? To get you started, here are *four approaches* found quite effective for unpacking the "Christology" of any passage. Any one of these sets of questions can help you plant in participants a more dynamic Biblical vision of the victorious Christ.

One of my "readers" who interacted with me on preliminary drafts of *Joyful Manifesto* is a busy wife and mother. By her own admission she does not consider herself a Bible scholar. Yet, without my asking her to do so she attempted to apply these four sets of questions to four separate passages of Scripture, just to see if they really made a difference for her. Enthusiastically she reported that each approach opened up God's Word for her in dynamic new ways. Maybe one of these "study guides" will do the same for you.

What do you think of the Bible study guide #1?

A SIMPLIFIED APPROACH

Choose a passage that articulates some hope or promise we have in Christ. Possibly start with a portion of Isaiah, or Ephesians, or Hebrews, or the Gospel of John. Or focus on one of the Messianic Psalms like Psalm 2, 24, 72 or 110. In any case, ask this set of questions about the text:

- What *promises* and *prospects* are contained in this passage?

- *What will be true* of those promises when they reach their *ultimate fulfillment* in the Consummation to come? What might the *display of their completion* look like *then*?

- What must I see God doing *here and now* for me to sense that these promises are being fulfilled in more immediate, *preliminary* ways? How might I experience *initial installments* or *foretastes* of each promise today? What might this look like, in specific terms, for me? For my church? For my city? For unreached peoples in the world?

- Whether in ultimate or preliminary forms, how will God's faithfulness to the promises presented in this passage *magnify Christ* even more? In other words, how does the hope it inspires zero in on *Him*? Why do Christians need to depend on Jesus to accomplish this hope fully?

- How might any of the previous answers help me *know Him better* in terms of His supremacy in my life or my world?

- What immediate *steps of obedience* do my discoveries require of me? How might this study impact my prayers, for example? Or my growth in Christ-likeness on the job? Or my priorities in financial spending? Or my ministry for Him to non-Christians?

Such questions can equip believers to study and share God's Word with refreshing insights. They can empower you in your mission as a Messenger of Hope! But you might want to come at it a second way.

What do you think of the Bible study guide #2?

USING SEVEN PREPOSITIONS

Here's an equally useful approach. Let's work with *seven prepositions* that capture seven dimensions of Christ's supremacy. The seven are: **to, for,**

through, before, over, within and **upon**. Seven little words, but they can help unpack even more of all we have in the person and work of Christ. They can help *reform* and *enlarge* our hope in Him. (These seven words are discussed in some detail in ***Appendix VI.***)

To start your study choose a favorite text. Ask yourself or the group you are leading: How do the promises and prospects in this text expand on one or more of these seven key expressions of Christ's supremacy? (Here's how I've learned to formulate my study questions.)

- Is there an insight or promise about who Christ is *to* us? (His nature and His character)

- Is there an insight or promise about who Christ is *for* us? (from His incarnation to His crucifixion and resurrection, to His ascension, through His intercession, to His return)

- Is there an insight or promise about who Christ is *through* us? (reaching out to the unreached world through us, either locally or beyond)

- Is there an insight or promise about who Christ is *before* us? (going ahead of us, opening doors, defeating enemies, leading us in victory)

- Is there an insight or promise about who Christ is *over* us? (Head of the Church, Lord of the Nations, King of my life)

- Is there an insight or promise about who Christ is *within* us? (reproducing His life within us, including His love, His holiness, His gifts for ministry)

- Is there an insight or promise about who Christ is *upon* us? (as He intensifies and deepens all the other dimensions of His work with His people through the power of the Holy Spirit)

- Finally, surveying the text again, to what extent are the promises in this passage *individual* in nature? To what extent are they *corporate* in nature? ("me" vs. "us")

- How might all these insights on God's Son help restore in our lives much more of the hope in God were meant to have?

Can you imagine the extent of changes these discoveries will engender? With these questions you can help others re-examine God's Word in order to transform how they view and value His Son.

What do you think of the Bible study guide #3?

USING THE FOUR DIMENSIONS

Let's explore another way to turn any text into a Message of Hope. Return to our original definition of supremacy. The four dimensions of Christ's lordship begin with the letter "F" — *Focus, Fulfillment, Fullness,* and *Fervency*. As suggested earlier, all 7,000-plus promises of Scripture could be subsumed under one or more of these four categories. Thus, these dimensions should help uncover all the hope any passage was meant to give us:

- ***Focus*** relates to hundreds of passages where God promises to clarify our vision of Christ, helping us focus on Him better for who He really is ***to*** us and ***for*** us. We're looking for what we can find in the text about who Christ is as the Son of God, and how that relates to any hope the passage offers to believers.

- ***Fulfillment*** speaks to multiple promises that impact our ministry in the world. These passages point to all Christ wants to be ***through*** us and ***before*** us in order to fulfill God's mission among the nations, and to weave our lives and our churches into the consummation of all things in Him. We're looking for what we can find in the text about where Christ leads in the Purposes of God.

- ***Fullness*** describes the countless promises about what Christ intends to do within the life of His followers — how He intends to give us His fullness as He reigns ***over*** us and lives ***within*** us. We're looking for what we can find in the text about how Christ imparts the Resources of God to the people of God.

- ***Fervency*** captures those passages promising that Christ will come ***upon*** us to quicken in us hope, faith and love toward Him, and to intensify our devotion and obedience in serving His Kingdom glory. We're looking for what the text tells us about the glory, zeal and service Jesus expects to receive from the People of God because He is Lord of all.

Most texts, you'll find, major on only one or two of the themes of Focus, Fulfillment, Fullness and Fervency. As you grow in our understanding of what is involved in each dimension, a fresh outlook on any passage of Scripture will be established and will increase hope in Christ and passion for serving His Kingdom's advance.

What do you think of the Bible study guide #4?

A MORE EXHAUSTIVE APPROACH

Here's a more in-depth progression of questions you might like to try. This approach may prove the most useful in helping you prepare a Bible study or sermon. At the same time, it can also turn daily devotional times into powerful encounters with the Lord of Glory. You don't need to use all of them. Choose only those that appear most helpful at the moment.

- How does this text, either directly or indirectly, promise that God will manifest to us more of the *glory* of His Son? In what ways does it encourage us to expect fresh encounters with Christ for who He really is? *(focus)*

- How does this text speak, directly or indirectly, to the *mission thrust* of God's people? How might it reinforce for us God's intention to advance Christ's kingdom by working with His people to lead us into the consummation of all things? How does it unfold additional dimensions of the Grand Climax? How does it point us toward foretastes of that wonderful hope as we serve Christ's global cause right now? *(fulfillment)*

- How does this text, directly or indirectly, highlight God's promise to involve His people in a deeper, healthier, more abundant life in Christ? How does it speak to ways Christ wants to pour more of His victorious life into His Church and exercise more of His sovereign ministry within His Church? Or, within my own life? *(fullness)*

- How does this text point us toward the kinds of *responses* we need to make to Christ as our Lord — for example: How we need to seek His glory; or yield to His call; or pursue His agenda; or be passionate for His Kingdom; or give Him our heart's devotion and praise? Even more, in what ways does this passage provide disciples with compelling reasons for an all-consuming passion for Christ as our hope? In what specific ways does it call us to be more wholly committed to magnifying His name and to sacrificing for His global cause? *(fervency)*

- Are there any supporting texts with *similar promises* that might be woven into the prospects offered in this immediate text? How might including other texts expand an understanding of the passage? *(understanding)*

- What does this text teach us to expect from *God* as He acts on our behalf to accomplish any of these promises (whether focus, fulfillment, fullness, fervency)? *(grace)*

- In what ways might this text give us the right to expect God's intervention in *extraordinary* ways? If it does, what might that look like, based on the teachings in the passage? *(supernatural)*

- Does this text reveal any *hindrances* we must deal with, whether inside or outside the Church, which might prevent a fuller expression of the hope the text offers? *(barriers)*

- What does this passage teach us about important steps we should take immediately to *prepare,* individually or corporately, for greater manifestations of Christ's supremacy among us? *(preparation)*

- How do the promises of this passage help us anticipate what we will experience in the Consummation itself? In other words, how would the hope highlighted here find its *climactic* expression when Jesus comes again? What might that look like then? How might this text enlarge and enrich our hope in the supremacy of Christ? *(Consummation)*

- How would a pursuit of the promises found in this text best express itself practically in our *daily discipleship*? Be as specific as you can. *(obedience)*

- Drawing from this text, what is it about Christ and His supremacy that we should proclaim to our hearers? How would *you* present Him as the One who embodies and guarantees the promises of God? (This is related, of course, to focus, fullness, fulfillment, and fervency.) How can you increase others' understanding of Christ's glorious greatness as the center and circumference of the hope this text sets before all of us? *(witness)*

- Using the insights from this passage, how would you address any crises of hope or passion that others may be facing right now? With this text in mind how would you challenge your hearers to re-engage with Christ for *all* that He is? What next steps do they need to take to implement renewed commitment to His lordship? *(ministry)*

- If the fulfillment of the promises of this text were given fuller expression right now by the power of the Holy Spirit, how might that help make Christ seem more *supreme* for others? How might this contribute to curing the crisis of supremacy where you live? Bottom line: What kind of "reforming" of your current perspectives on God's Son should this passage inspire? Where will you begin?

(campaign)

Opening up God's Word to believers in order to impact their vision of Christ and restore their hope in Christ is just one part of our mission as Messengers of Hope — the most critical part, to be sure. But there's more to the strategy if Messengers of Hope are to successfully accomplish their mission. I've boiled the rest down to four easy steps.

A Four-Part Strategy for Every Messenger of Hope
(Matthew 11:1-15, 25-30)

An amateur painter once tried to develop his own version of Leonardo daVinci's "The Last Supper". After giving it his best shot, he showed his efforts to a few friends. He was broken-hearted when one remarked: "My, what exquisite detail you have incorporated on the cups the disciples are holding!" Realizing he had failed to make Jesus the central focus of the painting as he intended from the outset, he destroyed the canvas and started all over again.

Messengers of Hope are like painters. Our mission is to pass along life-changing portraits of Jesus that make Him the major issue for other Christians. But how do we effectively deliver this message for maximum impact on God's people? What are the key ingredients to ensure that every Message of Hope reaches its goal? Is there a tested-and-proven strategy that, combined with God's Word, effectively awakens believers to reform their pursuit of Christ's glory?

I've discussed this question at length in a previous book titled *Messengers of Hope: Becoming Agents of Revival for the 21ˢᵗ Century* (available for free in digital format at my website). At this point let me distill from a number of those chapters a four-fold formula that comes out of nearly 30 years of being a Messenger of Hope myself. I base it on the acronym **H.O.P.E.** which stands for:

- **H** = *Hop On!* — a ministry of "inspiration"

- **O** = *Open Up!* — a ministry of "revelation"

- **P** = *Pray Back!* — a ministry of "intercession"

- **E** = *Enter Into!* — a ministry of "mobilization"

This four-part strategy provides a dynamic *delivery system* for any Message of Hope. Let's survey each guideline briefly. (In my book *Messengers of Hope* I spent a whole chapter on each part.)

THINK WITH ME ...

H **Is for** *Hop On!* — **How do you grow a ministry of** *inspiration*?

God cannot lead us on the basis of facts we do not have. That's obvious. Ignorance cripples hopefulness. We need to expose God's people to the ways He has been working (and still is) to execute His promises in power. How has He gone about manifesting greater displays of Christ's Kingdom over the generations? How is He currently doing so among the nations? Since God is always on the move toward completing Christ's global cause, we are obliged to help the saints "hop on" to His victorious "bandwagon". We need to inspire them with the stories. We want to motivate them to join up with Him — to "get with the program", so to speak.

Specifically you can expand a Christian's vision using any of the following:

- *Recount signs and activities* of renewal and awakening in the Church in different parts of the world today. Give accounts of how Christ is restoring and mobilizing Christians and churches across the globe. A variety of websites can help you. So will a number of books listed in *Appendix III.*

- *Report on breakthroughs* going on right now in the missionary cause among nations and unreached peoples. Give accounts of how Christ is manifesting His Kingdom authority in evangelism, social reform, compassion ministries and church planting. Again, use the web and *Appendix III*.

- *Comb back through the annals of Church history.* Uncover some of the hundreds of stories of people and movements who hoped in God and were not disappointed. Since Jesus Christ is the same yesterday, today and forever (Heb. 13), pass along concrete examples of how His supremacy was manifested in the past — with individuals, churches, nations — in order to encourage believers to expect Him to be able, willing and ready to do the same again. (See *Appendix III*)

- *Share stories of what God is doing locally* highlighting up-to-the-minute examples of "approximations of the Consummation" (see chapter 4) taking place right around you, maybe in another church or another part of your city.

- Of course, report on all the ways Christ is revealing His glory in various *spheres of concern within your own nation,* such as in government, business, education, media, and labor as well as in the challenges of our cities, or among the poor, or with immigrants. Certainly highlight every evidence that the Holy Spirit is turning back the crisis of supremacy inside our nation's churches.

- *Share your own story* to show how Christ has displayed His dominion and power in your own walk with God. Tell your own story of life lived under the supremacy of God's Son. Ask others in your congregation to do the same.

Whatever approach you take, the goal is to help God's people "hop on" to His forcefully advancing kingdom (Matt. 11). We must awaken them to activities of the Spirit, past and present, that show how the reign of Christ can break into the present. Don't let fellow Christians receive Scripture's teachings in a vacuum. Challenge them to expect manifestations of Christ's supremacy within their own settings not only in fulfillment of God's words but also in a manner similar to how He actually works in other places, with other people, at other times, within other parts of His Body. As the Bible says, our God is no respecter of persons. What He has done for others, He is able, willing and ready to do for us.

Reports and stories, vividly and enthusiastically told, can accelerate the saints' hope in Christ and inspire them to "get up to speed" with where He's headed. Remember: Every hope-filled account you share gives the Holy Spirit something to work with in your hearers that He didn't have to work with before — to take them where they have never gone with Christ before. What a tremendous ministry this is for the Kingdom.

THINK WITH ME ...
O is for *Open Up* — How do you grow a ministry of *revelation*?

Once you have whetted people's appetites with stories of promises-in-action, then open up the Scriptures for them in wonderfully fresh ways. Show them how the Bible is the foundation for the hope your reports have offered them. On God's Word all of God's work is grounded. Therefore, by that Word all His previous Kingdom activities must be interpreted. Make use of the approaches explored earlier in this chapter — such as the seven themes (seven prepositions) or the four F's (Focus, Fulfillment, Fullness, Fervency).

QUOTABLE QUOTE

From every text of Scripture there is a road to Christ. And my dear brother, your business is, when you get to a text, to say, now, what is the road to Christ? I have never found a text that did not have a road to Christ in it.

(CHARLES SPURGEON)

However you approach it, confirm from Scripture how Christ is Sovereign over our hope. Make the Bible indispensable as God's "book of hope" for them.

Look at *Appendix V*. It lists scores of passages that powerfully portray the preeminence of Jesus and the hope we are meant to have in Him as a result. Share from these Scriptures every chance you get. This will help fellow Christians internalize a vision for God's Son and a passion for His Kingdom.

THINK WITH ME ...
P is for *Pray Back* — How do you grow a ministry of *intercession*?

Now you're ready to help your hearers pray your message back to God. Once people have grasped how much the Father longs to manifest the greatness of His Son among them in new ways — once you've inspired them through compelling stories and expanded understandings of the Biblical promises — the most appropriate step is to help them seek God about these matters. By prayer Christians can worship the glory of God "in the face of Jesus Christ" (2 Cor. 4). By prayer they can petition Him to perform what He's promised for the honor of His Son. All prayer is intended by God to secure further demonstrations of Christ's lordship in heaven and earth.

Your role as a leader of prayer is critical to overall effectiveness as a Messenger of Hope. The blessing of seeking is equal in importance to the impact of speaking, when it comes to a Campaign of Hope (Acts 6). Beyond the amazing answers that result from Kingdom-driven praying, such activity brings significant changes in at least four areas:

- *It changes the way you share your Message of Hope.*
  When you know your message will be followed by your hearers' praying over the promises you presented to them and about your vision for the supremacy of God's Son, you will be even more committed to giving your message in a comprehensive, compelling and crystal clear way.

- *It changes the way your hearers listen to you.*
  If they know ahead of time that they will be asked to pray about the Message of Hope you share just as soon as you've laid it before them, their attention will be galvanized like never before on the vision you are saying and the hope you are urging.

- *It changes the way they obey your message.*
  Praying God's promises in Jesus back to Him always moves Kingdom-filled truths out of people's heads, down into their hearts and ultimately out into their daily walk with Jesus. Prayer over supremacy issues takes discipleship beyond the academic and translates it into a passion for the hope Christ's Kingship gives us.

- *Above all, it changes their encounter with Christ in His supremacy.*
  God is unalterably committed to answering any prayers that allow Him to reveal His Son more fully to those who have sought Him in hope. Your Message of Hope will incite your people to pray probably in ways they have never dared to pray previously regarding Kingdom issues. God will take full advantage of this unique openness to His Son and will invade their lives to reveal more of His glory even as they pray. He also will do so later as their prayers are answered. Now they will see even more reasons to put their hope in the supremacy of Christ.

But, you may ask, how does one shape hope-filled, Christ-exalting prayer derived from a Biblical text? We'll study this more in chapter 12. There we look at prayer as basic to "anticipatory discipleship". For now, remember: Strong praying begins by having your hearers retrace by prayer major truths in your Message of Hope. For example, you might have your group or congregation borrow phrases found in a text you've just explored with them, restating Scripture with their own words and praying (or praising) those insights back to the Father. Or you might have them shape their requests by using points from your teaching or sermon notes. You can have them pray over the main entries on the outline of your study. Whatever approach you take, encourage them to express to God — in prayers of rejoicing, repenting, requesting, recommitment — their growing hope in God based on His Kingdom promises in Jesus. *Appendix VII* gives you a tool that combines the proclaiming and the praying in a unique way.

Our ultimate goal should be to create a "culture of prayer" in our churches, where "pray[ing] without ceasing" (1 Thess. 5) becomes a way of life for our people. This can provide an "atmosphere of expectation" conducive to hearing and receiving every Message of Hope shared with them.

THINK WITH ME …
E is for *Enter Into* — **How do you grow**
a ministry of *mobilization*?

Prayer is not the final step, however. Once the hope has been proclaimed, illustrated and prayed back to God, our intention is to get our hearers involved in living out that hope.

The first priority is calling Christians to *prepare* for greater things to come, for the answers to their prayers. Just as the Bible exhorts us to get ready for the Second Coming of Christ, in the same way we should be poised for *preliminary out-workings* of that hope at any moment. Every Message of Hope should motivate disciples to pursue what I describe as "anticipatory discipleship". Here's a short definition: *Anticipatory discipleship defines the obedience to Christ that looks more to what is coming than to what has already been.* (This will be explored fully in chapter 12.)

We work to help our hearers interpret Biblical hope in a way that not only transforms their prayer lives but mobilizes every aspect of their *daily walk* with Christ around the fullest implications of His supremacy. They will learn to apply this hope to:

- Family-life activities

- Local church involvement

- Engagements in social reforms

- Issues of racial and denominational reconciliation

- Economic lifestyle choices

- Career directions

- Daily use of time

- Investments in entertainment and recreation

- Personal devotional life with God

Hope-filled Christians look for increased expressions of Christ's lordship in all these arenas. They must *"act as if"* great promises from a great Savior are about to find greater demonstrations. They must *"act as if"* the Father is ready at any moment, for the sake of His Son, to do unsearchable things which we have not yet experienced (Jer. 33). They must *"act as if"* the time for fresh demonstrations of Jesus' majesty are at hand (Mk. 1) as they daily "enter into" the reign of Christ and "enter into" the hope and passion His reign encourages them to have.

QUOTABLE QUOTE

We have preached ourselves, not Christ. We have preached too often so as to exalt ourselves instead of magnifying Christ, so as to draw men's eyes to ourselves instead of fixing them on Him and His Cross. Christ, in the sufferings of His first coming and the glory of His second, has not been the Alpha and Omega, the first and the last, of all our sermons.

(HORATIUS BONAR)

Eventually this fourth step will require us to help others become Messengers of Hope. Just as it is often true that "leaders don't create followers, they create more leaders", even so ultimately *Messengers of Hope don't create listeners, they create more messengers.* Reproducing messengers who join you in your wonderful mission is a key confirmation that you've effectively delivered your message and that they've begun to "enter into" it.

H.O.P.E. — These steps are not gimmicks. They really work! Decades of ministry have taught me that each ingredient is incredibly potent, *especially when packaged together to unleash a Message of Hope.* Each provides an effective approach for proclaiming Christ's Kingdom, as we do so from four directions: by a *look back* (hop on); a *look in* (open up); a *look up* (pray back); a *look out* (enter in). In using these ingredients you will become not only a more productive Christ-proclaimer, but you will also foster among fellow believers a lasting cure for the crisis of Christology.

Through it all, however, remember one thing: You *are* proclaiming. You're not simply giving counsel or advice, or expressing opinions. Your message is about a hope directly from Heaven, backed by every promise and purpose God has ever revealed in Jesus. It is shaped by the One Lord before whom everything must ultimately bow. So persevere in your mission. In love announce Christ's glory along with the wonderful hope that goes with it. Do so sensitively. Do so consistently. Do so with confidence your message will not return void (Isa. 5). Do so with believers and unbelievers alike. But do so first of all *inside* the Church.

Measuring the Success
of any Messenger of Hope
(Acts 20: 17-35)

At this point you may be wondering: How can I know for sure I've truly been successful as a Messenger of Hope? Perhaps you're uncertain about the Bible study approach you've chosen. Or you feel a need for confidence that you've actually delivered your message and made a difference. Knowing a little about possible responses to your message might help.

THINK WITH ME ...
What four responses to a Message of Hope might you expect?

First, remember that even Jesus faced mixed reactions to His own Message of Hope. Only one of four responses (listed below) would be termed *"successful"*. We must be prepared for similar diverse reactions.

In a parable about four different soils Jesus illustrated four possible responses to His "word of the Kingdom", a phrase highlighting His Kingship and its prospects (Mt. 13). I find it interesting that the first three soils make it clear that a "crisis of supremacy" already prevailed among God's people:

- The *hard-hearted* people (trodden path) concluded there was really no hope from God to begin with. So they refused to respond at all. Satan, chief opponent to God's promises, quickly moved in to seal their doom as they received the message from Jesus.

- The *weak-hearted* people (rocky dirt) settled for superficial understandings of Christ's Kingdom-filled word. This created a response unable to withstand challenges that seemed to contradict the grand hope He offered.

- The *half-hearted* people (thorny ground) supplemented their feeble passion for Christ's glory with temporal strategies for self-fulfillment, such as the pursuit of earthly riches and fleshly pleasures. In the end, "false hopes" choked out the promised productiveness of Christ's reign in their lives.

- Only with the *whole-hearted* people (fertile soil) did Jesus experience genuine success. Convinced God really had something more for them — something better and greater for them in the Kingdom of His Son — they gratefully received Christ's "Message of Hope" for themselves. They held on to it, not wavering in unbelief. They ended up bearing the fruits of hope-filled obedience. Truly, theirs was a lasting hope.

Serving as Messengers of Hope today, you will find it prudent to be ready for similar outcomes. When fellow believers hear you, some will appear hard-hearted. Others will turn weak-hearted. Still others will respond with half-hearted measures. This will disappoint you deeply. But, by God's grace, some *will* choose to be *whole-hearted!* They will grab hold of your Message of Hope with great expectations and determine to live in the light of its Kingdom promises. As it was for Jesus, so it will be for you: Whole-hearted disciples must remain our primary audience — ministry #1 in any Campaign of Hope. Be on the look out for them.

Regarding the other three soils, however, let me encourage you: Before your message about Jesus' glorious greatness was shared with them, most were locked-up in "boxes" of shrunken vision, feeble faith and dead-end prospects. *Now,* at least, your message about the supremacy of Jesus has them wrestling with possibilities of a whole new kind of existence in Jesus. Now, you have them wondering if a truly fulfilling life, a life lived in the wide-open spaces of Jesus' forcefully advancing Kingdom, might possibly happen for *them.*

As is often said, once it is *moving,* a bike (the disciple) can be steered where it needs to go (the vision of Christ). Through your Message of Hope the Spirit has a new way to guide your hearers into sensitive encounters with the glory of God's Son. Who wouldn't want to help launch new dreams in the hearts of fellow believers, formed around Kingdom promises for the praise of the King, even if your efforts must take some "flack" at the outset due to others' struggles with unhealthy fascinations or unresolved fears?

On the day of Pentecost when good soil turned up among thousands (including not a few priests, we're told), then all of Jesus' sowing finally paid off. It cost Him His life, of course. It will be costly for every Messenger of Hope, one way or another. But we can be sure that a Word from God not only sustains the universe and raises the dead but can transform resistant hearts into "Prisoners of Hope" (as the next chapter will show).

THINK WITH ME ...
What is the single most important measure of any messenger's *success?*

In John Bunyan's epic allegory *The Pilgrim's Progress* we meet a little fellow dubbed "Hopeful". Part way through his journey, our hero Christian loses his first traveling companion Faithful to martyrdom (a rather soul-wrenching moment). However, he soon finds himself joined by Hopeful who for the remainder of Christian's adventures provides a constant commentary of encouragements. By his witness to him Hopeful helps Christian defeat Giant Despair, survive a dungeon, discover the Key of Promise, fight off corrupting creatures like Ignorance, Little-Faith and Flatterer. It is Hopeful who keeps the ultimate vision of The End alive for Christian. It is Hopeful who points him to the Shining One and his Celestial City. It is Hopeful who proclaims such a hope-filled message for Christian that the pilgrim is able to progress (as Bunyan puts it) "from this world to that which is to come". Hopeful's mission is a thorough success.

All of us need at least one friend like Hopeful in our lives! More importantly, all of us need to become a Hopeful for someone else. Our churches need to be flooded with a *host* of Hopefuls! But how can we be certain we've successfully accomplished, like Christian's companion, our calling to be "Hopefuls" (Messengers of Hope) for other believers? Is it simply enough to ask: "Was my message relevant to someone?" Or: "Was my message practical and useful for someone?" Or even: "Was my message encouraging to someone?"

Bunyan's little Hopeful had far more in mind than these goals as he ministered to pilgrim Christian. Similarly, our primary evaluation must ask:

Did my hearers encounter
a larger vision of Christ and His supremacy,
and were they gripped by stronger reasons
to put their hope more fully in Him,
than they had before we came together?

Whatever the text, the context or the pretext; whatever the audience's make-up, size or agenda; whatever a meeting's immediate topic, issue, cause or concern may be, I must be confident that:

To the best of my ability,
I have helped my hearers leave my presence
with a deeper understanding of the glory of Christ
and a fuller hope shaped by the supremacy of Christ.

Do you recall the last time you raised spiritual issues with some of God's people? Maybe it was during a luncheon Bible study at the office; or in a conversation with a friend between church services; or during deliberations at the last missions committee meeting. Maybe it was last night at family devotions; or while visiting a friend in the hospital; or when you recently consoled a grieving widow. Whatever the situation, did your effort focus primarily on *Christ?* Did it lead to greater hope in Him? Ask yourself:

1) The last time I shared God's Word from my heart with other believers, did I unfold for them a *larger vision* of Christ and His supremacy than what they had before we met?

2) At the same time, did I lay out for them *more compelling reasons* to put their hope in Christ, and to do so with greater confidence, than what they had before we met?

For a Messenger of Hope saying "Yes" to such questions is the sign of success, as *God* measures success. We have succeeded anytime people can say, *"Through what you shared with me you opened up for me a larger vision of Christ's grace and glory than I had ever seen before! And, now my hope in Him and my passion for Him are stronger than ever."*

When God gives such a result, we've effectively achieved the one mission that really matters. We have taken a strategic step toward confronting and curing the crisis of supremacy. Our Campaign of Hope has found one more reason to press onward!

But being a Christ-proclaimer is only the start of the campaign. We must become successful on two other fronts as well. With those who respond to our Message of Hope our additional responsibility is to help *captivate* them as wholly as possible with a fuller vision of God's Son. Hearers of hope must eventually become *Prisoners* of Hope (see chapter 11) who ultimately draw together as *Vanguards* of Hope (see chapter 12) to become a dynamic force for the renewal of an entire congregation.

Let's start by finding out how captives are created.

QUOTABLE QUOTE

If I could stand on this platform and say, "I have received from heaven a secret of wealth and success which God will give freely, through my hand, to everybody who will take it," I am sure you would need a larger hall for the people who would come. But, dear friends, I show you in His Word a truth which is more precious, a great secret which is now disclosed to the saints. Paul went through the world just to tell it to those that were able to receive it. That simple secret is this: "Christ in you, the hope of glory." I feel I have only begun to learn how well it works.

(Dr. A.B. Simpson)

11

BECOMING PRISONERS OF HOPE

How to Re-capture the Church for the Supremacy of God's Son

It was near the end of the second hour, part of a six-hour convocation. More than one million men huddled across the vast expanses of the Mall in Washington, D.C. Called *Stand in the Gap*, this historic gathering convened to spend a day fasting and praying over the desperate need for revival in the churches of America.

Baking under a hot early October sun, participants obviously were ready to pray. My place in the program had come. My assignment was to prepare the men for the next season of intercession. Minutes before mounting the platform, however, I was overcome with a profound sense that what we really needed to do at that moment was to get *silent* before the Lord — making room for Christ to reveal Himself afresh to us. After I approached the microphone, I recited verses from Revelation 1. The passages reminded the crowd of the matchless, magnificent Master whom John saw. This vision of Christ caused the apostle to fall down in absolute silence like a dead man as John waited for his Savior to make the next move. I proceeded to invite a million strong to prostrate themselves on the ground in the very same way John did.

For the next three minutes that's precisely what we did. An awesome scene unfolded before me as participants responded — out-stretched, flat on their faces, humbled before the King in a holy hush — spanning the mall to the Washington monument! Everything became so eerily still that one could hear a faint breeze rustling trees along the walkways.

What happened to the participants during those sacred moments? Most of all, they experienced a fulfillment of Psalm 46: "Be still and know that I am God. I will be exalted in the earth." It was the Holy Spirit's wake-up call for us to seek the Kingdom of God's Son like never before. Before the day was over, not a few told me they had experienced a rebirth of hope at that point — hope that one day our nation might see genuine revival and be covered with the glory of Jesus Christ.

Over the years since, numerous times men from the Mall event have approached me to talk about the gathering and report that of the entire six hours, it was as they bowed to reaffirm the preeminence of our Lord Jesus Christ with a few minutes of total silence — when no one *did* anything! — that they were transformed forever with fresh confidence about the advance of Christ's purposes in our generation, and their place in it.

Stand in the Gap was convened by a national men's movement called Promise Keepers. PK founder Bill McCartney, a former university football coach, wrote me a personal note just before the gathering in which he said: "We need to know the playbook. We also need to understand the whole game. We need to understand the big picture of what God is doing. We need to understand our point in history. Then, we must step into position. There's an awesome move of God across our nation and the planet. We live in a day of great hope — hope of a genuine, Biblical revival. You and I are meant to be a part of it. All of us need to pray for and prepare for a God-given awakening to Christ. Millions of men and women are rising up to do so."

That represents the breadth of vision for Jesus that lies behind every Campaign of Hope. As we've begun to explore in **Volume Three,** Messengers of Hope seek to captivate fellow Christians with the same hope that flooded the Mall that day — the promise of the Church's awakening to the greatness of God's Son — reproducing what I call *Prisoners of Hope.* This phrase defines the second cure for the crisis of supremacy. Once we begin to herald the hope, we must move on to help our hearers understand that (as chapter 11 will explain):

- Every Christian must become such a prisoner to really thrive in his/her life in Jesus.

- God Himself is *determined* for us to be captivated by a much larger vision of His Son.

- We can learn to receive hope more fully in a daily walk with the King of Glory.

- There are effective ways to rebuild *confidence* in God's promises in Christ so that we are bold to receive what His reign offers.

- *Repentance* and *suffering* are keys to increasing our *capacity* to receive Kingdom promises.

- Recovering our hope in Christ always works best in the company of *other* Prisoners of Hope.

QUOTABLE QUOTE

Realize how great is the hope to which He is calling you — the magnificence and splendor of the inheritance promised to Christians—and how tremendous is the power available to us who believe in God. That power is the same divine energy which was demonstrated in Christ when He raised Him from the dead and gave Him the place of supreme honor in Heaven. The Church is His body, and in that body lives fully the One who fills the whole wide universe.

(EPHESIANS 1 — PHILLIPS TRANSLATION)

The Biblical Profile of a "Prisoner of Hope"
(Zechariah 9:9-10, 11-12, 13-17)

Captivity to hope — that was the unexpected gift the Father gave an avalanche of men that historic Fall afternoon in 1997, literally before the eyes of a watching nation (since it was broadcast on C-Span and hosts of TV outlets). From that day on, many began a new journey with Christ. They became what I call *"Prisoners of Hope"*. Where does the term come from?

It's hinted at in a number of passages. Take, for example, 2 Corinthians 2. There Paul designates Christians as "captives" to Christ, marching in a triumphal procession, moving forward with great expectations in His mighty power, spreading the fragrance of His glory everywhere they go. This picture comes from the defeated armies Rome paraded before the Emperor after a battle, now slaves of the Empire for the rest of their lives. That's how we share in our Holy Emperor's victorious inheritance! Out of His decisive defeat of sin and death, the New Covenant has made us Jesus' grateful bondservants for His royal purposes forever. In the same sense, Ephesians 4 urges Christians to "live a life worthy of the calling you have received", because we serve the Lord who "when he ascended on high, led captives in his train and gave gifts to men".

However, Zechariah 9 actually uses the phrase "prisoners of hope" to encourage a remnant of disheartened exiles:

> As for you, because of the blood of my covenant with you,
> I will free your prisoners from the waterless pit.
> Return to your fortress, *O prisoners of hope*.
> Even now I announce that I will restore twice as much to you.
> (verses 11-12 emphasis mine)

On this side of the Ascension, how does this promise apply? What do such captives look like? Come with me to three countries — South Africa, India and Afghanistan — and let me introduce you to modern-day Prisoners of Hope.

THINK WITH ME ...
What might Prisoners of Hope look like today?

Some years ago Zechariah's text was first introduced to me by a leading black Christian pastor in **South Africa**. Within the social ferment aimed at the scourge of apartheid, he witnessed repeatedly how ordinary Christians made courageous differences toward ending racial injustice, even in impoverished communities like Soweto. They labored in the hope that no matter how the government oppressed them, Christ's Kingdom would prevail. Hope in Christ became their daily passion. They couldn't help themselves, this pastor insisted to me. They were *prisoners* of that hope! As a result, disenfranchised believers helped transform the face of a nation, preserving it from massive bloodshed by their peaceful demonstrations and persistent negotiations — above all, by their prayers. They stunned the world with the impact of their efforts in spiritual, social and political liberation.

I've met similar prisoners in my travels across **India**. I've found hope's captives among many leaders of Indian missionary organizations. The founders of one mission society told me how years earlier, while still in their teens, six of them began to ask God to grant major breakthroughs for the Gospel among masses of Hindus around them. Their prayers and labors for Christ grew increasingly tenacious because God's Word filled them with great expectations for their nation. So, they set out to be Messengers of Hope. By proclaiming to Christians a larger vision of Christ and His Kingdom, they worked at renewing discouraged congregations across South India. Eventually hundreds of volunteers stepped forward for missionary service, men and women ready to serve Christ because they had recovered hope and passion for Him. The laborers were sent out, in turn, by the prayers and sacrifices of thousands of other Indian Christians quickened by the same promises. Despite their own financial poverty, these partners agreed to fund hundreds of new missionaries. Both senders and goers responded at great personal cost because they had become Prisoners of Hope.

In another part of the world at the opening of the 21st century, God miraculously set two young missionaries free who had been held hostage for months by terrorists in **Afghanistan**. Dayna and Heather left a safe, predictable life in America to obey their Savior's call to one of the most dangerous nations on earth, to work among impoverished Afghans. Imprisoned on the Taliban's death row, they became pawns in history-shattering events. Yet their utter confidence in Christ as Lord-of-All kept them hope-filled and faithful. After miraculously being freed from their iron chains, they set about to launch on behalf of the beleaguered nation a new avenue of ministry which they called the *Hope Afghanistan Foundation*. At the same time the young women published the best-selling *Prisoners of Hope* on their adventures for Christ's Kingdom. Still captive to *spiritual* chains, they continued to pursue Christ's call to serve the nations.

South Africa, India, Afghanistan ... In each arena hope was awakened within Christians enveloped in humanly hopeless situations. But vision for the supremacy of Christ took them captive so fully, that they prayed and prepared, served and sacrificed, in the unshakeable conviction that God's best lay still ahead. How does the Father harness His children to unquench-able zeal for the preeminence of His Son? Let's explore some answers.

THINK WITH ME ...

What is God's primary way to create Prisoners of Hope?

Have you ever sat in a courtroom and studied prisoners awaiting trial? Frequently the accused are dressed in street clothes, a suit and tie perhaps, so as not to prejudice the jury against them. They appear as normal and free as everyone else in attendance. But in truth, prisoners are not "normal" at all! Outside the courtroom they are completely at the disposal of the penal system. Decisions about what they eat, how they dress, where they sleep and where they reside are totally controlled by others. At trial they may look like you or me, but privately they are preoccupied with a very different agenda. They're ruled by forces and futures larger than themselves.

The same is true of every "Prisoner of Hope". Because of Christ's finished work for us, God is forever in the business of delivering Christians out of "waterless pits" (the dusty trenches of our own making, dry with hopelessness and despair) to soak in the Living Water. He imprisons us within a most extraordinary hope, as the context of Zechariah 9 indicates. The prophet describes nothing less than the supreme promise of Redemption's worldwide revolution under the reign of Messiah King (see verses 8-9, which the Gospels claim were put into motion at Christ's triumphal entry on Passion Week). *This* vision gets us out of waterless pits and holds us captive to hope. God's strategy for creating Prisoners of Hope comes down to vs. 12 (emphasis mine):

> Even now I *announce*
> that I will restore *twice* as much to you.

In anticipation of sending Israel's Deliverer (vs. 8-10), the living God commits *Himself* to step directly into the drama. Not only that, He broadcasts to Israel precisely what He's up to — God becomes the prime Messenger of Hope to a crowd of weary refugees. The prospects for them are amazing, He declares. He will not take them back to where they were before, even to the best of the pre-exilic days they had known. Instead, they will surge forward to where they've never gone before — into blessings they have never known before — "I will restore *twice* as much", He promises.

So, goodbye, *pits*! Hello, *hope*! God *announces* the hope. He *heralds* the hope. He *proclaims* the hope. And they become *Prisoners* of Hope.

"Faith comes by hearing, and what is heard is the message of Christ" (Rom. 10). When the Spirit shows us a future in Christ that's too wonderful for us to produce (creating in us desperation) but too wonderful for us to live without (creating in us anticipation), we have to surrender (creating in us subjugation), yielding to the blessed hope we have in Him.

The lordship of Jesus chains us to the Father's Plan for the Ages. As Zechariah testified, whenever the Head of the Church speaks His promise to His people, He invites us into "twice as much". By His power at work in us, God wants to do for us "exceedingly above and beyond all that we ask or think" so as to bring Himself far greater glory "in the Church and in Christ Jesus, throughout all generations, forever and ever" (Eph. 3).

So, how has this process unfolded in your walk with the Lord? How far along are you in becoming a Prisoner of Hope?

THINK WITH ME ...
How fully have you been taken captive to hope in Christ?

Stand in the Gap convened under the banner of a movement called Promise Keepers. Borrowing the motif of a "promise keeper", let me suggest a process I've watched unfold with many Christians to recover hope and passion for the Lord Jesus. This series of *transitions* could be regarded equally as *benchmarks* along the path as we follow the Master — a *metamorphosis* believers must go through to grow into full-fledged Prisoners of Hope.

There is nothing arbitrary about how we move through these phases. From the moment we commit ourselves to Christ, all of us are somewhere along this path. With each transition we grow to know Him more deeply, engage Him more passionately, and walk with Him more responsively. Passing through each phase we become more *captive* to our vision of Christ's supremacy.

Which benchmarks have already been set in your life? What does this tell you about your very next step in growing as a Prisoner of Hope?

- **PROMISE-SLEEPER ...**
  This describes believers who are *unaware* of most dimensions of a Biblical hope focused on Christ and His supremacy. As God awakens them for the first time to these realities, through His Word and His Spirit, they may choose to become a ...

- **PROMISE-PEEPER ...**
  For this phase any believer qualifies who initially senses he (or she) must put their hope in Christ *alone*. A Christian chooses not to turn

away to other possibilities, sensing it's time to ponder how to
respond appropriately. Next, God helps this person become a ...

• **PROMISE-SEEKER ...**
Every Christian worthy of this name has transitioned into actively
pursuing (by the Word, prayer and obedience) the meaning and
implications of God's promises for them in Christ. As each disciple
seeks more of Jesus' glory, God keeps her or him growing in a vision
of the Lord until each becomes a ...

• **PROMISE-KEEPER ...**
This title belongs to all believers who hold firmly to God's
promises with the intention of focusing every area of their lives
on Christ and the abounding hope His supremacy offers. They grow
in their passion to make Christ's Kingdom glory their highest
ambition. That's why God is able to transform anyone like this
into a ...

• **PROMISE-LEAPER ...**
Christians who respond with hope-filled praise, daily celebrating the
Redeemer toward whom the promises point, are "leapers" who
"rejoice in the hope of the glory of God" (Rom. 5). They also
celebrate all the ways God is preparing to reveal the glory of His Son
in days ahead. Simultaneously, however, each leaper grows into a ...

• **PROMISE-WEEPER ...**
Hope-ers with heart show it! They ache for individuals who are
weary with waterless pits, lacking any sense of the wonderful
prospects found in the Empire of the Son. At the same time, weepers
carry an intensified longing that God's extraordinary blessings be
fully revealed to the Church as a whole as well as to the nations. They
are very aware of how much grace many believers are still missing
and how much praise still awaits the Lord of Glory. A Prisoner of
Hope longs to take another Christian captive to the same hope by
being a ...

• **PROMISE-SPEAKER ...**
A hope-filled Christian will speak up and share God's Word in a way
that helps others find fresh promise in Jesus. He will speak out
about the King — proclaim Him — in order to awaken others to His
supremacy and to the glorious future He brings. She or he will

challenge fellow believers to be re-converted back to Christ for ALL that He is, and to reorient their walk in the light of Christ's Kingdom. Ultimately, every Messenger of Hope becomes a ...

- **PROMISE-REAPER ...**
  Prisoners of Hope want to harvest brand new "hope-ers" — first of all *inside* the Church. They sign-up other Prisoners of Hope to live out the full implications of Christ and His supremacy right now. They help shepherd new captives through the transitions listed above until each becomes a promise-reaper in his own right.

Sleepers. Peepers. Seekers. Keepers. Leapers. Weepers. Speakers. Reapers ... Once again let me ask: Where do you find yourself in this process? Toward which benchmark are you currently moving? How fully has hope in Christ's supremacy captivated you up to this point? How fully have you become a Prisoner of Hope thus far?

QUOTABLE QUOTE

O, My God! In all my dangers, temporal and spiritual, I will hope in thee who art Almighty power, and therefore able to relieve me; who art infinite goodness and therefore ready and willing to assist me.

O, precious blood of my Redeemer, O, gaping wounds of my crucified Savior. Who can contemplate the sufferings of God incarnate, and not raise his hope, and not put his trust in Him?

Blessed hope! Be thou my chief delight in life, and then I shall be steadfast and immovable, always abounding in the work of the Lord.

(*"A Prayer for Hope"* by RICHARD ALLEN — c. 1815)

THINK WITH ME ...
What makes any Christian a good *receiver* of the hope Christ brings?

To move from "promise-*peeper*" to "promise-*reaper*", every Prisoner of Hope must learn to become a better "promise-*receiver*". We must recognize the Spirit's voice. Then we must learn to receive His words of promise to us just as we received the Son of Promise the day we entered the Kingdom. We can start by nurturing an *attitude of readiness*.

Vigilant like city watchmen alert for the crack of dawn (Ps. 133), we need to anticipate what is coming, stay open to what lies ahead, remain prepared for more of God's grace (1 Pet. 1). The Father invites us to regularly *seek* more, not simply *do* more, so as to *receive* more of what He wants to give.

Are you growing every day in a spirit of *expectancy* toward Christ? Prisoners of Hope are always ready for Christ to take them where they have never gone before — always expecting more of His glory to be revealed; always preparing for God to give them "twice as much"; always welcoming fresh manifestations of Christ's Kingdom to draw them out of status quo dead-ends (in their lives and in their churches); always anticipating new advances of the Gospel. Walking with our sovereign Savior may carry no *risks,* but it creates plenty of *suspense*!

To what might we compare the experience of a good receiver? It's like standing near a runway and watching a plane's final approach. For a time it's almost impossible to discern if the plane is even moving because it seems to hover motionless while suspended in the mid-air. Only in the last few moments as it touches down on the runway does one realize that through the entire landing maneuver the plane was actually traveling nearly 150 miles per hour!

The advance of Christ's Kingdom is like an approaching aircraft. It never ceases to be constantly in motion as it moves toward us. To us it feels like the opposite — as if He may have become inactive or uninvolved. Prisoners of Hope remain patient, waiting without undue complaint, even when the vision they profess seems "suspended" between promise and fulfillment with little indication of any changes any time soon. Because they "walk by faith and not by sight" (2 Cor. 5), they know that at just the right moment He will wonderfully invade the present with His glory, one way or another. He will "touch down" in their lives with fresh foretastes of the Age-to-Come (Heb. 6). And there will be *no* disappointment when He does! So, they fend off the fatalism that says: "If nothing appears to be happening, then nothing is happening!" Under His reign something is *always* happening. Promises are always taking shape no matter what our eyes may tell us.

> QUOTABLE QUOTE
>
> **The secret of hope is that things can be all right at the center of our lives even if everything seems wrong at the edges. Because at the center, where we open our hearts to the living God, we are inseparably bound into a future for which He leads us, loves us and cares for us unconditionally. He gives, and we simply receive.**
>
> (DR. LEWIS SMEDES)

To become a good receiver of hope sometimes a Prisoner of Hope needs to stop everything and assume the *silent heart*. Shutting down the clutter, chaos and constant motion of their lives, they may need to practice what I call the *"strategy of silence"*. A choice can be made to set aside time to listen to God, maybe during a half-day prayer retreat or in a secluded corner of the train on a daily commute to work. Prisoners of Hope need to become enthralled with the word of Christ, be taken captive by the voice of Christ, spend time listening to the heart of Christ and be exposed to the Spirit of Christ. Whenever Christ imparts more *vision* of Himself to us, He imparts more of His *life* in us. "No eye has seen any God besides you, who acts on behalf of those who *wait* for him", Isaiah reminds us (Isa. 64).

The *Seven Confidence-Builders* to Help You Grow as a Prisoner of Hope
(John 20: 24-31)

For more than twenty-five years I've been sustained as a Prisoner of Hope by drawing on seven important insights on God's promises. They provide practical ways to organize and apply many of the perspectives on Christ's supremacy shared with you in this manifesto. Each principle is comprised of an *irrefutable reason* for any Christian to pray and prepare for greater demonstrations of Christ's lordship with the absolute confidence that God will not disappoint us. Any of the seven taken separately is enough to inspire a redoubling of commitment to a Campaign of Hope. Put together they provide unassailable assurance in the ultimate outcome of that campaign as well as the overall advance of Christ's Kingdom.

Above all, they enhance a strong Biblical Christology. They help us see God's Son more thoroughly in His rightful place as Supreme Sovereign of the Universe, Ruling Head of the Church, and Eternal Lord of life.

In similar fashion they provide stimulating "talking points" for pressing fellow believers to reconsider for themselves what a reclaimed vision for Christ's supremacy should include. Frankly, these points provide the compelling rationale for re-engaging Him with a healthy hope and passion based on what His lordship is all about.

The seven confidence builders include:

- The decisive person
- The divine pattern
- The dark prospects
- The disturbing paralysis
- The dramatic preparations
- The distinctive praying
- The determined people

A few years ago I treated each one separately with its own chapter in my book *The Hope At Hand*. Now, you can download those chapters for free at my website. Here is a very brief review of each concept:

- **The DECISIVE PERSON** — Who Christ is, in the full extent of His supremacy as the ordained centerpiece of everything in God's plan for the ages, *guarantees* the fulfillment of all the promises. God will never fail to respond thoroughly and unconditionally to the One to whom all the prophecies and promises ultimately belong. Because He is decisive, we can have hope.

- **The DIVINE PATTERN** — How God has consistently triumphed in Christ in the millennia-long history of His people, and through their witness among the nations, *guarantees* the fulfillment of all His promises. What God has done before to glorify His Son we can expect Him to do again and again and again. When we remind ourselves of His faithfulness to His own ways, we can have hope.

- **The DARK PROSPECTS** — God's unwavering desire for His Son's glory to be displayed among all the nations, especially in the midst of the raging spiritual battle with Satan's hosts, *guarantees* the fulfillment of all His promises. He intends for the nations to become the inheritance of the Lamb on the Throne. Because of His determination to dispel the Darkness we can have hope.

- **The DISTURBING PARALYSIS** — God's irrevocable intention is to liberate the Church thoroughly so that His people truly live before the nations as the Body of Christ. His commitment to heal our crisis of supremacy — to exorcise our debilitating disunity, suffocating self-sufficiency, missionary lethargy and spiritual impotency — *guarantees* the fulfillment of His promises to us. From eternity He has ordained to exalt His Son *through* His Church, not apart from it. Resting in His plan for His people, we can have hope.

- **The DRAMATIC PREPARATIONS** — The way God has set the stage so clearly in our generation both in the Church and throughout the world for major advances of Christ's Kingdom on all fronts *guarantees* the fulfillment of the promises. This is especially true among the three billion unreached people of Earth. He who has begun a good work will bring it to proper completion. He is preparing the way for all flesh to see the revelation of the Lord of Glory. Surely, we have hope.

- **The DISTINCTIVE PRAYING** — God's commitment to answer the current cries of millions of individual saints as well as whole movements of prayer within denominations, cities, regions and nations *guarantees* the fulfillment of the promises. He has stirred up bold prayers in Jesus' name, for Jesus' sake, that must now be answered to bring unto Jesus praise in all the earth. He takes our prayers seriously. Of course, we can have hope!

- **The DETERMINED PEOPLE** — God's recruitment and empowerment of millions of passionate believers everywhere today who, with great expectations, are already wholeheartedly committed to serving Christ at any cost for strategic breakthroughs of His Kingdom purposes, *guarantees* the fulfillment of His promises. In fact, these current Prisoners of Hope are the first wave throughout the Church of the promised awakening to Christ we so desperately need. They are the sign of good things to come. Thus, once again, we can have a sure and certain hope.

Such breadth of vision will cause any Campaign of Hope to thrive. Such confident perspectives will hold any Christian captive to hope in Jesus. Experience shows that as Christians spend time meditating on the realities behind each insight, these Confidence-Builders will naturally enlarge one's passion for Jesus by the huge boost in Kingdom-vision the seven give. They can inject into any congregation antidotes to cure the crisis of supremacy wherever it is found. They can give Messengers of Hope another way to shape their own "Message of Hope." Clearly, then, they ought to help *you* become and remain the Prisoner of Hope you are meant to be.

How *Repentance* and *Suffering*
Take Us Captive to Our Hope in Christ
(Joel 2:12-32)

Citizens of Pasadena, California (where I once lived) are grateful when the Santa Ana winds sweep in and blow suffocating smog out of the San Gabriel Valley on out to sea. As a result, people on the street are able to breathe more easily once again. They can also enjoy a view of the magnificent, multi-peaked San Gabriel mountains, previously veiled for days by brownish haze.

In the same way, the Holy Spirit — God's wholesome wind of hope (called "the promise from the Father" in Luke 24) — desires to fill every Prisoner of Hope with clear vistas on our Victorious One, removing all foggy thinking about Him and enlarging our horizons of hope as we breathe in the freshness of His Kingdom promises.

Sometimes we stifle the Spirit by *apathy* toward opportunities to grow in knowing and serving Jesus as Lord. Sometimes our joy in Jesus is suffocated by *arrogance* when we smugly assume we have Him pretty well figured out already and don't need to know that much more. However, if we're ever to experience an "abounding hope" restored in us by "the power of the Holy Spirit" (Rom. 15), God may need to re-capture us for Christ's supremacy by two dramatic developments: by leading us into *repentance* and by leading us through *suffering*.

To be sure, God's promises in Christ always present unlimited horizons. As we've seen throughout this manifesto, Biblical hope is as infinite, unfathomable, uncontainable and inexhaustible as our Lord is. However, that's not the whole story. We can experience temporary limits on the impact of Christ's supremacy by how well *prepared* we are to receive more of His greatness and glory. His *accessibility* must be coupled with our *ability* to encounter more of Him.

Not only must Prisoners of Hope become good receivers — anticipating and welcoming what God will do because Jesus reigns — but also they must grow their *capacity* to take in as large a vision of the Son as the Father wants to give them.

Just as enlarging a General Motors factory increases its capacity to build more cars; just as angioplasty increases an artery's capacity to handle an increased flow of blood; just as a clean windshield increases the driver's ability to arrive safely where he intends to go — even so the twin experiences we're about to explore (*repentance* and *suffering*) increase a believer's capacity to see, seek and speak about Christ for all that He is. Let's discover why this is so.

THINK WITH ME ...

**How does *repentance* increase our capacity
for more of Christ?**

The New Testament Greek word translated "repentance" — *metanoeo* — means "to think again, to retool one's perspective, to alter one's outlook on something". For the Christian, repentance acts as the *hinge* of hope. It swings us *from* destruction, despair and defeat *toward* all the promises offered under Jesus' reign. It turns us *from* whatever opposes God's Kingdom purposes and turns us *toward* a whole new identity and destiny related to the King. It shifts us from *self*-absorption over to the happy state of "Christ-absorption". That's why repentance must become a way of life for every Prisoner of Hope.

Repentance is not a synonym for self-loathing. By it we embrace the truth of our sinful depravity on the *inside,* to be sure. But repentance prepares us for so much more: to be seized by the hope-filled vision of Christ's majesty on the *outside*. As one pastor put it, repentance is motivated by "an awakened taste for pleasure in God". We take at face value what Scripture says about where God is headed in His Son. We desire to head in that same direction with Him. So we eliminate everything that might get in the way, laying aside every sin that could entangle us or distract us as we run toward Christ alone (Heb. 12).

Christ-filled repentance *renounces* the sin within us that hinders the promotion of God's glorious purposes in Christ. It *denounces* everything around us or among us that contradicts the exaltation of His Kingship. But it also *announces* (to all who will listen) our intention to share fully in delight-

ful displays of Christ's dominion in our daily walk now as well as in all the
ages to come.

Someone might ask: Which comes first,
hope or repentance? The answer is that the
Spirit works from both directions. But, His
starting point is always hope. As sinners we are
simply *not capable* of repentance without God's
preceding it with a larger vision of His Son.
More than unmasking the seriousness of sin's
offense against a righteous God (which must
happen, see Jn. 16), the Spirit's most powerful
way of breeding heartfelt repentance is by
filling us with greater expectations toward God
(Isa. 11; 61; Lk. 4). Peter says it well: We have
been given "very great and precious promises, so
that through them you may participate in the
divine nature and escape the corruption in the
world caused by evil desires" (2 Pet. 1). As our
hope in Christ abounds, this fact alone compels
us to repent, making us ready to receive more of
Him in our lives.

Jesus verified the wisdom of this approach by
how He constructed His own "Message of Hope"
in Mark 1:15. (Review our study of this in chapter 9.) Notice once again:
Three parts of His message emphasized hope ("the time is fulfilled", "the
Kingdom is at hand", "believe this good news"). Only one part underlined
repentance ("repent"). Furthermore, the repentance theme came third in
order. In other words, for Jesus repentance had to be in response to a hope-
filled vision for His redemptive purposes.

Here's the major reason, I submit, we do not see the level of ongoing
repentance in Christians today we know we should be experiencing: *We
have not been saturated with a grand enough, glorious enough, majestic
enough hope in our Supreme Savior to inspire such a response.* The Christ
we proclaim is simply too small to make us *dissatisfied* with sin (along with
our dead traditions and our religious flesh), to *want* to turn from sin and
turn toward Him. The lack of adequate daily repentance in my own life,
frankly, is simply the crisis of supremacy viewed from another direction.

There's another form of repentance, however, that also enlarges our capacity for a greater vision of God's Son. I call it "dismantling" — the laying aside of *good* things. These might include personal spiritual ambitions, or commendable ministry projects, or honorable denominational tradition — wonderful initiatives we may treasure for Jesus' sake but which, to our surprise, have begun to interfere with the sharper focus on His lordship we desperately need.

We may need to "dismantle" — to strip down, to repent of — dreams, activities, relationships and priorities that were useful once to the Kingdom but are now hindering (often unwittingly) full enthusiasm for Christ's glory. Maybe it is a worship style. Maybe it is a hobby. Maybe it is being too focused on the stock market, or television, or on theological nuances. No matter how well-intended or Christ-centered in its appearance, if something in our lives or our churches is not compatible with magnifying Jesus' majesty and extending His Monarchy, it must be dismantled with impunity. By setting aside distractions to our devotion to Christ true repentance becomes *proactive*. It increases our capacity to embrace and enter into God's eternal purposes wholeheartedly. Prisoners of Hope grow in captivity to Christ's glory by dismantling even the good (when necessary) to be ready to receive more of *God's best*.

THINK WITH ME ...
What Kingdom issues need to be addressed by hope-filled repentance?

True repentance will penetrate the core of a Christian's life as it confronts the crisis of supremacy head-on. The profound level of repentance — repenting for how we've diminished Christ's supremacy, wounding the heart of our Savior — will take us into the most disturbing experience of spiritual *brokenness* we'll ever know. But in doing so it will increase our *capacity* for more of Christ and allow us to receive more of His reign in our lives. It will cause us to entertain questions many Christians would never dare to ask, such as:

- How have I *neglected* Christ by my self-serving ways?

- How have I *diminished* Christ, bringing Him down to my own level?

- How have I *resisted* Christ's supremacy by half-hearted, partial obedience?

- How have I *hindered* Christ's work because of fears, selfish ambitions, or the need for control?

- How have I *substituted* other things for Christ's role in my life, maybe by religious activities performed in His name or by putting confidence in impressive personalities who claim His name?

- How have I *exploited* Him, that is, sought to appropriate His blessings for my own gratification and comfort?

- How have I *contradicted* Him by ignoring His Kingdom purposes, remaining indifferent to so many who live in injustice and without hope in Christ?

- How have I *abandoned* Him as I've bought into counterfeit promises, either offered by the world or propagated by other believers?

Take your answers to each of these questions and turn them into prayers of repentance and recommitment. Nothing may be more effective in taking you fully captive to Christ and His Kingdom. (Also, consider re-reading *Interlude II: A Prayer Over the Crisis of Supremacy*.)

THINK WITH ME ...
How does *suffering* increase our capacity for more of Christ?

That night so many years ago is still vivid to me. It came at the climax of months of personal agony. Mine was an inner pain. It rose out of unbearable ministry setbacks that overwhelmed me. Late one night I reached the point where I had nothing left to say or pray to the Father. I was out of tears. I was void of hope.

Then, in the stillness of my darkened room the Spirit brought my thoughts to 2 Corinthians 1:8-11. There Paul records how he too despaired of life itself because of his sufferings in Asia Minor. Paul felt, as I did, in his very soul "the sentence of death". He wondered if he could take another step. It was at this low point through what he suffered, Paul writes, that God taught him all over again to cease relying on himself and put his hope in the God who actually raises the dead (vs. 10).

The Holy Spirit seemed to apply Paul's conclusion to me directly in those moments. In my helplessness the following words formed in my mind:

You are right, David.
You have no ministry.
And you will never have a ministry,
unless I raise it with my Son from the dead,
day by day by day.

Then and there I embraced personal suffering as I never had done before. This was God's way to increase my capacity for more of Christ's resurrection power in my life. As He had done for Paul, God awakened me more fully to all of His promises, both for myself and my ministry. Those dark moments transformed me into a much richer (and freer) Prisoner of Hope. Paul concluded: "This happened [his agonies in Jesus' service] that we might not rely on ourselves but on God, who raises the dead".

Imagine that! Even a spiritual giant like Paul, after years of faithful missionary service, still needed to be awakened, by his *sufferings,* to a more comprehensive hope in Jesus as Lord. Certainly, then, how much more is it required in our own lives!

As it did for Paul, so for every Christian: suffering magnifies our *lack.* It confronts us with a sense of our futility apart from Christ. It amplifies the worth of the blessings from Heaven for which we groan. It convinces us that God has something *better* for us to be found in His Son and sends us seeking it. God is determined to do whatever it takes to prevent anything from sedating our deepest hungers for more of Christ. He loves us too much to let us feel *completely* satisfied with anything in this life apart from Him. *When suffering has exhausted for us every other alternative to Christ and His supremacy, then Biblical hope in Him can take on a compelling new force in our lives.*

Evangelical French philosopher Jacques Ellul wrote on this experience in *Hope in a Time of Abandonment.* In the book he documented how faith in the promises of God and in the God-of-Promises reaches its apex when everything seems to suggest God is no longer there, that He's forsaken us. Why? Because, as Ellul observed, when

QUOTABLE QUOTE

Suffering comes before laughter, the pain of birth precedes the wonder of new life, and questions must be asked before confidence develops. The Spirit of God must first disrupt something bad within us before he entices us with the promise of joy. The road to finding God takes us through darkness before it brings us to light. Disillusionment is the soil in which hope grows.

(DR. LARRY CRABB)

everything is stripped away — including a sense of God's intimate presence — we discover that Christ really is all the hope we have for deliverance. Hope in Him shines brightest in our darkest despair. It is then that we see Him to be all that remains, and truly all we need. As I sometimes say,

No pain, no gain.
But no pain is ever in vain.
All pain makes things plain.
My pain magnifies Christ's reign.

THINK WITH ME ...
How have you grown through the
"discipline of dis-illusionment"?

Our sufferings become God's opportunities to help us come to terms with our ultimate nothingness *apart from* the abounding hope He has given us in our Redeemer. We need to let God's Kingdom *overwhelm* our pain with the anticipation of things above and things to come, arriving from the Throne where Christ, who is our life, sits supreme (Col. 3).

Disappointment was quite a familiar companion for 19th century missionary statesman Oswald Chambers. He was distressed by debilitating experiences on the mission field that defied his ambitions to serve Christ. Working with orphans in England, recruiting young people to missionary service and eventually serving in Egypt, he often suffered what he described as the *"discipline of dis-illusionment"*. This experience was not in spite of, but more *because of,* his desire to proclaim Christ and to magnify Him. All suffering, he learned, *dis-illusions* us. That is, it unmasks the *illusions* in our lives. It exposes false hopes and dreams we've harbored (often mistakenly attributing their source to God). It forces us back to the time-tested truth of the living hope revealed in the Word.

Just as Chambers learned, amazing as it seems, illusions can rise out of misunderstandings (or misapplications) of God's Kingdom intentions toward us. Maybe we misread God's timing, or misinterpret a Biblical promise out of its context. In fact, illusions that seem to have scriptural warrant may be the hardest of all to forsake (like the claim that obedience guarantees a Christian health and prosperity). But illusions must be discarded if we're to see Christ more clearly for all that He is. Illusions clog up our capacity for more of His glory in our lives.

Once we've been *dis*-illusioned by suffering (whether through financial setbacks, or physical debilitations, or malicious rumors, or spurned love) we're ready to embrace the *true dreams* God sets before us in His Son. Like a sunrise, dis-illusioning experiences dispel silly shadows that shade our vision of Him. They help separate us from the fog of foolish fables that so often imprisons us in despair. Dis-illusioning experiences shake us and wake us to the rousing reality of all we have in Christ, bringing us into captivity to the hope of His Kingdom advances.

I think Chambers would have agreed with someone's suggestion to change one letter in the word dis-appointment: To replace the "d" with an "H" so that it reads *His*-appointment. That is to say that the very life-experiences that break our hearts are really, in the end, God's appointed moments to involve us more deeply in Christ's glorious reign, to draw us more fully into who He is, where He's headed, what He imparts and how He is blessed.

Bedridden for years while with a debilitating disease, a good friend of mine discovered one of her appointed moments of life. Despite relentless pain, her capacity for Christ's sovereign presence continues to expand. This internationally-respected Christian leader, a prime mover in one of today's great missionary societies, wrote me recently about how huge her hope in Christ has become:

> I will be eternally grateful for what I'm suffering!
> I'm not agonizing over the fact that
> God hasn't yet fulfilled His numerous promises to heal me.
> I am so utterly convinced that "as for God, His way is perfect."

> I am not [merely] living in the light of this little bit of time here on earth.
> How I pass this season of severe testing
> determines what God can do with me
> throughout the ages of eternity.
> I'm living and focusing upon the BIG PICTURE that's ahead.

> Besides all that,
> God has opened up a huge door of opportunity since my illness,
> to minister to many the truths of Christ He has entrusted to me.
> These understandings from His Word could have only been revealed
> through prolonged suffering.

> Furthermore, this long period ohysical pain and partial disability
> is conforming me so much more to the image of God's Son.
> Truly, I am blessed.

That's the beating heart of a Prisoner of Hope. That's the blessed impact of Son-saturated suffering, helping us become truly captive to the lordship of Jesus! His followers choose to lose — to exalt the Savior by giving themselves up to and over to His lordship alone, no matter what the price. Why? Because despite the cost Jesus assures us that in losing our lives for Him we will *find* life indeed (Mark 8). Such promises render believers His prisoners for now and forever. Indian evangelist Sadhu Sundar Singh, writing from a jail cell during the British Raj, understood the principle well: "Christ's presence has turned my prison into a blessed heaven. What then will His presence do for me in heaven itself?"

What is it we sometimes sing? "My *hope* is built on nothing less than Jesus *blood* and righteousness ... all other ground is sinking sand." That's where you'll find Prisoners of Hope standing whenever the floods of suffering start to swell!

Our Need for Other Prisoners of Hope
(Hebrews 10:19-25)

In *The Wall Street Journal* not long ago a brokerage firm rolled out a two-month ad campaign around an overused word: *"Vision"*. In a full-page ad with large, black letters they shared their definition for "vision":

> **Vision** is an acute sense of the possible.
> It is seeing what others don't see.
> And when those with vision come together,
> something extraordinary occurs.

They believed their organization was unlike many others because it was equipped to uncover promising investments in the stock market other brokers failed to see. They offered a bold but accurate fix on the future of the market. Clients who chose to invest with them could expect extraordinary returns. However, none of this would happen (so they claimed) unless investors pooled their resources *together,* assumed the same confident outlook and submitted their resources to the proven investment strategies of this one firm.

For disciples who are zealous for the Kingdom the wording of this ad highlights a vital spiritual principle. Committed to Christ and the glorifying of His name, Prisoners of Hope also are aware of God-ordained possibilities that other Christians don't see as yet. Thus, if these captives come together around the promises of God, extraordinary things can start to happen, both in them and through them. For our hope in Jesus to remain vibrant and productive, we need each other. We need to become *a company of hope-ers,* jointly investing in our shared vision of the supremacy of God's Son. Let's look at some of the reasons this is true.

THINK WITH ME ...
What does the infectious nature of hope say about our need for *community*?

In chapter 9 we noted that in Scripture hope is more often a noun than a verb, that with God hope is ultimately a person: His Son. The Bible suggests something similar about Christian community: *Hope is often another person in my life who is re-discovering and sharing with me the full extent of Christ's supremacy and the hope this brings.* God knows hope is infectious. It spreads life to life — from Christ to me; then from me to others. Where people gather around His Son, hope explodes so that they hold to a vision of His supremacy, living and serving with their eyes on the End Himself.

By contrast, *hopelessness* breeds best in an environment of *isolation.* Isolation keeps us from witnessing the promise-packed activity of God in other Christians' lives. When facing personal setbacks it is nearly impossible for isolated believers to envision on their own the fulfillment of Christ's reign in their circumstances.

Prisoners of Hope are in a battle. We're engaged in "the fight of faith" because we dare to "lay hold of eternal life" and nothing less (1 Timothy 6). Vigilance — watching for every evidence of the crisis of supremacy — is the price we must pay to grow in our captivity for Biblical hope. But we were never meant to triumph in the battle by ourselves. We need each other to *inspire* and *re-fire* each other; to stir up our faith and confidence toward God, to purify our passion for Christ and His global cause; to sustain our pursuit of His Kingdom advance in our generation; and to remain fully alive to all the hope we were meant to have.

Prisoners of Hope need a strategy to mobilize other captives to walk with them in their commitment to Jesus as Lord. There's something wonderful about serving alongside Christ-dominated companions. When our own desperate cries for more grace seem so futile, we can interact with others for whom God-given blessings seem for the moment to be in greater abundance. They infect us with their confidence. Our hope in Jesus is restored. In equal measure, at some later point when they begin to stumble and falter, we can return the favor! No wonder we're told in Hebrews 10 never give up coming together for a larger purpose. We're to encourage each other to follow Christ boldly because we see the Day of Christ itself (the Consummation) approaching.

THINK WITH ME ...
How can we go about building a community of hope-filled disciples?

How do we get this mobilization started? How do we *find* other Prisoners of Hope around us? Good news — you can! Here are *six simple principles* many have employed to successfully do so:

❖ **UNCOVER THEM** ... In point of fact a host of hope-ers — potential prisoners — *already* reside in our churches. God has gone ahead of us to raise them up. They are a gift from God just as much as the hope within them that so delights them. Many, however, are waiting to be discovered. Or more properly, they need to discover themselves! You could be the key to making this happen. One way to start is to begin sharing with fellow Christians the larger vision of Christ embodied in this manifesto. Watch for those who "light up" when you do. Note those who "open up" to express personal struggles with a spirit of hopelessness they want to conquer. Expect those who have a hunger to experience Christ's power and presence more fully in their lives to say so once they find out you're after the same thing. That's the primary clue that you are in touch with a Prisoner of Hope-in-the-making.

❖ **DEFINE THEM** ... With those who exhibit such initial responses begin to share more of your own pilgrimage as a Prisoner of Hope. In addition, expose to them some of the hundreds of Scriptures related to Christ and Consummation that have touched your heart. Consider taking them through this manifesto in a formal study, investigating some of its central themes. Above all, help them realize how *unique* their hunger for hope really is, and that it is God's gift to them for very special purposes.

❖ **INVITE THEM** ... Encourage them to join you in discovering all that it means to live a hope-centered life under Christ, to seek greater impacts of His supremacy. Invite them to take new steps in their conversion experience, to turn more fully toward Christ and His supremacy. Offer to walk out these changes with them. For example, you might discuss with them the various transactions outlined in this chapter. Help them pinpoint which phase they are in and ask them where they would like to go next as they grow from promise-sleepers to promise-reapers. Or you might read together the *Prelude* in this book *("Put Your Hope in Christ")* to see how they respond.

❖ **GATHER THEM** ... Show them they are not alone. Introduce them to others with the same passionate hope stirring in their hearts. Bring all your newfound Prisoners of Hope together, like coals gathered to start a fire. Set up regular meetings, perhaps in someone's home on a week night, or maybe during the Sunday school hour on Sunday morning. Again, rely on this Manifesto to start the journey together, possibly facilitating weekly discussion sessions to digest the book one chapter at a time. Or you can create a shorter curriculum using suggestions in chapter 9 based on "H.O.P.E."

❖ **EQUIP THEM** ... Teach them how to expand their vision of Christ and His supremacy, perhaps using one of the four approaches to Bible study in chapter 10. Lead them to explore a life of "anticipatory discipleship" (covered in the next chapter). Provide them with overtly Christ-exalting passages to explore during their daily devotions (see *Appendix V*). Challenge the group to grapple honestly with personal repentance, as needed, to release hope more fully in their lives. Or

debrief together the ways some of you may be suffering in your
Christian walk. Then explore how the suffering could make God's
promises in Christ more alive for you. Of high priority, mentor them in
prayer by teaching them how to pray in hope by doing it together.
(Chapter 12 has more details about this.)

❖ **RELEASE THEM** ... Rally them to join you in spreading their
emerging vision of Christ and Consummation among believers right
where you live. Encourage them to fulfill their special opportunity to be
a Messenger of Hope, both in your congregation and beyond. Discuss
using the H.O.P.E. strategy to reshape how they proclaim Christ and
teach about His supremacy within their families or among their friends.
Pray over them — better still, have them pray over each other — to send
each other into the glorious mission of spreading a vision for the
supremacy of God's Son in all things. Then, be ready to be a mentor and
a resource to them as their own ministries of hope unfold.

As suggested earlier one tool available to you is this *Joyful Manifesto*.
Christ Is All! offers a 13-week study on hope and the supremacy of Christ
that can become the perfect "launch point" for a gathering of potential
Prisoners of Hope. *Appendix I and II* provide guidelines on how to use it
effectively in a group setting.

THINK WITH ME ...
How would you shape a weekly gathering for
Prisoners of Hope?

Once you've uncovered a few other "hope-ers" to work with, you may
wonder what to do (in addition to activities suggested above) as you come
together. Here are a few ideas based on personal experiences of doing it
myself. These are very practical starting points any time you gather:

• *Above all, talk about Christ.* In what ways has your vision of
Christ expanded since you were last together? Perhaps use the "Four
F's" (focus, fulfillment, fullness, fervency) to organize your sharing
sessions. How is your Christology being transformed?

• *Share the hope* that is already growing in your own hearts. Talk
about what you anticipate God will do in your life (as well as in the
world beyond your own daily walk) in the days to come.

- *Talk about what you see God doing among others* even now, either where you are or in some other part of your community, nation or the world. Explain how this illustrates what "approximations" of the ultimate displays of Jesus' Kingly glory might look like for you or others. (Refer to examples in chapter 4.)

- *Work through barriers* that are currently robbing you and others of confidence in Christ. Talk honestly about your struggles, disappointments, sufferings, doubts and fears. You could refer to issues discussed in chapters 7 and 8.

- *Report on ways you are seeking to stir up hope in other believers.* Describe successes as well as specific challenges in doing so. Talk about how to improve your ministry as a Messenger of Hope.

- *Focus on building into each other fresh confidence toward God.* You might want to reflect on and discuss the seven Confidence-Builders outlined in this chapter. Which ones do you find most helpful? Which ones need to be better fortified in your own thinking?

- *Study specific Scripture passages* on hope and the supremacy of God's Son (see Appendix V). Or tackle major texts related to the Consummation itself to see how your vision of Christ and of your destiny in Him might be changed. Start with the inductive questions recommended in chapter 10. Also, talk about how each of you might share the focus of these verses with someone in your family or with one of your friends.

- *Discuss the implications* of all you've explored for your daily walk with Christ. Pinpoint specific aspects of "anticipatory discipleship" you need to work on (the focus of chapter 12). What practical changes do each of you need to make in light of the hope-filled insights into Christ you've just uncovered? In other words, make sure your meetings always lead to fruitful *action* for Christ and His Kingdom.

- *Spend much time praying together.* Pray that God will set you free of barriers to hope, fill you with renewed passion toward Christ, expand your vision of the work of His kingdom, and thus empower you to be a Messenger of Hope. Also, pray for a hope-filled awakening to Christ within your families, churches, communities and beyond.

- **End each session by re-commissioning each other** to herald this wonderful vision of Christ's supremacy to everyone you meet and to bring others with you into all the hope Christians were meant to have. Be prepared to invite some into your future gatherings.

Any group pursuing such activities will rapidly awaken to more of Christ and His supremacy. As a result, they will become a major stream of healing for the crises of supremacy in their churches. Your "band of captives" can help foster a reformation of Christology among other believers while serving together as Messengers of Hope, co-laboring to awaken hope fully for others, and thus helping empower them to be part of vital advances in the work of Christ. A Campaign of Hope can never be accomplished by a party-of-one! It wouldn't be a *campaign*!

But, you may ask, what should one call such weekly gatherings? Well, for starters, how about calling them *"Christ Huddles"*? At least that's how *Appendix II* refers to them.

By whatever name, this group will eventually begin to look like what the whole Church should look like: *"Vanguards of Hope"*. I use the word "vanguard" to describe Prisoners of Hope who are committed to serving as Messengers of Hope and who have begun to promote a Campaign of Hope right where they live.

"Vanguards of Hope". It has a rather intriguing ring to it, don't you think? Our final chapter is all about what it means and where it leads.

QUOTABLE QUOTE

We find ourselves standing where we always hoped we might stand — out in the wide open spaces of God's grace and glory, standing tall and shouting our praise. In alert expectancy such as this, we are never left feeling short-changed. Quite the contrary — we can't round up enough containers to hold everything God generously pours into our lives through the Holy Spirit.

(ROMANS 5 — THE MESSAGE)

12

BECOMING VANGUARDS OF HOPE

How to Re-mobilize the Church Around the Supremacy of God's Son

During World War II the German V2 rocket got things started. This was followed by the development of the Redstone/Jupiter missile by the United States around 1947. With that, the overture to the Space Age played its opening chords. In the early 50's the National Academy of Science concluded that within five to ten years satellites for geophysical research could become reality. Finally, in September 1955 the U.S. Department of Defense adopted a Navy proposal for a project given the code-name *Vanguard,* intent on launching a U.S. satellite as soon as possible.

As America's pioneer space venture *Vanguard* was the right word. Though plagued at first with serious mechanical deficiencies and frequent delays, the Vanguard Program pressed forward, driven by the reasonable hope that space exploration would open up an era of strategic discoveries, from military to mineral to medical. Vanguard was the USA's commitment to lead the way, not only for America but for the world. Finally, after two launch pad failures, on St. Patrick's Day 1958 the first successfully orbiting U.S. satellite was placed in space. Known as *Vanguard I,* it was the first wave of some of the greatest advances in the history of global science.

Taken captive to a "solar system" of stunning promises orbiting around the Lord Jesus Christ, *Christians must develop Vanguard-like lifestyles to match.* Living out a hope based on the full extent of Christ's supremacy, disciples ought to exhibit daily "previews of coming attractions", foretastes of victories up ahead. The *trajectory* of our existence as believers is nothing short of the Consummation itself. Our destination is an eternity focused on Jesus as Lord. We will be caught up forever in the unending outpouring of His presence and power, reflecting back the glories of His reign in ten thousand different ways.

QUOTABLE QUOTE

An enterprise which aims at the evangelization of the whole world in a generation, and contemplates the ultimate establishment of the kingdom of Christ, requires that its leaders be Christian statesmen — men with farseeing views, with comprehensive plans, with the power of the intuitive, and with victorious faith.

(JOHN R. MOTT)

Into all ages to come we will never, ever stop living for the Son of God or ever cease operating under the sway of His Throne! Such expectations should "radicalize" every dimension of the day-to-day ministries of believers. God has a wonderful plan for the nations to reveal the full extent of Christ's supremacy in all things, to all peoples, for all time. He loves His children enough to give each one a very significant place in it beginning right now. Every hour the hope of Christ's supremacy should keep us on the cutting edge of His ever-expanding global cause while we serve Him moment by moment as *"Vanguards of Hope"*.

In every sense Christians live at the forefront of the future. We are part of a much greater plan than most have ever contemplated. To borrow from Brother Lawrence's masterpiece on discipleship, *Practicing the Presence of God,* we are "practicing the presence" of the *future.* Such a hope in Christ can *empower* the Church's everyday obedience to Christ with thoughts, words and deeds — a "vanguard lifestyle" — motivated by the anticipation of how God will magnify His Son for generations to come.

This final chapter will clarify the third major cure for the crisis of supremacy — the rest of our strategy for a Campaign of Hope, by:

- **exploring the empowering impact of *anticipatory discipleship*.**

- **applying this approach to a variety of issues in a believer's daily walk with Christ.**

- describing a "daily discipline" that can transform you into a Vanguard of Hope.

- demonstrating how hope fixed on Christ puts prayer at the frontlines of His Kingdom advance.

- linking this third cure to the Campaign of Hope God's people desperately need to see right now.

The Joy of "Anticipatory Discipleship"
(1 John 2:28-3:3, 14)

The Gospel of the Kingdom is more than "good advice". It is the "good news" of a great hope. However, we need to do more than hear the hope, share the hope and grow the hope. We must remain *victorious* in the hope, learning to walk in the hope. This happens best by practicing what I call *"anticipatory discipleship"*.

The concept of *anticipatory discipleship* was suggested by our Lord, actually, in His original invitation (Mk. 1): "Leave everything. Come follow me" (His call to discipleship) "and I will make you fishers of men" (dramatic changes promised). In other words, obedience to Him *today* could anticipate significant transformations *tomorrow*. Following Him turned disciples into "vanguards" of the Kingdom, moving into a hope they would eventually proclaim to the nations.

THINK WITH ME ...
In what sense is this approach to discipleship truly *anticipatory* in nature?

Atheletes who trained for the 1984 Olympics were forced to experience something akin to anticipatory discipleship. Because of the American boycott of the 1980 Olympics in Russia (ordered by President Jimmy Carter) American Olympians had to postpone competition for eight full years. Having prepared from 1976 for the Russian Olympics in 1980, they were forced to press on for an additional four years of training to stay in shape for Los Angeles in 1984. What kept most going? One simple answer:

the desire to win along with the confidence they could. Convinced they could ultimately triumph, day after day for eight long years one hope drove them. Every part of their existence conformed to that vision. Dreams harnessed discipline. Hope dictated radical regimens. Future glories empowered them to stick with sacrifice despite the discouragement of unprecedented delays.

They became "vanguards" of the memorable victories America achieved when 1984 rolled around. You could define their pre-competition experience as "anticipatory *training*", a perseverance of the highest order. In the end, this outlook paid off as scores of medals trailed them out of the L.A. Coliseum.

Imitating Olympian training, *anticipatory discipleship* shapes every aspect of Christian obedience. We keep our eyes on the Prize! Anticipatory discipleship *integrates* the promises of God into our walk with His Son. Hope inspires and intensifies our desire to serve Him because we expect Him to prevail. Isn't that what John tells us? He writes that our hope in Christ should cause us to purify ourselves, even as Christ is pure, so that when He appears in glory we will greet Him without shame (1 John 2 and 3). Isn't that what Peter tells us? Describing the renovation of Heaven and earth by fire, he teaches that a vision for the Consummation ought to drive Christians toward purity of life right now, making it their commitment to live in a manner that hastens the coming of the Day of the Lord (2 Pet. 3). Isn't that what the book of Hebrews tells us when it says: "Let us hold unswervingly to the hope we profess ... Let us consider how we may spur one another on toward love and good deeds. Let us not give up meeting together ... Let us encourage one another — and all the more as you see the Day approaching" (Heb. 10).

By linking itself to the culmination of Christ's global cause, anticipatory discipleship impacts the most practical sides of service to our Master — which include everything from developing qualities of Christ-likeness, to worshipping God with abandon, to honing hallmarks of holiness, to standing with the poor, to increased missionary outreach — because we know we are moving from "here" to "there". No steps are "small" steps under

Jesus' lordship. Every step sets the stage for even more of Christ's reign to break through for us, our churches, our communities and our generation.

THINK WITH ME ...
In what sense is anticipatory discipleship always *preparatory* in nature?

The anticipatory approach to Christian discipleship naturally translates into a *lifestyle of preparation*. Grateful as we are for God's current blessings, hope in His Son keeps us preparing for His breakthroughs in new ways. He is the God-of-So-Much-More because He who "did not spare his own Son, but gave him up for us all, how will he not also, along with him, graciously give us all things?" (Rom. 8).

This is the God who, when it was time to cross Jordan, commanded Joshua to rally the people with this exhortation: "Consecrate yourselves, for tomorrow the Lord will do amazing things among you" (Joshua 3). Notice the sequence: A transformed lifestyle (consecrate) is motivated today by looking toward promised wonders for tomorrow — not years from now, but sooner: tomorrow! What if this vision were to fashion the agenda for weekly activities within every congregation? How many more groups of believers would become Vanguards of Hope as we followed our Joshua ("Yeshua" = "Jesus")?

We actually see this happening with the seven churches of Asia Minor (Rev. 1-3). In His resurrection glory, Jesus stirred them to exhibit new levels of faithfulness and fruitfulness. He did it not by calling them *back* but by calling them *forward*. If you study the verses listed below, you will see that our Lord appealed to them on the basis of what was *coming*. He focused them, first of all, on the unfolding of His glory in the Consummation. He urged them to anticipate more of God's grace and obey accordingly — to become pacesetters of the promises His supremacy offered them. The life of each congregation could be revolutionized — whether they faced heresy, persecution or spiritual lethargy — as each made the ultimate revelation of Christ's Kingdom the driving ambition for obeying Him

> ## QUOTABLE QUOTE
>
> **If you read history, you will find that the Christians who did most for the present world were just those who thought more of the next. It is since Christians have largely ceased to think of the other world that they have become so ineffective in this. Aim at Heaven and you will get Earth thrown in. Aim at Earth and you will get neither.**
>
> (C.S. LEWIS)

on the spot! [See Revelation 2:7 (the church in Ephesus); 2:11 (the church in Smyrna); 2:17 (the church in Pergamum); 2:26-29 (the church in Thyatira); 3:5-6 (the church in Sardis); 3:11-13 (the church in Philadelphia); 3:21-22 (the church in Laodicea).]

Should we expect Him to do less with us in forming us into Vanguards of Hope? So, how will my (our) next step of obedience *this* moment open a way for Him to demonstrate His supremacy in the *next* moment? How will it not only glorify Him *now*, but also help me (us) get ready to enter into more of His Kingdom advances *tomorrow*? How will it not only reveal *more* of the His presence and power now, but also point to even greater promises to pursue?

THINK WITH ME ...

If you knew Christ was coming tomorrow, what would you do differently today?

Apparently those are not priority concerns for many in our churches today. Most have probably never asked themselves such questions. Most simply strive to survive. There's little that's *anticipatory* about much that passes for discipleship. Ours is more *"maintenance* discipleship" with efforts to remain respectable church members, fulfilling basic Biblical obligations and maintaining morally respectable uprightness. By comparison, anticipatory discipleship nurtures a passion to prepare for — a readiness to receive — in-breakings of the powers of the Age that's ahead (Heb. 6). Christian disciples aren't saved to sit satisfied in ecclesiastical "dressing rooms" while fixing up for the Great Day coming. God wants so much more for us. He invites us to engage each day as one more *"dress rehearsal"* and "practice" the kind of holiness, and worship, and loving of others that will comprise our Command Performance when He appears.

To vary metaphors, someone has said the music of the future provides the tune to which

Christians are to dance right now. If we believe our Savior will be the theme of an eternal symphony of praise, then the way we live today must show it. We must "sing" and "dance" accordingly!

THINK WITH ME ...
How is "acting as if" a helpful way to grow as Vanguards of Hope?

Since by the Spirit the reigning Lord Jesus dwells among His people right now, it's worth asking: Should not disciples *"act as if"* the End-of-the-World had already come? Named by Paul as "Christ in you, the hope of glory" (Col. 1), He is as fully Lord today as He will be on That Day. As Son of God, He embodies at this moment all the glory of the Father He will ever have. In a very real sense the End *is* here, in Him — and *we* are in Him. What does that tell you?

Surely it is not far-fetched to encourage Christians to live-out each day ...

- *acting as if* Christ had raised us from the dead to reign with Him.

- *acting as if* Christ were magnifying Himself before the peoples of earth.

- *acting as if* Christ were destroying every form of Satanic rebellion against His name.

- *acting as if* Christ were receiving homage from inhabitants of Heaven and earth.

Because ... guess what? The New Testament teaches that *in principle* all of these dynamics are truly a part of our daily walk with God's Son in tangible though preliminary ways. (Consider these texts for starters: 2 Cor. 4, Rom. 6, Eph. 1-2, Col. 3, Heb. 12, 1 Pet. 1, Rev. 2-3).

Today the Savior is defeating powers of Darkness. Today He is retrieving churches from deadly lethargy. Today He is rending the heavens in thousands of communities to display redeeming glory in unexpected ways, even with signs and wonders. Today He is advancing His reputation among unreached peoples who until now never knew of His name. Today He is the central theme of worship, devotion, prayer and sacrifice for millions worldwide from a myriad of tribes and tongues. Therefore, we need to "act as if" the Consummation is upon us ... *because in Christ it is.*

We were meant to act as if we had almost reached the Climax; to act as if we were about to physically enter the Throne Room of Revelation 4-5 at any moment. We should shape every response to Christ right now with that unavoidable hope clearly in view, because, in principle, we've already begun to taste the Final Triumphs in Christ. Forming the footstool of His throne (Ps. 110), Christians are commanded to reckon themselves alive with Jesus from the dead, seated with Him in heavenly places this day, co-laboring with Him in His reign, and wrapped up with Him in His ascended glory (Rom. 6, Col. 3 and Eph. 2). This is no "virtual reality" from some Hollywood movie studio. Christians are born again to be vanguards of an Eternal Kingdom already among us — to be precursors of a future in which we already have a stake.

This might also be called the *"principle of compatibility"*. Any thoughts, words or deeds I know for sure would not be compatible with life in Jesus' presence at the full unveiling of His Kingdom must be challenged aggressively even now. Any current activities or attitudes that do not submit to the rule of Christ in a way that's compatible with how all creation (including me) will one day submit to Him, must be confessed, put under His blood and put out of my life. Put another way: When Christ comes in glory, do I want my daily living for Him to be *vindicated* and not *repudiated*?

In Colossians 3 when Paul urges those whose "life is hidden with Christ in God" to "dress up" in new creation clothes, he is calling for compatibility. There he exhorts Christians to eliminate all rage, slander, unforgiveness, greed, superstitions of all kinds, divisiveness and spiritual apathy. These things have no place in a people who have been "raised with Christ" and should therefore "set your hearts on things above, where Christ is seated at the right hand of God" (vs. 1-2). Anticipating the End, we should live *like* the End ... *until* the End. Believers choosing this path may expect substantial installments *of* the End's breaking in today by the power of the Holy Spirit.

Anticipatory discipleship could be compared to a woman's experience of pregnancy! A mother-to-be is easily motivated to take on whatever disciplines, diets, schedules, exercises and precautions would help ensure delivery of a healthy child. She fully cooperates with her doctors; she rarely complains. As each day brings her closer to the due date (the hope for which she endures), she takes additional steps to be ready for the marvelous event. This might even include the designing, months ahead of time, of a nursery in the spare bedroom where the little one will sleep.

Even so, Jesus' followers are "pregnant" with promises as big as the Kingdom of our Savior. In a very real sense the same Holy Spirit who worked the miracle of conception in Mary's womb, "overshadows" God's people to conceive in them and birth through them ministries for Christ that are "holy" (Lk. 1). Like a mother-to-be with her doctor, every "serious disciple" seeks to give our Lord full cooperation as He brings forth the advance of His Kingdom. Keeping ourselves in readiness, we assume daily disciplines that look toward every new way He intends to display His dominion.

THINK WITH ME ...

How could just four questions revitalize your walk with Jesus?

Farmers plowing a field, I'm told, try to keep their eyes fixed on some distant point, such as a tree at the edge of the property, to help them maintain straight furrows. If they look only down where the blade meets the soil, they will inevitably plow crooked rows. In the same way, the following four questions have helped me "plow" a much straighter line toward God's purposes. Each consists of two words which make them easy to recall: *What goes? What stays? What's new? What's next?* Let's look briefly at how they work.

1. **WHAT GOES? In other words ...**

   What things in my lifestyle, even now, are simply *incompatible* with the hope in Christ I profess? Incompatible with His Kingdom purposes? Incompatible with the focus, fulfillment, fullness and fervency of His supremacy? Incompatible with God's promises and with all I believe He is able, willing and ready to do to glorify His Son more fully in me? What steps must I take to remove these contradictions?

2. **WHAT STAYS? In other words ...**

   What is going on in my life today that *is* clearly compatible with the unfolding of God's purposes in Christ, so much so that I must embrace those areas and then develop them more fully? How can I go about making my Christian walk more intentionally focused on revealing Christ's glory through me as His follower — for example: my devotional life, my witness to neighbors, my marriage, my worship on Sunday, my investments in world missions?

3. WHAT'S NEW? In other words …

What new initiatives do I sense God is asking me to assume today in order to prepare for additional blessings and victories tomorrow? How can I pursue Christ and His supremacy in a manner that will enhance my involvement in His Kingdom as it unfolds in greater ways right where I live? What areas of obedience do I need to strengthen to shape a discipleship experience more in line with God's promises and purposes in Christ Jesus? How can I become more receptive to all that Christ wants to be for me, to accomplish in me and to share through me?

4. WHAT'S NEXT? In other words …

Based on answers to the first three questions, what should be my very next move? What one step of obedience must be taken *today* in anticipation of God's purposes in Christ *tomorrow*? Far more importantly: What do I expect to be *God's* very next move with me? What immediate adjustments in my lifestyle should I make at this very moment so that I'm ready to respond as He acts?

I realize these four questions are stated in very personal terms. But don't forget, they provide categories that also must be addressed *corporately* — by the leadership of a local congregation, for example.

VANGUARDS:
Mobilized by the Scope of Their Hope to Live Every Day for Christ
(Romans 4:16-24)

Around Southern California huge man-made arroyos were built to drain torrents of rainwater from nearby mountains into appropriate reservoirs for safe keeping. In the rainy seasons these mammoth ditches mercifully prevent houses in the valleys from being washed away by the runoff. Arroyos may sit bone dry for ten months a year, like gaping gutters — seemingly of no use to anyone and taking up precious space. Yet once the spring downpours begin, the construction of the arroyos is fully justified as they swell with life-threatening currents.

Similarly, Vanguards of Hope serve as "spiritual arroyos". Their obedience to God's Word prepares them to receive the fresh revelations of Christ's presence and power for the blessing and redeeming of others. To be sure, like empty arroyos at times we may experience spiritual dry spells. In those difficult seasons especially we must faithfully hold our ground, willing and wanting and waiting in hope for God's promises to unfold for us, confident that Jesus reigns. In His perfect timing, like spring rains, fresh outpourings of the Spirit will arrive (Isa. 44), bringing a fuller reality of Christ's supremacy to our lives and churches and communities in marvelous ways.

We need to live as if we believed that! So, let's get down to specifics on "anticipatory discipleship".

THINK WITH ME ...
How can hope in Christ empower your worship of God?

We worship more accurately and more passionately when we do so in hope in Christ. Not only should we praise Him for who He is or what He has done, but we also must celebrate what He's getting ready to do. We need to rejoice ahead of time over displays of Christ's dominion we know are promised. After all, He is not only the God who is and was, but also the God who is to come (Rev. 1). *Our worship should say so!*

Properly understood, worship is designed not only to be Christ-focused but also *Heaven-focused*. Our worship can prepare us for, and even approximate, the worship we expect to experience in His presence for the rest of eternity. We're called to be a vanguard of the kind of worship into which the entire universe has been invited!

Furthermore, hope-filled worship transforms every other aspect of discipleship. Take, for example, the Church's missionary outreach. Worship

QUOTABLE QUOTE

WORSHIP must recount divine action of the past in ways that anticipate divine action in the future. Whatever style of ownership you employ you should ask: "Does this worship recount the history of God's gracious saving action in this world and proclaim that our hope both now and forevermore is to be found in Jesus Christ alone?" The great danger is to settle for petition, thanksgiving and proclamation that is almost completely focused upon the present moment and our present feelings. For us to live in the riches of full biblical worship, our prayer, praise and proclamation should be carried out as if we stand before a cosmic timeline of God's actions, fully aware of divine faithfulness from the creation of the world to its full restoration in Christ.

(DR. JOHN ARMSTRONG)

among the nations is actually a "preview of coming attractions", of an Hour not long from now when people from every tongue, tribe and peoples will shout their redemption before Him who sits on the throne and before the Lamb (Rev. 5). True worship, therefore, must stir up in us greater determination to extend His praises right now among friends or neighbors or unreached peoples. All evangelism is ultimately about expanding eternal adoration for God's Son into the midst of those who do not know Him ... yet. Dick Eastman puts it well: "Missionaries are filling Heaven with worshippers of Jesus".

THINK WITH ME ...
How can hope in Christ reinvigorate your approach to scripture?

We simply must learn to study and teach the Bible differently, by highlighting its themes of supremacy and hope. We must uncover in God's Word everything we can about the four dimensions of Christ's supremacy: who He is as the Son of God; where He leads in the Purposes of God; how He imparts the Resources of God; and what He receives from the People of God.

As noted in chapter 10, God cannot lead us on the basis of facts we do not have. As we bring a Biblical vision of Jesus' greatness and glory to fellow Christians, they will discover a hope they may never have considered previously. Immediately the Spirit will have new possibilities to work with — facts in their hearts by which He can take them further with Christ than ever before. He will begin filling them with a holy anticipation that inspires hope-filled obedience to Christ. There are many effective ways to unlock the truth of Scripture along these lines. As you already know, chapter 10 suggests a variety of approaches from which to choose. (Also, see *Appendixes V and VII*)

THINK WITH ME ...
How can hope in Christ reshape your financial strategies?

Anticipatory discipleship empowers us to reevaluate the extent of our financial obligations. We ask: How do my giving patterns — to my church, to ministries, to missions, to the poor — reflect the supremacy of Christ? How do they mirror the values that will count with Him when the Consummation rolls around?

We're often told that Christian giving should be *"proportionate* giving". Proportionate to what? To our excess reserves? To our credit debt load? To our social status? To our sense of obligation to church and society? To the pressing demands of the neediest people or ministries around us? To the snappiest fund appeal letters in the afternoon mail?

What if I measured my giving in proportion to major themes of Christ's lordship, instead? What if I asked myself:

- How does this particular expenditure or investment I'm about to make reflect to others my confident hope in the supremacy of Christ over all of my life?

- In what ways does my philosophy of consumption tie into what I expect to be doing with Jesus 10,000 years from now?

- What financial choices made today might free up funds to help promote greater "approximations of the Consummation" where I live? For example: By serving the homeless? By comforting the sick? By lobbying for social change like prison reforms? By educating teens on sexual abstinence? By providing care for the elderly?

- What material sacrifices should I be willing to make in order to help proclaim Christ's redemptive reign among peoples currently beyond the reach of the Gospel?

- What specific Biblical promises focused on God's Son should guide the consumption choices and material purchases I intend to make today?

- How might some form of renouncing or redirecting earthly treasures help me more effectively see, seek and speak about the supremacy of God's Son?

In the end, "simplicity" of Christian lifestyle rises best out of a discipleship full of anticipation, caught up with a view of the eternal Kingdom, taken up preeminently (thus, *simply*) on advancing current and future displays of

---

QUOTABLE QUOTE

Tell those who are rich in this present world not to be contemptuous of others, not to rest the weight of their confidence on the transitory power of wealth, but on the living God who generously gives us everything for our enjoyment. Tell them to do good, to be rich in kindly actions, to be ready to give to others and to sympathize with those in distress. Their security should be invested in the life to come, so that they may be sure of holding a share in the life which is permanent.

(1 TIMOTHY 6 — PHILLIPS TRANSLATION)

Christ's dominion. It is a way of ordering priorities and possessions so that we remain unencumbered. It allows us to stay flexible enough to respond adequately to all the new directions God may take us. It keeps us mobile the way any "vanguard" needs to be.

THINK WITH ME ...
How can hope in Christ reinforce your efforts at evangelism?

In terms of outreach, evangelism is about delivering a Message of Hope to unbelievers so they can be reconciled to God and begin to follow Jesus as the everlasting Hope of Glory. Gospel promises address the deepest longings in the heart of every sinner. Biblical hope brings lost people to the One who consummates those longings in Himself (Isa. 61).

At the same time, a vision for Christ's supremacy has significant impact on the *evangelizers,* too. It provides us the confidence we need to reach out to the lost. It instills faith for increased breakthroughs of the Holy Spirit. It fosters a liberty to take risks because we know the Son of God will back us and multiply our efforts. It stabilizes our resolve to move forward in outreach, even in the face of opposition, because we are assured of the ultimate victories. ("We will reap if we faint not", says Gal. 6.)

Caught up in an expanding hope in Christ, believers find themselves empowered to present God's promises to unbelievers in a much more convincing way. Furthermore, as Peter says, Christians can live in such a manner that even before we open our mouths to share the Gospel, people see in our words and deeds an incomparable confidence about the hope of eternal life that can only be explained by the sovereignty of the Savior. They sense our passion for the Kingdom. Therefore, Peter says, *they* end up demanding from us reasons for our hope (1 Pet. 3).

This is why Christians should learn to be witnesses by ministering the word of Christ *inside* the Church. That's one of the best ways to get equipped for sharing and defending the news of His saving supremacy to people *outside* the Church.

THINK WITH ME ...
How can hope in Christ lead to acts of reconciliation?

If we expect wholesale peace to reign at the End, should we not strive for a measure of it among ourselves even now? A vision for the *future* that shapes relationships in the present is what Martin Luther King appealed for in his famous "I Have a Dream" message at the Lincoln Memorial in 1963. He was on to something. And the nation knew it.

As Christians we may not see eye to eye on many issues, but we can all turn and face the same direction. Since we hold to the same hope and are called to the same destiny, this vision should shape how we welcome one another as well as how we work for Christ with one another.

Anticipatory discipleship always drives us toward reconciliation, including racial and denominational. That's because we've already begun to live in anticipation of a Day of unqualified unity that will those gathered around the Lamb on the Throne. The uniqueness of Jesus — the finality of His sovereignty — provides us common ground found no other place. Since He is the foundation on which lasting harmony will be built, His supremacy — as we enter into who *He* is, where *He* is headed, what *He* is doing and how *He* is blessed — creates the perfect platform on which believers can stand side by side in Kingdom work now. We should come together in coalitions — across racial, cultural, traditional, social boundaries — to labor for Kingdom agenda. We should strive to reflect in significant measure how we soon will be joined universally to serve Jesus at His return in glory. Doing so can help us fulfill our role as Vanguards of Hope. We can pioneer the "shalom" of the future, so to speak. Not only will we draw people into a foretaste of the promised reconciliation of Heaven and earth under God's Son but also, in a very real sense, we will be inviting that future right into the present.

THINK WITH ME ...
How can hope in Christ foster courageous decisions about congregational activities?

In Luke 14 Jesus taught that even an ordinary potluck supper at church must be measured by its relationship to His final reign in glory. Listen: "When you give a banquet, invite the poor, the crippled, the lame, the blind, and you will be blessed. Although they cannot repay you, you will be repaid at the resurrection of the righteous" (vs. 13-14). In equal fashion, the Day of Resurrection should challenge churches to re-adjust schedules, re-shape programs and re-organize activities in a way that focuses its members more directly on Christ's consummate victory.

For example, when elders meet to handle church-related business (to review priorities and procedures and programs), a prime agenda might be: How can we prepare our people to become more strategically involved in

Christ's advancing Kingdom? Why not measure activities in your congregation by how well they help God's people pursue and experience "approximations of the Consummation" through their worship, or youth programs, or shut-in visitation, or capital campaigns, or prayer meetings, or community outreach?

Let me illustrate. One church on the West Coast begins every staff meeting by placing an empty chair in the middle of the room. They call it the "Jesus chair". (I'd probably call it the "King Jesus chair"!) As they begin in prayer, the staff declares to the Father that as far as they are concerned, His Son occupies that chair for the rest of the meeting. His throne is in their midst. From that point on, in all deliberations they refuse to lose sight of the chair and of the presence of the Lord who is in it. They see Christ as the One for whom the meeting is taking place, the One who is guiding all decisions, the One for whom decisions are made and the One prepared to lead their church where they have never gone before (and never would, if left to themselves).

Or, take another issue: How should we view Sundays? In New Testament times saints gathered on the first day of the week, resting and rejoicing in Christ's finished work in order to go forth the next six days to invest in Kingdom purposes. The fact is, the phrase for the Christian day of rest — "the Lord's Day" — hearkened back to Old Testament prophets who talked a lot about *the* Day of the Lord. It was one of the seers' favorite descriptions for the Consummation. For Christians, every weekly gathering was intended to be an opportunity to taste of, and prepare for, the coming Final Celebration. Sunday pointed them like a laser to the final *Son's*-Day, the culmination of all things when Heaven and earth would resound forever with praise for Him. Then it summoned them to live accordingly this day.

How could a local church develop activities on Sunday (the Lord's Day) to enhance everyone's commitment to, and training for, service as Vanguards of Christ's Kingdom purposes? How might holy hope, shaped by Jesus' reign, be re-ignited for them each Lord's Day? What would happen if members left your sanctuary fired up, eager to walk into the next six days looking for increased displays of Christ's dominion around them? What if, as a result, people returned the next Sunday full of reports on where they had witnessed revelations of Christ's supremacy — in their lives as well as the lives of others?

THINK WITH ME ...

How can hope in Christ undergird your daily battle with sin?

All sin (envy, anger, lust, greed, gluttony, to name just a few) detours believers from fully engaging Christ for all that He is. But hope in Christ supplies an effective antidote to the deceitfulness of sin. It defies sin by making much of God's promises to contrast with sin's enticements. Hope motivates us for holy living by reminding us of our ultimate destiny when Jesus will fully reveal Himself to be our all in all, leaving sin powerless to counteract. The promise of tasting now as well as later the powers of the age to come (Heb. 6) should fortify each of us to flee ungodliness and "lay hold of eternal life" (1 Tim. 6). We may need to "crucify the flesh". But we know that by "sowing to the Spirit" Christians will reap eternal life with all its fruits (Gal. 5 and 6).

In one sense, anticipatory discipleship encourages a form of *voluntary abstinence,* a phrase frequently used today to describe a young person's commitment to sexual purity. On a far more profound level, Christians are called to *abstain* from all counterfeit hopes offered them by the world, the flesh and the devil (1 Jn. 2). We are to renounce shallow substitutes for the promises of God. Backing off temporary gratifications, we are to allow God to fulfill our lives by His ways, in His timing and out of His riches in glory in Christ Jesus (Phil. 4).

Of course, if we're responding to Kingdom promises, the battle with sin forces us to tackle evils of other kinds such as social injustices, poverty, corporate greed, religious scandal, moral relativism, political oppression or domestic terrorism. Proclaiming hope in Christ to the poor, for example, must be coupled with efforts to overcome poverty at its systemic roots. Christ's battle-call includes a healthy combination of both telling and showing the full extent of His supremacy.

QUOTABLE QUOTE

New Testament Christianity is essentially two-worldly: not other-worldly in the sense of lacking interest in this world, but seeing life here as travel to, and preparation for, and indeed a foretaste of, a life hereafter in which all without exception will reap what they sowed here in terms of their attitude and decision God-ward.

(J.I. PACKER)

THINK WITH ME ...

How can hope in Christ re-ignite your zeal for world outreach?

A forward-looking obedience to Christ will always produce sacrificial service for advancing the Great Commission. Christians understand that the missionary task impinges on fuller demonstrations of Christ's lordship among the nations by the spread of the Gospel. We acknowledge, as well, that the task must be completed to usher in the fullest revelation of His consummate glory at His triumphant return (Matthew 24:14, 30-31). Since we endorse the chorus sung by the Church Universal in Heaven (Rev. 5), should not the highest priority of the Church Militant be the planting of congregations among every people group on Planet Earth? Shouldn't we resolve to bring the Gospel especially to those currently beyond its reach?

For generations missionary statesmen have urged the Church consistently to pursue their goal by this appeal: *"Finish the task, in order to bring back the King!"* This motto has challenged thousands to become Vanguards of Hope by embracing the missionary enterprise as the straightest road to travel in order to reach the Day when our Supreme Commander returns to put everything under His feet (Ps. 110).

I wonder how many local churches in America today have set priorities on the basis of how congregational life will ultimately connect with unreached peoples — and, how the church's efforts will further the spreading of Christ and His reign among the poor — and, how their activities may help bring our generation closer to the Grand Finale among the nations? Should not hope about the culmination of Christ's global cause shape how a church defines success? Would not effectiveness be measured best by how many people a congregation *sends* rather than by how many people it seats?

THINK WITH ME ...

How can hope in Christ inspire the way we love one another?

Worship, Scripture, possessions, evangelism, reconciliation, church activities, righteous living, world outreach — all of these find new meaning in the context of anticipatory discipleship. Preeminently, however, hope expresses itself best in how we *love* one another. Hope in Christ and His supremacy will cause Christians to explore Christ's love in fuller dimensions.

"Vanguard love" might show itself uniquely as:

- A constant longing for other people to discover with us all the hope we were meant to have, in order that together we might enjoy every purpose God has for us in Christ.

- A willingness to do whatever it takes as Messengers of Hope to help God's promises come alive for others.

- An investing in others by using the gifts God has built into our lives in order to help others discover and hone their own gifts, to fulfill their destiny in Christ.

- The effort to view all people not only for who they are today but also for who the Father intends them to become for eternity — and then to serve them with that grander perspective.

- A commitment to settle for nothing less than God's best in Christ for others, no matter what price God may ask of us to bring it to pass.

Maybe the most telling demonstration of a "vanguard love" is this: Responding to you here and now in a manner reflective of how I would expect to show you my love *if we were both suddenly standing together in glory, in the Final Hour, in full view of the Savior on His throne.* One day that is precisely what will happen to both of us! Should I not determine, therefore, how God would expect me to love you *there* (in That Day) and then strive to show you no less of a love *now* (even though I fall short of that goal many times)?

Among other things, I've found that this perspective provides whole new incentives for seeking and giving forgiveness. After all, do I really expect to hold grudges toward brothers and sisters in Christ in that Glorious Appearing when we all behold our glorious Lord? Will I be able to close my heart to them once we all surround Him in His everlasting triumphs? If not in that moment, then how can I justify holding unresolved grudges toward any of them in this moment?

True, Paul concludes three godly qualities will remain with us forever: faith, hope and love. He also says the greatest of these is love (1 Cor. 13). But let's not forget that *love* is the outworking of *faith* (Gal. 5) which is, in turn, the evidence of things *hoped* for (Heb. 11). To follow New Testament logic, therefore, the *starting point* for love must be hope — hope which incites a daily faith in Jesus and His purposes that leads me to want to love anyone the way Jesus does, as well as the way He always will. After it has had its full impact, hope "morphs" into love.

Bottom line: Wherever the Spirit of Christ abides, you will find hearts passionate for others, along with a desire for God's promises to unfold for others, and a sensitivity to help others discover a fuller vision of God's Son for all He is. Hope-filled disciples are uniquely empowered to reach out, to forgive, to serve, to bless — and to stick with their efforts with the knowledge such labors never will be in vain in the Lord (1 Cor. 15). Vanguards of Hope spread a "preview" of the love that will someday fill the entire universe!

Vanguards of Hope:
Blast Off with the "20-Minute Ticker"!
(Matthew 5:3-12; 7:21-25)

Sleep is a condition in which the real seems unreal and the unreal real. The Bible summons us to put off garments of sleep, to be armed instead for the coming Day. We're to wake up, to live every aspect of discipleship in the light of Christ's coming. We're to put on Christ as we walk in the broad daylight of His victories — past, present, future (Rom. 13). So how might Vanguards of Hope fire up more aggressive involvement in the sunrise of Christ's global cause? What are some *personal* applications of anticipatory discipleship that can get a vanguard off the launch pad, sooner rather than later?

Consider the possibilities offered by the following daily discipline. It's arbitrary, I know. But for the moment, view it as training wheels for a child's bike. Learning to ride requires the devices for a time to keep one's balance. So the first thing Dad does is bolt the wheels onto the bike. Before long such crutches are no longer necessary. The youngster achieves enough skill to stay upright entirely on his/her own. And the training wheels can go into storage until the next child is ready to learn.

The same applies regarding the **Twenty Minute Ticker** I'm about to give you. This discipline has proven to be quite useful for Vanguards of Hope eager to blast into new orbits in following the Lord Jesus. Often all they needed was a way to get their balance. The *Twenty Minute Ticker* did this for them. Here's how it works:

6 – Build ...

For *six minutes a day,* using Scripture primarily, build your own vision of hope — your personal outlook on the supremacy of God's Son. Review some of the thousands of texts that look at our God-given hope. (See *Appendix V* for suggestions.) Consider how each one ultimately exalts Christ, amplifying some aspect of who He is as God's Son; or where He's headed in God's purposes; or how He imparts God's resources; or what He receives from God's people. At the same time, don't hesitate to make use of supplementary literature (such as this book) to help open your eyes and reform your Christology! (You might read portions of key books listed in *Appendix III,* too.)

5 – Pray ...

For *five minutes a day* pray hope-filled prayers of your own making. Ask God to unleash His promises in greater ways for you and for others, both now and in ages to come. Pray particularly about some of the perspectives you uncovered in the previous six minutes of reading God's Word and/or other Christ-exalting literature. (Feel free to draw on insights for prayer explored toward the end of this chapter.)

4 – Strategize ...

For *four minutes a day* reflect on how you might combine your hope in Christ more fully with one particular area in your walk with Christ. In other words, *apply* what you discovered the first six minutes, and prayed about the next five minutes, to some practical dimension of discipleship. Be as specific as you can. Then go out to make it happen the rest of the day.

For example, you might ask: What adjustment in the use of my finances is needed to prepare the way for the Father to reveal more of

His Son in me? Or, how do I need to love my spouse better to encourage him or her to enter more fully into the promises of God? Or, how
might my growing vision of Christ's supremacy impact this day how I
answer one or more of the decisive questions explored earlier? ("What
goes? What stays? What's new? What's next?")

3 – Proclaim ...

For *three minutes a day* share with another Christian the hope in
Christ you've uncovered that day as you studied it, prayed over it, and
incorporated it into your walk with Him. Become a Messenger of
Hope to someone during the course of the day. You could be a
messenger by writing a Christian friend a brief note; or phoning
someone to give a short report on what God is teaching you; or by
striking up a quick conversation with a friend at church or on the job.
For many there's the option of sharing a growing hope with one's
family around the evening meal. The point is this: Let the supremacy
of Christ increasingly become an issue in your interaction with other
believers.

2 – Listen ...

For *two minutes a day* sit quietly at the feet of your Lord Jesus. (This
might work best at the close of the day.) In absolute silence, based on
all that has happened in you throughout the earlier eighteen minutes of
your *Ticker,* let your King speak into your heart by His Spirit deeper
insights into who He is as the Hope of Glory. Keep this question in
mind: "What more has the Father revealed in my life *this* day of the
glory of His Son and the work of His Kingdom?"

This might be a good time to start a *diary.* Take one of your two
minutes of silence to write down in a couple of sentences a thought
that best summarizes God's work in you that day. Record how you've
grown as a Prisoner of Hope. Document whatever sense of promise is
bubbling up in you about some facet of your life in Christ. Summarize
what more of Christ you have discovered today that wasn't there
yesterday?

After a month of doing this, review your diary. Look for common
patterns or themes. Identify how you have grown in various aspects of
anticipatory discipleship. At the same time, rejoice over how the Holy
Spirit is transforming your vision of God's Son and increasingly delivering you from the crisis of supremacy.

Twenty minutes a day. That's just ten hours a month. But notice, *in the end it adds up to a 120 hours a year!* Ask yourself: All other things being equal, between now and a year from now, if I were to add to my life 120 hours of growth as a Vanguard of Hope, what kinds of delightful changes might I expect in my vision of Jesus, my hope toward Him and my service to Him?

Vanguard Praying: Shaped by Hope in Christ's Supremacy
(Ephesians 3:14-21; 4:1-6)

Dag Hammerskjold, former Secretary General of the United Nations, was a strong follower of the Lord Jesus Christ. He defined prayer's agenda one time by simply stating: "For what has been, pray *thanks!* For what shall be, pray *yes!*"

Let's call this *anticipatory* praying. Taken up with Christ's supremacy, our prayers should be marked not only by spontaneous thanksgivings for previous Kingdom blessings but also by strong affirmations for promised Kingdom advances. Every hope-filled prayer meeting should ring with the "Yes!" of God's people.

THINK WITH ME ...
Why is a church's prayer life a barometer of its hope in Christ?

Prayerfulness and hopefulness are inseparably linked. First, God gives us a vision for the future that is so wonderful we conclude we cannot live without it. But then He helps us realize that it is so wonderful we cannot personally produce it. Can't live without it, can't produce it? That's when our primary option becomes to seek it — to pray for it.

To say it another way: The joy of the blessings He promises convinces us we never want to *go back* to wherever we were before Christ opened this vision to us. But the magnitude of the blessings He promises also convinces us we never can *go forward* into their fulfillment by our own strength, apart from Christ. We have no other option but to *go down* onto our knees before the Throne. We are compelled to ask the Father to accomplish for us the hope we long for and the promises we are so helpless to produce by ourselves.

That's what makes prayer such a dependable barometer of what's happening with hope inside any congregation. An *absence of prayer* in church priorities — corporate prayer and prayer as a way of life — should ring an alarm. The pall of hopelessness may be hanging over us more than we thought. Previous disappointments, for example — what seemed to us like God's failures to be faithful to us regarding some of His promises — may have taken more of a toll than we suspected. Fears of defeat fasten onto a people clutched by the crisis of supremacy.

The good news is that we don't have to remain stuck in these waterless pits. If I've learned anything over the past 30 years of working with prayer leaders and prayer movements all over the world, it is this:

The single most important ingredient
for igniting and sustaining a united work of prayer
is simply to clarify for everyone, at every opportunity,
the hope that Christ's supremacy calls us to pray toward.

That's why Messengers of Hope inside a congregation will usually double as *mobilizers of prayer* without hardly trying. Prayer becomes the necessary response of anyone who seriously heeds a message of the hope the supremacy of Christ is for us.

THINK WITH ME ...
In what sense is prayer always at the vanguard of God's purposes in Christ?

Prayer is more than a scheduled *interlude* in Christianly activities (though in many churches that's what it has become). Prayer is the *prelude* to a fresh work of God. As we call on Him to come and do for us what we cannot do for ourselves, prayer makes room for Jesus to take center stage. When we use phrases like "in Jesus' Name", "for Jesus' sake", or "for Christ's glory alone" in our prayers, we signal our desire for God to unleash His promises in a way that opens wide the door for more of Christ and His supremacy. When we pray "Your Kingdom come, your will be done on earth as it is in Heaven", we lobby the Throne of the universe to give fullest expression to every facet of Christ's lordship. We appeal to the Father to stamp the very nature and character of His Son on everything that matters to us — to mark with His Kingdom concerns all of our personal concerns.

Throughout history, concerted prayer movements have provided launching pads for major advances of Christ's Kingdom. This was certainly true with four major religious awakenings in our nation the past two centuries. As God's people *kept* praying, each awakening overflowed into revitalized churches and denominations, significant social reforms, widespread evangelistic in-gatherings, and the creation of scores of new mission sending societies. Today the scope and urgency of prayers going up from literally millions of saints in many nations is committed to a similar awakening to the glory of God's Son. The historical pattern should forewarn us: Get ready! Extraordinary new displays of Christ's dominion are on their way!

In fact, it would be correct to describe prayer as one of the most hopeful *signs* God gives His people. Nothing in our natural selves (the flesh) wants to seek God at all. Left to ourselves our wayward hearts want to run from Him. Whenever Christians intensify their praying, therefore, you know that *God* is up to something. Only He can create soul-hunger for more of Christ in our hearts, and He never moves His people to pray in vain. He fully intends to answer them. Every prayer meeting in every local church is the vanguard of coming advances of Christ's Kingdom. None of His praying saints will be disappointed.

During the "First Great Awakening" Jonathan Edwards exhorted his readers in his 1747 volume on "concerts of prayer": "For undoubtedly, that which God abundantly makes the subject of His *promises,* God's people should abundantly make the subject of their *prayers.* It also affords them the strongest assurances that their prayers shall be *successful*" (italics his).

To better understand the unique outlook that supremacy and hope give to prayer, let's explore briefly the **four dimensions** of prayer, **six responses** of prayer and **three answers** to prayer which encourage Vanguards of Hope in their life of prayer under the lordship of Jesus. (*Appendix VII* puts the dimensions and responses in the form of a tool to help you grow your experience of "anticipatory prayer".)

THINK WITH ME ...
Are you incorporating the *four dimensions* of vanguard praying?

Hope-filled prayer draws on the **four major dimensions** of Christ's supremacy as a summary of all God's promises to us:

- **Focus**

- **Fulfillment**

- **Fullness**

- **Fervency**

Recall what we learned about each in chapter 1:

Who Christ is as the Son of God
    makes up the FOCUS of His supremacy.
Where Christ leads us in the Purposes of God
    speaks of the FULFILLMENT of His supremacy.
How Christ imparts the Resources of God
    comprises the FULLNESS of His supremacy.
What Christ receives from the People of God
    defines the FERVENCY of His supremacy.

When Vanguards of Hope pray, they lay hold onto four concerns to shape their praises and prayers before the Throne. Put simply:

- Many of God's promises encourage us to seek Him for a fresh *focus* on Christ Himself, that we might know Him better for *ALL* that He is. Our prayers must seize on this grand prospect, asking the Father to reveal more of His Son's glory to us, in a whole variety of ways, as well as to our churches and the nations.

- Other passages reassure us that God intends to grant greater *fulfillments* of Christ's mission — in evangelism, justice, healing, church planting, feeding the hungry, etc. Our Father encourages us to intercede for powerful in-breakings that can advance Christ's redeeming work. We're even told to pray for the Consummation itself. Anticipatory praying asks the Father to carry us on into the completion of His ultimate Kingdom purposes in His Son.

- A host of other promises invite us to pray for fresh experiences of Christ's *fullness* in our lives and in our churches as He lives out His reign among us. Our prayers should ask the Father to pour out on us everything for growing in the life of His Son — including Christ's gifts for ministry (1 Cor. 12), the fruit of His Spirit (Gal. 5), His wisdom and counsel (Eph. 1) and His empowerment for outreach (Acts 1).

- Other texts compel intercession for renewed *fervency*. We ask the Father to ignite within us deeper devotion for His Son, to strengthen us by His Spirit to live for Jesus, and to impact others through all the gifts and resources He has given us. Not only do we pray for the Lord of Glory to bless us (fullness), but also for us to be a blessing to Him and for His Kingdom, none of which is possible apart from the grace of God working through us in resurrection power.

Every Biblically-based prayer a Christian expresses must incorporate one or more of these primary dimensions of Christ's supremacy. In similar fashion, we may expect every answer to our prayers to advance Christ's glory in one or more of these same four dimensions.

The next time you conclude a season of prayer, either alone or with others, debrief the time by asking:

- Which of these four dimensions surfaced most often in my/our time of prayer?

- Was there a good balance among all four as I/we prayed?

- What adjustments do I/we need to make next time I/we pray to ensure greater accuracy, balance, breadth and effectiveness in my/our prayers?

THINK WITH ME ...
Are you practicing the *six responses* of vanguard praying?

On top of the four dimensions of prayer, Vanguards of Hope should also incorporate the *six major responses* of prayer. Let me highlight them with six words — six "R's" that summarize all that Scripture teaches on the major ways we can *express* hearts of hope when we pray:

- **Rejoice**
- **Repent**
- **Resist**

- **Request**
- **Receive**
- **Recommit**

Let's look at what each response might include:

❖ **REJOICE means that you:**

- Praise the Father as the God who is, who was, and who is to come — the God of all hope.

- Celebrate the various dimensions of hope that He has set before you.

- Rejoice in the prospects of greater glory for Christ up ahead, both in this world and in the world to come.

- Thank Him for so many promises already fulfilled in the past.

- Praise Him for what you believe He is getting ready to do, even before you see it all accomplished.

- Celebrate how He will bring greater honor to His Son as He accomplishes His purposes in the Church and among the nations.

- Delight in the prospects you hold to, inherent in both the Consummation as well as current approximations of the Consummation.

- Above all, proclaim in prayer all that Christ means to you — who He is to you, for you, over you, within you, through you, before you, upon you.

❖ **REPENT means that you:**

- Make specific confession of both the individual and corporate sins that quench your passion for Christ's glory, diminish your spirit of hope in Him, hinder your enthusiasm for His Kingdom, or diminish your joy over the Consummation itself (the final display of His Lordship).

- Declare your willingness to turn away from everything that might hinder the full realization of God's promises in your life in Christ.

- Repent for whatever you find in yourself or in your church that is incompatible with the hope Scripture sets before us.

- Make similar confession over the besetting sins of your nation as well.

- Acknowledge how your sins, relationships, ambitions, even Christianly traditions, may hinder the outworking of God's promises by quenching, grieving and resisting the Holy Spirit.

- Plead for God's mercy for all His people because we have diminished, distorted and dishonored Christ for who He really is.

❖ **RESIST means that you:**

- Intercede over every situation where you sense the Enemy seeks to thwart the unfolding of God's promises.

- Pray for thorough victories over Satan's strategies against advances of Christ's kingdom.

- Combat strongholds raised up against the vision of Christ and His supremacy, both inside and outside the Church.

- Resist Satan's efforts to rob us of hope and distract us from the Consummation as well as from approximations of it now.

❖ **REQUEST means that you:**

- Offer bold prayers for the promises of God to be fulfilled in greater measure. Apply specific promises to specific situations.

- Intercede for the supremacy of Christ to be more clearly revealed in your life, your church, your community, your nation, and the world.

- Seek God's outpouring of refreshing encounters with any and all four dimensions of God's promises: Focus, Fulfillment, Fullness and Fervency.

- Target many prayers on your desire for God to increase specific "approximations of the Consummation" among us.

- Ask for renewal, revival, awakening in the Church.

- Plead for a powerful increase in the worldwide missionary endeavor.

- Remember always to intercede for the return of Christ in glory!

❖ **RECEIVE means that you:**

- Pinpoint periods of silence simply to listen to what God may want to say back to you as you pray. Prayer is a two-way conversation!

- Let Him enlarge your understanding of the hope that stirred you to pray originally, expanding your vision of Christ and the fullest implications of His reign *while you pray*.

- Expect Him also to reinforce your hope about what you've already prayed by increasing your confidence in what the future holds as the answers come.

- Prepare for Him to summon you to new acts of obedience in anticipation of those answers as He calls you to get ready to engage what is coming.

- Receive fresh clarifications from the Holy Spirit for your daily discipleship and ministry so that everything you do will be conducted in anticipation of more to come.

- Above all, look for your passion for Christ to be fanned aflame as you listen while waiting to receive His responses to your prayers.

❖ **RECOMMIT means that you:**

- Offer yourself anew to the Lord Jesus Christ in view of the promises that you have just prayed about.

- Express readiness to be involved in the answers to your prayers, no matter what it may cost.

- Invite the Holy Spirit to empower you for everything that ongoing anticipatory discipleship may demand of you.

- Seek the Spirit's (re)filling so that you can live consistently with the vision and concerns around which you prayed.

- Above all, surrender to the Spirit to re-ignite your passion for Christ alone and for the great hope you have in Him — a passion consistent with the rest of your prayers.

Combined with the *four dimensions*, these *six responses* of prayer represent everything a Vanguard of Hope would ever choose to pray! When

Vanguards of Hope put the four and six together (as *Appendix VII* illustrates), the power of their actions places them at the frontline advance of the Kingdom of God's dear Son. We move forward with Him in all directions. We step into all the hope we are meant to have.

THINK WITH ME ...
Are you watching for the *three answers* to vanguard praying?

Whatever we pray for, from now to eternity, ultimately has only *one* answer: increased manifestation of the greatness and glory of the Lord Jesus Christ. Just as He is our hope before we pray, so He embodies the final outcome of all our prayers. This truth will be thoroughly vindicated in the Last Day. But it also holds true all along the way as the Father gives us approximations of the Last Day — *because* we have prayed. As noted before, God's promises are always "Yes" to us *in Christ Jesus* (2 Cor. 1) because Christ Jesus is His ultimate answer to all of our prayers. All the promises of God are summed up in Him.

Accordingly, we could say that God answers *every* Biblically-grounded, hope-filled, Christ-exalting prayer with a plain and simple *"Yes!"* However, this "yes" must manifest itself in one or more of three ways:

Immediate Answers
Intermediate Answers
Consummate Answers

Let's look at each briefly:

1) **IMMEDIATE ANSWERS ...**
   The Father is eager to reveal more of His Son *while we pray*. Since the Kingdom-vision around which we pray is about Him, the simple act of praying causes us to engage with God's Son more fully during the very activity of praying. Because all answered prayer results in decisive demonstrations of Christ's dominion to someone, somewhere, it should come as no surprise that God begins to grant that ultimate answer to His praying children in more *immediate* ways the very moment we begin to seek Him. When we draw near, He draws near (James 4). When we ask, seek and knock, the Father's initial answer is to open to us deepening encounters with the very One whose Kingdom and glory we are praying about.

Christ will meet us *personally* in prayer even when wider, more tangible out-workings of our requests don't seem to occur, at least in our timetable. The greatest answer to *any* prayer — whether it comes at this very moment or in some future age — takes the form of an increased manifestation of the person and purposes of our preeminent Lord every time. The good news is this: The supreme answer of all answers can begin to unfold the very hour we start to pray, if not for others (and often it *does* for others) at least within the intercessor's own heart — as firstfruits of more to come. What encouragement to keep praying this holds for all of us!

2) INTERMEDIATE ANSWERS …

As laid out in chapter 4, God enjoys granting His Church approximations of the Consummation. Every day the Church may expect substantial foretastes of how His promises will be culminated. Therefore, we may watch also for preliminary installments of those promises as answers to prayers whenever we set ourselves to the task.

Heaven's initial breakthroughs — even if it is not yet all we are longing for, all we know Jesus is reigning for — are evidences of God at work for the intercessors. He is giving "down payments" on the Age-to-Come, as it were. Miracles, healings, financial supplies, restored relationships, opened doors for ministry, relief for the poor, victories over besetting sins — we must be vigilant so we don't miss any such *intermediate* answers. We must remain on the lookout for the ways God is accelerating, expanding, multiplying and deepening the advance of Christ's Kingdom. Then, we must praise the Father every time intermediate answers appear. This can become an act of extraordinary worship, especially if, in the midst of our praises, we also proclaim to the Father our longings for so much more of His Son exalted among us and among the nations. As we continue to seek Him for more of what He has promised, we bring Him even greater pleasure.

3) CONSUMMATE ANSWERS …

Every Christ-exalted, Biblically-grounded prayer we have ever prayed will be thoroughly answered. Count on it. It will happen on the day Christ returns. In this life no prayer has ever been answered to the *full extent* that Christ's supremacy guarantees. In the

Consummation, however, there will be no disappointment with God or with how He has responded to our cries. Whether prayers for justice, or for defeat of dark powers, or for racial reconciliation, or for unity in the Church, or for revival, or for unreached peoples — all of them will finally and fully be realized. All of them will be consummated in a manner exceedingly beyond what we might dare to imagine today (Eph. 3). Just as the saints at the Throne praise the Lamb for answered prayers that touch nations, so we too will be utterly satisfied!

Now, let me give you one example that incorporates all three forms of answered prayer:

When Jesus visited Lazarus' tomb (Jn. 11), He gave to Mary and Martha an *immediate* answer to their pleas for Lazarus: He revealed to them that He Himself was "the Resurrection and the Life" walking among them (that is, He claimed to be the "consummation" of their hope). In Him their eternal future stood in front of them. They met Him in a new way. In one sense, this was all they needed at that moment to find comfort — by knowing Him more fully as Lord of all. But, in addition, Christ gave them an *intermediate* answer by raising their brother from the dead right before their eyes. A marvelous miracle to be sure. It was a true "approximation" of their ultimate hope!

Yet, a few years later Lazarus died again of old age. At that point, what would we expect the sisters to do? Fall into despair? Interpret his death as unanswered prayer for them? Charge Jesus with betraying them? Not at all!

In the Eternal Kingdom when Lazarus is raised physically into immortality at Christ's return, Lazarus' siblings will behold the greatest answer to their petitions for healing — the *consummate* answer. No questions or concerns will be left in their minds when that moment rolls around. Instead, they will enter with Lazarus into the ceaseless joy of the sovereign Son's presence. They will find their Lord to be the same Jesus who came to them as resurrection hope during earthly days, thousands of years before. He brought them an *immediate* answer, followed by an *intermediate* answer, all of which pointed them to the *ultimate* answer for which their hearts longed.

Which leads to the most crucial insight on hope and supremacy as it relates to answered prayer: Everything we pray for is, in one way or another, an appeal for the Consummation to prevail. All prayers, spoken in a thousand different ways, are ultimately one prayer, echoing the final prayer of the Bible: *"Come, Lord Jesus"* (Rev. 22).

In other words, *every* petition is a cry for Christ to take the pre-eminence and reveal His glory, whether in a marriage, a ministry, a career decision, in physical sufferings, justice for the oppressed, or, in the reach of Muslims and Hindus. No matter the issue, we invite Him to work as thoroughly with us now as He is willing to. We anticipate that His responses will be similar, though preliminary, to what He promises to unleash before all Heaven and earth at His coming again. Furthermore, when the Consummation dawns, we will discover to our great joy that our work of intercession became one of *God's chief means* to reach that wonderful End.

Plain and simple, all prayer is about extending the supremacy of Christ from here to eternity. Therefore, all prayers to the Father about the Kingdom can be distilled into one word: *Come!* And all answers — immediate, intermediate, consummate — boil down to one person: *Christ!*

God has ordained the End. He also has ordained the means to that End. And chief among those means is the powerful impact of our prayers — especially when we pray together as Vanguards of Hope.

Back to the Future:
Vanguards on a Campaign of Hope
(Habakkuk 3)

Now and then in our walk with Christ it is important for us to take time to survey the great parade of hope-filled saints who have served so sacrificially in Christ's mission among the nations. Vanguards of Hope — the multitudes of believers over the centuries who have been able to lay their heads on the pillow at night and say:

**I know that this day
my life has counted strategically for Christ and His Kingdom,
promoting the hope of His supremacy,
in the Church and among the nations,
for my generation as well as for the ages to come.**

As we near the close of *Joyful Manifesto,* I pray that each of us will have discovered the excitement of living with Christ in such a way that this conviction defines *every* day we walk with Him.

I wrote in chapter 8 about how I gave my life to Christ while sitting on a tombstone in a 200-year old Moravian cemetery. Let me tell you a little more about the Moravians.

As a result of a 24-hours-a-day prayer watch for revival and missions, an effort that eventually continued every day for over 100 years (!), these German missionaries circled the globe throughout the 1700's. First, they sent out teams all over Europe to spur Christians toward prayer for a Christ-awakening in their churches. This raised awareness across many nations that God desired spiritual renewal for His people. Additionally, at tremendous sacrifice they launched teams to evangelize unreached peoples in Asia, Africa and North America.

In both endeavors the Moravians (named for an area of Germany called Moravia) labored to reclaim a more comprehensive Christology for themselves and others. Hundreds eventually lost their lives for the cause, especially on the mission field. They did so joyfully, however. They were convinced about the triumphs of God's grace yet to come. Their eyes were constantly focused on the supremacy of His Son and the power of His Cross. We may rightfully call them *Prisoners* of Hope, who sent forth *Messengers* of Hope to begin a *Campaign* of Hope among Christians around the globe.

It is no surprise, therefore, that their sending base developed into a *Vanguard* of Hope. Together their community pioneered fresh works of renewal and mission for Jesus' sake, based on Jesus' right to lay claim to all the promises of God. They inspired subsequent generations to follow in their wake.

In fact, they practiced "anticipatory discipleship" to such a radical extent it even transformed the way they *died!* Anywhere they were buried Moravians asked for their bodies to be laid facing *east*. They interpreted Scripture to teach that at the Second Coming Jesus would reappear in the eastern sky to bring in the consummation of the ages. They were so anxious to meet Him, so set on the Climax, that they decided to avoid any need to "turn around" to greet Him when their bodies were raised incorruptible. What magnitude of vision for Christ's supremacy! It propelled one of the greatest "Campaigns of Hope" of all time.

THINK WITH ME ...
Are you "facing east" as you serve God's Son?

The Moravians challenge me to examine carefully how I want to position my relationship with the King of Kings. Even before Jesus comes back, long before we enter Heaven, Vanguards of Hope "face east". Are you "facing east"? Ask yourself:

- Do I believe that what I'm doing right now will truly matter when that Final Hour arrives? In other words: *Am I facing east?*

- Do I believe my activities today have a direct bearing on what my life will be about ages from now? Again, *am I facing east?*

- Am I committed to developing a greater capacity to know Christ and to enjoy Him forever by the choices I make moment by moment? *Am I facing east?*

- Am I increasing my ability to worship and serve the Lord ten thousand years from now by how I give myself *today* to Kingdom business? *Am I facing east?*

- Am I seeking to live more fully in the power and presence of God's Son, engaging His supremacy on all fronts, just as I expect to do when I join Him in glory? *Am I facing east?*

- Am I determined to know and love the Lord of Glory in His coronation splendor, not waiting until I die but doing so now with every move I make, day after day? *Am I facing east?*

- Am I willing to help others "face east" with me? Am I willing to labor among God's people, beginning with my own congregation, to call Christians back to a hope and passion that's shaped around the full extent of Christ's supremacy? *Will we face east together?*

Countless saints throughout the ages have lived like the Moravians, "facing East" — serving Christ in the sunrise of His coming Kingdom, and finding Him to be their "all and in all" (Col. 3).

Learning to live "facing east" — experiencing in practical ways what it means to give Christ the supremacy in everything because He is our hope of glory (Col. 1) — is what sustains every Campaign of Hope. It is key to the cure for the crisis of supremacy.

Now I invite you to take a few moments to meditate on the last couple of pages of *Joyful Manifesto*. **Postlude: Refrain for a Campaign** can help you identify your level of readiness to join in a Campaign of Hope. It will bring you back to reason for the title of this book:

Christ is All!

Postlude

REFRAIN
For a Campaign

"Let this motto be upon your whole ministry: 'Christ is all.' "

(Cotton Mather, c. 1720)

"Christ is All!" Surely, among the nations this phrase represents the most profound truth a human tongue can express. Surely, within a Church caught up in a crisis of supremacy, this phrase must form the clarion call from Christians to Christians everywhere. Surely, there's no better message for any Campaign of Hope to proclaim ...

We must aim our campaign

toward those who name the Name,

to reclaim in them the flame

of this radical refrain:

"Christ is all!"

In many ways these three words mirror the chief confession of another great campaign: the historic Protestant Reformation. Their cry was *solus christus* — declaring that eternal salvation could come through *Christ alone*. *"Christ is ALL!"* provides a motto for reforming 21st century believers. The vision is the same. Since God imparts every one of His promises through Christ *alone,* in the final analysis *only* Christ could ever be called our *all*. How could it be otherwise?

"Christ is All!"
Refrain for a Campaign of Hope.

Should this be our refrain? Think about it:

- *Christ is all!* He brings life down to utter simplicity. Everything that matters is reduced to this one Person. Therefore, He is the only hope we *can* proclaim.

- *Christ is all!* He is thoroughly sufficient for the needs of a whole universe. He can satisfy the longings of the nations. He can infuse the saints with the power of resurrection life. Consequently, He is the only hope we *should* proclaim.

- *Christ is all!* He's everything we have. He's everything we need. We can actually make it with Him alone. So He is the only hope we *need* to proclaim.

- *Christ is all!* He belongs fully and equally, in His totality, to all who trust in Him, without exception. He is the only hope we could ever *want* to proclaim.

- *Christ is all!* He is our destiny. His throne is our home. He is the one with whom we will be preoccupied forever. That's why there is *no other hope* for us to proclaim.

"Christit is All!"

Refrain for a Campaign of Hope.

So, what is this Campaign of Hope inside the Church *really* about? Is it about fostering a vision of the full extent of the supremacy of Christ? Is it about encouraging an awakening to the greater glory of Christ? Is it about re-converting God's people back to Christ for all that He is? The refrain holds the answer. It's about all of the above! Here's why.

- In the Savior we have become eternal beneficiaries of the Triune God. Through Him we have inherited precious provisions — given by the Father to the Son to be endowed lavishly on the redeemed by the Spirit. **But** ... many Christians today have little sense of what this means and express little desire to seek God for more. Therefore, we need a Campaign of Hope that declares to them: *"Discover how fully Christ is all. Recover the hope you are meant to have!"*

- In Christ the promises and the Promise-er are forged inseparable. All of Heaven's riches are bound up in our Lord *exclusively*. Each of God's purposes will be culminated in our Lord *conclusively*. **But** ... many Christians today fumble in fogginess of vision while wandering in a wilderness of self-reliance, self-sufficiency, self-absorption, self-promotion. To reverse this trend, our Lord is worthy of a Campaign of Hope that urges believers: *"Discover why Christ is all. Recover the hope you are meant to have!"*

- Christ is able by virtue of Who He is to permanently and wondrously transform hosts of saints in Heaven and earth. No prospect of lasting blessings for any one, anywhere, at any time, exists outside of God's Son. **But** ... many Christians today have put their hope in a vast array of other resources, even Christianly ones, and have made Christ mainly supplemental. How vital, then, is a Campaign of Hope that exclaims: *"Discover that only Christ is all. Recover the hope you are meant to have!"*

- The Kingdom that Christ brings is absolute, universal and all-encompassing. He is both the consummation and the consuming passion of every form of Christian hope. **But** ... many Christians today are more zealous for personal dreams and ambitions. They often pursue Christ only as He is useful for achieving those goals. That is why a Campaign of Hope must sound the warning: *"Discover now that Christ is all. Recover the hope you are meant to have!"*

The time has come. We must spread a vision of the magnificent greatness of Jesus among *Christians* once again! The time has come. We must help *one another* be consumed with His glory as a way of life. The time has come. We must focus on reforming *disciples* into strategic bases of operation, men and women who are passionate for the advance of His Kingdom among the nations.

Soon, *"Christ is all!"* will bear witness to a fresh movement of God across the Body of Christ. Soon, *"Christ is all!"* will define the greatest answer to the prayers of an entire generation. Soon, *"Christ is all!"* will resound throughout the Church, heard on the lips of all who have re-engaged their Savior in the full extent of His supremacy. Soon, *"Christ is all!"* will become the trademark of those who have recovered the hope we are meant to have.

"Christ is All!" proclaims even more, however. It announces the consummation of all things just ahead. It composes Heaven's testimony of triumph to be sung for ages to come. It's the pledge that will emblazon our banners on that unending Day when we rally to this uncontested Conqueror — when every hope will be perfectly consummated in Him.

"Christ is All!"
Refrain for a Campaign of Hope.

If you intend to claim such a refrain for your campaign, you must respond first the way John did in Revelation 1. On Patmos Island he encountered an unexpected revelation of his majestic Master looming before him as Alpha and Omega. What did John do? He fell down like a dead man — *in silence*. Trembling, in silence. Overwhelmed, in silence. Surrendered, in silence. Expectant, in silence. Waiting, in silence.

So it must be for you. To prepare for the Campaign of Hope that beckons, I invite you to respond the same as John did — in a moment of absolute, awe-struck ...

... SILENCE.

Set aside this book. Quiet your soul before the living Lord of Glory. Kneel, even. Worship your Supreme Commander. Be joyful in the courts of His Royal Highness. But, before anything else, be silent ...

> *Silent* — alert for Him to come near to you as the hope we are meant to have ...

> *Silent* — looking for Him to shine on you with the hope we are meant to have ...

> *Silent* — listening for Him to speak to you about the hope we are meant to have ...

> *Silent* — waiting for Him to draw you on toward the hope we are meant to have ...

> *Silent* — eager to join Him to promote the hope we are meant to have ...

> *Silent* — ready to help other believers recover the hope we are meant to have ...

> *Silent* — poised for the rest of your life to proclaim the full extent of His supremacy because it is all the hope we are meant to have.

Then, as you begin your very own Campaign of Hope right where you live among those you love, make sure this one refrain remains the message you share and the identity you bear:

"Christ is All!"

APPENDICES

APPENDIX I
EQUIPPED!
How to Make This Book
Work for You

The volume you hold serves two purposes. (1) It is, as it claims, a *"Joyful Manifesto"*, meant to be shared with believers everywhere. It proclaims a vision of God's Son for *all* that He is. It magnifies His supremacy. It announces fresh possibilities for those ready to re-engage Him as Lord in deeply meaningful ways. It lays out a promising pathway for those who are seeking a restoration of hope and passion toward Christ, both for themselves and their churches. It provides the blueprint for a *Campaign of Hope* aimed at fulfilling the cries of many hearts like yours — a campaign that could change the face of the Church in our generation.

"Joyful" is not *too* strong a word for this document. It provides scores of reasons to celebrate *Christ:* to celebrate the multiple dimensions of His dominion; to celebrate the everlasting prospects He offers the nations; to celebrate with anticipation a fuller revelation of His glory to God's people many believe is at hand. As Paul exhorts in Romans 5, there are times when Christians simply *must* "rejoice in the hope of the glory of God". *Joyful Manifesto* confirms that such a time has come.

However, we might also call it a *"Jewel-Filled Manual"*. This book holds a treasure-trove of what I hope you will agree are refreshing insights, stimulating vision, reflective questions, supportive Scriptures, useful hints on living, as well as practical steps toward discovering what the glory of God's Son really means. Its value as a Christian discipling tool should not be underestimated either, for individual readers or for groups that decide to discuss the book together.

If, in fact, you would like to lead a weekly group discussion of *Joyful Manifesto,* turn to **Appendix II: Christ Huddles** for further helps and insights on facilitating small group discussions.

Call this instrument you are holding a *manifesto-doubling-as-a-manual,* designed to really *work* for you. Its impact can be seen, first of all, by the fact that **CHRIST IS ALL!** is divided into three volumes. Actually, it gives you three books in one.

The Emphasis of Each Volume

First, **Volume One** (ch. 1-5) maps out a larger vision of the glory and supremacy of God's Son. It investigates what Christian leaders for centuries have termed *Christology* — that is, the study of who Christ is as God's Son, where He leads in the Purposes of God, how He imparts as the Resources of God and what He receives from the People of God. I describe this as the Focus, Fulfillment, Fullness and Fervency of His supremacy. Though just a beginning, these five chapters unveil an overview on Jesus that is both stunning and stretching. Here you'll encounter Him in four wonderfully amazing ways (supported by hundreds of Scriptures): The Summation, Consummation, Approximation and Consuming Passion of all Christian hope.

Think of *Volume One* as a "short course on supremacy", designed for anyone ready to join a campaign to confront and cure the crisis of supremacy in today's Church — a course designed to help you recover all the *hope* you are meant to have. The exquisite insights on God's Son contained here will revitalize your *walk* with Him in surprising ways. At the same time, they will give you a hope-filled, life-changing *message* about Him to share with fellow Christians so that the Spirit might begin to "re-convert" them back to Christ in the same way He's doing for you. Above everything, the opening chapters encourage enduring praise to the One whom the Bible calls "Christ in you, the hope of glory" (Col. 1:27).

Next, in **Volume Two** (the middle three chapters) we explore the *"crisis of supremacy"* surfacing throughout the Christian movement, including its attendant impact on our hope and passion toward Christ. We uncover who and what this crisis is about; how it touches every aspect of life and ministry for Christ; and what it will take to cure the crisis and reawaken the Church to Christ for *all* that He is. You'll learn why concerned Christians today are eager to — indeed, must — deal with this challenge straight-on and without delay. *Volume Two* concludes by calling for a *Campaign of Hope* to confront and cure the crisis.

Finally, **Volume Three** (ch. 9-12) brings us to the campaign itself. It surveys the greater message about Christ we must deliver to the Body of Christ. It unpacks a three-fold strategy for any *Campaign of Hope* — what I call three compelling "cures" for the crisis. We can launch this campaign in three ways: As *Messengers* of Hope, as *Prisoners* of Hope and as *Vanguards* of Hope. *Volume Three* helps you get a practical handle on how to grow a dynamic life of discipleship for yourself and fellow believers. It will increase your confidence that God's people can be set free from their paralysis of hope and passion, and be reawakened to Christ for *all* that He is.

The Layout of Each Chapter

You'll find each chapter divided into *major sub-sections.* Under the heading for each sub-section appears *a corresponding Scripture reference,* suggesting a key Biblical perspective on the issues raised within that portion of the chapter.

At what point should one look up the Scripture text? You might do so either before you read each sub-section or immediately after you've completed one. Or you might choose to read them one after another, after you've grappled with various issues raised throughout the entire chapter. Either way the passages help bring your thoughts and reactions back to God's Word. They also provide a way to pray over the issues from a Biblical perspective. The main reasons for suggesting these passages are to alert you to how much the book attempts to root everything in the Word of God and to challenge *you* to test every insight by the truth of Scripture as our final authority. (*Appendix V* provides significantly more texts to consider at some later time.)

If you're working in a small group setting, you might begin each weekly session (covering one chapter a week) by reading around the circle some or all of the suggested Scriptures before you actually begin your time of discussion. Later, you might refer to the passages as you discuss the chapter. An equally effective approach is to read them separately before interacting over each individual sub-section. Or you can simply read them, one after another, at the close of your session before going into a brief season of prayer. Again, the main objective for giving these texts remains the same: to keep God's Word at the heart of your study and reflection.

Next, notice that each sub-section is divided into bite-sized units of a few paragraphs with *side headings* used to flag each unit. Each one is introduced with the phrase **"THINK WITH ME"**. Unlike other books you may have studied, here every side heading is put in the form of a *question.* You'll soon discover that these questions make the *Joyful Manifesto* work for you in two vital ways:

(1) For the individual reader the side headings double as *reflection questions.* I've formatted them this way in order to encourage you to pause a moment to consider what you think about the subject at hand before you read what the *author* thinks. In addition, you might choose to take a few moments *after* completing each unit to respond to what you've read — using the questions to wrestle with analyses or truths found there. Most of all, before moving on to the next unit, you might want to use the side headings to help you pray about how the Father wants you to respond to His Son in light of what you've just read. You've probably never read through a book with quite this approach. It will make a huge difference in how the material impacts your life.

(2) To help stimulate small group interaction on the content of each unit, I recommend your group use the side headings as *study/discussion questions.* The group facilitator can employ the questions to instigate lively exchanges over issues addressed in each unit of that chapter, taking them in sequence until you've covered the chapter. The benefit is that you will have right in front of you the precise content that addresses that particular question, in case your group wants to reference the author's thoughts. This whole approach is most effective, of course, if group members have read the assigned chapter prior to gathering to discuss it.

But for both individual and group, the side headings demonstrate a basic assumption behind this book: I intend to help Christians uncover *what they already believe about the supremacy of Christ* — including issues touching the crisis of supremacy as well as its cures. It is my way of honoring you. Each *"THINK WITH ME"* says to you: I know God has already begun to minister to you about these concerns. You bring important perspectives to *Joyful Manifesto* that can enrich your study. Start your thinking, therefore, with what God has placed in you before you take on anything additional that I suggest.

Next, you'll find what I call four *"Ludes"* — specifically, *Prelude, Interlude I, Interlude II* and *Postlude.* Whether privately or as a group, please do not by-pass these sections. Each *"Lude"* plays an important role, bringing *Joyful Manifesto* down to the heart level.

Before you start to read, use the *Prelude* to prepare yourself to experience the kind of encounter with Christ this book encourages. Use *Interlude I* and *II* to examine how fully you're prepared on a personal level to respond to the issues in the preceding chapters, and then move on to the next volume. Use the *Postlude* to close your study of the book on a note that brings you back to the title. One other suggestion: Each *"lude"* is composed in such a way that it may be more effective if read aloud, whether in a room alone or with your *"Christ Huddle".*

Other features of *Joyful Manifesto* include the many *"Quotable Quotes"* that appear throughout each chapter. Some are taken directly from Scripture (primarily in chapters 2-5). Most draw from the writings of Christian leaders past and present. Be aware of this: The quotes do not necessarily relate directly with the content of the paragraphs nearest where they appear. There are reasons, however, for why they are placed where you find them. Each quote serves as supplemental reinforcement, enriching some dimension of the basic theme of that section of the chapter. The reader should feel free to make applications as appropriate.

Whether you're alone or in a *"Christ Huddle",* you might pause from time to time to reflect on the thoughts of a particular *"Quotable Quote".* Or you might choose to read all of them before beginning a particular chapter to get an overview of upcoming themes. Another stimulating approach is to use them to help review the themes of a chapter once you've completed reading it. (Consult the *"Giving Credit"* appendix for sources from which many of these quotes were taken.)

Incidentally, the *Appendices (I-IX)* provide a variety of supplementary materials, some of which will continue serving you long after you've finished the book.

NOW ... Can you understand why I offer this book to you as not only a *joyful manifesto* but also a *jewel-filled manual?* It is ready to *work* for you!

APPENDIX II
CHRIST HUDDLES:
Facilitating Small Group
Discussions of the Book

This book was designed to double as a discussion guide to help a small group can explore the book together.

This effort might take place weekly in private living rooms, with a quarterly Sunday school class, during weekly gatherings in a college dorm or at a regular local ministerial meeting. Whatever the setting, I recommend that this short-term group, convened for such a specialized focus, be called a **CHRIST HUDDLE**, stating right up front that Christ is the reason you're gathered together.

If you want to facilitate such a group, the following will prove useful. First, note that various components within each chapter — described in detail in *Appendix I: EQUIPPED! How to Make This Book Work for You* — lend themselves quite easily to guiding group interaction. If you have not yet read *Appendix I* you may want to do so at this time.

Joyful Manifesto can be broken down into a thirteen-week curriculum on the supremacy of Christ. The series consists of an opening "orientation session" (see suggestions below), followed by one week for each of the twelve chapters.

A 13-Week Study Curriculum

First, to prepare between sessions each participant should own her or his copy of the book in which to write personal reflections and questions. Each participant should commit to other group members to spend time reading an estimated 40 minutes a week in the next session's assigned chapter or section. Along with Bibles bring copies of **CHRIST IS ALL!**

to each session because much of your conversation will draw from the text surrounding each *"THINK WITH ME"* question.

Whenever your *CHRIST HUDDLE* meets, open every session with a brief time of worship and prayer, possibly praising God for all you've learned about Christ and His supremacy over the past week, or thanking Him for new vistas of hope and passion toward Christ that the Spirit has given you in recent days. Praise the Father for ways you see the "crisis of supremacy" being confronted in the Church already. Pray for God to use your group to help cure that crisis even more.

On the first of your thirteen weeks (the orientation session) the approach is necessarily a-typical. This gathering allows participants to receive their copies of the book. Then, the facilitator guides the group through an overview of the entire *Joyful Manifesto,* beginning with a look at the *"Contents"* outline. The facilitator should explain how and why the book is put together the way it is (the logic in the flow of the chapter topics) and how participants can best make it work for them, sharing suggestions as found in *Appendix I.*

The orientation time should focus as well on the need for accountability to one another during the remaining twelve weeks. Indicate a commitment to one another about fulfilling assigned weekly reading before coming.

Next, read the two opening passages on "supremacy": *Joyful Manifesto's* definition and the one Paul gives in Colossians 1. Then share initial thoughts, questions, surprises or concerns that either perspective on Christ might stir up for you. In addition, you might read out loud from **Appendix IV** which provides **Nine Theses** behind the entire book. Discuss initial responses to any of them. (Do they make sense or not? Why or why not? Do you disagree for some reason with any one of them? Why or why not?)

You should try to discuss the key points of the **Look Beyond the Threshold (An Introduction)**. If the group has not had opportunity to read that section, then walk through it together, summarizing main ideas and asking them to read it on their own before you re-convene.

Conclude by reading the **Prelude** aloud. It will provide a worshipful beginning for your next twelve weeks. Try doing it responsively the way that's suggested there. Conclude the first session with a brief time of worship and prayer, using ideas from the Prelude *(Put Your Hope in Christ)*. Pray especially about the rest of that first week of your Christ Huddle.

For the remaining twelve weeks, here's one approach you might try with your *CHRIST HUDDLE* (which can be adapted, expanded or collapsed depending on the amount of time you have each week):

- After an opening time of worship and prayer, let the facilitator begin with *a summary overview of the chapter for that week,* possibly highlighting one or two statements or paragraphs in the chapter that pinpoint major issues that could form primary talking-points during the discussion time. Or the facilitator might read aloud sentences (or a paragraph) that are more intellectually provocative, or even potentially controversial. Ask for initial, preliminary reactions to get people engaged at the outset.

- *Then, ask someone to read selected Scriptures* listed under the center headings in the chapter for that session. Ask for a few initial reactions or reflections on the verses as they relate to the overall theme of that chapter. (Time will probably not allow you to read all the verses highlighted throughout the chapter.)

- *Next, work through the reflection questions* (side headings), asking participants to respond first to the questions themselves and then to bring additional responses and reflections on the issues raised in that unit of the chapter. The facilitator also might select ahead of time certain statements in a section to highlight for more directed interaction. Whatever approach, ask people where they agree or disagree, and always ask them *why* they think the way they do. And remember: Depending on the time allotted to each meeting, you may need to skip over some of the side headings to cover what you feel are the most relevant sections for your particular group.

- *Once the whole chapter has been explored, work on application.* Ask the group to determine what practical changes might be implemented — either individually or collectively — based on what has been discovered and discussed. For example: Where are changes needed in how they *see* Christ, or *seek* Him, or *speak about* Him? How might they want to *hope* in Him in new ways? How might they change the way they *obey* Him in the coming weeks? How has the chapter touched them personally regarding any shortfall of hope or passion in their own lives? Based on insights from this chapter, what could they do about any crisis of supremacy they see in themselves or in their churches? The goal is this: to get each participant to determine at least one next step she or he will take the following week in response to the discussion (along with reading the next assigned material).

- **Conclude with a time of prayer** regarding all that has unfolded during the session. Pray about how your vision of Christ and His supremacy needs to grow stronger. Ask the Father to give you a greater hope shaped around Christ's Kingdom and His global cause. Pray for a revitalization of your hope and passion toward Him. Pray equally for such a re-awakening to Jesus to impact your local church or the Christian movement to which you belong. Finally, pray for the spread of Jesus' reign and glory among the nations in specific ways.

- *Use the "Ludes".* When you finish a chapter that concludes one of the *Volumes*, be sure to save time at the end of that session to share the wrap-up, whether *Interlude I or Interlude II or Postlude*. Try reading them aloud (or at least portions). You might let them shape your concluding prayer time as well

The facilitator must watch the time and keep the conversation rolling. For example, if you have 90 minutes together, it might break down into something like this:

A season of general worship and prayers ... **10 minutes**
Overview the chapter, summarizing its main points ... **5 minutes**
Present introductory thoughts for opening discussions ... **5 minutes**
Read Scriptures related to that chapter ... **5 minutes**
Guide deeper discussion of sub-sections ... **50 minutes**
Draw discussions to a close with some final thoughts ... **5 minutes**
Conclude by facilitating a time of prayer over the issues ... **10 minutes**

This is just a sample. Feel free to make adjustments to fit the timeframe you have.

CHRIST HUDDLES are a first step — but it no small step — in a *Campaign of Hope* right where you live! However you put them to use, they provide an effective way to help believers re-discover Christ for *all* that He is and recover *all* the hope they are meant to have.

APPENDIX III

GIVING CREDIT
The People Behind the Book

In a recent issue of *AAAWorld* magazine an article called "To Build a Big Jesus" told of a team of workmen laboring outside Tijuana, Mexico. Their goal? To create a statue for their city the size of the famous sculpture that dominates the skyline of Rio de Janeiro. In a sense, my vision for the greatness of Jesus has been "under construction" over many decades — but no more so than over the last eight years as I've worked on this *Joyful Manifesto*. Like the project in Tijuana, however, it really took a *team* effort.

To switch metaphors: For years I've matriculated through a "college of Christology", mentored by a distinguished "faculty". Without them I could not have written about the Lord of Glory the way I have.

Let Me Introduce You to My "Personal Mentors"!

First of all, for over 15 years I was tutored by nearly two dozen board members under the chairmanships of John Kyle (a close spiritual father) and Richard Griggs (a true spiritual brother). Guiding the ministry of *PROCLAIM HOPE!* (previously called *Concerts of Prayer International*), this board exhibited a sacrificial love for the lordship of Jesus I can never forget.

Second, across the decades additional clusters of Christian leaders have deeply affected my heart for the glory of Christ, my hope in His promises and my passion for His Kingdom. Some of my best teachers have included members of the following: America's

National Prayer Committee (founded by Vonette Bright); the Mission America Coalition (served ably by Paul Cedar); the National Revival Network (chaired by Dale Schlafer); and Concerts of Prayer Greater New York (a coalition of hundreds of pastors mobilized by Mac Pier). I must also include the leaders of a number of organizations involved with the Evangelicals for Social Action (facilitated by Ron Sider); the Christian Community Development Association (spearheaded by John Perkins); the Lausanne Committee for World Evangelization (particularly during the tenure of Leighton Ford); the A.D. 2000 and Beyond Movement (coordinated by Luis Bush); and the U.S. Center for World Mission (founded by Ralph Winter).

I've gained so much from my church family, too: The Presbyterian Church at New Providence (New Jersey). They served as a Christ-exalting "sending base", empowering me to proclaim this Message of Hope across the world over the past decade. I'm especially grateful for the members who have met with me weekly to pray for Kingdom-sized breakthroughs. How much I've learned from them!

I find myself indebted daily to Juli Kuhl, Director of Operations for *PROCLAIM HOPE!*, whose down-to-earth wisdom as well as love for Jesus has been poured into this ministry (and into this book) through an extraordinary mosaic of gifts.

Let me thank Curt Olson, for 15 years the post-producer for our national radio program *Hope for America*, broadcast on over 300 stations daily. I hasten to list a cadre who worked with me to bring this book into being, including a team of 15 "readers" consisting of pastors, scholars, lay leaders, ministry heads, and youth. They went through the manuscript with me chapter by chapter to provide invaluable input. (You know who you are!) I'm grateful for additional assistance from Brad Bush, Kathy Davis, Steve Hall, Rick Kress, Bill Sahlman and Eddie Smith.

A special word of thanks is extended to Roland and Lila Hinz, John and Wendy Beckett, Bob and Carolyn Ernest, Jerry and Nancy Jackson, Howard and Katie Williams, and Dick and Lois Griggs whose faithful Christ-ward involvement with me helped keep this manifesto project alive over the long haul.

Never could I overestimate how my vision for Christ's glory has been profoundly shaped by the spiritual depth of my precious life-partner, Robyne. I have no greater earthly teacher.

Now, Please Meet My More "Formal Faculty"!

Credit is due to a team of servant-scholars whose hearts and minds lie behind many of my insights on the Christ, the crisis and the cure. During my sojourn in God's "university on supremacy", these key women and men have sharpened my understanding of what it really means to say *Christ Is ALL!* Their perspectives were and are invaluable.

Most of the volumes listed below can be ordered on-line through **Amazon.com** or **Barnes&Noble.com**. Obviously, as indicated by older copyright dates on some, I've been enrolled in the "school of hope" for quite a few years! Still, I'm convinced each book remains relevant to anyone's efforts at proclaiming God's Son to the 21ˢᵗ century.

To this "formal faculty" — *and above all to the Holy Spirit-inspired authors of the 66 books of the Bible* — I am indebted for my growing understanding on the Biblical, theological, historical, contemporary, practical, existential and eternal dimensions of the supremacy of Christ. **To each one I want to say:** For whatever positive blessings *Joyful Manifesto* brings to the Body of Christ, you are to be thanked. For wherever it misses the mark, I alone assume full responsibility.

BIBLICAL AND THEOLOGICAL FOUNDATIONS

Armstrong, John H., Editor, *The Glory of Christ* (2002)

Blackaby, Henry, *Experiencing God: How to Live the Full Adventure of Knowing and Doing the Will of God* (1994)

Blauw, Johannes, *The Missionary Nature of the Church* (1962)

Bloesch, Donald G., *The Struggle of Prayer: Taking Hold of God's Outstretched Hand* (1988)

Bonhoeffer, Dietrich, *Christ the Center* (1960), *The Cost of Discipleship* (1934)

Bright, John, *The Kingdom of God: The Biblical Concept and Its Meaning for the Church* (1953), *A History of Israel* (1974)

Brown, Raymond, *Christ ABOVE All: The Message of Hebrews* (1982)

Buchanon, Mark, *Things Unseen: Living in Light of Forever* (2002)

Cantalamessa, Raniero, *Life in the Lordship of Christ* (1990)

Chapell, Bryan, *Christ-Centered Preaching: Redeeming the Expository Sermon* (1994)

Clouse, Robert G., Editor, *The Meaning of the Millennium: Four Views* (1977)

Clowney, Edmund, *Preaching Christ in All of Scripture* (2003)

Coleman, Robert E., *The Mind of the Master* (2000)

Conn, Harvie M., *Evangelism: Doing Justice and Preaching Grace* (1982)

Crabb, Larry, *Finding God* (1993)

David, John Jefferson, *Christ's Victorious Kingdom: Postmillennialism Reconsidered* (1986)

Dyrness, William, *Themes in Old Testament Theology* (1979)

Eastman, Dick, *Heights of Delight* (2002), *Patterns of Delight* (2002), *Rivers of Delight* (2002)

Edwards, James R., *The Divine Intruder: When God Breaks into Your Life* (2000)

Eldredge, John, *The Sacred Romance: Drawing Closer to the Heart of God* (1997)

Ellul, Jacques, *Hope in Time of Abandonment* (1972)

Fernando, Ajith, *The Supremacy of Christ* (1995)

Frangipane, Francis, *The Days of His Presence* (1997), *The House of the Lord* (1992)

Fry, Steve, *I AM: The Unveiling of God* (2000), *Rekindled Flame* (2002)

Fuller, Daniel P., *The Unity of the Bible: Unfolding God's Plan for Humanity* (1992)

George, Timothy, *Theology of the Reformers* (1999), *Amazing Grace: God's Initiative — Our Response* (2000), *For All the Saints: Evangelical Theology and Christian Spirituality* (2003)

Glasser, Arthur F., *Announcing the Kingdom: The Story of God's Mission in the Bible* (2003)

Goerner, H. Cornell, *All Nations in God's Purpose: What the Bible Teaches about Missions* (1979)

Goldsworthy, Graeme, *Preaching the Whole Bible as Christian Scripture* (2000)

Green, Michael, *I Believe in Satan's Downfall* (1981)

Greidanus, Sidney, *Preaching Christ from the Old Testament* (1999)

Gruber, Darrell, *The Continuing Conversion of the Church* (2000)

Hahn, Scott, *The Supper of the Lamb: The Mass as Heaven on Earth* (1999)

Hayford, Jack, *Glory on Your House: Welcoming God's Radiant Presence in Your Home and Church* (1995), *Worship His Majesty: How Praising the King of Kings Will Change Your Life* (2000), *A Passion for Fullness* (1994), *Pastors of Promise: Pointing to Character and Hope as the Keys to Fruitful Shepherding* (1993), *The Anatomy of Seduction: Defending Your Heart for God* (2004),

Hettinga, Jan David, *Follow Me: Experience the Loving Leadership of Jesus* (1996)

Hockema, Anthony, *The Bible and the Future* (1979)

Jones, E. Stanley, *The Unshakeable Kingdom and the Unchanging Person* (1972), *The Christ of the Roundtable* (1937)

Ladd, George Eldon, *A Theology of the New Testament (1974), Jesus Christ and History* (1963)

Langman III, Tremper, *God Is a Warrior: Studies in Old Testament Biblical Theology* (1995)

Lewis, C. S., This Cambridge don authored classic books on the Christian faith that impacted my thinking. Titles include: *Mere Christianity, The Problem of Pain, Miracles, The Four Loves, The Great Divorce* and his *Tales of Narnia* (six books) that explore the implications of the supremacy of Christ from a child's perspective.

Lloyd-Jones, Martyn, *The Kingdom of God* (1992), *The Christian Warfare: An Exposition of Ephesians 6:10-13* (1976), *Revival* (1987), *Joy Unspeakable: Power and Renewal in the Holy Spirit* (1984)

Lovelace, Richard F., *Dynamics of Spiritual Life: An Evangelical Theology of Renewal* (1979)

Lucas, R. C., *Fullness and Freedom: The Message of Colossians and Philemon* (1980)**Lutzer, Erwin**, *Your Eternal Reward: Triumph and Tears at the Judgment Seat of Christ* (1998), *The Vanishing Power of Death* (2004)

MacLeod, Donald, *The Person of Christ: Contours of Christian Theology* (1998)

Manning, Brennan, *The Ragamuffin Gospel* (2000)

McGrath, Alister, *A Brief History of Heaven* (2003), *Knowing Christ* (2002)

Miller, Paul E., *Love Walked Among Us: Learning to Love Like Jesus* (2001)

Morris, Leon, *The Apostolic Preaching of the Cross* (1955)

Mostrom, Donald G., *Spiritual Privileges You Didn't Know Were Yours* (1986)

Mounce, Robert H., *The Book of Revelation* (1998)

Neill, Stephen, *The Supremacy of Jesus* (1984)

Newbigin, Leslie, *Signs Amid the Rubble: The Purposes of God in Human History* (2003)

Packer, J.I., *Celebrating the Saving Work of God* (1998), *Serving the People of God* (1998), *Knowing God* (1973), *Evangelism and the Sovereignty of God* (1969), *A Quest for Godliness* (1994)

Payne, J. Barton, *The Theology of the Older Testament* (1962)

Peterson, Eugene, *The Message: The Bible in Contemporary Language* (2002)

Pink, Arthur W., *The Sovereignty of God* (1928)

Piper, John, This pastor/scholar and author of over 30 books has greatly influenced my thinking on Christ at many points. I recommend: *The Supremacy of God in Preaching, Seeing and Savoring Jesus Christ, Let the Nations Be Glad, God's Passion for His Glory, The Passion of Jesus Christ, Desiring God*, along with many others. A full listing can be found by going to www.desiringGOD.org.

Ramm, Bernard L., *An Evangelical Christology: Ecumenic and Historic* (1985)

Rhodes, Tricia McCary, *Contemplating the Cross: A Life-Changing Encounter with the Crucified Christ* (1998), *At the Name of Jesus: Meditations on the Exalted Christ* (2003)

Simpson, A.B., *The Christ in the Bible Commentary, Volumes I-VI* (1993)

Snyder, Howard S., *The Community of the King* (1997), *A Kingdom Manifesto: Calling the Church to Live under God's Reign* (1985)

Stafford, Tim, *Knowing the Face of God* (1996)

Stott, John. R.W., *The Cross of Christ* (1986), *God's New Society: The Message of Ephesians* (1979)

Strobel, Lee, *The Case for Christ: A Journalist's Personal investigation of the Evidence for Jesus* (1998)

Swindoll, Charles A., *The Grace Awakening* (1996)

Tada, Joni Eareckson, *When God Weeps: Why Our Sufferings Matter to the Almighty* (1997)

Tippett, Alan R., *Verdict Theology in Missionary Theory* (1972)

Tozer, A.W., *Jesus, Author of Our Faith* (1988), *The Pursuit of God* (1948), *Worship: The Missing Jewel* (1992), *The Divine Conquest* (1952)

Travis, Stephen H., *Christian Hope and the Future* (1980)

Trueblood, Elton, *The Validity of the Christian Mission* (1972)

Warren, Rick, *The Purpose Driven Life: What On Earth Am I Here For?* (2002)

Wells, David F., *The Person of Christ: A Biblical and Historical Analysis of the Incarnation* (1984)

Willard, Dallas, *The Divine Conspiracy: Rediscovering Our Hidden Life in God* (1998)

Woodbridge, John (Editor, with others), *This We Believe: The Good News of Jesus Christ for the World* (2000)

Wright, N.T., *The Challenge of Jesus: Rediscovering Who Jesus Was and Is* (1999)

Yancy, Philip, *The Jesus I Never Knew* (1995), *Disappointment with God: Three Questions No One Asks Aloud* (1988)

Zacharias, Ravi, *Jesus Among Other Gods: The Absolute Claims of the Christian Faith* (2000)

HISTORICAL BACKGROUND

Bakke, Robert O., *The Power of Extraordinary Prayer: The Concert of Prayer* (2000)

Bercot, David W., Editor, *A Dictionary of Early Christian Beliefs* (1998)

Bettenson, Henry, *Documents of the Christian Church* (1963)

Dallimore, Arnold A., *George Whitefield: The Life and Times of the Great Evangelist of the Eighteenth-Century Revival, Volumes I, II* (1979)

DeBase, Francis M., Editor, *Classics of Christian Mission* (1979)

Drewery, Mary, *William Carey: A Biography* (1978)

Edwards, Jonathan, *An Humble Attempt to Promote Explicit Agreement and Visible Union of God's People, in Extraordinary Prayer, for the Revival of Religion and the Advancement of Christ's Kingdom on Earth, Pursuant to Scripture Promises and Prophecies Concerning the Last Time* (1747)

Fox, Richard, *Jesus in America: A History* (2004)

Graham, Billy, *Just As I Am: The Autobiography of Billy Graham* (1997)

Hopkins, C. Howard, *John R. Mott: A Biography* (1979)

Fox, Richard Wightman, *Jesus in America: Personal Savior, Cultural Hero, National Obsession* (2004)

Latourette, Kenneth Scott, *A History of Christianity* (1953)

Lawson, John, *The Wesley Hymns: A Guide to Scriptural Teaching* (1987)

Maus, Cynthia Pearl, Editor, *Christ and the Fine Arts: An Anthology of Pictures, Poetry, Music and Stories Centering on the Life of Christ* (1938)

McCasland, David, Oswald Chambers: *Abandoned to God* (1993)

Murray, Andrew, *The Key to the Missionary Problem* (1900), *The State of the Church* (1910)

Murray, Iain, *The Puritan Hope: Revival and the Interpretation of Prophecy* (1971)

Noll, Mark A. (Editor, with others), *Eerdmans' Handbook to Christianity in America* (1983)

Porter, Ebenezer, *Letters on Revival* (1830)

Prothero, Stephen, *American Jesus: How the Son of God Became a National Icon* (2003)

Smith, Michael A., *From Christ to Constantine* (1971)

Ton, Josef, *Suffering, Martyrdom and Rewards in Heaven* (1997)

Tucker, Ruth A., *From Jerusalem to Irian Jaya: A Biographical History of Christian Missions* (1983)**Webber, Robert**, *The Majestic Tapestry: How the Power of Early Christian Tradition Can Enrich Contemporary Faith* (1986)

Whitefield, George, *Journals* (1947), *Letters* (1771)

CONTEMPORARY ISSUES

Armstrong, John H., Editor, *The Coming Evangelical Crisis: Current Challenges to the Authority of Scripture and the Gospel* (1996), *When God Moves: Preparing for True Revival* (1998)

Bakke, Raymond, *A Theology as Big as the City* (1997)

Barna, George, *The Second Coming of the Church: A Blueprint for Survival* (1998), *The Power of Vision: How You Can Capture and Apply God's Vision for Your Ministry* (1992), *Today's Pastor: A Revealing Look at What Pastors Are Saying about Themselves, Their Peers and the Pressures they Face* (1993), *Think Like Jesus (2003), Grow Your Church from Outside in* (2002). See further at *www.barna.org*.

Barrett, David, *World Christian Encyclopedia* (1998)

Bloesch, Donald G., *Faith and Its Counterfeits* (1981)

Bryant, David, *In the Gap: What It Means to Be a World Christian* (1979), *Concerts of Prayer: Christians United for Spiritual Awakening and World Evangelization* (1986), *The Hope at Hand: National and World Revival for the Twenty-First Century* (1995), *Messengers of Hope: Agents of Revival for the Twenty First Century* (1997), *Stand in the Gap: How to Prepare for the Coming World Revival* (1997)

Clegg, Tom; Bird, Warren, *Lost in America: How You and Your Church Can Impact the World Next Door* (2001)

Colson, Charles, *Kingdoms in Conflict: An insider's Challenging View of Politics, Power and the Pulpit* (1997), *Against the Night: Living in the New Dark Ages* (1989), *The Body: Being Light in the Darkness* (1992)

Dawson, John, *Healing America's Wounds* (1994)

Delbanco, Andrew, *The Real American Dream: A Meditation on Hope* (1999)

Dennison, Jack, *City Reaching: On the Road to Community Transformation* (1999)

Gallup, George H. Jr., *The Saints Among Us: How the Spiritually Committed Are Changing Our World* (1992); *Surveying the Religious Landscape* (2001)

Gaudzwaard, Bob, *Idols of Our Time* (1981)

Gellmand, Rabbi Marc; Hartman, Monsignor Thomas, *Religion for Dummies: A Reference for the Rest of Us* (2002)

Gladwell, Malcolm, *The Tipping Point: How Little Things Can Make a Big Difference* (2000)

Graham, Franklin, *The Name* (2002)

Greenway, Roger, *Discipling the City: A Comprehensive Approach to Urban Mission* (1992)

Guinness, Os, *No God But God: Breaking with the Idols of Our Age* (1992)

Henry, Carl F. H., *Twilight of a Great Civilization: The Drift toward Neo-Paganism* (1988)

Hunter, James Davidson, *American Evangelicalism: Conservative Religion and the Quandary of Modernity* (1983), *Evangelicalism: The Coming Generation* (1987)

Jenkins, Philip, *The Next Generation: The Coming of Global Christianity* (2002)

John Paul II, *Crossing the Threshold of Hope* (1994); *Jesus: Son and Savior* (1996).

Johnson, Jon, *Will Evangelicalism Survive Its Own Popularity?* (1980)

Johnstone, Patrick, *Operation World: A Country by Country Analysis of Global Christianity* (2001)

Kimbell, Dan, *The Emerging Church: Vintage Christianity for New Generations* (2003)

Kroll, Woodrow, *Hope Grows in Winter: Inspiring Real-life Stories of How Hope Changes Lives* (2000)

Kuster, Volker, *The Many Faces of Jesus Christ: Intercultural Christology* (1999)

Lucado, Max, *And the Angels Were Silent* (1998)

Lutzer, Erwin, *Christ Among Other Gods: A Defense of Christ in an Age of Tolerance* (1994), *Seven Convincing Miracles: Understanding the Claims of Christ in Today's Culture* (1999)

McCullough, Donald W., *The Trivialization of God: The Dangerous Illusion of a Manageable Deity* (1995)

MacDonald, Gordon, *The Life God Blesses: Weathering the Storms of Life that Threaten the Soul* (1997), *Christ Followers in the Real World* (1991), *In Search of Resilience* (2004)

Myers, David G., *The American Paradox: Spiritual Hunger in an Age of Plenty* (2001)

Neill, Stephen, *Christian Faith and Other Faiths: The Christian Dialogue with Other Religions* (1970)

Neuhaus, Richard John, *The Naked Public Square: Religion and Democracy in America* (1984)

Padilla, C. Rene, Editor, *The New Face of Evangelicalism: An International Symposium on the Lausanne Covenant* (1976)

Pier, Mackenzie; **Sweeting, Katie**, *The Power of a City at Prayer: What Happens When Churches Unite for Renewal* (2002)

Schaeffer, Francis A., *The Great Evangelical Disaster* (1984)

Schaller, Lyle, *Discontinuity and Hope: Radical Change and the Path to the Future* (1999)

Sider, Ronald J., *One-Sided Christianity? Uniting the Church to Heal a Lost and Broken World* (1994), *Evangelicals and Development: Toward a Theology of Social Change* (1981)

Silvoso, Ed, *That None Should Perish: How to Reach Entire Cities for Christ Through Prayer Evangelism* (1994)

Sine, Tom, Wild Hope: *Crises Facing the Human Community on the Threshold of the Twenty-First Century* (1991)

Slaughter, Michael, *Unlearning Church: Just When You Thought You Had Leadership All Figured Out!* (2002)

Smail, Thomas A., *The Forgotten Father* (2001)

Sweet, Leonard, *First Century Passion for the Twenty-First Century World* (2000)

Tutu, Archbishop Desmond, *Suffering and Hope* (1985)

Wallis, Jim, *The Call to Conversion: Rediscovering the Gospel for These Times* (1981)

White, John, *The Golden Cow: Materialism in the Twentieth Century Church* (1979)

Wolfe, Alan, *The Transformation of American Religion: How We Actually Live Our Faith* (2003)

APPENDIX IV
NINE THESES
That Support the Book

Many have asked about the underlying assumptions on which CHRIST IS ALL! is built. Actually there are nine, woven throughout the twelve chapters. I call them the "Nine Theses". Both a Summary Version *and an* Expanded Version *are presented below.*

THE SUMMARY VERSION

Thesis One

We can have everlasting hope in *Christ* based on all that He is as Lord: This hope is one of God's primary *gifts* to the nations through His Son.

Thesis Two

Christ dominates the *focus* of our hope: This defines the *glory* of His supremacy.

Thesis Three

Christ rules over the *fulfillment* of our hope: This defines the *magnitude* of His supremacy.

Thesis Four

Christ embodies the *fullness* of our hope: This defines the *riches* of His supremacy.

Thesis Five

Christ shapes the *fervency* of our hope: This defines the *intensity* of His supremacy.

Thesis Six

A *crisis* of supremacy exists throughout the Church today: It is a crisis of Christology. It is robbing us of the *hope* and *passion* toward Christ and His Kingdom that He rightfully desires and deserves.

Thesis Seven

The crisis of supremacy can be effectively *cured:* Hope and passion toward Christ, for *all* that He is, can be reawakened and restored throughout the Church.

Thesis Eight

The cure for the crisis consists of *proclaiming* Christ inside the Church for all that He is, taking Christians *captive* to the hope we have in His supremacy and helping them to *get ready* for greater displays of His Kingdom.

Thesis Nine

The cure calls for a new initiative — a *Campaign of Hope* that involves Christians in three strategic roles: Messengers of Hope, Prisoners of Hope and Vanguards of Hope.

THE EXPANDED VERSION

1. **I believe that ...** one of the greatest gifts God offers, both to His people and to the nations, is a comprehensive *hope,* for now and forever, based on Christ and the full extent of His *supremacy.* This hope is tied to who He is as the Son of God, where He leads in the Purposes of God, how He imparts the Resources of God and what He receives from the People of God.

2. **I believe that ...** for the Church to experience the deepest impact of God-given hope, our vision of Christ and His supremacy must be shaped by nothing less than the thousands of Biblical promises that give expression to His supremacy — to its Focus (Son), Fulfillment (Purpose), Fullness (Resources) and Fervency (People).

3. **This is true because ...** every promise that Christ will fulfill when His supremacy is manifested in the consummation of all things, He embodies *already,* making *Him* the supreme hope for our generation, just as fully as He will be in the End.

4. **This is true because ...** whatever Christ will be Lord of when His supremacy is manifested in the consummation of all things, He is Lord of *already,* making *Him* the supreme hope for our generation, just as fully as He will be in the End.

5. **This is true because ...** in the same way Christ will be seen as both center and circumference for the life of the redeemed when His supremacy is manifested in the consummation of all things, He reigns *already* as the center and circumference of His Church today — once again making *Him* the supreme hope for our generation, just as fully as He will be in the End.

6. **Therefore, I'm convinced that** ... wherever this larger vision of Christ and His supremacy has been diminished and neglected in the Church — wherever Christians struggle with a shortfall of hope about God's promises in Christ as well as succumb to sagging passion for the advancement of God's Kingdom in Christ — we face a critical *crisis* that impacts every facet of the Church's life of worship, prayer, discipleship, community, compassion, service and mission.

7. **Therefore, I'm convinced that** ... for the sake of God's glory in His people and among the nations, this crisis calls for multitudes throughout the Church to be *re-awakened* to fresh hope and passion, focused on Christ and the full extent of His supremacy; and, to be *re-converted* back to Christ for ALL that He is.

8. **Consequently, I urge that** ... for the sake of God's glory in His people and among the nations, committed Christians everywhere must render to Christ *strategic service on three fronts:*

   - We must **proclaim** among fellow believers a message of hope that *redirects their faith* toward Christ and His supremacy.

   - We must **awaken** fully within fellow believers the call of hope that *re-ignites their passion* for Christ and His supremacy.

   - We must **empower** fellow believers with a strategy of hope that *reorders their daily discipleship* under Christ and His supremacy.

9. **Consequently, I urge that** ... a broad-based **Campaign of Hope** be mobilized immediately throughout the Body of Christ, summoning believers to assume *three primary roles:*

   - To become **Messengers of Hope** who take every opportunity to proclaim to fellow Christians the full extent of Christ's supremacy and the hope we have in Him.

   - To become **Prisoners of Hope** who expand and deepen their own vision of Christ, growing with a consuming passion for Christ and the hope based on His supremacy.

   - To become **Vanguards of Hope** who band together as *Messengers* and *Prisoners,* sharing a lifestyle focused on the supremacy of Christ and pursuing among the nations greater manifestations of the hope of His Kingdom.

APPENDIX V
KEY PASSAGES
on Hope and the
Supremacy of God's Son

The next few pages contain samplings from Scripture that set forth the two great themes of this *Joyful Manifesto: supremacy* and *hope*.

Referencing certain Old Testament customs and traditions, the Apostle Paul reminds us: "These are a shadow of the things that were to come; the reality, however, is found in Christ" (Col. 2). A shadow can be useful in providing shade or in alerting us that someone is approaching. But ultimately a shadow calls attention to something beyond itself — to the object that casts it. In the end, shadows suggest the shape of something far more vivid and tangible and useful and lasting. Similarly, Old Testament texts on God's supremacy as well as the hope shaped around that supremacy, foreshadow (point us toward) the fuller revelation of New Testament teachings on His Son. For millennia God's covenant promises were anchored exclusively in the sovereignty of His character and actions.

But then, in the "fullness of times" (Gal. 4) the promises burst forth with a whole new level of reality, in clear view of the nations. They sprang into the foreground of world history by the incarnation of our Savior who, by virtue of His preeminence at the Father's right hand, elicited one unanimous confession from the Church: "Jesus is Lord" (1 Cor. 12; Rom. 10). Early Christians were convinced that Jesus embodied in Himself everything the Bible claimed about God's greatness and everything His Kingdom guaranteed. The closing verses of Isaiah 45, for example, compared with the opening verses of Philippians 2 provide just one of a thousand illustrations of how 1st century believers linked the "shadows of supremacy" with the exaltation of the risen Jesus over all.

Thus, as you study Old Testament selections below, let this be one of your major goals:

to determine how ancient visions of God's awesomeness — whether from Moses or David, Job or Malachi — along with dramatic stories of God's activities, as recorded in Exodus or 2 Chronicles or Daniel, provide hints of more to come. How are they shadows *when compared* to how the visions ultimately found expression and culmination in the person and reign of His Son? In other words, how does our Lord Jesus "sum up" and "flesh out" what the Old Testament sets forth about supremacy and hope?

If more in-depth analysis of any passage is desired, try using one of the guides to inductive Bible study outlined in Chapter 10 *(Messengers of Hope)*. They are designed to help you unlock the teaching of God's Word on the glory of Jesus, both Old and New Testaments.

Whatever approach you use to dig into the texts below, in the end make it your mission to mine-out of each at least one insight on the four major dimensions of Christ's supremacy defined by *Joyful Manifesto*. Focus, Fulfillment, Fullness and Fervency. And as you do, ask yourself: How does this insight increase my *hope* in Him as well as my *passion* for Him?

One final note: I've given you chapter references only for each theme. Even though in some cases the title I've suggested for a text applies to just a portion of a chapter, reading the entire chapter will ensure a better grasp of context and thus a more faithful interpretation of the relevant verses.

THE OLD TESTAMENT: CHRIST'S SUPREMACY FORESHADOWED

GENESIS

EXODUS

LEVITICUS

NUMBERS

9-10 — Led by God with a Cloud and a Trumpet

16-17 — God Vindicates Aaron as High Priest

24 — Two Oracles from Balaam about God's Kingdom

DEUTERONOMY

8 — Honor God for His Supremacy

10-11 — Hold Fast to God in His Supremacy

30 — Return to God and His Supremacy

33 — Moses Sets Great Hope in God Before the People

JOSHUA

1-4 — God's Commission and Mission for Joshua

5-6 — God's Supremacy Manifested over a City

24 — Renewing a Covenant with God Full of Hope

JUDGES

5 — Deborah's Song about God's Deliverance

6-7 — God Leads the People Through Gideon

1 SAMUEL

7 — Samuel Rules the People at Mizpah

16-17 — David Anointed as King of All God's People

2 SAMUEL

5 — The Nation Unites under the Headship of David

7 — God's Covenant with His King

23 — How God's King Rules

1 KINGS

8 — The King Dedicates a Center of Worship

18-19 — The Prophet Proclaims the Supremacy of God

2 KINGS

4-5 — The Prophet Demonstrates the Supremacy of God

1 CHRONICLES

12 — The King and His Army

28-29 — Focusing the People on the Glory of God

2 CHRONICLES

14-15 — God's King Experiences His Sovereignty in Revival

17, 20 — God's King Experiences His Sovereignty in Battle

29-32 — God's King Experiences His Sovereignty in Transformation

34-35 — God's King Experiences His Sovereignty in Reformation

EZRA

1, 3, 9 — Recovery and Renewal under God's Chosen Leader

NEHEMIAH

1, 2, 4 — Restoration and Reconstruction under God's Chosen Leader

THE NEW TESTAMENT:
CHRIST'S SUPREMACY REVEALED

Note: Gospel texts that are repeated by more than one writer are presented in only one of the samplings from the Gospels.

APPENDIX VI
ANOTHER APPROACH
To Defining "Supremacy"

The core of Christ's supremacy — what gives increased substance to who He is as the Son of God, where He leads in the Purposes of God, how He imparts the Resources of God, and what He receives from the People of God — could be expressed in an entirely different way than we've explained it in this book. Sometimes I like to distill it down to just a few *prepositions*. Actually, these seven words might provide a strong outline for a follow-up book to *CHRIST IS ALL!* But for now, let me provide you with this brief summary of my thoughts.

Christ's supremacy incorporates ALL He is in seven key areas:

- **TO us**
- **FOR us**
- **OVER us**
- **BEFORE us**
- **WITHIN us**
- **THROUGH us**
- **UPON us**

Such simple words! Yet, I submit to you, *everything* Scripture presents to us about the glory of the Savior — everything about the Focus, Fulfillment, Fullness and Fervency of His reign — can be sliced a whole other way by these seven phrases. Each preposition proclaims the primacy of the Person whom we must adore through endless ages ... and why He is to be adored. The phrases provide working material for constructing an exciting Biblical "resumé" for God's Son, a resumé we can freely share with others.

To show you how quickly each preposition opens up magnificent vistas on our Victor, let me retrace each with you. Using verses from Colossians 1 to illustrate, let me highlight what is implied by each. I'll show you how they can enhance the four-part definition of Christ's lordship established in this book.

TO us ... This speaks of how His supremacy is eternally rooted in His nature, His character, and His Trinitarian existence as the Son of the Father. This is one way to describe our FOCUS on who He is to us. We read in Colossians 1 — "God was pleased to have all His fullness dwell in Him" (vs. 19).

FOR us ... This includes how His supremacy became fully visible through His incarnation: His righteous life, Spirit-filled ministry and teachings; as well as His Crucifixion, Resurrection, Ascension, and on-going intercession. This is another example of how He is the FOCUS of supremacy. We read in Colossians 1 — "through Him to reconcile to Himself all things ... through His blood" (vs. 20).

OVER us ... He is supreme-to-the-max as Ruler of history and Lord over the nations. But above all, He reigns as Head of the Church, called "the fullness of Him who fills all in all" (Eph. 1). Paul writes of the FULFILLMENT that comes to all over whom He rules — "rescued ... brought into the Kingdom of the Son He loves ... firstborn over all creation ... from among the dead ... head of the body, the Church ... all things whether things on earth or things in heaven" (vs. 13, 15, 18).

BEFORE us ... Supremacy is displayed also by His pioneering leadership. He endows His people with new dreams and visions for serving His cause. Then He strikes out ahead of us to open doors for the Kingdom. He scatters the strongholds of dark powers to take us where we've never gone before. He brings God's purposes to their ordained climax. With other phrases from Colossians 1 Paul encourages us to expect the FULFILLMENT of Christ's grand designs as He goes before us — "in Him all things hold together ... He is the firstborn from among the dead ... all over the world this gospel is bearing fruit and growing" (vs. 17, 18, 6)

WITHIN us ... He reveals His supremacy wherever His saving presence, holy God-like characteristic, inexhaustible wisdom and multiple ministry gifts are lived out by His Spirit within the community of His people. He changes them individually and corporately. Paul also teaches the Colossians of the FULLNESS Jesus puts within us — "Christ in [among] you, the hope of glory ... asking God to fill you ... share in the inheritance of the saints in the kingdom of light ... live a life a life worthy of the Lord" (vs. 27, 9, 12, 10).

THROUGH us ... This points to how His reign reaches out by His Spirit through His Church to the unreached of the earth, both neighbors and nations. He works in union with

His people to further His mission worldwide. Here's another demonstration of Christ's FULLNESS in our life with Him — "The commission God gave me ... to make known among the nations the glorious riches of this mystery, which is Christ ... to this end I labor, struggling with all His energy He so powerfully works in me" (vs. 29).

UPON us ... This reminds us that He is passionate for the consummation of all things in His reign. Sometimes His glory breaks through by frequent outpourings of the Holy Spirit for the renewal and revival of His Church. At these times He intensifies and accelerates the previous six displays of His supremacy. The "upon us" dimension, however, awaits its climax in His spectacular, bodily return to bring His victories to bear upon all Creation forever. One way we embrace this all-consuming destiny is by our FERVENCY for Him now. Paul speaks of this — "Him we proclaim, teaching every person and warning every person that we might present every person complete in Christ ... please him in every way: bearing fruit in every good work, being strengthened with all power according to his glorious might" (28, 10-11).

What a resumé this is! No wonder Paul sums up the magnitude of this seven-fold vision of God's Son with that one decisive declaration in vs. 18:

" ... that in everything He might have the supremacy."

APPENDIX VII

HOW TO PROCLAIM AND PRAY
Our Hope in the Supremacy of God's Son

In one form or another the grid presented below has been shared with audiences around the world over the past 20 years. In one picture it represents everything a Christian might speak or seek related to the supremacy of God's Son. Most of the topics and truths included in what Paul calls "the whole counsel of God" (Acts 20) are captured in one or more of the 24 boxes you see there. *It's that simple!*

Of course, an appendix isn't the place to go into detail on how the grid works. For now let me give you the following guidelines:

THE SIX R's —
SIX RESPONSES TO CHRIST'S SUPREMACY

The six R's down the side represent major responses to the glorious greatness of our Grand King, whether in the hearts of our hearers (as we speak — see chapter 10) or in their prayers (as we seek — see chapter 12).

Our prayers, for example, may take the form of worship, praise and celebration regarding one or more of the four dimensions of the supremacy of Christ (the **Rejoice** expression). At the same time, any message we proclaim about the Savior (whether in personal conversation or before a larger group) ought to elicit from our hearers the same spirit of rejoicing — delight, excitement, praise — over who the Lord Jesus is. Quite naturally a heart response to a vision of hope and supremacy can be translated easily into a prayer response by helping our hearers take our message back to God with expressions of thanksgiving and joy.

Similarly, enlarging peoples' outlook on Christ will stir conviction over sin (or systems) that, either individually or corporately, grieve the Holy Spirit — or quench His revelations to us of the glory of the King, or rob others of the blessing of beholding Christ's supremacy in the life of His people. That's when the **Repent** response becomes appropriate. Every Message of Hope should call for repentance at some point (see chapter 11), and then help Christians express broken hearts by how they pray.

This same approach applies to the other responses: **Resist** (pinpointing where Satan opposes the advance of Christ's Kingdom as well as praying for his strongholds to be broken); **Request** (proclaiming and praying some of the thousands of promises regarding each facet of Christ's supremacy and how God intends to manifest each to the Church and before the nations); **Receive** (calling our audiences to live every day expecting fresh demonstrations of Jesus' lordship, and then helping the people identify how He is already glorifying Himself — already exhibiting the focus, or fulfillment, or fullness, or fervency of His supremacy — in answer to our obedient prayers); **Recommit** (urging believers to yield to every implication of Christ's reign in our lives, leading them to consecrate themselves to the advance of His Kingdom and helping them to offer themselves to be used in any way God chooses to be an answer to any of our prayers, no matter what it costs us).

THE FOUR *F's* —
FOUR DIMENSIONS OF
CHRIST'S SUPREMACY

Look at the grid again. Please notice that any one of these six responses, whether expressed by prayer or through a ministry of the Word, can be (and should be) shaped by one or more of the key dimensions of Christ's supremacy, explored in-depth in this book (especially chapters 1-5).

For example, our worship (rejoicing) might celebrate some aspect of the nature and saving work of the Son of God *(Focus)*; or ways He is working victoriously to extend the Father's purposes for all the earth *(Fulfillment)*; or His manifest presence and activity with His people into whom He is pouring the resources of Heaven *(Fullness)*; or how He has been and is being glorified by the devotion and passion and service of the subjects of His Kingdom *(Fervency)*.

A similar approach works for each of the other six responses. We might call the people to repent and pray about indifference to His glory *(Focus)*; or apathy toward His mission *(Fulfillment)*, or hoarding His blessings *(Fullness)*, or withholding affections from Him *(Fervency)*.

In the same vein, we might proclaim some of the Kingdom promises touching each dimension of supremacy. Then we might move on to encourage fellow Christians to make it their priority (Request); summon them to greater hope over the ways God will manifest these four dimensions (Receive); and urge them to choose to live more fully at the center of who Christ is, where He is headed, what He does and how He is blessed. Then we could say so to God (Recommit).

The Grid

Just 24 squares ... representing everything Christians can speak and seek regarding the supremacy of God's Son!

Certainly, no one message — and no one prayer meeting — could cover all the issues at one time. But over time, in a congregation's experience of various proclamation ministries and prayer ministries, Christians should see themselves growing in the balance and breadth of knowing Christ and responding to Him along the lines suggested by this grid. I hope you find this tool helpful in serving those to whom God has sent you as a "Messenger of Hope."

	FOCUS	FULFILLMENT	FULLNESS	FERVENCY
REJOICE				
REPENT				
RESIST				
REQUEST				
RECEIVE				
RECOMMIT				

Appendix VIII
David Bryant

A Glimpse at the Man
Behind the Message

Former president of Concerts of Prayer International (COPI) and chairman of America's National Prayer Committee, over the past 30 years David Bryant has been defined as a "messenger of hope" and a "proclaimer of Christ" to the Church throughout the world.

Capitalizing on city-wide mass rallies; national and international conferences; training videos, seminars and manuals; development of leadership coalitions; the mentoring of younger leaders; and media outreach (both TV and radio), David has played a widely visible role in the emergence of an unprecedented, worldwide prayer movement. Many testify, however, that his key contribution to this movement always has been to help set its primary agenda: the hope of a God-given awakening among Christians everywhere to Christ for ALL that He is.

To that end, since January 2003 David Bryant has concentrated his efforts exclusively on his new mission outreach called *PROCLAIM HOPE!* The ministry emphasizes four major goals:

To proclaim a more comprehensive vision of Christ and His supremacy throughout the Church.

To awaken for all believers a life-changing hope focused on this larger vision of Christ and His supremacy.

To empower Christians and churches, and especially their leaders, by helping them grasp the dynamic hope in Christ that mobilizes God's people for new advances of Christ's Kingdom among the nations.

To equip other "Messengers of Hope" who are able to replicate the same mission: to proclaim, to awaken, to empower and to equip.

Taking his cue from Colossians 1:24-29, in every facet of **PROCLAIM HOPE!** he spreads this hope-filled message through a variety of outreaches: from city-wide *Christ Awakenings,* to *Christ Roundtables* for leaders, to a national daily radio broadcast called *Hope For America,* to the publishing of books and articles on the supremacy of Christ, to leadership mentoring, to national training activities such as *Christ Summits.*

David Bryant gives priority both to *proclaiming* a vision that promotes nothing less than a national (and even international) awakening to Christ and the full extent of His supremacy; as well as to *mobilizing* many others (especially leaders, at every level) to join him in what he calls a *Campaign of Hope.*

To follow-up his daily coast-to-coast radio program **(Hope for America)** David Bryant provides a one-of-a-kind website: **www.DavidBryantDirect.com**. There he offers a variety of his tools and books to be downloaded, many for free, in order to foster as widely as possible his message about Christ throughout the Body of Christ.

A popular speaker and author, David Bryant holds graduate degrees in both Biblical Studies and Missiology. A senior pastor in Ohio for six years; a missions trainer for three years in southern California; and minister-at-large with the Madison (WI)-based InterVarsity Christian Fellowship for twelve years, David founded and guided Concerts of Prayer International for 15 years. He also chaired America's National Prayer Committee for nine years (on which he still serves as a National Senior Advisor), and currently holds leadership roles with **PRAY! Magazine**, the **Mission America Coalition** and the **National Revival Network**. Among his writings are four key books: *In the Gap, With Concerts of Prayer, The Hope at Hand,* and *Messengers of Hope.*

David and his wife Robyne call metropolitan New York City their home. Their three grown children, Adam, Bethany and Benjamin, were all adopted as infants from India.

APPENDIX IX
DAVID BRYANT DIRECT
How to Benefit from David's Ministry and Website

Only a God-given reawakening to Christ and the full extent of His supremacy can resuscitate the Church's hope and passion, and re-engage her effectively in the worldwide advance of His Kingdom.

— **David Bryant**

Thank you for visiting ***www.DAVID BRYANT DIRECT.com***. Here we offer you a menu on David Bryant's multi-faceted ministry for Christ to the Church worldwide. First of all, we want you to know: In all we do, our main theme remains ...

"Awake To Christ For ALL That He Is!"

The icons you will find along the side of the home-page when you visit our website represent the fruits of David Bryant's 30-year ministry to the Body of Christ. There is much here that David would now like to share with YOU — freely!

To find out about our flagship ministry, click on the icon called **PROCLAIM HOPE!** There you'll learn more about David Bryant and his current outreaches. Also, you'll read about the reasons for the recent launch of our "National Campaign of Hope" to restore to the Church a dynamic hope based on the supremacy of Christ. You'll discover strategies for how this campaign might unfold right where you live.

OUR VISION
A Church awakened to the full extent of Christ's supremacy.

OUR MISSION
To awaken throughout the Church
fresh hope, passion, prayer and mission,
centered on the Lord Jesus Christ,
by proclaiming the full extent of His supremacy
and *by empowering* others to do the same.

OUR STRATEGIES
"Christ Awakenings"
(Vision-casting with larger audiences)

"Christ Roundtables"
(Vision-casting locally with strategic leaders)

"Christ Summits"
(Intensive leadership training)

"Christ Huddles"
(Curricula for small groups)

Website Resources
(Includes many of David's writings)

Strategic Alliances
"Hope For America"
(Daily national radio broadcast)

PROCLAIM HOPE!
PO Box 770
New Providence, New Jersey 07974

Phone 908.771.0146
Fax 908.665.4199

APPENDIX X
THINK WITH ME:

A Chapter by Chapter Outline Using the Embedded Reflection/Discussion Questions

As explained in Appendix I and II, the side-headings double as questions for personal reflection and small group discussion. This Appendix simply gives you an overview of all the issues waiting to be explored throughout the book. This can be especially helpful to the facilitator of a small group. Or, use the outline as a way of reflecting back over the book once you have finished reading it.

Chapter 1:
What are different ways Christian leaders identify the current crisis?
How much do we actually talk about God's Son to one another?
In what sense is Jesus missing in the evangelical movement today?
How does one demonstrate a "Person-driven" approach to discipleship?
In what other ways does our stumbling over supremacy show itself among us?
In what sense do we view Jesus as a mascot more than a monarch?
How might we begin to recover a vision for the supremacy of God's Son?
How would you define a Biblical vision of the supremacy of Christ?
What are the four dimensions of a "wide-angled vision" of Christ?
How can snapshots of supremacy ever capture the "mystery of God"?
Where does the suffering of Jesus fit into the supremacy of Jesus?
How does the supremacy of Christ take us beyond the centrality of Christ?
In what sense does Jesus' supremacy make Him the circumference of our lives?
How does Colossians picture the pinnacle of Jesus' preeminence?

Why does a vision of Christ's supremacy always cause hope to grow?

How could a campaign to recover hope become the antidote to the crisis of supremacy?

Is God calling you to move forward with such a campaign?

Chapter 2:

In what sense is it Christ's very nature to be the summation of all hope?

Who do you say that He is and what words would you use to say it?

In what ways is Christ the only focus for every bit of hope we have?

Why does it make sense to say our hope in God is "summed up" in Christ?

Where does the Trinity fit into the hope in Christ we confess?

How do Old Testament texts on creation prepare us for Jesus' majesty?

How does Jesus sum up the Old Testament's "shadows of supremacy"?

How did Christians look at the Old Testament through "Jesus' glasses"?

How does calling Jesus the "Son of Man" magnify hope in His supremacy?

How does the Incarnation touch our personal experiences of hopelessness?

Why is the Cross the great crossroads for our future?

How has the Cross eliminated every false hope for us?

Why do Christ's sufferings crown Him supreme over every hope we have?

How many victories did His Resurrection achieve?

In what sense is Christ also now the firstfruits of all our hope?

In what way does the Resurrection anchor every other hope for us?

What practical difference should it make that Christ is on the throne?

Why is Psalm 110 quoted so frequently in the New Testament?

How are we a part of Christ's missionary invasion among the nations?

What does opposition to His mission tell us about His supremacy?

Why is our Ascended Ruler also our chief prayer partner?

How does hope inaugurated become hope consummated?

Chapter 3:

How should the hope of "consummation" affect our daily lives with Christ?

How much do you feel a part of history's grand and glorious goal?

What Biblical themes define the Consummation of Christ's supremacy?

How does Christ's second coming add weight to His supremacy now?

What will the Consummation of Christ's supremacy not include?

What will the Consummation of Christ's supremacy include for sure?

In what ways will Christ's reign require both continuity and discontinuity?

How will the fulfillment of Christ's supremacy be expressed in community?

Why must Christ's reign climax in a ravishing vision of the Godhead?

So, who will be consumed with Christ and who will just be consumed?

Why does the Consummation project a perfect portrait of our Lord Jesus?

What if we acted as if the Consummation was here and now?

What if we acted as if the Consummation could arrive soon?

Chapter 4:

Why should Christ's supremacy feel like the future invading the present?

How has God applied the future to our relationship with Christ today?

What does the word "justification" tell us about the fullness of Christ's supremacy?

In what sense does the Spirit provide us the power of the future?

How does the filling of the Spirit connect us with Christ's supremacy?

How does the Spirit consecrate us for Christ's reign, both present and future?

What can happen when a congregation sees itself gathered around the King?

Why ought any church bear witness daily to the climax of Christ's reign?

What was the vision behind the beginnings of the modern missionary movement?

How is missions an extension of Christ's hope-filled reign among nations?

How can hope in Christ's supremacy impact earth's unreached poor?

Why should a vision for the future drive our mission to the nations today?

Why does revival under Christ always ignite a forward look?

What words help describe the hope in Christ that revival brings?

What does it look like when Christ rules a people through revival?

Why might "arrival" be the best metaphor to use for revival?

Why should Christ Himself form the central definition of revival?

Where around us do we see the judgments of the Lord revealed already?

How did you discover Christ's opposition to the unseen dark powers?

Why must preliminary installments of Christ's victory often be so costly for us?

Chapter 5:

Where do you see evidences of consuming passion today?

How can passion for Christ right now reflect what it will ultimately become?

What does our passion reveal about the content of our Christology?

Why does greater hope in Christ help increase our passion for His Kingdom?

What does sagging passion for Christ tell me about my relationship to Him?

What kind of passion is owed to Jesus as our Supreme Commander?

How passionate was the King about you from the beginning?

Why must the Father's passion for His Son deepen ours?

How do we go about consuming God's Son day by day?

How do we go about being consumed with God's Son day by day?

What might a congregation look like if it was controlled by consuming passion?

How did Paul exhibit the consuming passion we can all experience?

How do you respond to these probes on passion?

Chapter 6:

What should we call the overarching crisis we face inside the Church?

In what sense might the Church have an "identity crisis"?

What is our most strategic response to the "crisis of supremacy"?

What are some ways that the crisis has manifested itself over the ages?

Who is Jesus in America, and how much hope do Americans place in Him?

What are some ways this crisis is making its appearance inside the Church?

What are other tangible ways to measure the crisis among us?

In what ways does this crisis manifest itself in the Church worldwide?

Where do you see the crisis manifesting itself in your church?

What is the crux of the evangelical movement's "identity crisis"?

Why is the Ascension key to rebuilding our vision of Christ as our Monarch?

Chapter 7:

What is the relationship between hope and human survival?

What is responsible for today's disappearance of hope?

How does hopelessness hit us at the heart level?

Why do the world's crises of hope impact Christians even harder?

How does a spirit of hopelessness show itself as spiritual paralysis?

How does the evangelical "rat race" exhaust our hope in Christ?

How has our hope in Christ been paralyzed by the magnitude of the task?

How have we lost hope due to personal disappointments with Christ?

What happens if we don't get to debrief our disappointments with Christ?

How is all this paralysis evidenced in the Church's prayerlessness?

How much do Christians need to be re-awakened to a larger hope in Christ?

How is passion affected by the battle for hope?

Chapter 8:

What three essential choices in conversion are fundamental to Christian passion?

Why does a life of continual conversion prevent a loss of passion?

How would John Wesley confront a loss of passion?

How do life experiences fight against our fervency for Christ?

How does sin suffocate passion for Christ and His supremacy?

Why would Christians fear a passion for Christ's supremacy?

What primary fears often restrict passion for Christ and His supremacy?

In what sense is a loss of passion a result of "spiritual warfare"?

What overriding disconnect often triggers our loss of passion?

How need-centered is the message about Christ most Christians have heard?

What are some forms which "trite Christologies" take inside today's Church?

What is the greatest tragedy shortsighted messages create?

How did Jesus confront "trite Christologies" in His own ministry?

Why might Chinese and Hebrew words for "crisis" encourage us?

Are you willing to join me in a Campaign of Hope?

Chapter 9

How does our message stack up against other "hopes" the world talks about?

How did Paul proclaim Christ as the great "Message of Hope" for every Christian?

Why should our message about Christ point Christians to an abounding hope?

Why should our message of Christ also point Christians to an apocalyptic hope?

How did Jesus transform churches with a message about abounding, apocalyptic hope?

How often do our churches hear a message about Christ that sounds like this?

How did the supreme Proclaimer of hope shape His "campaign"?

How have multiple campaigns in the past impacted the advance of Christ's Kingdom?

Is it time for you to join in with a movement of proclaimers?

Why do pray-ers of the hope often become the best proclaimers of the hope?

How might a prayer meeting become a starting point for a Campaign of Hope?

Chapter 10

How does Paul demonstrate the strategic mission of a "Messenger of Hope"?

What does it mean to be a proclaimer of Christ inside the Church?

What does it mean to be a witness to Christ inside the Church?

What topics are people talking about these days in your congregation?

Which of these 13 characteristics are already found in your life?

How would you deliver to Christians God's Word on the supremacy of His Son?

H is for Hop On! — How do you grow a ministry of inspiration?

O is for Open Up — How do you grow a ministry of revelation?

P is for Pray Back — How do you grow a ministry of intercession?

E is for Enter Into — How do you grow a ministry of mobilization?

What four responses to a Message of Hope might you expect?

What is the single most important measure of any messenger's success?

Chapter 11

What might Prisoners of Hope look like today?

What is God's primary way to create Prisoners of Hope?

How fully have you been taken captive to hope in Christ?

What makes any Christian a good receiver of the hope Christ brings?

How does repentance increase our capacity for more of Christ?

What Kingdom issues need to be addressed by hope-filled repentance?

How does suffering increase our capacity for more of Christ?

How have you grown through the "discipline of dis-illusionment"?

What does the infectious nature of hope say about our need for community?

How can we go about building a community of hope-filled disciples?

How would you shape a weekly gathering for Prisoners of Hope?

Chapter 12

In what sense is this approach to discipleship truly anticipatory in nature?

In what sense is anticipatory discipleship always preparatory in nature?

If you knew Christ was coming tomorrow, what would you do differently today?

How is "acting as if" a helpful way to grow as Vanguards of Hope?

How could just four questions revitalize your walk with Jesus?

How can hope in Christ empower your worship of God?

How can hope in Christ reinvigorate your approach to scripture?

How can hope in Christ reshape your financial strategies?

How can hope in Christ reinforce your efforts at evangelism?

How can hope in Christ lead to acts of reconciliation?

How can hope in Christ foster courageous decisions about congregational activities?

How can hope in Christ undergird your daily battle with sin?

How can hope in Christ re-ignite your zeal for world outreach?

How can hope in Christ inspire the way we love one another?

Why is a church's prayer life a barometer of its hope in Christ?

In what sense is prayer always at the vanguard of God's purposes in Christ?

Are you incorporating the four dimensions of vanguard praying?

Are you practicing the six responses of vanguard praying?

Are you watching for the three answers to vanguard praying?

Are you "facing east" as you serve God's Son?